A Castle on Green Street

To Lisa, with all best wishes, Hoggy X

The Champions!

The 1958 Second Division Championship winners line up against the backcloth of the fine architectural lines of the West Stand. Back-row, L-R: Andy Malcolm, Ken Brown, John Bond, Ernie Gregory, Noel Cantwell, Bill Landsdowne. Front-row, L-R: Mike Grice, Johnny Smith, Vic Keeble, Johnny Dick, Malcolm Musgrove.

A Castle on Green Street

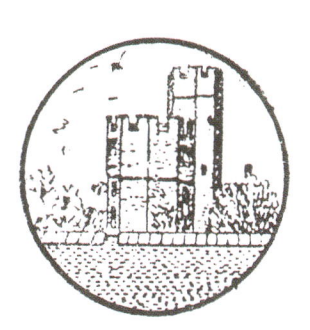

– An alternative history of West Ham United's 112 year tenure at The Boleyn Ground

1904-1966

E.C.W.C. WINNERS 1965

By Tony Hogg

With a foreword by Eddie Bovington, 1964 FA Cup Winner

© Tony Hogg 2018
First published in Great Britain in 2018 by the Author
and Bert Dog Design

All rights reserved. No part of this publication may be
reproduced, stored in a retrieval system, or transmitted,
in any form or by any means, without the prior permission
in writing of the publisher, nor be otherwise circulated in
any form of binding or cover other than that in which it is
published and without a similar condition including the said
condition, being imposed on the subsequent purchaser.

British Library Cataloguing applied for.

Hogg, Tony

A Castle on Green Street.

Origination the Author

Print managed by
Biddles Books Limited, King's Lynn, Norfolk, England

Contents

Acknowledgements	08
Dedications	09
Foreword by Eddie Bovington	10
Introduction by Barry Parham	13
Chapter 1. In The Beginning	17
Chapter 2. New Era Dawns	43
Chapter 3. War Almost Stops Play	84
Chapter 4. A New Beginning	109
Cover Stars	165
Chapter 5. Back At The Top	188
Chapter 6. The Silver Sixties	216
Chapter 7. Europe Beckons	294
Chapter 8. 1966 And All That	327

Acknowledgements

The completion of *A Castle on Green Street* has only been possible because of the help and encouragement of a great number of people and the author would like to thank them all accordingly.

Barry Parham for keying in the whole manuscript with great diligence and attention to detail which only a former typesetter from the hot lead days could bring to a project of this nature. It helped enormously that he is also a massive West Ham fan from the old school.

Steve Marsh of *theyflysohigh* fame for going above and beyond the call of duty on so many occasions and generously raiding his vast archive of memorabilia which included pictures, newspaper reports, tickets, programmes and cigarette cards which you will see here.

Dave Alexander of *Football Wanted* for lending me his collection of press photos, many of which are published here for the first time and without which this book would have been much poorer.

Thanks also to John Northcutt for images he sent me and his help over the years. Tony McDonald and his good lady Suzy of the late lamented *Ex Magazine* who both went the extra mile to help me. Also Tim Crane for sending images and general encouragement. Steve Blowers and his wife Lyn for their amazing support. They'll know what I mean. Also Chris Duncan for constant encouragement. My life-long pal Barry Nunn for his financial help. Barry, a goalkeeper in his younger years, holds the signal honour of being the oldest ever custodian to appear at the Boleyn in a specially arranged match in the summer of 2016. Also Mark Hudson, better known as Huddy to his many friends both here and in his native New Zealand, for financial help. Something of a legend in the world of Rugby Union, Huddy played for the Maori All Blacks and was a member of the Wellington team which won the Championship in 1986. Thanks also to Denis Lamb and my old mate Terry Connelly for their help over the years, and my great pals, Geoff Pointer, Dave Gibbs who played for Spurs, and Sean. I must also thank the good people who bought the book before it was published – Michael Oliver, Tony Clement of Sheerness who also sent a donation to go towards print costs, Andy Bish, Gary Bush, Don Hanley, Steve Burton, Julian Halliday, Alister Mackilligin, Chas Sturton, Kevin and Ben Jenkins, Dave Gibbs and finally my wing man on this project, Barry Parham who ordered books for his son Robert, son-in-law Steve Golding, and pal Mick Cardwell. I thank you all. Also my pal Roger Webb and wife Sandra who purchased two books before publication from Australia.

Dedications

This book is dedicated to the following people: Daniel Christopher May, his father Lindsay and mother Anne. Dylan Tombides, my great pal Geoffrey Thompson (Tommo) who bought me so many football books over the years to help me with research and his good lady Lucia, sister Linda, niece Vanessa and nephew Andrew. Also Gina Allen who helped West Ham's disabled fans on matchdays so compassionately. Also Kelly and Lisa who were part of the team behind the team for so many years. Ray Tuck (who ran the West Ham United Supporters' Club for the best part of three decades) and his son Chris. Big Chris who ran the door at the East Ham Working Mens' Club. Special thanks to my former partner, Lorraine Skingle, who went out scouring the charity shops looking for football books to add to my vast collection and also famously "libratised" them for me. As far as I know, there is no such word, but there is now! Also Craig Voyce, Sam, Joel, Jodie, Brian and Sonia. Finally, my dear sister Val and father George who took me to the Boleyn Ground for the first time against Burnley in April 1961 and all the other fine "West Ham" people we have left behind at the Boleyn Ground, E13.

The Law Man Cometh: Dennis Law sets up Les Massie for one of Huddersfield Town's five goals in the sensational 5-1 FA Cup victory at a snow-bound Upton Park in January 1960, watched by Andy Malcolm (left) and John Bond (right) who are helpless to intervene.

Foreword

By Eddie Bovington, FA Cup Winner, 1964

Although it seems a lifetime ago now and my memory sometimes fails me these days, I can remember everything about the day when I first walked through those famous gates into the Boleyn Ground in April, 1957.

I should do, because I didn't even know where West Ham United played. I was a North London boy, you see, and my uncle had to take me there.

I had been recommended to the Hammers' Chief Scout, Wally St. Pier, by the manager of the boys team I played for – Darwen – Alan Durrance, whose own son also Alan, had failed to impress in his trial. Wally, apparently, had asked him if he had any other players who might be suitable for a try-out and he put my name forward.

The author with Eddie "The Bov" Bovington (right) and pal Geoff (left) at the auction to raise money for the Bobby Moore Cancer Fund at the well-known West Ham pub in Brentwood, The Brewery Tap, which was run by the late, popular mine host Ron and now his good wife Marita and son Ian. The Tap was formerly run by another staunch West Ham supporter the late Ken Faulkner, who also used to run the Lacy Lady in Seven Kings.

We had been instructed to wait at the ground to pick up a coach to take us to play in a specially arranged trial game against Fulham at a company called Green & Silley Weir's sports ground at Wanstead.

If I remember rightly, George Cohen and Alan Mullery were in the Fulham team. They both went on to play for England, of course.

I must have done alright because although I didn't have any representative honours, I played a few more games after that and was given expenses. I also trained on Tuesday and Thursday evenings.

There was a handful of us North London boys taken on at the time – Micky Brooks, Bobby Keetch, Jack Burkett, Tony Scott and me. As I didn't have a job, I asked if I could be taken on the Groundstaff and was accepted – much to my relief.

I was really chuffed because I got on so well with all the other lads at Upton Park at that time like Bobby Moore, Andy Smillie, Johnny Cartwright and the North London gang I have already mentioned. They were exciting times for us all.

Being a Groundstaff lad wasn't all fun and games though. On Monday mornings after a weekend match at the stadium, there were a host of tasks to get through, like cleaning the baths, dressing rooms and then cleaning the corridors before taking on the major task of the day – sweeping the terraces.

When you think of some of the jobs we had to take on in those days, you wonder what Health & Safety would have made of it all.

IT'S OURS! Eddie lifts the Cup with Skipper Bobby Moore.

We had to get underneath the old wooden and corrugated iron built Chicken Run, for example, and clean out all the newspapers, programmes, peanut shells and other rubbish that had accumulated over several months and constituted a fire risk.

It was a job that literally had a silver lining though, because of all the two-bob-bits and "tosheroons" (half-crowns) we would find and even more shillings and sixpenny pieces, three-penny-bits, pennies, half-pennies and farthings. It was a handy supplement to our wages as apprentices.

We deserved everything we found because it was infested with rats, mice and cockroaches under there. We also had to get up ladders to clean windows that were really high and in summer we would also have to repaint everything.

We would "moonlight" by doing other jobs in the summer months. I remember, for instance, Bobby Moore's mum got us a job where she worked at William Warnes Rubber Company in Barking.

They also had their own sports ground and me, Mooro and Scotty were given the task of grass cutting there with scythes, It was hard graft as the grass was two feet high. After a couple of hours doing this we were tired and decided to have a kip because we were exhausted. But a security guard saw us "sleeping on the job" and bubbled us to the foreman, who was very upset and said, "you've all let me down lads". We all felt terribly guilty about that, I recall. The other workers there were a bit jealous of us because they thought we were favoured because we played for West Ham – especially as we turned up for work in Scotty's Sunbeam Talbot Convertible. It made us look a bit flash, I suppose. But we weren't really. We were just normal teenagers.

At the ground the old Boiler Room was our unofficial office and where the Head Groundsman, George Izatt, would dispatch us on our tasks. I would sometimes still turn out for my old team Darwin if they were short. But I would have been for it if I'd got injured, luckily I didn't.

Obviously the halcyon days of the mid-sixties were the highlight of my decade as a West Ham United player, when we won the FA Cup by defeating Preston North End in 1964, then became only the second English team to win a major European trophy in 1965 when we defeated TSV Munich 1860 at Wembley again and then reached the semi-finals when we went down gallantly against another top German side, Borussia Dortmund, who fielded three of their country's World Cup Final side that same year of 1966 – Hans Tilkowski, Siggi Held and Lothar Emmerich.

We also reached the final of the Football League Cup earlier that year, but went down to West Bromwich Albion.

Yes, they were wonderful days and now you can read all about them in Tony's book.
Enjoy.

Eddie Bovington

Introduction

By lifelong Hammers fan Barry Parham

Defining the decade. What an overused cliché! But for me that's just what the 60s were.

And what a decade it was! Leaving school, first job, starting an apprenticeship, amazing music that will last forever, girlfriends and then meeting my wife. Oh, how could I forget to mention – West Ham United?

The West Ham part is very well documented in this brilliantly created book.

Cleverly written in a non-chronicled and easy-flowing style, it is packed with a wonderful collection of photographs. This book allows the reader to be reminded of when, who and why the Boleyn Ground and its graceful guests of the decades are so special in all Hammers' fans memories.

Managers from the past, local celebrities like Paddy and Monty and tales from both would-be players and professionals are well represented in the following pages.

All Hammers' fans expect so much at the start of each new season. More senior supporters have been blessed with quite a few magical moments at our E13 cradle. Even a few at the famous old Wembley Stadium. Especially really memorable afternoons in the early 60s. Who can forget that match in 1966 when three of our heroes had the game of their and our lives!

I remember the crowds that would gather all around the ground for a glimpse of their favourites when they paraded their cups from Wembley successes. I am sure we were even allowed into the ground to see the team holding up their trophies.

I probably share similar memories with a host of fans of those days following the Hammers at the old Boleyn Ground.

Meeting up with pals in a pub or on some corner near the ground before matches.

We all had favourite players of course. Bobby Moore, Geoff Hurst, Johnny Sissons, Peter Brabrook and Johnny Byrne, to name but a few.

Regulars in the Chicken Run even had their own soccer team, Hartley FC I think it was named. Surely, some of the old fans that played in this team could meet up to go over those wonderful days at the Boleyn Ground? I expect most are still following their idols at the new Stratford ground. The Chicken Run regulars even had their own song, penned by Olly. I can't quite remember what the lyrics were. I wonder where Olly is now, writing songs for West End musicals no doubt? When the afternoon sun shone in the faces of the supporters in the west-facing Chicken Run, hands would be raised to shield their eyes. It was affectionately known as the Chicken Run Salute! I wonder who remembers that?

This book contains many anecdotes from fans' memories from their days in the E13 ground.

Mine included. I sometimes met with mates and stood on the terraces of the old North Bank. If you got there early enough, you would be able to get to a certain step that was twice as high as the others. A must for a better view!

Before matches, I often went to Nathans in the Barking Road for a delicious pie and mash meal or to the nearby chippy on the corner. But then again we all had our favourite eateries before the matches.

No doubt these locally famous food shops must miss the years of home matches which would bring in so much income. Now it's Stratford's turn to reap the rewards of match-day crowds seeking food and drink before matches at the new London Stadium.

Local pubs featured in the match day ritual too. Famously, The Hammers Supporters Club, The Black Lion, Boleyn Tavern, The Duke of Edinburgh, The Queens, The Wakefield Arms, The Hammers, The Denmark Arms, The Victoria, The Lord Stanley, The Central and, of course, the East Ham Working Mens' Club, just a few yards from the ground. It's sad to hear rumours of that old club closing its doors sometime soon.

My family have been Hammers supporters since before the First World War.

Granddad Henry was a Canning Town lad living in Mona Street with his extremely large family. He once told me of his journey to the 1923 Cup Final on a tram. My father Henry (aka Bob) served on destroyers in the Royal Navy during the Second World War and would ask for wartime results in letters and went to home matches when he was on leave. My brother Colin and I have always gone to games, both as schoolboys and later as Season Ticket holders.

We lived in Lawrence Road, Upton Park as my 90 year old Mum Jeanne still does. On a home game evening as a kid, if the wind was just right, you could hear the crowd noise slightly. This increased to a crescendo when a home goal was scored.

My wife Barbara, friends with players such as Trevor Hartley and Bobby Howe in her teenage days is an ardent follower. My son, Rob and son-in-law Steve complete the loyal band of family Hammers' fans.

Claret and Blue through and through, even my old headmaster at Harold Road Secondary Modern School played for West Ham in the early years of the 20th century – Vivian Gibbins. He joined the Hammers in 1923 and was a prolific forward. I remember that he had quite a collection of England caps in his office cupboard. A real gentleman!

As an apprentice Compositor at Curwen Press in Plaistow, I used to work by a window looking out onto North Street Passage which was a short cut between Plaistow and Green Street. Travelling Hammers' fans would use this passage on match evenings. We did a silent "thumbs up" or "thumbs down" with each other as they were passing after the games, depending on the result.

Almost everyone I knew was a Hammers' fan in those days. Who wouldn't be with the unforgettable 1964, 1965 and 1966 years of so much success.

Younger Hammers' fans who may not have been about during the successful 1960's years will find this book a virtual history lesson of their club's endeavours and will cherish it alongside future West Ham United literature.

Since the relocation to the Stratford site, the E13 area has lost some of its nostalgic buzz. I now live in Essex and travel to matches by train. This journey only takes about 30 minutes, but then its a 25 minute walk to my seat in the London Stadium. I used to be able to walk to the Boleyn Ground in 10 minutes when I was young.

Now for more about the concept and creation of this informative and compelling book by Tony Hogg.

I first met Tony when I answered an ad from him, enquiring about any Hammers' or general soccer memorabilia. I had a huge collection of programmes, both Hammers, Internationals and away games, and some early 60s annuals.

Obviously, Tony already had all the Hammers' programmes he needed, but found the magazines and annuals more interesting as he had worked on some of them in his early career in the industry.

These magazines included Charles Buchan and Soccer Star titles amongst others. I had previously loaned them to a good friend and fellow Hammer, Mick Cardwell, while he was recovering at home from a hip operation. He and his twin brother Tubbs, have been going to the Boleyn Ground since 1958!

When Tony and I met, we spent quite a time talking "West Ham stuff". During these chats, he told me of his desire to write a history of the old Boleyn Ground, which was also his second home in the past.

I offered to typeset the text and give a few memories of my own. This was over 3 and a half years ago on a snowy day early in 2015 and now the final product is ready. It's a must for all serious West Ham United fans to have in their bookcases.

Barry

Barry's old school master, the famous England International Vivian Gibbins (on ground), scores in the 5-5 thriller with the Villa at Upton Park in the 1930s.

Johnny Byrne (second from left) says 'More good news lads, our horse won the 4.30'. Johnny Sissons (left) and Geoff Hurst (centre) after completing the lap of honour following the 3-2 FA Cup Final victory over Preston North End at Wembley in May 1964. Jack Burkett (right).

In the Beginning
Chapter 1

Liverpool had its Kop, Chelsea their Shed and Spurs the Shelf, but seldom can a football ground have been blessed with as many endearing and romantic features as West Ham United's very own Boleyn Ground.

The fact that there have been three different enclosures bearing that magical name over the ground's 112 year history on the same site, straddling two millennia, has only served to cement its irrevocable claim on being East London's most famous footballing arena.

The foundations for well over a century of sporting excellence were laid amid uncertain beginnings in the summer of 1904 when the nascent West Ham United Football Club grabbed a piece of land off Green Street, Upton Park. Variously described as a cabbage patch, a potato patch, or more salubriously, the Boleyn Castle Field, within two months it was transformed into an arena capable of hosting a crowd of 10,000 for the visit of Millwall.

But no one waved a magic wand, although the homeless Hammers were said to have met a good fairy in their quest to secure a new home in the face of seemingly insurmountable odds.

The need for a new abode became apparent by the close season of 1903-04 when the club was enmeshed in dire financial difficulties. The board, who had known from the start of the year that the occupancy of the Memorial Grounds in West Ham was up for renewal in the summer, failed to reach an agreement with Arnold Hills (the Thames Ironworks owner who had done so much for the club in their embryonic years) for an extension of the tenure for seven, fourteen or twenty-one years at a rent the club could afford while still exercising sole control.

At this point the club were homeless, penniless and in grave and real danger of being bankrupt. They then made the acquaintance of a benefactor in the form of a local brewery, however, which advanced them a loan to buy a new ground, but still their troubles prevailed.

An area of wasteland was offered by West Ham Corporation but was considered unsuitable with the 1904-05 season approaching and the SL authorities anxious that the Hammers would be able to fulfil their fixtures, the future was looking decidedly uncertain.

The outlook was bleak when a match was being played between boys of the two Home Office schools. One of the Catholic Brothers, who attended the Boleyn Castle Roman Catholic Reformatory School, was watching the game alongside officials from West Ham. In conversation, the Irons' problems were discussed and a spontaneous arrangement was made for the club's representatives to view Boleyn Castle Field, East Ham. There they found a crowd of some 2,000 watching two pub teams and were left in no doubt about the site's accessibility to the public). The club's delegation, led by secretary Syd King, eagerly agreed to rent the ground from the Catholic Ecclesiastical Authorities, but were thrown into despair when they found out that the Home Office disapproved of the Brother's action. But Syd King persevered undaunted, explaining, "A deputation of directors waited upon MP Sir Ernest Gray

*West Ham United FC 1905-6: S. Hammond, A. McCartney, G. Kitchen, C. Cotton, D. Gardner, W. White
E.S. King, T. Allison, H. Hindle, F. Piercy, L. Jarvis, T. Robinson, C. Paynter, W. Ford, H. Winterhalder
C. Mackie, G. Hilsdon, W. Bridgeman, H. Wilkinson, L. Watson, F. Blackburn, A. Winterhalder*

and, through his good offices, subject to certain conditions, we were finally allowed to take possession of Boleyn Castle".

Further light may be shed on the nature of the "certain conditions" and the identity of the Brother who was West Ham's mystery saviour in the following extract from Colm Kerrigan's excellent biography, *Gatling Gun George Hilsdon*.

"George made his first recorded appearance in local club football early in 1904. The club he played for was Boleyn Castle FC, near to his house in East Ham and getting its name from a castle alongside the ground that was supposed to have associations with Anne Boleyn.

"The ground was owned by the Catholic diocese of Westminster and was also used by Boleyn Castle Reformatory. The boys in this institution had a very strong team and in 1903 beat all the local Board Schools in an open competition.

"Brother Norbert of the reformatory, when interviewed by the *East Ham and Barking Free Press*, was found to have been a football enthusiast on principle. And here is the reason he gave: 'A few years ago, before the introduction of football – and cricket – into the school, it required ten masters to control the boys, where only one master suffices now,'

"The move made provision for Boleyn Castle FC to join up with West Ham United, with their best players getting the chance to play in West Ham's reserve team. Hurried improvements were undertaken during the summer to have the ground ready for the new season. While they were not finished on time, the ground was able to accommodate the 10,000 who came to see West Ham beat Millwall 3-0 on the opening day of the 1904-05 season. The exact date? Thursday, September 1, 1904.

"It is not known how many of Boleyn Castle's 'best players' were invited to join West Ham's playing staff at the Boleyn Ground, but at least two, Vettini and Rayment, appeared during the 1904-05 season for West Ham's reserves".

A mystery yet to be solved is the identity of Hammers scorers in their victory over already bitter rivals Millwall.

Some reports claimed that centre-forward Billy Bridgeman scored all three, while others credited Jack Flynn with one of the goals.

Boleyn Castle. Upton Park.

    Certainly the actual match report that appeared in the *Daily Mirror* of September 2, 1904 and reproduced here, credits Jack Flynn with one of the goals.

    "Favoured by the weather turning fine after the heavy rains of the morning, West Ham United began their season most auspiciously yesterday evening, when they beat Millwall by 3 goals to 0 on their new enclosure at Upton Park.

    "The Boleyn Castle ground is situated in a densely populated neighbourhood where the keenest interest is taken in football, and the crowd to see the first match was estimated at fully 10,000. Compact and well furnished with stands, the ground can probably accommodate twice that number of people.

    "Much enthusiasm prevailed yesterday and the winning side fully deserved the cheers that rewarded their efforts. Almost entirely composed of new players from the north, among whom Kingsley, the former Newcastle United goalkeeper, and Simmons, the West Bromwich Albion forward, are the best known, the team at once settled down to a strong fast game and, despite the rather heavy going, they kept up their pace and form in a manner quite wonderful for the start of the long campaign.

    "Millwall, though their halves, particularly McLean, worked very hard, were completely outplayed. About 15 minutes from the kick-off Bridgeman, a local player, who earned his promotion from the reserves last season, scored a capital goal from a pass by Flynn, and the dashing centre-forward put in two other shots that almost scored, one hitting underneath the bar and the other being well stopped by Joyce.

Green Street House and Boleyn Castle (left).

"Flynn obtained a second goal about half an hour after change of ends, his clever shot from the left-wing sending the ball just under the bar. From a pass by McCartney, Bridgeman got the last point, this piece of combined work, perhaps, the smartest in the match".

Whoever scored the goals against him, the Millwall goalkeeper Tiny Joyce was so annoyed he reputedly punched a hole through the dressing room door.

So what was the Boleyn Ground like in 1904? In short, it was a ramshackle affair. The dressing rooms that 6ft, 16 stone "Tiny" vented his fury on were located in the north-west corner, and were little more than a glorified Nissen hut. The length of the west side was served by a small grandstand with a narrow enclosure fronted by advertising boards like most lower league clubs still utilise today. One of the adverts appears to be for "Three Little Maids" – a show maybe? The front of the stand was also covered in adverts, one for Bovril, a product personally endorsed by club secretary Syd King.

The covered bank on the east side would have made its future Chicken Run replacement positively "State of the Art". The south-west corner housed the directors' box complete with press facilities and bearing the prominent slogan on its roof: "Ask 4 Claymore Whisky". The North and South banks were rudimentary earthen mounds with rough terracing of ash and slag from Beckton Gasworks.

But despite the venue's make-shift appearance, there can be no denying the contractor's tremendous achievement in preparing the ground for SL football at such short notice.

The board's decision to move was vindicated when attendances in 1904-05 improved

1904-1905: The ground, after it had first been laid out.

dramatically compared to those at the Memorial Ground to set a trend that would continue up to the outbreak of WWI. Even more encouraging, the club posted an end of season profit of £400 – the first time they'd ended a campaign in the black. An occurrence that would also continue unabated until the outbreak of war.

Although West Ham's SL form after the move to Boleyn Castle was steady, but not spectacular, some games were lively affairs and marred by bad sportsmanship and fist fights with rival players, particularly those involving Millwall – bitter rivals even then.

In September 1906, for instance, a bad-tempered Western League match with the Dockers erupted into violence at Upton Park. As the *East Ham Echo* reported: "From the very first kick it was seen that there was likely to be trouble. All attempts at football were ignored".

The situation deteriorated when West Ham's Len Jarvis clattered Deans of Millwall hard against a metal advertising board. He retired badly hurt and took no further part. Jarvis got off with only a caution from referee Case, but the incident was reported to the FA. They suspended Jarvis for 14 days and ordered West Ham to post warning notices, as fist fights in the crowd had been sparked by events on the field. The referee was also suspended for the rest of the season.

On November 15, 1906 an indication of the esteem trainer Charlie Paynter was held in at the Hammers was revealed when he became the first West Ham employee to be awarded a

Benefit Match, against Woolwich Arsenal.

With ever-increasing crowds flocking to Upton Park to see Syd King's men in action, it became apparent that ground improvements were needed with increased capacity a priority. Hammers' growing love affair with the FA Cup had the Boleyn Ground bursting at the seams as FL giants like Blackpool, Everton and Newcastle United visited the East End.

After disposing of Blackpool in the First Round in 1906-07 by a 2-1 scoreline in front of 13,000 at Boleyn Castle, after they'd induced the Lancastrians with £250 to switch the tie to the East End, Hammers cup luck held as they were drawn at home in the Second Round to First Division Everton. The board cannily increased the admission fee to one shilling which kept the gate down to 14,000. It is recorded that Mr. Will Cutt, a director of Everton and later President of the Football League, came down to Upton Park to measure the pitch before the match to ensure it complied with regulations.

He had no complaints when the Toffees won 2-1 and progressed to the Final at the old Crystal Palace where they lost to Sheffield Wednesday.

The Merseysiders then rubbed salt into the wounds when they signed the promising winger Arthur Winterhalder who had impressed in the cup-tie against them. He made a mere four First Division appearances at Goodison Park before being transferred to Preston North End for the 1907-1908 season.

Entrance to West Ham Football Club c. 1911. The banking on this Castle Street side is not covered.

A letter sent to programme editor Jack Helliar by reader Mr. E. Walker in 1975 and published in the programme versus Arsenal in March that year, gives a fascinating glimpse of what life was like around the ground in the early 1900s.

"I worked for A.W. May, Bill-Posters of East Ham, a good many years. I used to go out with my brother early on Sunday mornings, all round the 'Old Marsh' and down the 'Back Road' to Silvertown before the war. I used to take the bill for posting to Mr. Bowen or Mr. Syd King in the office at the top of the old grandstand.

"Later I used to work at Castle Street, opposite the present ground. All those houses used to have boards in their gardens advertising match reports in the Sunday papers.

"I had the job on Saturday mornings to post these boards and tie them on the railings where I could, and do a bit of "flyposting" all round".

"I then went to see the matches when West Ham were at home. All the 'Fleet Street Boys' used to be around. I used to enjoy myself then, and have a good laugh".

Although West Ham's SL results were poor in 1908-09, attendances at the Boleyn Ground continued to rise with eight "gates" exceeding 10,000, while over 41,000 saw the Hammers in FA Cup ties against QPR, Leeds City and Newcastle United at Upton Park.

In 1909-10 West Ham reached the third round of the FA Cup for the first time and again the

PROMINENT FOOTBALLERS.

T. BRANDON,
WEST HAM UNITED.

match versus QPR necessitated a replay.

A remarkably large crowd turned up for a midweek match at the Boleyn of 18,000 in the return and witnessed the game being stopped when a barrier broke, but luckily no one was injured. QPR, however, got their revenge in winning 1-0.

The 1910-1911 season saw the signing on of all the previous campaign's first team and the much needed extensions to the Boleyn Ground.

The old dressing rooms were removed to the front end of the grandstand and the offices were rebuilt on iron supports over the enclosure. The space left vacant by the demolition of the offices was banked up for 3,000 additional spectators on the left side of the South Bank.

The work was carried out by West Ham United director, J.W.Y. Cearns, who owned a company of the same name at a cost of £4,000.

There was also a major change in the club's boardroom personnel that close season with Chairman Joseph Grisdale being elevated to President status and William (Bill) White installed as his replacement. The new incumbent's powers of diplomacy were soon put to the test when on September 17, 1910 West Ham hosted Syd King's old team, New Brompton, at Boleyn Castle. A section of the crowd became incensed at the way the visiting defenders were treating the home fan's favourite, diminutive winger Herbert (Tiddler) Aston. They were ready to take

West Ham proudly displaying the Western League trophy which they won in 1906-7. Back row L-R: W. Wildman, G. Kitchen, S. Hammond. Middle row: T. Robinson (Trainer), T. Allison, F. Piercy, L. Jarvis, E.S. King (Secretary). Front row: D. Lindsay, W. Grassam, H. Stapley, L. Watson, F. Blackburn.

matters into their own hands before the new Hammers Chairman left his seat in the Directors' Pavilion and went among them in a timely intervention to calm what was rapidly descending into an ugly situation.

The FA Cup again brought glory as the Hammers reached the Fourth Round for the first time ever. Victories over Nottingham Forest (2-1) and Preston North End (3-0), then known as "the Invincibles", set up the prospect of another mouth-watering clash in the Third Round with another home draw.

The visit of Manchester United on February 25, 1911 set a new attendance record of 27,000 – 9,000 more than the previous high in another FA Cup tie against Queen's Park Rangers the year before.

East Ham Echo correspondent "Rambler" reported: "Every vantage point was seized upon by the spectators. Some climbed up the telegraph pole, others sat on the top of the advertisement hoardings and looked every minute as if they would topple over. While others seated themselves on the top of the covered stand. Around the banks there was one huge mass of humanity, packed like sardines in a box but all as happy as could be".

So delighted were the Hammers' fans with the 2-1 victory and Tommy Caldwell's winning goal two minutes from the end that they invaded the pitch and carried the left-winger to the dressing room.

Hammers lost 3-2 at home to one of the Football League's founder members, Blackburn Rovers in the quarter-finals, but their success in the tournament through the turnstiles and on the pitch made that £4,000 they had invested on ground extensions and improvements seem money well spent.

Attendances had also been healthy in the Southern League with 15,000 turning up for the opening day for a 3-3 draw with Southend United and 20,000 for the 3-0 win over QPR a month later. Hammers finished fifth with a best-ever points total of 45.

A contribution sent to the West Ham programme editor Jack Helliar for the Football League Cup Third Round tie with Southend United on September 25, 1979 by a Mr. Malcolm Fletcher, a freelance journalist, who was also a Southend season ticket holder, succinctly summarises Iron's two meetings with the Shrimpers of the 1910-11 season:

SATURDAY 3 SEPTEMBER 1910

West Ham United 3 Southend United 3

The 14,000 spectators who turned up at the Boleyn Ground on the opening day of the new season witnessed a remarkable match.

After only 12 minutes West Ham were 3-0 up and set for an emphatic victory. However, Southend had other ideas. The visitors pulled back a goal just before the interval and added two more during the second half to force a draw.

Southend full-back, Tommy Murray, had a nightmare start to the game and was in part responsible for all three West Ham goals. After only 2 minutes he completely missed his kick to let in George Webb – Hammers' amateur centre-forward who was to be capped twice for the full England side later in the season, and shortly afterwards slipped as he shaped to tackle little winger Bert Ashton, who ran on to blast the ball past Southend goalkeeper David Clark, a former West Ham player. The visitors' Scottish full-back was again at fault as he allowed Webb to gain possession; Hammers' burly leader passed to Fred Blackburn, who touched the ball past the advancing Clark.

Southend who had themselves gone close to scoring during this period when Alec "Nutty" King shot against the West Ham crossbar, appeared dead and buried.

Then, five minutes before the interval, they got a break when Hammers' right-back Shreeve handled a cross from Southend left-winger Dunn. Referee Tom Robertson awarded a spot-kick, which Murray, atoning for earlier errors, calmly converted, while goalkeeper George Kitchen jumped up and down on his line. (The rule requiring 'keepers to stand still until a penalty taker had touched the ball, was still a long way off from being introduced).

Southend dominated the second half, and it was no surprise when they netted a second goal after 65 minutes. "Gonger" Frost robbed Danny Shea before sending away centre-forward King, who beat Kitchen with a ferocious shot.

Eight minutes later Southend's comeback was complete when they hit their third. Once again the marksman was King, playing against one of his former clubs. The lanky Massey attempted to pass back to his 'keeper, but the centre-forward nipped in, steered the ball round Kitchen, who got a hand to it, but could not prevent it entering the net.

West Ham Utd.: Kitchen (*capt.*), Shreeve, Fairman, Randall, Piercy, Massey, Ashton, Shea, G. W. Webb, Blackburn, Caldwell.

Back row: *J Cearns, G. Fundell, J. Moss, G. Handley, T. Williamson.* ***Second row:*** *G. Eccles, A. Kay, F. Griffiths, C. Cotton, A. Fair.* ***Third row:*** *G. Hone, E.S. King (Secretary) J. Bigden, E. Watts, J. Blythe, T. Allison, W. Johnson (Trainer) T. Tappin, A.C. Davis.* ***Fourth row:*** *J. Grisdale (Chairman) T. Duckworth, H. Lyon, J. Butchart, W. Kirby, C. Satterwaite, W. Barnes, W. White.* ***Fifth row:*** *C. Paynter, J. Johnson, W. Ingham, G. Davis, H. Simins.*

Southend Utd.: Clark, Murray, Molyneux (*capt.*), Emery, Lavers, Craig, Parke, Frost, King, McKenna, Dunn.

SATURDAY 31 DECEMBER 1910

Southend United 0 West Ham United 6

Another sensational game, with West Ham, generally outplayed for the first hour, hitting six goals between the 60th and 80th minutes for an away win at fog-bound Roots Hall.

The match was a personal triumph for Danny Shea, or "The Wapping Pet" as the press called him; he netted four times to enhance his reputation as one of the deadliest marksmen in English football.

Southend, who had trounced Millwall 7-0 in their previous home match, were well on top for the first hour, but unable to score.

Then, immediately after Southend had seen a shot cleared off the West Ham line, Hammers took the lead 15 minutes into the second half. The scorer was Shea, who found the net with a clever hook shot after goalkeeper Clark had beaten out his first effort.

As one contemporary newspaper account put it: "*After this it was simply a procession of goals.*" Clark presented Hammers with their second, dropping a soft shot at the feet of Bill Kennedy (once an amateur on Southend's books) who shot into an empty net. Kennedy, a schoolmaster from Grays, was to tragically lose his life in the First World War.

The third goal came from Shea, after he waltzed round Southend skipper George Molyneux (the former England full-back), who, in his mid-thirties, was having his last season in first-class football.

Shea, soon to play for England, netted the fourth and fifth, and Tom Caldwell – a winger who had joined Hammers from Southend – completed the scoring by converting a centre from Ashton.

The fog, so thick at half-time there were fears the game would have to be abandoned, kept the attendance down to just over 3,000.

Southend Utd.: Clark, Thomson, Molyneux (*capt.*), Emery, Harwood, Chalkley, Evans, Sutherland, King, Curtis, Dunn.

West Ham Utd.: Kitchen (*capt.*), Shreeve, Lavery, Whiteman, Woodards, Randall, Ashton, Shea, Kennedy, Butcher, Caldwell.

West Ham finished the season in fifth place, eight points behind champions Swindon Town; while Southend ended 19th (out of 20 teams), and were relegated to Division II together with bottom-placed club Portsmouth.

There was a pleasant surprise for spectators who frequented the North Bank and attended the opening game of 1911-12 at the Boleyn Ground between Hammers reserves and their Woolwich Arsenal counterparts.

With the first team playing away at Crystal Palace, those who came to see the "stiffs" must have been delighted to discover that the terracing had been concreted and a concrete boundary wall erected at that end.

As the official club programme commented: "Considerable expense has been incurred, but the public will have a splendid uninterrupted view of the game from that end of the field".

The club's *Official Handbook for 1911-12* also noted the improvements commenting favourably in the "Preview": "During the summer months a contract for terracing the North Bank and building a retaining wall has been entered into, and it is expected that the work will be completed before the opening match; those who are in the habit of taking up their positions on that part of the ground will find the terracing much more comfortable than the ordinary slope". Prices for season tickets 15/-, (Shareholders 12/6), numbered and reserved seats being One Guinea.

On the administrative side in those days the club had a President, 18 Vice-Presidents, ten Directors, a Ground Committee of three, a Secretary-Manager and a Financial Secretary.

On the eve of Guy Fawkes Night 1911, another attendance mark was set with the visit of old foes Millwall, when 23,000 assembled at Upton Park to create a new record for SL matches.

There were fireworks on the pitch as Hammers came back from a goal down to win 2-1 with two strikes from Fred Harrison. Millwall's goal was scored by W. Davies, ironically the son of West Ham's Deputy Mayor.

The visit of Plymouth Argyle on January 20, 1912 was allocated as Tommy Randall's benefit match and from a crowd of 10,000 he received a hefty sum, but was injured during the game which was lost 0-2. Also crocked was Frank Piercy and this match would be the last of his 214

* Excerpt taken from '**The Thoughts of Chairman Alf - Alf Garnett's Little Blue Book or Where England Went Wrong**' by Johnny Speight, published by Robson Books

Illustration by Stanley Franklin

*I mean, one day when Elizabeth was down at Tilbury with Drake an' his lads, and with the Armada coming up the channel, she said, 'My loving people', she said, 'All you here of dockland – supporters of my father's team, West Ham. They have told us,' she said, 'to be careful of our safety...to take heed how we commit ourselves to armed multitudes, for fear of treachery from you, my people, my loyal subjects who have followed my father's team – West Ham – to victories in ten cup finals.' (That was before the Football League, when football was football, and your defence wore armour and carried bloody swords an' no bloody foreign team dared to meet us.) 'But I assure you,' she went on, 'I do not desire to live to distrust my faithful, loving people. Let tyrants fear...I am come among you, as you see, (it's true – West Ham were playing away that week) 'but being resolved, in the midst of the heat of battle, to live and die amongst you all. I know that I have the body of a weak woman.' (You see, there was no women's lib about her, mate, and she was the Queen of England.) 'But I have the heart and stomach of a King... and a King of England too. And I think foul scorn that any Prince of Europe or Spain should dare to invade the borders of my realm. Rather than any dishonour should grow by me, I will myself take up arms, I myself will be your general, judge and rewarder of every one of your virtues in the field. Up the Hammers! And death to the Spanish King and his bloody Armada!'

'Could you imagine darling bloody Harold doing that eh? he'd run a mile. Look at him with Gibraltar. He should have stuffed Franco's Paella down his dago throat! And I mean, just after that speech, she was having her dinner, Elizabeth was, when Essex came in and told her they was raising armed rebellion in the city streets, and she didn't even bat and eyelid. She finished her dinner, and then took a bloody great carving knife and a rolling pin and went out on the street and said, 'Where is the rebel who will dare to face me?' And she was sixty-seven then. And the rebels, they might well have quailed, 'cos she could be a bloody rough handful when she liked. She had a piercing eye and could see through any of 'em who was after something for nothing. And when the bloody scouse gits and geordies rebelled she ordered hangings on every village green and market-place where the rebels had assembled. And the bodies, she said, was to remain there and rot till they fell to pieces where they hung. And when she was in a rage, mate, with all the rubbish around her, she left no doubt whose daughter she was, and laid about her with a big old rusty sword she kept handy. (The rust was caused by the damp of the blood that Henry her father had drawn with it.) But when she smiled – perhaps at the glad tidings that West Ham had won again – it was pure sunshine. And her sister, Henry's other daughter, bloody Mary, was just the same. She put a few down, but only unbelievers, to save their souls. They was the good times of England they was.

SL games for the Irons. Having had his own benefit in 1910, Frank was appointed Assistant Trainer in place of Tom Robinson. A post he held until his death in 1931.

Iron's SL form was patchy to say the least this season, but a highlight occurred with a cracking goal from an unexpected quarter in a 2-2 draw at Norwich.

It came from the normally defensive boot of centre-half Dan Woodards who put his side 2-1 ahead with a tremendous "30 yarder" at the Nest.

One of the only 3 goals he scored in over a hundred SL games, we will hear more of him later in the Boleyn Ground story.

Once again the FA Cup proved to be West Ham's saviour as they enjoyed another good run which pulled in 44,400 extra paying customers for three ties at home, one a 2-1 replay win over First Division Middlesbrough achieved with 10 men, which attracted a crowd of 10,000 despite admission prices being doubled.

Double that again turned up for the Third Round against SL Champions Swindon Town, who were followed by many from Wiltshire to create an electric atmosphere.

When George Butcher put the Irons in front following an exciting move between Tommy Caldwell and crowd favourite "Tiddler" Ashton after only 5 minutes, the crowd gave out "a long drawn out yell, its echo to be heard a mile off", according to the East Ham paper of the same name. So it would appear that the "Upton Park Roar" was already well established even at this early stage of the ramshackle ground's development. Although the depleted Hammers lost the replay 4-0 at the County Ground, the FA Cup competition (at this time more commonly referred to as the English Cup) had helped the club to survive, flourish and now prosper financially in uncertain times.

Fans arriving for the opening fixture of 1912-13 would no doubt have been pleased to note that in line with the North Bank, the South Bank terraces had been newly concreted to replace the cinder, ash and slag surface edged with timber in use since the ground's inception in 1904.

The team, too, got off on a firm footing by defeating the Devonians 4-0 with established hot shots Danny Shea and Fred Harrison again in amongst the goals.

At season's end the Irons occupied third spot in the SL table, their highest ever finish, level on 48 points with second place Swindon Town and only two behind Champions Plymouth Argyle. But it was in the FA Cup that they grabbed the national headlines after eliminating the previous year's finalists, West Bromwich Albion, thanks mostly to four goals from the returnee from Chelsea, "Gatling Gun" George Hilsdon, over the three ties.

In the following round the Irons went down 5-0 to the team they had copied their claret and blue livery from, Aston Villa, in front of the biggest crowd they had appeared before thus far – 50,000 at Villa Park.

So, although short, the cup run had again proved lucrative with over 62,000 watching the three ties with the Throstles, as Albion were then nicknamed. Villa went on to win the trophy that year, so no disgrace.

As Colm Kerrigan explained in his minutely detailed biography of "Gatling Gun" George Hilsdon, "There had been changes outside and inside the Boleyn Ground in the six years George had been on the opposite side of London. The population of the Borough of East Ham had continued to grow, increasing from 116,000 in 1906 to nearly 140,000 in 1912. The High Street, along which hedges had grown forty years before, was now a crowded metropolitan thoroughfare".

So the public was there, all West Ham had to do was draw them in, and by punching above their weight against established Football League clubs in the FA Cup, they were doing just that.

Many were critical however, and a report on Hilsdon's first game back at the Boleyn against Merthyr Town in September, 1912, showed how little traits of spectators had changed over more than a century.

The *East Ham Echo* reporter noted Hilsdon "had to run the gauntlet of some very uncomplimentary remarks from part of the stand". As his passing and shooting were still of a high standard, as we've seen, his fitness may have been called into doubt by his detractors, as he was known to be a heavy drinker.

His judgment was unimpaired a month later for sure as he scored three times from the penalty spot in former trainer Tom Robinson's benefit game against QPR which Irons edged 3-2 before just 2,000 spectators.

West Ham's first home match of the 1913-14 season against Swindon Town kicked off amid a blaze of excitement in front of the biggest crowd ever to watch the Hammers in a SL fixture at the Boleyn Ground – 25,000.

Almost as soon as the last ball had been kicked in the last match of the previous season, the Boleyn Ground had witnessed a hive of activity. When the curtain opened on the new campaign, a brand new West Stand was revealed.

Built by Cearns & Co., it was an impressive structure by SL standards, prompting the reporter of the *East Ham Echo* at the Swindon Town game to note that: "the magnificent new stand came in for much favourable comment".

Author John Powles in his exhaustive definitive history of West Ham United in the Southern League: *Irons of the South*, noted that:

"At 300ft in length and 20ft in depth, it was estimated to hold around 7,000, all under cover. There was to be a terraced enclosure 320ft long and 25ft deep in front of the stand. The

---

For **Sidney Garner**, a loyal supporter of the London team West Ham, football provided 'relief from work, from war... it was a way out. In the late 1920s the times were very hard'.

The football industry was growing quickly and becoming increasingly commercial, but the ritual gathering of fans and their passionate team loyalties remained. Sidney Garner would turn up at matches to support West Ham wearing a hat and scarf in the team colours, brandishing his rattle. Football became a focal point for whole communities, with friends meeting regularly at the weekly match to enjoy themselves together. 'I would go with most of my footballing pals.... Saturday or Sunday we'd all go together,' Sidney Garner recalls. As more and more fans flocked into spectator stands, new and larger stadiums were needed to accommodate them. In 1923 a new stadium complex opened at Wembley, in the London suburbs. It catered not only for football matches but for other events including tennis, boxing, ice hockey and greyhound racing. That year, a huge crowd flocked to Wembley to watch the Football Association Cup Final. 'All everybody wanted to see was the big game. It was the first cup final played at Wembley,' recalls Sidney Garner, who went to the match with his friends. So many people were trying to get in that the crowds overflowed on to the pitch. 'We made our way towards the main gates, and there were literally thousands of people. We couldn't go where we wanted to go. We had to go where the crowd pushed us... All of a sudden there was a great surge at the back, fences went down... a lot of people fell, got trampled on.' Mounted police, led by just one policeman on a white horse, managed to push the crowds back off the pitch so the match could begin. Nothing like this had ever happened before, and it confirmed the enormous popularity that professional football had now acquired.

Excerpt from 'People's Century' by Godfrey Hodgson.

Sidney Garner

structure would be divided into five bays, A, B, C, D and E. C bay in the centre would be for reserved seat holders. A and E would be for spectators who pay a shilling and prefer to sit rather than stand on the terrace, and B and D would be reserved at an extra charge. A main staircase would lead up to the distributing area, leading up five staircases to the various blocks. Those finding blocks A and E full would be able to descend another staircase at the far end of the stand down to the terracing. Under the structure were to be the offices, dressing rooms and other facilities, with a passage leading out on to the pitch for the players and referee to enter the playing field.

Yet it appears, over the passage of time, the existence of the second West Stand was largely forgotten – until, that is, a letter was submitted to the Correspondence page of the official club programme in early November 1971, from a Mr. D. N. Gillies of Leigh-on-Sea – the contents of which are well worth repeating here:

"Browsing through the Hammers' Handbook for last year, I spotted an omission from the history of the Boleyn Ground. There was no reference to a West Stand built in 1913. Prior to that there was a grandstand (as the history stated) built of wood and uncovered. In those days the dressing rooms were in the North-West corner, between the West Stand and the North Bank.

"During the summer of 1913, a new West Stand was built – concrete and roofed over entirely, with terracing in front of the seats. The dressing rooms were underneath in the new stand and the players emerged from a tunnel in the centre of the stand.

"Incidentally, does anyone remember an old chap who occupied a seat in the front row of the stand I have described? He had a white moustache and wore a peaked cap, from which we youngsters deduced that he was a retired sea captain! But he had an unmistakeable 'trademark', in that he always wore an enormous chrysanthemum, perhaps five inches in diameter. He must have grown prize blooms.

"If the Hammers were in need of encouragement, we would appeal to him from the terracing below, 'Come on, give them a shout!' and he would respond with a stentorian roar of 'Up the Iron!' I did not see him again after the First World War."

So a story well worth recalling before it is lost forever, shrouded in the mists of time, or one of those pea-souper fogs that used to roll in over the North Bank.

Unfortunately, the Hammers couldn't christen the new stand with a victory, or even a draw, as "Gatling Gun" misfired from the penalty spot to leave champions-elect Town 3-2 winners of a pulsating match.

It's unlikely the club's shareholders would have been lastingly disappointed by the narrow defeat, secure in the knowledge that they had been paid their first dividend, despite the huge cost of the impressive new structure.

It was crowd favourite Herbert "Tiddler" Ashton's turn for a benefit game this season and the match against Bristol Rovers on January 3, 1914 was duly allocated to the Blackburn born flankman.

But before this, manager-secretary Syd King's lads had to negotiate a nightmare fixture list typical of the day.

First they entertained Exeter City before an 18,000 crowd at the Boleyn on Christmas Day which was drawn 1-1 thanks to a goal from new goalscoring sensation Syd Puddefoot who had taken over the mantle of Danny Shea who had transferred to First Division Blackburn Rovers for a world record fee of £2,000 where he would win a First Division Championship medal in 1914.

On Boxing Day Hammers would make the long journey to Devon for the return with the Grecians with whom they again drew 1-1 thanks to a goal from winger Dick Leafe who would later be appointed assistant secretary when he retired from playing.

What were the West Ham player's thoughts, I wonder, as they gazed out of the window of the steam train clinging to the Devon cliffs on Brunel's masterpiece of engineering with each mile taking them further from home and the prospect of another match at Swindon Town the next day?

As there's little chance of proving otherwise, I can only presume that Hammers' party called off at Swindon on their journey where, however they got there, they lost 4-1 with just another Puddefoot goal to show for their travels.

A very good crowd of 14,000 paying spectators turned up to cheer the team and bolster "Tiddler's" benefit fund at Upton Park for the SL fixture with Bristol Rovers. They were rewarded handsomely with a thumping 6-1 win over the Pirates with "Puddey", as he was affectionately known, notching a hat-trick.

Then it was back to the serious business of making money in the FA Cup as three consecutive home ties attracted over 50,000 fans to the Boleyn as Irons romped home against Chesterfield 8-1, with Puddey scoring a club record five times in an FA cup tie – Crystal Palace, 2-0 and drew 1-1 with First Division Liverpool in Round Three.

Although the Hammers lost the replay with just a solitary Puddefoot goal to show for their efforts, the blow was considerably lessened by another big payday as 45,000 squeezed into Anfield before the gates were closed. Receipts totalled £1,430.

Finishing in sixth place in the SL in 1913-1914 looked respectable enough, but it was in fact, a huge disappointment as the team had gleaned just 4 points from their last 11 matches. But the fans weren't to know at the time it was destined to be their penultimate campaign in the competition.

On June 18, 1914, an event took place in the then Yugoslavia that would put football – and indeed almost everything else – to the back of people's minds for the next four years. Archduke Ferdinand of Austria and his consort were assassinated in Sarajevo. It proved to be the spark that ignited the powder-keg of Europe and would transplant the young men of Great Britain from the football fields of home to the killing fields of France.

As players reported back for training in August 1914 the "war to end all wars" had been declared on the 4th of that fateful month and by the time the season kicked off, the British Expeditionary Force was already in France helping the French to stem the German invasion into the country through Belgium.

Despite opposition from some quarters, it was decided to allow the 1914-15 season to continue on the grounds that some form of normality at home would help morale at the front and also because the large crowds attracted by matches were also seen as an ideal opportunity to stage recruitment drives by the authorities.

Yet again, Hammers met Newcastle in the cup, this time in the First Round and after resisting the Magpie's director's inducement of £1,000 to switch the tie to St. James Park, fought back from 2-0 down to draw 2-2. Another goal from Leafe (who scored twice in the first game), who was now playing at outside-right, and another from his opposite flankman Jack Casey wasn't enough to overcome the Novocastrians in the replay which was unluckily lost 3-2 before a crowd of 28,000 – the biggest which would watch the Hammers for another six years.

Puddefoot was the Hammers top scorer with 18 goals as the side finished in fourth place, seven points behind champions Watford against whom they were the only team to achieve the "double". The great "Puddy" was forced to move from the centre-forward position to inside-right to make way for the highly rated Arthur Stallard for the last 11 matches, a switch more than vindicated by the latter's seven goals in that period.

Although no one realised it at the time, West Ham's 1-1 draw at home to Norwich City on April 24, 1915, was destined to be their last ever match in the Southern League.

Watched by a meagre crowd of just 3,000, the attendance was the lowest to assemble at Upton Park for a SL match since 1908-09 when a similar number had witnessed home games versus Luton Town and Gillingham, both of which were also preceded by three successive defeats. The all-time low of 2,500 occurred against Northampton Town in 1904.

To Stallard goes the honour of scoring the club's last goal in the competition they graced for 15 years, but it could so easily have been Hilsdon, who missed a penalty and the chance to make it 2-1. He may have found consolation in the knowledge that even if his spot kick had not been saved by the keeper, it would not have placed his team any higher in the table behind Watford, Reading and Cardiff City. Stallard's rich promise was further underlined by 17 goals in 24 wartime appearances in the London Combination.

Action on the football fields was obviously completely overshadowed as events in the Great War unfolded on the battlefields of Europe and predictions that the conflict would be "all over by Christmas", proved to be hopelessly over optimistic.

Although football continued in its makeshift form throughout the battle, thousands of fans from areas which provided the groundswell of the West Ham support enlisted en-masse to join the fight for freedom.

Many enrolled with the 13th Service Battalion of the Essex Regiment, predominantly made up of East Londoners. Enrolment posters were posted up at the Boleyn Ground by the County Borough of West Ham on the regiment's behalf urging: "Join the 'HAMMERS' and HAMMER the Hun".

The recruitment drive was very effective with many hundreds joining up from areas such as Barking, Bow, Stepney and Silvertown.

The battalion became known as the "West Ham Pals". Arriving in France in December 1915, they had their first taste of action on June 1, 1916 and fought on the Somme, at Ypres, Cambrai and Vimy Ridge. "Up the Irons" was said to be their battle cry.

Trevor Brooking attended an unveiling of a memorial plaque to "The West Ham Pals", in November 2009 at the Boleyn Ground.

West Ham goalkeeper Joe Webster joined the so called Footballers' Battalion after Lord Kitchener gave an assurance that any professional that joined would be able to complete any playing commitments for his club until the season's end.

Another who enlisted was Hammers wing-half Jack Tresadern, who reached the rank of lieutenant in the Royal Garrison Artillery and would later go on to play in the 1923 FA Cup Final at Wembley.

Others were not so fortunate.

Sadly, Arthur Stallard was destined to die while serving his country during the conflict – falling on the front line in France on November 30, 1917. William Jones, a member of the Royal

Jack Tresadern against the backdrop of the West Stand built in 1913.

Welsh Fusiliers, lost his life in Macedonia on May 6, 1918. He had been the club's first full international when capped for Wales v England and Scotland in 1902.

The ill-fated Bill Kennedy, who had his West Ham career cut short by injury, also perished in battle while serving the London Scottish Regiment on October 13, 1915. Although his body was never recovered, his name appears on the memorial at Loos.

So, too, did Frank Costello, an inside-forward with the club in 1908-09 – killed in action early in the war and Frank Cannon, a centre-forward in 1908-10, who fell in action on the Western Front at Ypres on February 15, 1916. He was a member of the Bedfordshire and later the Essex Regiment, rising to the rank of sergeant-major. Welsh international goalkeeper Fred Griffiths also failed to return, killed in action on the Western Front. He held the rank of sergeant in the 15th Battalion Sherwood Foresters. He played for Hammers in 1902-04.

Their six names complete a sad, but heroic, Roll of Honour. WE WILL REMEMBER THEM.

George Hilsdon did not escape unscathed, suffering the effects of mustard gas poisoning while serving the East Surrey Regiment at Arras in 1917. Fred Harrison, whose forceful forward play and goals had played such a big part in the Hammers' performances before the war, suffered the same fate on the Western Front and never played again.

Lancashire-born winger, turned half-back, Harry Bradshaw was awarded the Military Medal when serving as a brigade runner in France during the war and after his safe return from service played 15 times for Hammers between 1919 and 1921. He was also a member of Hammers' relay team which won the professional footballers' 4x400 yards at Stamford Bridge, when such races were often a part of the programme at Sports meetings.

Although Southern League football was suspended for the duration of the war after 1914-15, the game still continued, albeit in the somewhat ersatz form of the London Combination. Made up of SL and Southern-based Football League clubs, team selection often relied on the availability of "guest" players who could be from any team in the country, but billeted in the south.

West Ham, in particular, made full use of the system and some famous names appeared in claret and blue to supplement their often depleted ranks. Danny Shea was a welcome returnee along with Percy Smith from Blackburn Rovers, and were joined by other star performers such as later Hammers legend Ted Hufton, when on leave from the Coldstream Guards, and Bill Masterman from Sheffield United. Third Lanark's Scottish international goalkeeper James Brownlie, Andy Cunningham from Glasgow Rangers, Liverpool's Bob McDougal and George Harrison, John Macconachie, Billy Kirsop and Sam Chedyzoy, who were all members of Everton's 1914-15 Championship winning team. Chedyzoy, who was a winger, was credited for being responsible for forcing a change in the laws of the game. On one occasion when Everton were awarded a corner kick, he dribbled the ball into the opposing penalty area, rightly claiming that there was nothing in the rule book at that time outlawing such an act.

With such radical reformers on board, it was hardly surprising that the Hammers had an impressive record in the London Combination which read: 1915-16 – 4th; Supplementary Tournament – 2nd; 1916-17 – 1st; 1917-18 – 2nd; 1918-19 – 3rd. Attendances at Upton Park were understandably low in this makeshift competition apart from 1918-19 when 26,000 gathered for the clash with Chelsea and 25,000 for the usual "blood and thunder" meeting with deadly rivals Millwall. Those two high "gates" provided a stark contrast to the paltry attendances which turned up at Boleyn Castle for the final match of the previous season, when only 7,000 showed to witness West Ham finish 1917-18 with a flourish as they dispatched Crystal Palace 11-0, with "Our Syd", as Puddefoot was now known to his adoring fans, grabbing a record seven of the goals.

There's no doubt that Hammers good track record during WWI helped considerably when the club successfully applied to join the enlarged Second Division of the Football League following the signing of the Armistice in Versailles in November 1918, to open a new and exciting chapter in the club's history.

Only one SL club sent Irons a congratulatory telegram – Swindon Town, the team of Charlie Paynter's birthplace.

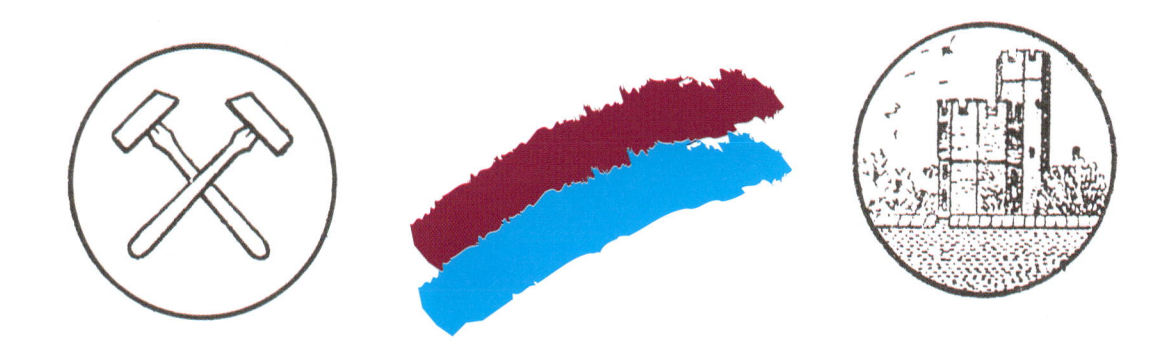

West Ham United's famous England International goalkeeper Ted 'Tiger' Hufton.

New Era Dawns
Chapter 2

The excitement leading up to the Irons first ever match in the Football League can only be imagined, but it was sufficient enough for 20,000 fans to fork out double the amount they had paid before the war.

They obviously thought it well worth the increased one shilling admission fee to witness their favourites' opening match with Lincoln City on that historic red letter day of August 30, 1919.

Amid a carnival atmosphere, the proceedings became an anti-climax when the Imps inside-left, Billy Chesser, became the party pooper by converting a first half penalty to ruin the script by sending Ted "Penalty King" Hufton the wrong way and earn the honour of scoring the first ever goal in a Football League match at Upton Park.

It was typical West Ham, but the fans went home in a far happier mood after Scottish inside-right James Moyes earned himself immortality by scoring the equaliser and Hammers first ever FL goal at the Boleyn in the 65th minute.

A former Scots Guard, signed from Dundee, Jimmy's star was destined to shine only briefly in East London, as he donned the claret and blue just once more before returning north of the border to sign for Clackmannan.

Despite the shortage of labour and materials in the wake of the Great War, Upton Park had been a hive of activity during the summer of 1919 as an army of workers toiled tirelessly to get the ground "up to scratch" to meet the strict Football League requirements and regulations. More than £4,000 was spent on general alterations and further stadium developments – a huge outlay for those austere times. Most of the money went towards moving the East Stand (Chicken Run) back towards Priory Road to make way for more standing accommodation on that side of the ground to house 4,000 spectators. The North Bank was also extended and raised to bring overall capacity up to 30,000 to ensure that Upton Park was now fit for purpose and a stadium to be proud of.

They would be more exciting still as survivors from the pre war days like tough tackling full-back Billy Cope and his regular partner Frank "Bronco" Burton "got stuck in" – the latter having recovered from shrapnel wounds received while serving the Royal Fusiliers during the conflict.

Also still among the ranks were wing-half Alf Fenwick, "Dapper Dan" Woodards, winger Dick Leafe, veteran Jack Macksey, Jack Tresadern, Dan Bailey, George Butcher and the great Syd Puddefoot.

Syd became a coincidental beneficiary of an amazing sequence of events which took place during a match against Derby County on December 17, 1921 at the Boleyn Ground in Irons' second season in the Football League.

The drama unfolded after the ball had been kicked out of the ground into Castle Street which, of course, ran behind the then uncovered South Bank. When it was returned it came down into the Rams' penalty area and one of their players picked it up, whereupon the referee awarded a penalty to West Ham from which Puddefoot duly scored.

With two balls on the pitch at the same time, was the ref right to give the penalty? The reaction of the Derby players is not recorded, but can well be imagined.

Coincidentally, the Castle Street end of the ground was known at the time as "Puddy's End" due to the high amount of penalties converted there by the prolific Hammers' marksman.

To add further intrigue, it was discovered after Syd's sensational world record £5,000 transfer to Scottish side Falkirk that the penalty spot was 10 inches nearer the goal line than regulations demanded.

Hammers won that match with County 3-1 despite being reduced to 10 men when full-back Jack Hebden broke a leg. But the game was remembered more for the controversial penalty award than anything else that occurred during the 90 minutes.

Had these highly unusual and remarkable events occurred at the other end and the ball been kicked over the North Bank, the same situation could have happened in reverse; as a playing pitch known locally as Robert's football ground backed on to the brick wall of the old North Bank.

The following Easter there was more penalty drama at the Boleyn as 30,000 crammed in for the local derby with Clapton Orient.

The Good Friday clash was finely poised when Hammers were again awarded a penalty. Percy Allen, the West Ham right-half stepped up to take the kick and was noted for a terrific shot, but the legendary Arthur Wood made a marvellous save and O's won 2-1.

Although the Hammers had a healthy FA Cup run in their first season as a Football League club in 1919-20, eliminating Southampton, after a Boleyn replay, and Bury before losing 3-0 before a 47,646 crowd at White Hart Lane in the Third Round; they uncharacteristically exited in the First Round in 1921 and 1922.

They more than made amends for those two barren years in 1923, however, as they embarked on their most successful campaign in the grand old competition to that date and battled through to the first-ever final to be played at Wembley against First Division Bolton Wanderers.

The fact that West Ham lost 2-0 to Bolton in the game that became universally known as the "White Horse Final", became almost incidental by the events surrounding their defeat and the financial compensation gained from their share of the gate provided by the 126,047 paying customers.

The untold thousands of half-crowns and florins paid at the turnstiles by the heaving, cloth-capped and trilby wearing multitudes who besieged the gatemen until they could take no more, literally gave West Ham a solid silver lining in defeat.

An extract from the club's 1924-25 Handbook gave a financial breakdown: "All gate records were broken on April 28, 1923 in the FA

George Kay shakes hands with his opposite number.

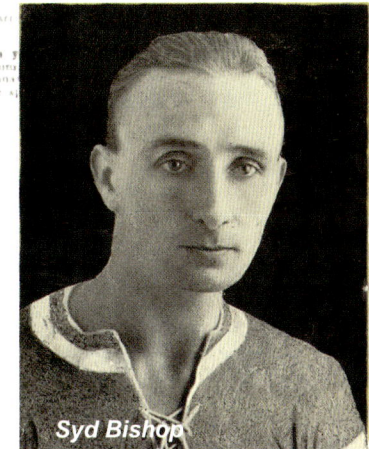

Syd Bishop

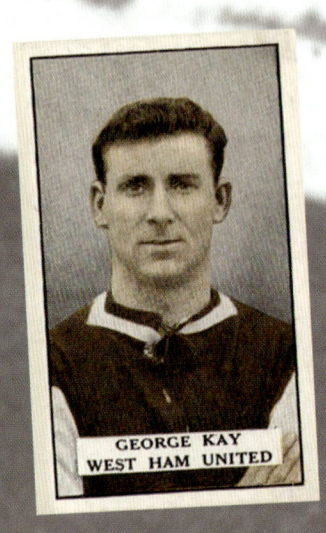

Billy Moore is put through by Ruffell in 1923 Cup Final.

MY FATHER WAS THERE!

Says souvenir hunter Bob Parham

Bob Parham, whose father, Henry, had travelled to Wembley in 1923 to watch the White Horse Final, and father of Barry who helped with the text for this book, took his other son, Colin, to the 1965 ECWC final at Wembley.

On the way out of the ground after that great win, he saw a bloke with a German scarf on.

He approached him with the intention of asking for a swap with his own West Ham United scarf. Unable to converse in German, he made arm-waving gestures, meant to give the chap an idea of what he would like to do.

"You swap scarves, my friend?", he asked.

The reply came as a complete surprise. "Leave orf mate, I've only just got this one myself!"

No souvenirs this time!

Bob was second in line of five generations to support West Ham United.

Cup Final between West Ham United and Bolton Wanderers. No correct return was possible, owing to crowds breaking in. The official figures returned by the Exhibition authorities were that 90,520 persons paid through the turnstiles and 35,527 ticket holders were admitted, making a total of 126,047. Various estimates were made of the crowd, whose actual number will ever remain a mystery, but it is probable that 200,000 persons were at Wembley on that memorable day.

"The gross gate was £27,776.

Entertainment tax was £4,206.

The British Empire Exhibition share was £4,714.

West Ham United, Bolton Wanderers and the Football Association each received £6,365 1s 8d.

The FA refunded to ticket holders who were unable to get to their seats £2,797".

The reason for this scribe's attention to minutae will become apparent later, but for the Hammers' gallant losing heroes, the season was not yet over…

Just 48 hours after the chaotic scenes and fiasco of Wembley, King's leg weary troops pulled off a tremendous 2-0 victory over Sheffield Wednesday at Hillsborough to go top of the Second Division ahead of Leicester on goal average and ensure that the promotion issue would go down to the wire on the last day of the season on Saturday May 5, 1923.

West Ham, Leicester and Notts County went into the final fixture level at the top with 51 points each. As if anything was needed to heighten the excitement of the final day, Notts

1923: Cup Final v. First Division Bolton Wanderers, at the first ever Cup Final to be played at Wembley.

were the visitors to Upton Park. Leicester were playing at Bury the same afternoon, but kicking off earlier. For Hammers the equation was simple enough – if they won, the Championship was theirs. If Leicester and County both won they went up, if it was a draw and Leicester won, they would be Champions and West Ham would be promoted with a better goal average than County. If Leicester lost, County and Hammers would win promotion regardless of the result at Upton Park.

With tensions and expectations continuing at an almost unbearably high level, only the exclusion of Hufton in goal differed from the Wembley XI as West Ham lined up: Hampson, Henderson, Young, Bishop, Kay, Tresadern, Richards, Moore, Watson, Brown and Ruffell.

In a party-like atmosphere, the majority of the "full-house" crowd of 26,000 had come to pay homage to West Ham's unlucky cup finalists and urge them to make the last effort needed to join football's elite.

Reporting on the match for the *Daily Graphic*, "Corinthian" timed the first goal as coming seven minutes before half-time, but unfortunately for Hammers and the wildly partisan crowd, it was scored by Hill of County. Hammers toiled tirelessly in the second half for what they believed might be a vital equaliser, but they needn't have worried as "Corinthian" explained so eloquently, "The news of Leicester's loss was signalled from the veranda of the director's pavilion whilst a fierce struggle was going on around Notts' goal. Immediately there was a cheer, which swelled to a mighty roar as it was taken up all around the ground.

"For the moment the players were confounded and the play seemed to hang in suspense,

RESERVED SEATS
& ENCLOSURE
TICKETS ONLY
RESERVED SE
& ENCLOSU
TICKETS O

RESERVED SEATS
& ENCLOSURE
TICKETS ONLY

Ted Hufton

Above: David Jack scores the first ever goal at Wembley to put Bolton 1-0 ahead in the 1923 FA Cup Final.

Left: Jack is foiled by the West Ham defenders.

The Football Association Challenge Cup Competition

FINAL TIE.

BOLTON WANDERERS v. WEST HAM UNITED

TO BE PLAYED AT

THE EMPIRE STADIUM, WEMBLEY

ON

SATURDAY, 28th APRIL, 1923.

KICK-OFF 3 P.M.

ADMIT **MESSENGER** TO PRESS GALLERY.

(ENTRANCE BY PRIVATE STAIRCASE from Main Terrace on NORTH SIDE OF STADIUM).

This Ticket is issued subject to the Rules, Regulations and Bye-Laws of The Football Association.

TO BE RETAINED BY MESSENGER.

F. Wall, Secretary

SOUTH STAND

British Empire Exhibition.

THE EMPIRE STADIUM WEMBLEY

The Football Association Cup Competition.

FINAL TIE.

SATURDAY, APRIL 28th, 1923,

Kick-off 3 p.m.

Block **FF**   Row **28**   Seat **1**

A. Henry McMahon, Chairman, Management Committee

Price 15/-
Including Tax.   SEE BACK.

This portion to be retained.

Back row: Manager Syd King, Henderson, Bishop, Kay, Hufton, Young, Tresadern, Trainer, Charlie Paynter.
Front row: Richards, Brown, Watson, Moore, Ruffell.

but immediately the loss of enthusiasm became apparent – it was a thrilling scene. An interesting touch was added when Donald Cock, the Notts County centre, found the opportunity on the field to shake hands with George Kay, the West Ham Captain".

Veteran supporter George Kerr who was at Wembley and standing on the North Bank for this match, saw things from a slightly different angle as he explained in *The Essential History of West Ham*: "The second half began much as before, with Hammers striving hard but creating little in the way of scoring chances.

"As time began to run out, the crowd became more and more subdued, there was high drama, but not on the pitch. The half-time scoreboard was situated in an elevated position at the rear of the North Bank. At the extreme right as we looked at it was a cubby-hole with a telephone and in which the operator was housed. We noticed that he was walking along the gang-plank to the opposite end and having reached it adjacent to the sign which would indicate the score of the Leicester v Bury match, he marked the full-time result – 0-1 to Bury. Immediately the mood of the crowd was transformed from one of utter dejection to complete ecstasy".

"We were in the First Division!"

Had the club's finances not been furthest from an ecstatic George's thoughts on that joyous occasion, he could have added: "and in the money!".

From a financial aspect, the club's performance had been the equal to the players' efforts on the field and a best-ever profit of £8,382 was announced by a buoyant board to prove it.

Showing a balance of £5,000 in its transfer of Puddefoot to Falkirk, the directors secured an extension of 34 years on their lease of the Boleyn Grounds from their landlords, the

Archdiocese of Westminster.

Since the end of the war, the company had expended more than £21,000 on ground improvements, making a grand total of £35,000 since it had accepted the tenancy in 1904.

But with the unforeseen successes in cup and league, the decision of Cearns Construction Ltd. to defer payment on future contracts and the agreement of Barclays Bank to extend their overdraft facility, the club felt confident enough to go ahead with the construction of a new West Stand.

Although the board of directors put out other tenders for what was an extensive project, it could have been small surprise when one of their number, W.J. Cearns' company won the contract.

There was nothing sinister about this, however, it just made sense to be dealing with one of the "West Ham Family", should any problems, financial or otherwise, arise during the normal

Birmingham's England International Goalkeeper Harry Hibbs punches clear from the legend Vic Watson.

course of events.

Make no mistake, this was a big build, an 81ft high edifice from ground level to the top of the roof; 332ft in length, boasting unrestricted sight-lines, scoreboards and an unheard of in those days, refreshment room that took reservations via telephone.

The magnificent two tier structure was opened in time for the opening fixture of the 1925-26 season versus Manchester United and was christened with a 1-0 victory over the Reds by courtesy of a goal from Stanley Earle in front of 30,000 fans – of whom 12,600 watched from the West Stand.

The report of the game in the *East Ham Echo* boasted that "West Ham now had the largest grandstand in London" and wouldn't have looked out of place in *Construction News* as it gave a running commentary on its construction which it claimed "used 780 tons of steel, 840 tons of cement and 18,000 bricks".

The *Echo* report added: "The roof protecting the supporters from the elements weighed over 300 tons".

So, once again, the spoils of success in the FA Cup had provided Upton Park with a lasting legacy in bricks and mortar for countless thousands of her patrons to enjoy for many generations to come.

The importance West Ham United attached to the unveiling of the new West Stand was borne out by a statement made by Chairman W.F. White at a civic event hosted by the club for local dignitaries and businessmen:

"Today is the second red letter day in the history of the club… The first was getting into the First Division and the third will be when we win the English Cup".

A feature in the 1925-26 *Official Club Handbook* gave further details on the exciting new development at the Boleyn Ground and went on to extol the virtues of the then state of the art structure under the heading of: The New Grandstand.

"West Ham will commence the new season with what is probably the most imposing grandstand in the country. When it is finally completed, no other stand will cover so many spectators under one roof. At present accommodation has been provided for 4,800 people seated, and 10,000 standing. A comfortable spacing has been allowed with 22 inches for distinguished visitors' seats, 20 inches for the centre block, and 18 inches for the remainder. The Directors have kept foremost in their minds the necessity for using up the maximum amount of the limited space available to accommodate spectators, but with a keen sense of the advisability of looking after the comfort of their potential regular patrons.

"The refreshments and the sanitary arrangements, both of which perhaps, left something to be desired in the old stand, have received special attention in the new stand, both being ample and easy to access from any part. Even from far distant parts of the district, the structure presents an arresting feature with its 81ft of height and fine architectural lines.

"Extra expense has been freely met by the Directors to give as far as possible an uninterrupted view of the game to the maximum number of people by adopting a scheme of very wide spaces between the columns supporting the roof and the unusually big overhang of

West Ham team 1925-1926.

the front portion of the roof. The distance between the columns reaches as much as 81ft and the roof, which is over 100ft wide, overhangs the columns for a distance of 38ft. The covered portion of the stand when completed will be 352ft long by 100ft deep, with the standing terrace carried on under the seating terrace to form a double deck, increasing the accommodation by many thousands.

"The terraces will be approached by entering through a block of turnstiles in the new private 50ft wide road from Green Street. Beautifully appointed dressing rooms, recreation room and gymnasium, are situated on the ground floor with a running track extending the length of the stand, allowing proper training during wet weather. This track will also be used on match days for passing spectators through to the North Bank. On the second floor the officials of the club have their quarters conveniently arranged to be easily approached from their allocated seats. The press representatives are given the convenience and position equal to that which they have with other big clubs. Most of the roof of the old stand has been transferred to the South Bank, and provides a striking contrast compared with the new structure.

"Sir E. Owen Williams, KBE, of Wembley fame, was the designing engineer, and Mr. W.J. Cearns of Stratford carried out both the constructional steel work and the general building work".

Vice Chairman Johnson added "that it had always been the policy of the club to put all

Vic Watson about to shoulder charge an opposing goalkeeper.

the money gained through the turnstiles back into football after it had met certain obligations to charity".

One such charity was the Catholic Ecclesiastical Society who ran the school in the Boleyn Castle grounds and it was certainly in the club's best interests to raise funds for this institution as it was under the auspices of the club's landlords, the Archdiocese of Westminster.

This they did in spectacular fashion by arranging a friendly match with the famous Glasgow Celtic at Upton Park on April 10, 1924. Thus Celtic became the first Scottish club to play at the Boleyn Ground.

That man George Kerr was at the match and his letter to programme editor Jack Helliar that was reproduced in the issue for the First Division match with Ipswich Town on March 20, 1971, helped to clear up some confusion over the year of the Glasgow giants' visit.

George wrote: "I also well remember this game, but unless my memory is playing tricks, it took place in 1924 and not 1922. I feel sure that, at the time, the Hammers were a Division I side and the game took place towards the end of their first season in the top division.

"It was Victor Watson's first First Division outing after a long lay off through injury; he had suffered a broken toe in the opening match of the 1923-24 season at Sunderland, and I remember being a little worried towards the end of the game as it got a little rough and I felt that Vic might get another injury.

"What I particularly remember about the game was the display of a little inside-right, Patsy Gallagher – an Irish international, who was reputed to weigh no more than 8 stone and looked like a bag of bones – but his ball control and dribbling ability was marvellous; he looked as if the ball was tied to his toes".

The match ended in a 2-2 draw.

The loss of records during WWII made it difficult to track down details until George's timely intervention, the "team book" in which matches were recorded having been destroyed by enemy action when a V1 rocket hit the Boleyn Ground in August 1944.

The Hammers team was: Hampson, Henderson, F. Blake, Bishop, Kay, Cadwell, Edwards, Watson, Gibbins, Moore, and Ruffell. West Ham's scorers were Viv Gibbins, and Billy Moore.

This, of course, was before the building of the West Stand was completed, but when the work was done the club had spent over £48,000 for major work on the ground thus far and had contracted £26,000 for more work to be completed by June 1926.

Meanwhile, Leicester City, the club that the Hammers had pipped for promotion to the First Division in 1923, were so impressed with Upton Park's new West Stand that they commissioned Cearns Construction Ltd. to build them an identical structure behind one of the goals at Filbert Street for the substantial cost of £31,000 in 1927.

It's likely that Dickie Pudan, a former West Ham full-back, who was a successful Midlands businessman and a Leicester City director at that time, played a prominent part in the proceedings leading up to the building of Leicester's replica, as he would have known the Cearnses well.

As West Ham became an established member of the First Division elite in the "Roaring Twenties", their stock rose and so, too, did their home attendances as Hammers very own "Upton Park Roar" became more and more vociferous as the decade unfolded.

Buried among the facts and figures for the 1926-27 season in John Northcutt and Roy Shoesmith's excellent *Complete Record of West Ham United*, one statistic stands out like a gold tooth in the tramp's mouth – the 44,417 attendance listed for the FA Cup Third Round clash with Spurs at Upton Park on January 8, 1927.

If that figure is indeed the correct number assembled to witness Hammers defeat their North London rivals 3-2 by dint of yet another Vic Watson hat trick, it easily eclipses subsequent figures.

During the epic FA Cup run of 1933, for instance, a crowd of 44,232 were recorded as attending the sixth round meeting with Birmingham at the Boleyn, but this figure was later called into doubt when it was thought that 4,000 spectators transferred from the North Bank into the "Chicken Run" were counted twice, even so, it was still given as West Ham's record attendance right up to, and throughout the 60s, in publications like the *Playfair Football Annual*.

To further muddy the waters, it was claimed that the gates were closed 40 minutes before kick-off on a 43,328 assembly for Hammers vital Second Division promotion battle with South

Falkirk paid West Ham United a record £5000 for Syd Puddefoot in 1922.

London rivals Charlton Athletic on April 18, 1936, which was lost 3-1 and hopes of returning to the top flight with it.

Although neither of these attendances can be officially verified due to loss of club records by enemy action in August, 1944, when the club's offices were destroyed, our mentor, Jack Helliar, later inferred that the Charlton match may well have been a separate record for a Second Division match at Upton Park.

But back to the twenties. Another huge crowd of 40,000 gathered at the Boleyn following the win over Spurs for a Fourth Round tie with Brentford which ended all square at 1-1.

Hammers surprisingly lost the replay against their Third Division South opponents 2-0 at Griffin Park.

An amazing crowd of 42,000 turned up for the Fourth Round FA Cup tie with the famous amateur side Corinthians at Upton park on January 26, 1929, many of whom were hoping for an upset, but Hammers ran out convincing winners by 3-0 with goals from Watson, Tommy Yews and Hammers own staunch amateur, Stanley Earle, who had also scored the only goal in front of 35,000 in the previous round versus high-flying Sunderland at Boleyn Castle.

Yet only 18,000 turned up to see their favourites destroy Leeds United 8-2 two weeks later, with English international centre-forward Watson scoring a club record breaking six times against the hapless Yorkshiremen.

CARRERAS CIGARETTES
J. BARRETT
WEST HAM U. (2ND DIVISION)

The home crowd swelled to 35,000 for the next match versus Arsenal which was lost thrillingly 3-4, but then plummeted to an all season low of 10,000 for the following Saturday's visit of Leicester City.

West Ham's biggest win of 1928-29 was achieved by the reserves in the London Combination with a 13-2 victory over Fulham reserves in December 1928. Among the goalscorers were two individuals who scored five goals each: Johnny Campbell and George Robson with Jock Rutherford (2) and Billy Moore (1) notching the others of the "baker's dozen".

The following campaign of 1929-30 was Vic Watson's season, and the crowds flocked to Upton Park to witness him break his previous season's total of 30 goals by a stupendous 20 tallies. He hit 9 against Leeds alone to make it 16 in his last five outings against the Yorkshiremen.

Thirty five thousand fans turned out to see the Hammers defeat Middlesbrough 5-3 in the first home match at Upton Park and that attendance figure was equalled in further wins versus Derby (2-0) and Arsenal (3-2).

Rightly returned to England duty, he duly repaid the selector's faith by scoring twice in the 5-2 defeat of Scotland at Wembley as he led the line with a dashing display of verve and vim worthy of the man he had replaced – the legendary Dixie Dean.

Hammers finished 1929-30 7th in the First Division and had again reached the FA Cup Sixth Round. Worthy achievements which pale into insignificance when compared to the individual scoring exploits of the centre-forward, whose 50 goals in league and cup have remained a record ever since. A contentious aspect of the cup run came in the 5th Round versus Millwall. The Lions wanted the tie to be switched to Wembley to meet an unprecedented demand for tickets. West Ham refused and raised admittance to two shillings with the result that only 24,000 paid to see Irons win 2-0, compared to the 28,389, and 34,000 who had turned out for the 3rd and 4th rounds against Notts County (4-0) and Leeds United (4-1), respectively.

The successive home fixtures at the commencement of the 1930-31 season at Upton Park gave a classic example of how a team's drawing power can ebb and flow just like changing fortunes over the decades.

First up, were Huddersfield Town on the opening day, their visit attracting a crowd of 24,000, by no means a full house, but compare it to that assembled for the visit of Liverpool on the August Bank Holiday just two days later on September 1, 1930.

Despite having defeated Town 2-1 with a brace from Watson, only 14,000 turned up at a half-empty Boleyn for the Reds' visit. In contrast, should the same two teams visit Upton Park today, the disproportionate attendance figures would no doubt be reversed.

The comfortable manner of Irons 7-0 defeat of the Liverpudlians, with Watson bagging another four goals, seems to speak volumes for the home crowd's knowledge of respective opposition strengths of the day,

ARTHUR E. HUFTON
WEST HAM UNITED

March 1933: West Ham United supporters at an FA Cup Semi-final against Everton. West Ham lost 2-1.

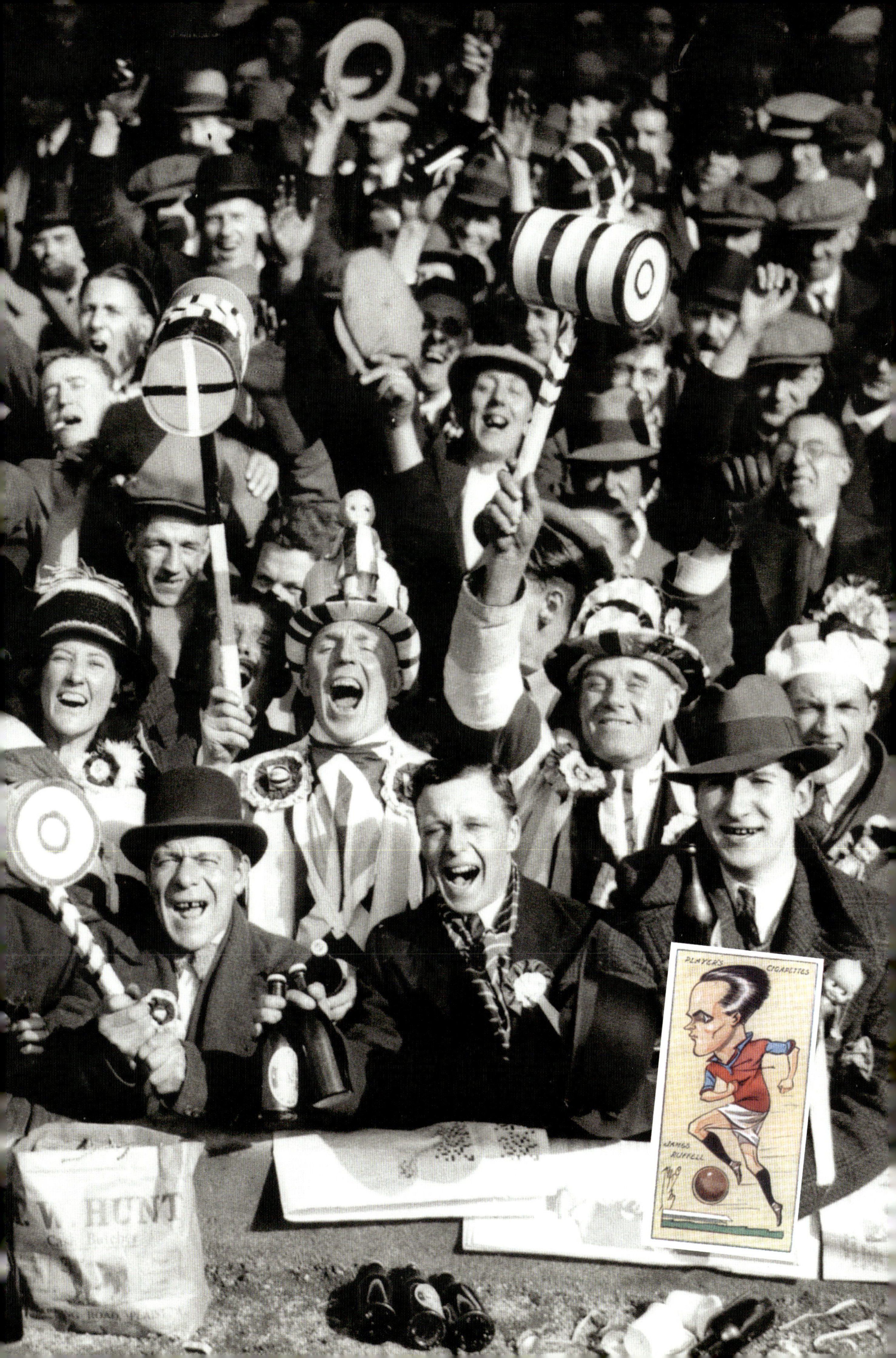
PLAYER'S CIGARETTES
JAMES RUFFELL
HUNT

15.9.34 Birch (Fulham) heads clear of Jim Barrett and Len Goulden (right).

but bizarrely, both finished well above their victor's in the final First Division placings –Town occupying fifth position, Liverpool eighth and Hammers a disappointing eighteenth; following an injury to Watson after seven games during which he had scored eleven times.

So the portents weren't good.

And so it proved. After a bright start when they secured a first-ever win over their old adversaries Bolton Wanderers at Burnden Park by 1-0 on the opening day of 1931-32, followed by a 3-1 victory over Chelsea before 35,000 at the Boleyn two days later, results deteriorated rapidly.

Even so, they didn't look likely to be relegated until losing their last seven games to plunge back into the Second Division they had left so elatedly eleven years earlier.

When West Ham won only one of their first nine matches at the start of 1932-33, it looked likely they would suffer successive relegations as attendances fell alarmingly.

At least that one victory had the added cache of being against old rivals Millwall in front of 30,000 at Boleyn Castle by 3-0, courtesy of goals from Watson (2) and new wing star Jackie Morton.

But they didn't get out of trouble until winning four games on the trot, to leave the final game at Plymouth, purely academic. As it was, they avoided relegation to the Third Division South by just one point.

Survival was secured by the grace of a 1-0 Upton Park victory over Spurs in the penultimate

3.10.34 Burns (Newcastle goalie) saves from Goulden.

ARTHUR WILSON

HE IS THE OLDEST SURVIVING EX-HAMMER, HE SCORED THE GOAL THAT SAVED WEST HAM FROM RELEGATION TO DIVISION THREE (SOUTH) AND HE NETTED A WINNER AT OLD TRAFFORD! 87-YEAR-OLD ARTHUR WILSON TALKS ABOUT HIS LIFETIME IN FOOTBALL TO TONY HOGG

BORN: NEWCASTLE-UPON-TYNE, 1908
HAMMERS CAREER: 1932-34
HAMMERS LEAGUE APPS: 29 (14 GOALS)
HAMMERS CUP APPS: 6 (2 GOALS)

vintage **CLARET**

WEST HAM UNITED's oldest surviving ex-player, 87-year-old former inside-forward Arthur Wilson, is still 'alive and kicking' in his native Newcastle.

Despite losing his treasured football medals to thieves recently, Arthur was in good spirits when he spoke to *Hammers News Magazine*.

"I well remember the events leading up to my transfer to West Ham from Southampton," he recalls. "I'd been to the races at Ascot during the close season of 1932, when I got a telegram instructing me to rendezvous at Kings Cross railway station with my Saints manager, former Hammers centre-half George Kay.

"When I met him there at 7.30pm that evening he told me West Ham wanted to sign me and I was to be at their ground at 10am sharp the following day to meet Hammers boss Syd King and complete the transfer.

"The deal went through okay, and I believe the fee was £500, but the trouble was I'd lost heavily at the races and didn't have my train fare back to Newcastle!

"I didn't like to ask Syd King for any money but when the negotiations were completed, I asked about the £10 signing-on fee. 'It will be forwarded to you in due course,' Mr King informed me.

"I then had to tell him of my predicament. Luckily he was sympathetic and told the secretary to give me the money there and then – it would have been a long walk back to Newcastle!

"I made my debut in the first match of the 1932-33 season against Swansea Town in a 1-0 defeat at Vetch Field, playing at inside-right, and two days later I was back there, playing for the reserves!"

But Arthur was soon back in the first team, taking over from the legendary Syd Puddefoot at inside-left, who was in his second spell at Upton Park and in the twilight of his career.

Nicknamed 'Sarser', for reasons even he doesn't know the origin of, Arthur took his opportunity with such aplomb that England international Puddefoot played only one more match for West Ham, while his replacement went on to enjoy the finest season of his career.

The genial Geordie scored twice in his first match back in a 5-2 Boleyn win over Grimsby Town and repeated that feat in three more emphatic Second Division home victories, against Charlton (7-3), Port Vale (5-0) and satisfyingly against his old team Southampton (3-1).

These victories were among the few bright spots in a disappointing league season for West Ham, however, and the part Arthur played in the club's battle against relegation to the Third Division has been largely overlooked by historians until now.

Not only did Arthur play a major part in Hammers progress to the semi-finals of the FA Cup, playing in every tie and scoring twice, he also scored two vital goals to become the club's saviour from certain relegation and descent into the hinterland of Division Three (South).

"Although we were nearly relegated, it was still a memorable season," Arthur recalls. "The cup run caused a lot of excitement and the press were clamouring for interviews and pictures as we came within a whisker of Wembley."

The fervour of the cup run, during which Hammers defeated Corinthians (2-0), West Brom (2-0), Brighton (1-0), after a 2-2 draw, and Birmingham (4-0) before failing gallantly (2-1) to Everton at Molineux, gave way to the anxiety of relegation as four out of six Second Division matches were lost following the cup exit.

Boleyn wins over Nottingham Forest (4-3) and Chesterfield (3-1) left Hammers needing to get six points from their final three matches.

"I can still remember my winner when we beat Manchester United 2-1 at Old Trafford," says Arthur with obvious relish. "It was a real 'belter' from 30 yards.

"The ball hit the underside of the bar and came back down and hit the goalkeeper on the back of the neck before crossing the line. The force of the shot knocked him to the floor."

If that goal was vital, Arthur's next strike in the claret and blue was even more crucial. It was the only goal of the game before a packed Boleyn crowd of 35,000 versus north London rivals Spurs, who needed to win to take the Second Division championship.

In the event, they missed out by one point and had to be content with the runners-up spot behind Stoke, while at the other end of the table Hammers missed relegation by one precious point, thanks to Arthur's opportunism in front of goal.

"The club promised us a continental tour as a reward for our efforts," laments Arthur. "But we had to make do with an extra day in Devon when we lost 1-0 at Plymouth in the last match of the season, travelling down on the Thursday instead of the Friday as we normally would."

Arthur finished the eventful 1932-33 season as the club's second top goalscorer with 15 goals in 33 league and cup games

Arthur (right) with West Ham's England winger John Morton in 1932

> "I CAN STILL REMEMBER MY WINNER WHEN WE BEAT MANCHESTER UNITED 2-1 AT OLD TRAFFORD. IT WAS A REAL 'BELTER' FROM 30 YARDS"

vintage CLARET

behind the great Vic Watson who hit 27 in 41 matches.

Something of a prodigy for Newcastle and Northumberland schools, young Arthur was snapped up by Newcastle United Swifts (effectively the Magpies' third team) for the 1926-27 season when the Geordies won the First Division championship, from the local Scotswood FC.

"I was at Newcastle from 1926 to 1927, the last time they won the league. I played in the reserves, but trained with all the greats, including Hughie Gallacher, Stan Seymour and Charlie Spencer.

"My starting wage was £2.10/- (£2.50) a week. It was like being a millionaire then."

"I was a 17-year-old when I was spotted playing for Scotswood. Huddersfield wanted to sign me as a professional, but my father advised me to go to Newcastle."

Unable to break into the first team at Gallowgate, Arthur made the long trek south to swap the black and white stripes of Newcastle for the red and white ones of Southampton and regular Second Division football at The Dell.

In five seasons on the South Coast he made 65 league and cup outings, scoring 12 goals playing at wing-half or sometimes at inside-forward.

Following the eventful 1932-33 season at Hammers, Arthur made just two league appearances the next season scoring once before transferring to Chester in March 1934.

Playing in the old Third Division North under the managership of Charlie Hewitt, Chester never finished out of the top three with Arthur as captain in his three full seasons at Sealand Road.

The Blues also reached the final of the Welsh Cup during that time, losing 1-0 to Tranmere Rovers in 1935 and 2-0 to Crewe Alexander the following year, both at Chester.

The two runners-up medals awarded to Arthur after those finals were among the haul stolen by heartless thieves during a robbery at his Heaton bungalow home, along with his pension book.

Despite pleading with the crooks to return the treasured items, he has heard nothing since the break-in late last year.

"The Welsh Cup Final medals were of great sentimental value to me," explains Arthur, who has been a widower since his wife Peggy died in 1973. "They had my name on them and I kept them with my nine schoolboy medals which were also taken.

"I would ask anyone who may know where they are to contact the police."

Since the theft, all Arthur has to remind him of his glory days is a faded photo album from when he rubbed shoulders with the greats.

"I remember the great Stanley Matthews knocking on my dressing room door before a Chester v Port Vale match, asking for two tickets for the game!

"Imagine, the great Sir Stan couldn't get in! He'd had a fall out with the Port Vale manager, Warney Cresswell, who incidentally played left-back for Everton v Hammers in that 1933 semi-final. Stan was then a big star with Stoke, who were big rivals to Vale.

"But as visiting captain I was able to get him a couple.

"The great 'Dixie' Dean of Everton was another pal of mine, who of course also played against us in that West Ham v Everton semi-final at Wolves, although legendary Hammers centre-half 'Big' Jim Barrett, who was another big buddy of mine, kept him scoreless on that occasion.

"I particularly remember a Southampton versus Everton match when I was a shock choice on the wing and we won 2-1.

"I scored twice and 'Dixie' got Everton's goal. But the situation was reversed in the return match when they won 2-1 at Goodison Park, with him scoring Everton's two and me getting our goal. Everton won the Second Division title that year.

"When I joined Wolves on the invitation of the great Wolves manager, 'Major' Frank Buckley, to player-coach their reserve side in 1937, mine and 'Dixie's paths crossed again in a reserve match between Wolves and Everton at Molineux.

"It caused a lot of amusement among the young Wolves players when he greeted me with a friendly 'Hello, son,' before the kick-off, as I was tagged 'Grandfather' by them!

"Another drinking pal of mine was the great Wolves and Welsh international Bryn Jones, whose £14,000 transfer to Arsenal broke the British transfer record.

"I remember getting very big-headed when my former manager at Chester, Charlie Hewitt, said when James Allen was involved in an earlier move from Portsmouth to Villa: 'If Allen is worth £10,000, Arthur Wilson must be worth £20,000!'"

In January 1939, Arthur was involved in his last peace-time transfer when he joined Torquay United in the Third Division South.

A year after war was declared in September 1940, he enlisted in the RAF and worked as a rigger on AA balloons for the duration of the conflict. But even during war-time, fate was to decide that he would continue playing football.

"Our unit were stationed at Long Benton near Newcastle and I got a terrific surprise one day when I discovered that 'Big' Jim Barrett was posted literally in the next field to us with his army unit.

"Jim, who held the rank of sergeant, asked me if I was still with a club. All I was doing football-wise was running the camp side. So Jim said he would ask the manager of Bradford City, Fred Westgarth, who had signed him as a war-time guest player, if he wanted me as well. Before I knew it I was earning an extra 30/- a week at Valley Parade.

"'Big' Jim was a great character who I used to go to the races with while at West Ham. He was the only bloke I knew who could back the first five winners and still come out losing!"

Arthur continued playing for Hartlepool when Fred Westgarth moved there as manager in 1943, and also played for South Shields and Carlisle United where he finally finished his playing career at the end of the war at the age of 37.

On the resumption of peace-time, Arthur was employed by Northern Club's Federation Brewery, situated in the same street where he started work at 16 as an apprentice cabinet-maker, and remained there until completing 25 years service in 1971 when he was awarded a gold wristwatch on his well-deserved retirement.

Arthur has had some good news recently to brighten the gloom of losing his medals and his older brother, William Wilson, who also played for Newcastle as well as Merthyr Tydfil, and who died just five days short of his 100th birthday last month.

Arthur's late wife's daughter, Pearl, has recently seen her daughter Jane give birth to twins, bouncing boys William and James. So there could be a new generation of footballers in the family in the new millennium.

I'm sure all West Ham fans will join us in hoping that in this, our centenary season, this grand old man reaches a centenary of his own.

FOOTNOTE: If any Hammers fans attending memorabilia fairs or auctions spot Arthur's medals, please contact detectives at Newcastle's East End, Clifford Street Station on (0191) 232 3451.

game. Geordie winger Arthur Wilson was the Hammers' saviour, having already scored the winner in the equally important 2-1 win over Manchester United at Old Trafford the week beforehand.

But there had been even more excitement and drama going on in tandem with the struggle for points in that grand old competition so close to the Hammers' hearts… the FA Cup.

Just as their lower status was shrugged aside in their old Southern League days as they accumulated a pile of First Division scalps in their quest for greater glory, a mere drop in divisions wasn't going to stop their dream of another Wembley trip on the 10th anniversary of their last visit to the famous Twin Towers.

The cup run began, appropriately enough, at The Crystal Palace, where all FA Cup Finals were staged between 1895 and the start of the Great War.

The Hammers' opponents were once again the famous Corinthian FC, whom they had defeated at Boleyn Castle in the Fourth Round in 1929.

With a crowd of only 16,421 scattered around the grand old ground which had once hosted 120,081 for the FA Cup Final there between Aston Villa and Sunderland in 1913, goals from Walter Pollard and Vic Watson saw Hammers through a tricky tie against the plucky amateurs.

Next up were West Bromwich Albion to visit East London and with memories of the Throstles's previous appearance at Upton Park the season before still fresh in their minds, Hammers had the utmost respect for the Midlanders… And one man in particular, W.G. "Ginger" Richardson, who had scored four times within the first ten minutes of Albion's 5-1 victory in November, 1932.

But there was no repeat on this occasion for happy Hammers who must have felt like they were back in the First Division as they put the 1931 FA Cup winners to the sword to win 2-0 with goals from Watson and Arthur Wilson in front of 37,222 at a bulging Boleyn.

The omens looked good when Irons were drawn away to another Albion – this time Brighton & Hove in the Fifth Round, then mid-table in the Third Division South and whom they had beaten on the way to Wembley in 1923.

There were even more feelings of *déjà vu* when a record Goldstone Ground crowd of 32,310 witnessed Irons come back from two goals down to force a replay. Watson (who else) reduced the arrears before right-half Joe Musgrave struck a memorable leveller in a repeat of events ten years previously.

In an exact replica of the 1923 result, but this time after extra time, 36,742 saw Hammers go through thanks to a solitary goal from the exciting young left-wing prospect Morton, to set up a plum home draw against First Division Birmingham in the quarter-finals. Hammers were optimistic at the prospect of meeting the Blues until an off-field incident lengthened the odds against them.

Returning from a postponed Second Division fixture at Oldham Athletic on February 25, 1933 in foul weather, Big Jim Barrett and goalkeeper George Watson were involved in a car accident. Jim got away with shock and bruising, but George sustained serious head injuries

Jim Barrett Senior

J. COCKROFT

Leonard Goulden

which would rule him out of the forthcoming cup tie.

Paynter was forced to draft in an untried rookie, Pat McMahon, who had been signed from Glasgow junior side St. Anthony's. After soaking up half an hour of Birmingham pressure and looking distinctly second best, Hammers had two strokes of luck.

First, full-back Syd Barkas put an own goal past his England goalkeeper Harry Hibbs, then the latter was injured trying to stop Morton scoring directly from a corner at the South Bank End just two minutes later.

Further goals from Wilson and Walter Pollard – picked ahead of the now returned Puddefoot in a gamble by Paynter – compounded the Brummie's blues and sealed a sensational result to set up the club's biggest match since the 1923 final; a semi-final meeting with Everton – Dixie Dean et al – at Molineux.

The overlooked legend Puddefoot, was back in the side two days later on March 6, 1933 to make his last ever appearance in a claret and blue shirt against Preston North End and scored Irons' goal in the 1-1 draw to earn a priceless point which would ultimately prove crucial in the fight against relegation to the Third Division South.

It is not recorded if his final goal at his beloved Upton Park was scored at his favoured South Bank end or, as the fans called it – Puddy's end. But, whichever end it went in, only 12,000 were there to see the last of his 107 goals as a true Hammers' hero.

Happy Hammer: Ronald Alliss being passed to the front at Upton Park in 1936, from *Football the Golden[Age]*

Picture brought a reminder of the way things were at Upton Park

RONALD Alliss has not watched his beloved West Ham United in east London for more than 20 years, but he is unlikely to forget the three times he was passed over the heads of a capacity crowd at Upton Park for a better view at the front.

The picture of Alliss, which was included in John Tennant's collection, *Football the Golden Age*, was spotted by his son-in-law, Mike Tucker, when it appeared in *Telegraph Sport* on Nov 28.

Alliss, 78, estimated that the picture was taken around 1936 when he regularly visited West Ham to stand in the Priory Road end with his father William, who worked in the fur trade, and his brother, also called William.

"The crowd in those days used to be packed in like animals. I was actually born in Bow but we moved to West Ham in 1923," Alliss said.

"I remember there was a bus garage and a synagogue behind the Priory Road end of the ground. If you weren't tall enough to see, you were passed forward. Later they built a place at the back just for children.

"Whether you were passed to the front just depended on whether it was a cup tie or a very good visiting team. It's not like now, where they are all sitting down."

Alliss went on to serve with

as he is today, aged 78

Picture: HULTON GETTY

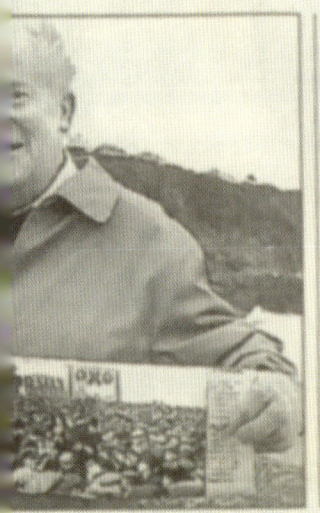

the Royal Artillery in the Second World War and is now retired and living with his wife in Cornwall.

"I think in the old days there was just one type of person, now they turn up with all types of scarves and shirts," he said.

"I suppose people didn't have money in those days and you didn't get a lot of visiting fans. Everyone had caps because if you wore a trilby it would be knocked off by the person behind if they couldn't see."

Sam Wallace

James Ruffell

Jim Barrett

Stan Foxall

Charlie Bicknell

Despite putting up a gallant display against Everton on Wolves's famous old ground, the history books tell us West Ham lost, and they did 2-1.

Watson, as ever, equalised before Hammers this time, were undone by a reserve, Everton's right-winger Ted Critchley, who scored a "soft" winner.

Hammers had no time to dwell on what might have been as they proceeded to successfully fight off relegation, as we know, and the curtain fell on another tumultuous season at the Boleyn Ground.

As is often the way in football, just as one star starts to fade, another begins to sparkle and just as Shea was replaced by Puddefoot and then Puddy himself by the emerging goal machine Watson, now, just one month after Puddy had departed for the last time, a new star was born… his name was Leonard Goulden, or, more simply, Len as he would become known to a generation of fawning Hammers' fans.

He had made his debut the week after another great favourite of the inter-war years, right-winger Tommy Yews, had left the Upton Park stage for the last time, against Charlton at the Valley on April 8, 1933.

Yews, along with opposite wingman Ruffell, had made countless goals for the prolific Watson inspiring manager Paynter's classic quote: "Tommy could knock a fly off Vic's eyebrow".

Following their brush with relegation, Irons finished a far healthier seventh in the final Second Division table of 1933-34 and with Jackie Morton and Goulden forming a formidable left-sided triangle with the consistent Joe Cockroft at left-half, Hammers never slumped as alarmingly again finishing third in 1934-35, fourth in 1935-36, sixth in 1936-37, ninth in 1937-38 and eleventh in 1938-39.

In 1934-35 they were pipped at the post by old adversaries Bolton, whose superior goal average of 96:48 saw them promoted over Hammers' 80:63 as both teams finished with 56 points.

The following season Hammers were again denied when they lost their final home match to South London rivals Charlton Athletic, 3-1.

A report from the official West Ham United programme from the similarly important Second Division clash on April 5, 1958 gave a resume of the 1936 meeting which took place 32 years earlier to the month.

"This afternoon's clash bears resemblance to the Robins-Hammers dual of April 18, 1936, for on that occasion we were likewise both concerned in the promotion hunt. The position at the head of the table before that match read:

	P	W	D	L	F	A	PTS
Manchester United	38	20	10	8	78	38	50
West Ham United	39	21	8	10	84	59	50
Charlton Athletic	39	20	10	9	78	55	50
Sheffield United	39	18	11	10	70	46	47

Joseph Foxall

James Ruffell

WILL'S CIGARETTES

L. GOULDEN (WEST HAM UNITED)

DR. J. MARSHALL

J. MORTON (WEST HAM UNITED) J. S. FOXALL (WEST HAM UNITED) J. BARRETT

"The importance of the game therefore required no underlining, and a record attendance for a league match at the Boleyn Ground was set up when 43,528 spectators packed the accommodation to capacity.

"The teams that day lined up: *West Ham United*: Conway, Chalkley, Walker (A), Fenton (E), Barrett, Cockroft, Morton, Marshall and Simpson. *Charlton Athletic*: Bartram, Cann, Turner, Jobling, Oakes (J), Welsh, Wilkinson, Robinson, Prior, Boulter and Hobbis.

"Charlton went into the lead within 10 minutes through Prior, but Peter Simpson equalised after half an hour by heading in Ted Fenton's cross pass. However, in the 62nd minute George Robinson put the visitors in front once more, and six minutes from time Harold Hobbis decided the issue by making it 3-1.

"A match report in the *Stratford Express* recorded that it was a poor game and that 'on this form neither side was worthy of going into the First Division'.

"However, the victory gave Charlton the advantage over us, and they consolidated this lead by gaining another win and a draw to finish with 55 points, one behind champions Manchester United. A 3-2 away win over Port Vale on the following Saturday had kept us in the running, but a 2-4 defeat by Sheffield United on the final day of the season also meant the Blades ousting us from third place on goal average – both of us having a total of 52 points".

Two days after the Charlton defeat, West Ham director A.C. "Bert" Davis seemed to have conceded promotion hopes when he unwisely stated in the *London Evening News*: "From a monetary point of view it might be better for the club to stay in the Second Division".

Harry Medhurst collects, watched by Albert Walker at Upton Park v Spurs.

Harry Medhurst saves at White Hart Lane, shielded by Dick Walker.

WEST HA

NITED F.C.

Stars of the 30s. Archie MaCaulay (centre).

Jackie Morton

L. GOULDEN (WEST HAM UNITED)

In the same article, the blundering Davis compounded the damage caused by his naïve "own goal" when he was further quoted as saying he preferred to have West Ham near the top of the Second Division rather than in the First "because it is a better paying proposition".

Although the board passed a resolution distancing themselves from their colleague's "purported" statement, the damage was done and Bert Davis' comments helped to perpetuate a myth that persisted until well after WWII that West Ham didn't really want First Division football.

Ted Fenton later recalled in his book: *At Home with the Hammers*, "We got together a fine side and we were always there or thereabouts at the top of the Second Division without quite making promotion. One year Charlton pipped us by winning 3-1 at Upton Park at the end of the season. That Charlton game brought abusive letters from so-called 'supporters' of West Ham, some of whom accused us of 'selling the game'. I wish they could have seen us in the dressing room. We took it hard – yet still the accusations and sneers continued. One fellow stopped me in the street and tried to make the point about us being in the hands of the bookies and big business. I ended that conversation with a sharp punch on the nose – my boxing background came in handy!"

With war clouds once again gathering over Europe and inevitable conflict with Hitler's Nazi Germany looming, competitive football was booked for an enforced absence from the social map for the foreseeable future.

But before the ever increasing likelihood of all-out war became grim reality, West Ham had a "going away" gift to their fans, all entranced by the romance and mystique of the FA Cup.

But before the FA Cup run interrupted, Irons hosted their smallest and largest League crowds of the season, just before and after the last peace-time Christmas of 1938. The first of the two London Derbies against Fulham on Christmas Eve attracted just 8,000 spectators to a snow-bound Boleyn Ground and some unwanted headlines, too.

That master boxing and football commentator Peter Wilson told the story in his match report which appeared on Christmas Day under the huge banner headline: "ANGRY FANS RAID PITCH", in the *Sunday Pictorial*:

"More will undoubtedly be heard of an incident which interrupted the match at the Boleyn Ground – a match which, in my opinion, should never have been played at all.

"In the first-half a nicely-angled shot from Morton cannoned off Bacuzzi, apparently into goal, and referee Wiltshire seemed to have awarded a goal.

"But after some of the Fulham players had spoken to him, he consulted a linesman (Mr. H.F. Hauxwell) and disallowed the score, presumably because of off-side.

"Immediately about ten spectators behind the Fulham goal scaled the rails and dashed onto the pitch. Players and police collared them before they could do any harm, but there was a little indiscriminate snowballing, and it was noticeable that for some time two policemen patrolled the touchline, keeping Mr. Hauxwell between them.

"It was a particularly disgraceful performance on the spectators' behalf. If the players managed to keep their heads and their tempers – if not always their feet – it should have not been outside the crowd's ability to behave with ordinary common decency. The ground was blanketed with snow and it never stopped snowing all through the match, so that when the ball went out to the corners, where it was thickest, it looked like a Christmas Pudding with sifted sugar on it.

"But although any sort of accurate kicking was absolutely impossible, there was no doubt as to West Ham's superiority. They must have forced quite thirty corners and, had their forwards not tip-tapped in front of goal, they would have got at least three goals in each half.

"Great credit was due to Keeping and Bacuzzi, who played a grand defensive game while Turner was positively magnificent. One of his saves from a Goulden drive stands out. But the attack never got going at all.

"Foxall was magnificent on the West Ham right-wing and Morton improved as the game went on. Indeed, all the West Ham forwards adapted themselves remarkably well, failing only in their choices of a method of attack.

"Macaulay got the goal after almost every forward had taken a pot-shot and Turner had saved brilliantly from Small. But the conditions really were too bad for football. My old friend Prince Poking Fire, the snow-shoeing Red Indian in the Winter Calvalcade at Earl's Court, would have enjoyed himself.

"Outside the ground there were posters announcing that West Ham may tour Russia. Yesterday's game was a good rehearsal!"

For the record, the West Ham team was: Medhurst, Bicknell, Walker (C), Corbett (N),

Walker (R), Cockroft, Foxall, Macaulay, Small, Goulden and Morton.

Three days later, the same team ran out of the tunnel (with the exception of Sammy Small, who was replaced by Tommy Green) to do battle with bitter rivals Millwall in front of a massive 41,300 at the heaving Boleyn. But this time there were no goals at all in the typically hard-fought battle with the Dockers. Just plenty of bruises, no doubt.

Surprisingly, no action was forthcoming over the indiscretions of a minority of spectators at the Fulham match on Christmas Eve, 1938, but further crowd problems during the 0-1 home defeat to Luton Town on March 18, 1939 brought the following warning from the Football Association which was printed in the last home match of the season's programme for the game with Manchester City on May 6, 1939, headed: "A WARNING" and commenced, "We have been instructed by the FA that misconduct on the part of spectators of a similar nature to that shown during our League match here versus Luton Town will be severely dealt with.

There is surely no need for us to stress how painful came this instruction to us and that overwhelming majority of Hammers' spectators who for years have enjoyed a reputation envied almost all over the football world, and we ask all to be particularly vigilant that no brainless and unsporting lout shall be allowed to spoil the sport of real sportsmen".

Making most impact in a side built around the graft, guile and sublime skills of by now established England international Goulden were flame haired Scottish forward Archie Macaulay and another import from Midland League Gainsborough Trinity, winger Stan Foxall, who was bang in form during what would be the last peace-time season of 1938-39 before WWII intervened.

Having partnered his colleague Goulden on England's right wing against Czechoslovakia at White Hart Lane in 1937, Jackie Morton, too, was in sparkling form that campaign and got on the scoresheet in the 5-4 victory over the Czechs – his solitary cap.

Having disposed of West London rivals Queen's Park Rangers 2-1 at Shepherd's Bush with goals from Foxall and Morton in the Third Round, Hammers were drawn at home to Spurs in the next.

Foxall, who had already scored in a 2-1 Second Division defeat at Tottenham back in October, 1938, was on the right-wing in the West Ham team printed in the match programme of January 21, 1939 for the Fourth Round tie before another capacity crowd at Upton Park which numbered 42,716, but still short of the Boleyn Ground's record of 44,417 set at the time of Spurs previous FA Cup visit in 1927.

The Times reported on the tie which had caught the imagination of the public, "on a pitch that was so generously covered in sand as to suggest spades and donkey rides rather than football, not only did Foxall score two brilliant goals, but his mere presence in the centre – after a somewhat unprofitable time on the right wing until West Ham were two down – seemed to revitalise the team. Almost immediately he scored a magnificent goal after a long dribble and, when he did very much the same thing again ten minutes from the end, West Ham drew level". In the replay at White Hart Lane, this time watched by a crowd of 50,798, Foxall and Sammy Small (who would score Hammers' goal in the 1-0 War Cup

Final win over Blackburn Rovers in 1940 at Wembley) again swapped roles. After Archie Macaulay had missed a spot-kick, Spurs went in front after 29 minutes through Sargent, but four minutes later Foxall equalised for the third time in three matches against Spurs when he got on the end of a Charlie Walker free kick.

Next the epic saga moved to neutral Highbury where again Tottenham led through Morrison after 15 minutes and Small missed a "sitter". The Spurs held the advantage until the last quarter of an hour's play when Foxall, again in the centre of attack, beat three Spurs' defenders to the ball to equalise yet again and pave the way for Macaulay's winner before another 50,000 plus crowd.

But Hammers lost 3-2 to Portsmouth at Fratton Park in the next round with the comforting knowledge that over 214,000 fans had paid to see the fixtures.

The Football League programme for 1939-40 kicked off on August 26 in as normal fashion as could be expected given the uncertain background to ever more perilous events in Europe.

West Ham travelled to Plymouth to face Argyle who were managed by former Hammer Jack Tresadern and returned from the West Country two points and three goals to the good by courtesy of two tallies from new signing from Hull City, Cliff Hubbard, and another from the club joker, Jackie Wood to a solitary reply from the Pilgrims. Two days later another goal from Woody and one from Ted Fenton, who now had brother Ben on the staff with him, secured a 2-1 home win over Fulham which seemed to justify the optimism of fans, players and neutral observers alike that this really could be Hammers' year. True to form, the same XI who had started so well went down 2-1 to Leicester City at Upton Park on September 2, 1939 to cast doubts over the high hopes held.

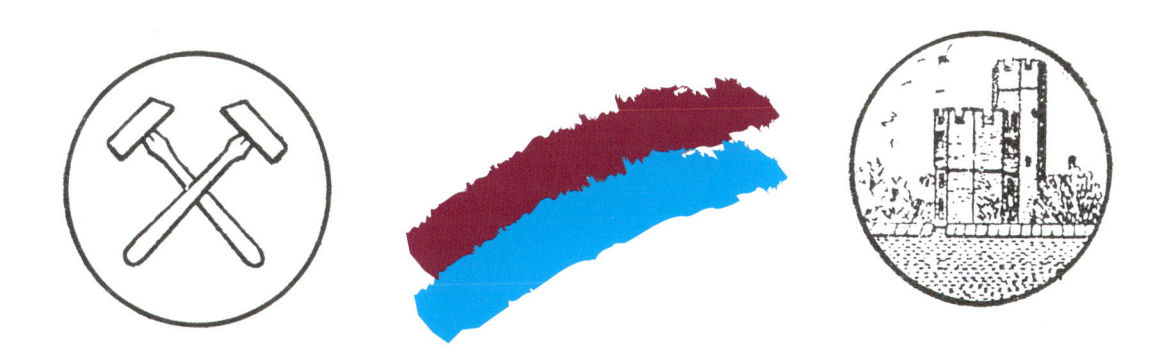

War almost stops play

Chapter 3

The above photograph shows an incident from the match versus the Foxes. The ball is being played towards the north-west corner by the Leicester City player for his colleagues on the right to intercept between the Hammers' defenders Ted Fenton (left) and captain Charlie Bicknell.

The action on the field is overshadowed, however, by those watching, for everyone of the spectators in view is a British soldier in full uniform; a sure sign that all is not well in the world.

The next day Great Britain declared war on Germany.

On Monday, September 4, the *Daily Mail* headlined on its sports section: "All Sport Brought to a Halt".

That same morning, 16 year old player and office boy Eddie Chapman (who later became West Ham's secretary and served the club for 50 years) was welcomed in the Upton Park forecourt with a bayonet at his throat.

"When I was confronted with the command 'Halt, who goes there?' and a bayonet pressed against my skin, I was shaking, I can tell you.

2—West Ham United F.C.

The only man on duty when the V1 hit the South East corner of the ground in August '44

D. WOODARDS
(Groundsman)

"But it was okay when I convinced the guard that I worked there", he recalled during an interview with *Hammers Monthly Magazine* in 1982.

"The infantry had requisitioned our ground and were using it as a barracks. They did the same thing at Highbury and Arsenal were forced to play all their home matches at Spurs' stadium, White Hart Lane.

"At Upton Park the scenes were unbelievable", continued Eddie. "They took over the Director's Lounge and turned it into the Officer's Mess, the place was riddled with army boots and you can imagine the horror of groundsman Dan Woodards and his assistant David Baillie when soldiers wearing them used our sacred turf for their own matches.

"They also put blankets down in the dressing rooms, trainer's and referee's rooms in case of gas leaking following an attack.

"In fact, the Football Combination offices, which were then situated in Barking Road, were bombed and for many years they used Upton Park as their headquarters.

"So you can see that the Boleyn Ground was put to completely different uses from the start of the war. I suppose its appeal to the military was its vastness and the fact that it was well equipped for the soldier's entertainment.

"In those early days of the conflict the administration was shared between Charlie Paynter, who was the Secretary-Manager and myself. I recall Charlie used to make weekly trips to Ramsey, Huntingdonshire, where most of Hammers' professionals were stationed in 442

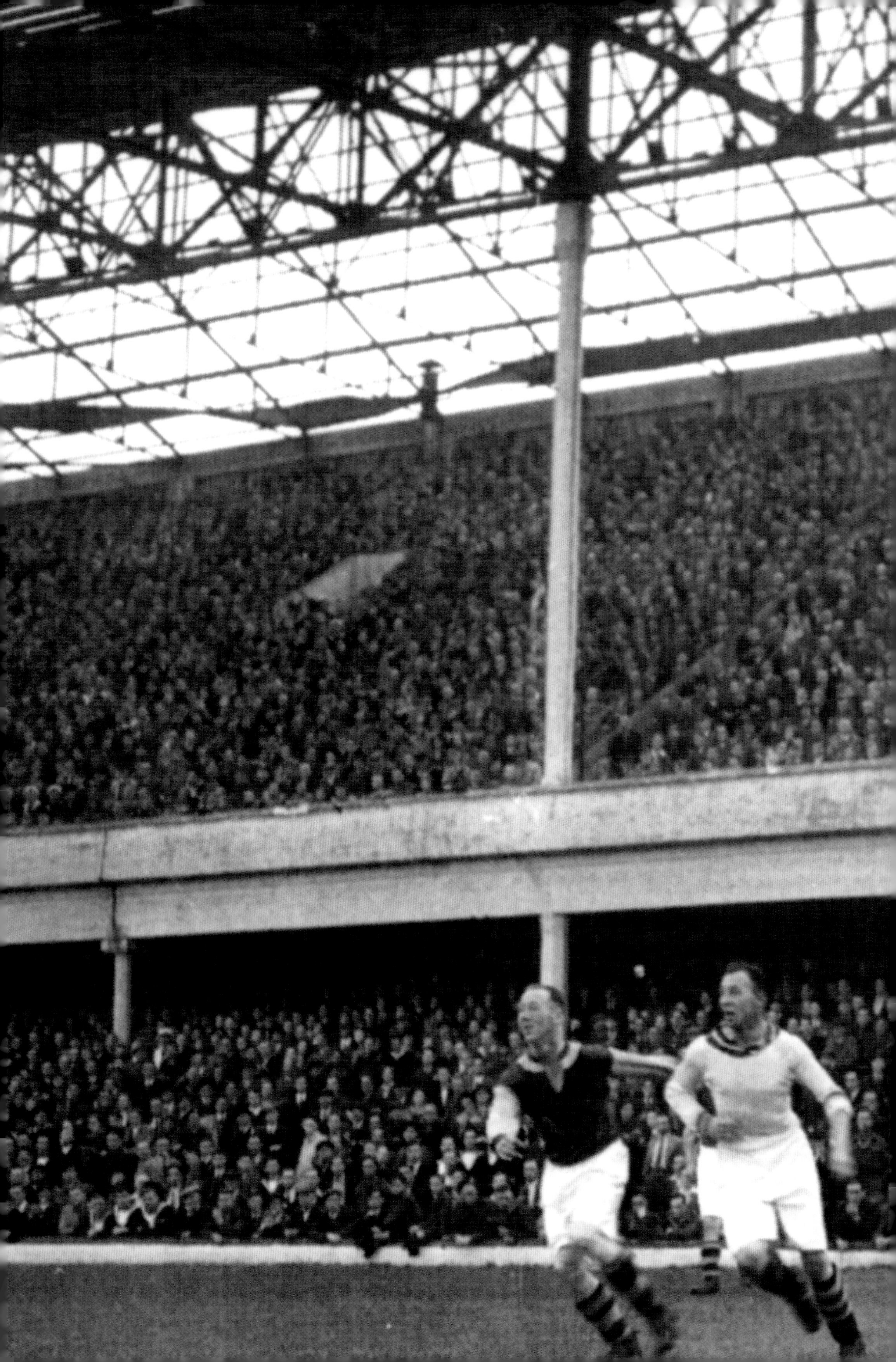

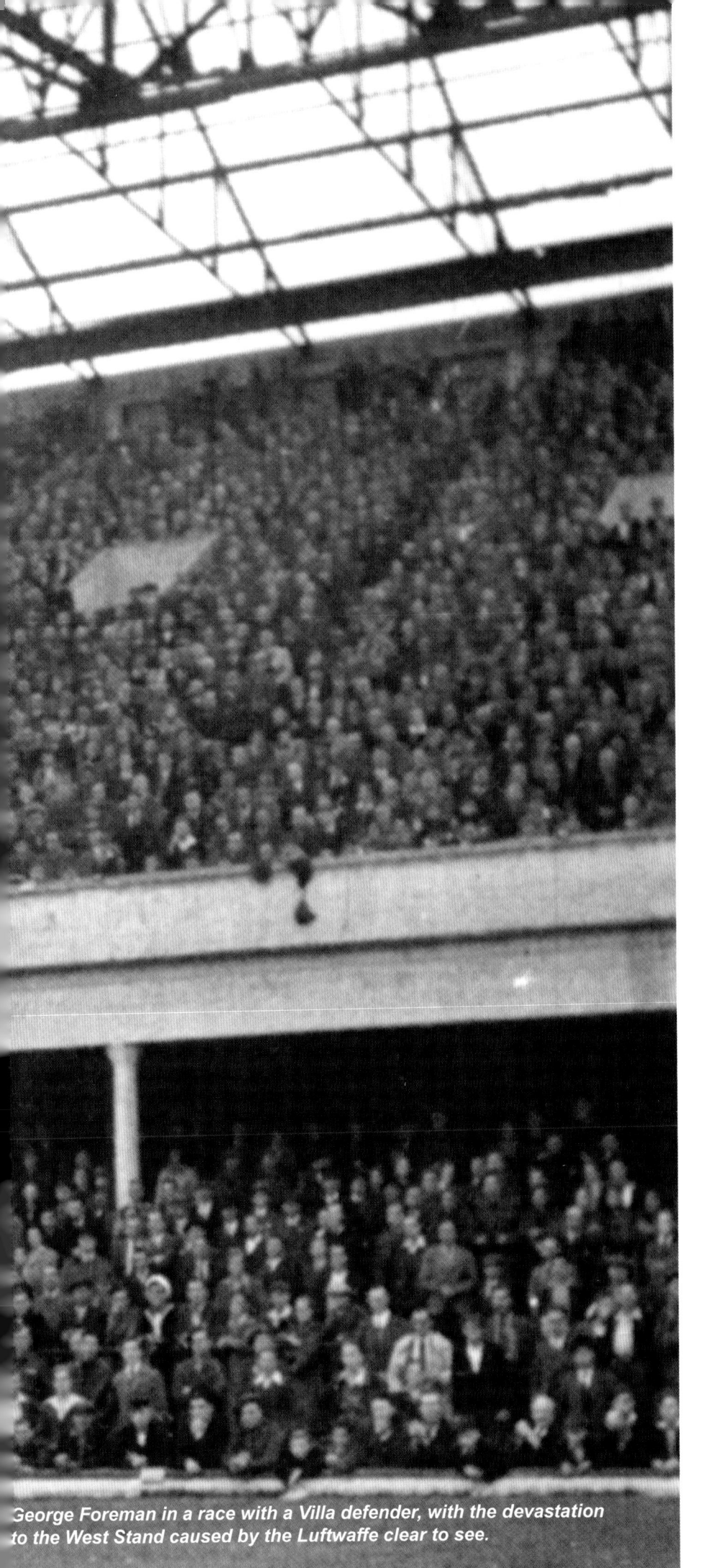

George Foreman in a race with a Villa defender, with the devastation to the West Stand caused by the Luftwaffe clear to see.

The Road To Wembley
Football League War Cup 1940

Round 1 (1st leg)
Apr 20 v Chelsea (h) 3-2
Fenton, Macaulay, og.
Attendance 15,200

Round 1 (2nd leg)
Apr 27 v Chelsea (a) 2-0
(agg 5-2)
Foreman, Small
Att 14,897

Round 2 (1st leg)
May 4 v Leicester C (a) 1-1
Macaulay
Att 6,320

Round 2 (2nd leg)
May 11 v Leicester C (h) 3-0
(agg 4-1)
Foreman 2, Foxall
Att 15,500

Round 3
May 18 v Huddersfield T (a) 3-3
Foreman, Foxall, Macaulay
Att 7,550

Replay
May 22 v Huddersfield T (h) 3-1
Foreman, Foxall, Macaulay
Att 20,000

Round 4
May 25 v Birmingham (h) 4-2
Foreman, Goulden, Macaulay, Small
Att 18,500

Semi-final (Stamford Bridge)
June 1 v Fulham 4-3
Foxall, Goulden, Small, og
Att 32,799

Final (Wembley)
June 8 v Blackburn R 1-0
Small
Att 42,399

Dick Walker

CLOSING PRICES EVENING STANDARD JUNE 1940 FINAL NIG

Evening Standard

Cocoa keeps better in a tin
When you buy your wartime packet of Bournville Cocoa, transfer the contents to an old Bournville tin—or any tin with a well-fitting lid. That's the best way to preserve Bournville Cocoa's rich aroma to the last spoonful.

ONE PENNY

BLACK-OU
MOON Sets 7.2

335,000 SAVED
DUNKIRK IN 1000
Churchill on Epic
Calais

...UNCED IN THE HOUSE OF
...AND SHIPS HAD TAKEN
...OPS FROM DUNKIRK.

...this deliverance the attributes

er, told the
is afternoon
or service in
ted and the
n be trained
n, giving an
ormal rate.
ings for
9½ in certain
the Home
Defence battalions, Mr. Eden added.

Sir Arnold Wilson, M.P., is Missing
Lady Wilson, wife of Sir Arnold Wilson, 55-year-old Conservative M.P. for Hitchin, Hertfordshire, has been notified by the Air Ministry that her husband has

armies of the north. They consisted of eight or nine armoured divisions each of about 400 armoured vehicles of different kinds.

EMPIRE STADIUM

WEMBLEY

THE FOOTBALL LEAGUE
WAR
CUP FINAL

BLACKBURN ROVERS
v
WEST HAM UNITED

SATURDAY, JUNE 8TH, 1940

OFFICIAL PROGRAMME   •   SIXPENCE

NORTH GRAND STAND
Reserved Seat (Unnumbered)
ENTER AT TURNSTILES (See Plan on back)
E
ENTRANCE 85

EMPIRE STADIUM, WEMBLEY
Football League CUP FINAL
SATURDAY, JUNE 8th, 1940
KICK-OFF 6.30 p.m.
Price 3/- (Including Tax)
A. J. Elvin
MANAGING DIRECTOR
Wembley Stadium Limited
THIS PORTION TO BE RETAINED
(See Conditions on back)

They
Toss
Leagu
— AFTER

It looks as if West
for the Football
it at Wembley on S
The Management
level at the end of
pegging after the ex
thought application
on favourably.

SPORT S

One West H
in West Ha

There will be one
in the West Ha
final Regional "C"
Charlton, at Cha
(7.0) — Jim Barrett
Millwall, who smas
championship cha

J. Barrett

Cocoa keeps better in a tin

When you buy your wartime packet of Bournville Cocoa, transfer the contents to an old Bournville tin—or any tin with a well-fitting lid. That's the best way to preserve Bournville Cocoa's rich aroma to the last spoonful.

...ROM ...SHIPS

...ht Have to Football ...up

...OURS PLAY IN FINAL

...nd Blackburn Rovers might have to toss ...up after they have played two hours for ...ing, says Roland Allen.

...ve arranged for half an hour extra if they are ... No provision is made if they remain even ... The season ends on Saturday, and it is not ...xtension, to fit in a replay, would be looked ...

It is provided that the Cup – a much more handsome affair than the F.A. piece of silver I am told – becomes the absolute property of the club whose players win it on Saturday.

If West Ham play all the way through with the brilliant directness they produced in the first half against Fulham there will be no question of a replay, anyhow. I understand that all the way through Mr. Charles Paynter, the West Ham manager, trainer, player-collector and "Uncle" to all of them has set out to win this Cup to celebrate his 40 years unbroken service with the club.

That question of which win could, if necessary, be settled in the Scots way of deciding on corner kicks if goals are level. What to do if they also are level on corner kicks is beyond me – and, no doubt, also Mr Paynter and the distinguished members of the Management Committee.

SUNDAY PICTORIAL

The Bantam Brothers: Over the Top!

WEST HAM SUPER MOVE DOES IT!

West Ham 1, Blackburn 0 (at Wembley)

League Results

WAR SOCCER HONOURS—South A champions Arsenal, South B QP Rangers, South C, Spurs South D Crystal Palace
Midland Wolves East Midland, Chesterfield
Western Stoke North Western Bury South Western Plymouth North Eastern Huddersfield
SOUTH C—Southampton 1 Charlton 3
SOUTH D—Bournemouth 2 Aldershot 1 Brighton 3 Orient 0, Norwich 1 Palace 3 Southend 2 Watford 2
MIDLAND—Birmingham 8 Walsall 1 Leicester 2 Northampton 0 Coventry 4 WBA 0
EAST MIDLAND—Grimsby 4 Notts F 3 Mansfield 2 Sheffield Utd 2
NTH WESTERN—Oldham 4 Blackpool 2
SOUTH WESTERN—Newport 5 Plymouth 2 Swansea 4 Bristol City 1
NORTH EASTERN—Hull 4 Darlington 4 Leeds 1 Newcastle 3 Newcastle 4 Bradford C 1
SOUTH B—Reading 2 Portsmouth 2
LANCS CUP FINAL—Bury 2 Everton 4

WEST Ham have won the War Cup Final—but even in this joyful moment (writes George Casey) there is probably some head scratching going on! Just seventeen years ago West Ham and Bolton inaugurated the opening of Wembley as a Cup Final ground, and on that never-to-be-forgotten day 150,000 people stormed into the Stadium—25,000 gate-crashed—and created a scene that has a place all its own in football history.

Yesterday only 43,000 turned up. Roughly 7,000 short of the crowd limit granted by the police.

Did people fear being turned away?

Is a night match at Wembley a failure? Or were too many enthusiasts engaged in work of national importance? There's a multiple problem confronting the authorities if ever they have again to arrange a big match in war-time.

As to the play the boys who like their sport tough will say it's the grandest final they've ever seen. No quarter asked—and no quarter given. But purists will raise their monocles and deplore the lack of skill and artistry. The classic touches in the whole ninety minutes can be counted almost on one hand!

One of these isolated moves produced the goal which won the match. Apart from the first save of the Blackburn goalkeeper, Barron, not a Rovers man touched the ball while it was being executed.

Small it was who sent in the smashing shot that eventually ended Blackburn's hopes—but this right winger will admit that nearly all the credit should go to the men who made his shot possible.

It all began with West Ham nearly conceding a goal! A free kick was taken on the left. Conway ran across the goal to collect the ball and left an open goal for a bunch of Blackburn men

George Foreman and Archie Macaulay attack the Blackburn Rovers goal.

Battery of the 1/6 Essex Regiment Territorials, to pick the team.

"About 20 of our players had joined the TA and Charlie had obtained the services of three goalkeepers who played on alternative weeks in the hastily arranged war-time competitions, George Taylor, Henry Medhurst and young Ernie Gregory. In the early years of the war a maximum 8,000 gate was permitted because the government did not want more than that number of people assembled at any one time in the event of an air attack.

"The only exception I can recall was the 43,000 allowed into the war-time Cup Final between West Ham and Blackburn Rovers at Wembley", he concluded his fascinating reminisce.

Later in the conflict when Britain came under ever more heavy attacks from the Luftwaffe, the government urged clubs to employ "spotters", armed with binoculars to warn of the approach of enemy aircraft.

West Ham didn't have far to look for the man to fill that post as the aforementioned Assistant Groundsman David Baillie volunteered for the role.

A local man from Ilford, Dave was a former Hammers goalkeeper during the 20s utilised mostly as an understudy to England international Ted Hufton and was said to have had an outside chance of playing in the 1923 FA Cup Final until Ted recovered from injury in time to take his place at Wembley. But on reflection, this seems doubtful as he didn't sign for the club until 1924.

Left: The War Cup is West Hams! Sam Small hits the winner in the 1940 Final at Wembley, watched by a restricted crowd of 43,000.

Right: Captain Charlie Bicknell receives the handsome trophy from Lord Alexander of Hillsborough following the 1-0 victory over Blackburn Rovers. Charlie Walker looks on.

Below: L-R Ted Fenton, Norman Corbett (in uniform), skipper Charlie Bicknell, Archie Macaulay, Stan Foxall (in background) and George Foreman inspect their medals and the trophy, which still remained in the Upton Park trophy cabinet until the Club left in the summer of 2016.

Dick Walker watches the ball go out of play, following a Blackburn raid on Hammers goal.

The victorious War Cup winners. L-R: Foxall, Fenton, Conway, Bicknell, Macaulay, Walker C, Foreman.

BLAST FROM THE PAST — WEST HAM v CHELSEA 1940

Daily Mail: Saturday May 3rd 2003. The ARW on the roof is ex-Hammers goalkeeper David Baillie.

David Baillie as a West Ham player.

During WWII, all companies and institutions had their own roof spotters, usually members of staff who did an extra shift. His job was to act as an early warning system to those inside the building of an impending attack by enemy aircraft.

The man allocated the task at Upton Park was assistant groundsman David Bailie, the former Hammers goalkeeper who we've mentioned earlier in the Boleyn Ground story regarding his help in training Ernie Gregory.

He would have had to have had his "eyes peeled" when this shot above was taken in 1940 when squadrons of Luftwaffe Heinkel and Dornier bombers used to follow the route of the Thames to drop their deadly cargo on London – especially the docks.

Ironically, the spot where David is standing in the south-east corner of the ground in the picture is just yards from where a V1 hit with devastating effect in August 1944.

Mostly understudy to Ted Hufton during his five years with Irons between 1924 and 1929 in which time he made 16 First Division appearances and one in the FA Cup, he transferred to Chester where he was under the autocratic management of Charlie Hewitt at Sealand Road. There is no record of Ilford-born David playing for the Blues after their elevation to the Football League in 1931, however.

In 2013, Steve Marsh, the founder of the award-winning website, theyflysohigh, was contacted by the nephew of our subject who told how he inherited a suitcase full of memorabilia when his great uncle passed away in 1967, including the original war-time photograph we have used here to illustrate this fascinating story.

Back row L-R: Alf Chalkley, Ted Fenton, Herman Conway, Albert Walker, Joe Cockcroft.
Front row L-R: Johnny Morton, Dr Jimmy Marshall, Big Jim Barrett, Dave Mangnall, Len Goulden, Jimmy Ruffell.

Baillie played 17 times for the first team before joining Chester in 1929, but when he hung up his gloves he returned to Upton Park to look after the pitch he had graced so many times.

Ernie Gregory who joined West Ham as a gangling young goalkeeper in 1936, had good reason to be thankful for Baillie's return early in his career.

In an age when goalkeeping coaches were unheard of, Baillie was one of the first big influences on the up and coming Ernie. He took Ernie for unofficial coaching sessions on the rough piece of training ground behind the main West Stand backing on to Green Street by the old castle.

Each dinner hour he would spend time improving his work in stopping shots on the ground. "I was OK in the air, but not so hot on the deck at the time because of my height", recalled Ernie in 1969.

Dave Baillie was unexpectedly back on the sports pages on Saturday, May 3, 2003 in a photo feature tagged "Blast From The Past" in the *Daily Mail*.

The photograph (previous page) shows Dave scanning the horizon over the "Chicken Run" for approaching enemy planes with a war-time match versus Chelsea going on below. He is standing on a precarious looking asbestos roof adjacent to the West Stand with the South Bank to his right.

It wasn't until comparatively recently that the identity of West Ham's war-time guardian resurfaced when historian Steve Marsh was sent the original photograph by Dave's nephew, Stephen Jones, who inherited it when his great uncle passed away in 1967.

Maybe it was the dramatic events of Saturday, September 7, 1940, with the Battle of Britain at its height, that decided manager Charlie Paynter to employ Baillie in his new role.

Hosting Spurs in a Regional League South fixture at Upton Park before 3,000 edgy spectators, goalkeeper Harry Medhurst would remember this day for much more than the four goals he'd conceded when the match was halted by one of the Luftwaffe's first daylight raids on the East End.

"The sirens started to wail and the drone of Heinkels could be heard coming up the Thames", Medhurst later recalled.

"The crowd dispersed in an orderly fashion, leaving the players behind to change.

"I remember pulling off my goalie jersey and running to help my sister who was a nurse; incendiary bombs were falling, there were many casualties".

In his book: *At Home With The Hammers,* former player and manager Ted Fenton remembered things slightly differently:

"We were playing Spurs and the referee called us off because German bombers were approaching. I was under the massage table when the dressing room windows came in from an explosion that was as near as we were likely to want it.

"But, as soon as the danger passed, we trooped back onto the pitch and got on with the job of chasing that little bit of leather, as if our lives depended on it".

West Ham had won the Football League War Cup with a 1-0 victory over Blackburn Rovers courtesy of a Sammy Small goal before a 43,000 crowd at Wembley, in a somewhat forced, unreal atmosphere.

As Jack Rollin concluded in the introduction to his classic work, *Soccer at War,* in 1985:

"Naturally in such traumatic times the game did not always fall easily on the ear. A seaman told me of the understandingly unfavourable reaction on board ship in the wake of the Dunkirk evacuation, listening to a radio broadcast of the first War Cup Final while fishing bodies out of the English Channel. But just as life went on, so did soccer".

At this stage in the Boleyn Ground story it might be pertinent to step back a moment to before WWII was declared to late summer, 1939.

The club's annual handbook was issued as usual.

In its foreword the anonymous writer began:

"All league clubs contemplate a coming season with visions of Cup Final and Championship. Indeed, it would be a dull game if pessimism were the prevailing influence, but it is with more than ordinary optimism that we Hammers face 1939-40 season's prospects".

It has been well documented that manager Charlie Paynter expected great things for the campaign with his playing staff bolstered by three new signings, a plentiful supply of exciting young players and first class men like Dick Walker, Ted Fenton and Joe Cockroft established in defence and England internationals Len Goulden and Jackie Morton in the forward line.

But as ever the devil is in the detail to be found in the penultimate paragraph of the foreword:

"Preparatory training will assume a rather unusual aspect this year, as only about a third will present themselves at Upton Park on July 31, the rest being in camp with the Territorials."

The writer got his Cup Final, but not the one he envisaged or wanted.

Despite the fact that the East End was hit harder than any other area of London by Goëring's Luftwaffe, the Boleyn Ground remained largely unscathed until the fateful day of August 2, 1944.

The accompanying photographs of the devastation wrought by the V1 flying-bomb (aka Doodle-bug) strike were not allowed to be published at the time by the government censor.

The only permitted location to be given or published on flying bomb incidents would be "Southern England".

Needless to say, everyone in the East End soon knew what had happened, though the direct hit on the Upton Park pitch was variously rumoured to have been caused by a parachute mine, bombs or, as proved correct, a V1.

Ted Fenton, for instance, in his book tells of how: "When I was playing at Inverness in the Army's Scottish tour, Sir Stanley Rous brought across a telegram to show me. Five bombs had fallen on Upton Park".

Luckily, only one man was on duty that August day when the missile struck, the head groundsman Dan Woodards, also known as "Dapper Dan" or "Beau Brummel" because of his well-groomed appearance when not attending his beloved Boleyn greensward. He was said to have been badly shaken and incandescent with rage over the blast which had caused a huge crater in the South/West corner of the well manicured pitch.

The impact blew the roofs off the South Bank, West Stand and Chicken Run, but the North Bank, which was uncovered, was spared.

Boundary walls, retaining walls and crush barriers were all destroyed as well as the club's offices situated in the wrecked West Stand. All the club's records were also lost.

The offices were evacuated along with what was left of the club administration, and re-located to Green Street House, the oft-referred-to Boleyn Castle.

It was extremely fortunate that the first V1s were not launched until June 13, 1944, as Upton Park was again requisitioned by the Army and from May 28 until D-Day on June 6, many hundreds of soldiers, awaiting orders to go to France, were billeted there in utmost secrecy.

In his book, *London Under Fire,* Leonard Mosley revealed the extraordinary events which unfolded at Upton Park in the build up to the biggest seaborne invasion the world had ever seen.

"Over Whit weekend (May 28-30, 1944) one of the biggest contingents of troops arrived from Scotland and the north of England, and these were shepherded into West Ham Football Stadium (*sic*). As in all the other camps, barbed wire fences were set up and sentries posted, and the troops cut off from the civilian world outside. That was how the trouble began.

"On June 1, the troops inside the stadium were divided up into groups and addressed in turn by their commanding officer. They were told that they were going to France 'any

The bomb ravaged Chicken Run, courtesy of the Luftwaffe.

day now' and given a rough idea of their landing. They were afterwards allowed to come forward in groups to study maps of the Ouistreham beaches in Normandy where their tank landing craft would soon be taking them. Then they were told to queue up before their supply sergeants, and were issued, and signed for, their first payment in French money for use when they got to the other side. After this they assembled in midfield and were addressed by an Army Chaplain, but his gloomy tone of voice and even gloomier forecast of the 'perils that lie ahead of us all' drove the soldiers off the field in the direction of the canteen in search of a soothing drink and a smoke.

"By seven in the evening the beer had run out and there was not a cigarette to be had in the stadium. Angry soldiers who approached the supply sergeants had it pointed out to them, in no uncertain terms, that this was Whit weekend and the NAAFI depots were closed.

"So, with the prospect of a dry and worrying weekend before them, several scores of D-Day soldiers did the logical thing. They crept past the sentries and crawled under the barbed wire. They snipped their way through it. They climbed on each other's shoulders and leaped over it. Some of them who knew the ground and had smuggled themselves into it to see the game as kids, now tunnelled their way out of it in search of a beer. Soon every pub in the vicinity was filled with British troops.

"Clamouring for drinks and smokes and even offering to pay for it with French francs, which the landlords were taking in as souvenirs.

Roofless, but not toothless. The Hammers attack the Spurs goal. Ted Ditchburn goes up to collect, supported by Bill Nicholson with Ken Wright to the right and Eddie Chapman on the left.

"By this time everybody from Montgomery down was telling us to get the soldiers back inside the stadium", said Chief Inspector Reg Smith. "My office had already been on the job and the bulk of the AWOLs had gone back quietly. Only about 30 remained, but they were carousing in pubs as widely apart as Limehouse and Canning Town and were in no mood to respond to the orders of the military and civilian police who had been sent to round them up".

And then, in Canning Town police station, Smith found the man who did the trick for him. He was an old retired police sergeant who had come back into the force as a volunteer for the duration of the war. He had sons of his own in the forces.

" 'If you'll just give me a truck and a driver, sir', the sergeant said, 'I think I can get the boys back for you. No rough stuff either'.

"It was a measure of his achievement that by five o'clock next morning not only had he got them all back, but there were six more soldiers in the stadium than there were before the thirsty invasion troops decided to make a break for it. A half-dozen ordinary soldiers not concerned with the invasion had fallen for the old sergeant's persuasive line and decided to come too.

"They had to be held in custody until after the D-Day barges were scraping the beaches of Normandy. So did a couple of East End pubkeepers. But they were allowed to keep the 'invasion francs' with which they had been paid when they were released".

So the mutiny had turned into an unwanted recruitment drive, and the most remarkable

Joslin, the Cardiff goalkeeper dives as the ball is cleared from Ken Wright by one of his defenders, watched by Eddie Chapman.

chapter in the history of the Boleyn Ground ended without a shot being fired or a single soldier disciplined.

Having "done its bit" for the invasion force and receiving a direct hit from the common enemy for its troubles, Upton Park was deemed unsafe to stage Football League South fare at the start of the 1944-45 season. As a result, the team was forced to play their first 14 fixtures on opponents' grounds to enable a team of volunteer workers to carry out "emergency repairs" at the badly damaged Boleyn.

This assistance was crucial at the tumultuous time due to the shortage of regular man-power and the club owed much to Chairman W.J. Cearns (who's company had originally built the West Stand in 1925) and Charlie Paynter who organised this help to bring back soccer to Upton Park before Christmas, 1944.

A letter sent to Hammers' programme editor and PRO, Jack Helliar, in 1974, shed further light on this group of unpaid heroes.

It came from a Mr. E.J. Talbot of Johnstone Road, East Ham, who wrote:

"This group of volunteers was made up of a small party of students, myself included, mostly from Plaistow Grammar School and aged about 15. Upon reading of the need for assistance they duly reported to the ground and proceeded with the work in hand under the expert supervision of the then groundsman, Mr. Dan Woodards.

War damaged Upton Park

The extent of the damage to the Chicken Run can be clearly seen in this photograph, showing action of a match against Portsmouth in 1945.

Archie Macaulay, the driving force in Hammers midfield in the 1930s and early Post War era. The flame haired Scot moved to Brentford, who were then in the First Division in 1947 and then on to Arsenal where he won an F.A. Cup finalist medal in 1950. He then moved across to West London, to join Fulham before taking up the managerial reins at Norwich City, although in the Third Division, he steered the Canaries to the semi-finals of the F.A. Cup where they lost to Luton Town 1-0 after defeating giants Manchester United and Spurs, in '59.

Below: Charlie Paynter shows Director A. C. Davis the badly damaged roof of the South Bank End, which took many years to repair because of restrictions on non essential works at this time.

"Being in the middle of the school holidays, we were able to help out on most days, and continued our help on Saturday mornings until the ground was able to be opened for home matches.

"During the remainder of that season, repairing goal nets, cleaning the stand and terraces, and when necessary, sweeping the puddles of water left behind due to the roofless stands.

"On looking back I can recall the occasions when the "Chicken Run" was unsafe to take spectators, and we were assigned as ball boys for the afternoon to patrol that section of the ground.

"We were all most gratified to receive a complimentary ticket for admission to the enclosure for the following season.

"Finally, I should like to place on record the great respect we all had for Mr. Dan Woodards during this difficult period".

Incidentally, Jack Helliar, who in 1986 published with me the first *Who's Who of West Ham* book, enlisted with the Essex Regiment Territorials in 1939 in company with many of the Hammers players of that time who joined up en-masse.

His paternal grandfather was a brassfounder at TIW and a member of the committee which in 1895 laid the foundations that led to the formation of West Ham United FC. His son John has for many years worked as a historian on the club programme and also succeeded his father as mine host and PRO in the pressroom at Upton Park, a role he still fills with some panache.

But back to that freezing precarious war-time season of 1944-45. Thanks to the unstinting efforts of those unpaid helpers, Upton Park was declared "open for business" again for the League South fixture with Spurs on December 2, 1944.

Then in true Hammers' fashion, having lost just three of 14 consecutive "away" matches, Hammers proceeded to lose that first home game of the campaign 1-0, in front of 25,000 soccer-starved fans, some of whom broke in at the South Bank end after the gates had been closed for safety reasons.

Spurs tally was scored in the second half by forward Harold Gilbery who had spent most of the war playing as a guest with Southend United and Charlton Athletic.

Hammers included two guests themselves against Tottenham, Dai Jones of Leicester City at left-back and Jock Dodds of Sheffield United who made 17 and 10 guest appearances for Irons respectively in that 1944-45 season, with Dodds finding the net an incredible 11 times.

The following Saturday, Irons were at long last able to record their first home win of the season with a 2-0 win over Charlton Athletic before a restricted crowd of just 9,500. Right winger Terry Woodgate scored the first just before half-time after shots by him and Ted Fenton had been blocked, then, six minutes after the interval, the prolific George Foreman scored when he intercepted a lobbed back pass and headed it home.

Home and away League South fixtures with Chelsea were scheduled on Christmas Day and Boxing Day that last war-time festive season. But the matches were postponed. War-time censorship did not permit a reason to be given in the club programme, but was probably due to the adverse weather conditions in Europe at that time which had a salutary effect on

A graphic picture of the damage caused to the West Stand by the V1 on August 2nd 1944 which wasn't able to be shown at the time due to censorship. The crater in the south west corner of the pitch can be clearly seen.

WWII operations prior to the German offensive in the Ardennes and brought restrictions on service-leave that left clubs short of personnel. Normal service was resumed on December 30, however, as a crowd of 9,000 watched Hammers defeat Queen's Park Rangers 4-2 at the Boleyn with Foreman (3) and Woodgate getting the goals to say goodbye to a traumatic year in style.

By February, the German's last offensive of WWII in what became known as the "Battle of the Bulge" had been repelled and although southern England was still under constant attack from Hitler's new "Terror Weapon" – the V2 Rocket, reporter Roy Peskett was able to draft the following account of West Ham's League South Cup qualifier with Spurs at Upton Park on the 10th of the month before a 21,000 attendance: "The final 20 minutes of this match were just about the most exciting I have seen this war. The last two minutes were played with Ted Fenton of West Ham, unconscious in the middle of the field, and play milling around him; in fact, the ball bounced on his prone body once, but play was not stopped. Spurs suffered their first away defeat since March. Len Goulden, who headed the vital goal in the 32nd minute was the star of a game which, although not a classic, continuously touched the high spots".

Hammers subsequently won their group and qualified to meet Chelsea in the semi-final at White Hart Lane where they lost 2-1 and with it the chance of anymore silverware during the rapidly ending war games.

West Ham's goal was scored by Len Townsend, a guest from Brentford. But, perhaps significantly, Len Goulden didn't appear in the Hammers' line-up although he had played in earlier ties. Had his transfer to the Blues already been earmarked and was just awaiting a rubber stamp?

It certainly looked to be the case as he appeared for Chelsea along with seven other guests in the Football League South Cup Final against Millwall at Wembley the following month, which was won by the West Londoners 2-0.

He was back in a Chelsea shirt following VE Day on June 3, 1945 as the Pensioners were defeated 2-1 at Stamford Bridge by the winners of the Football League North Cup, Bolton Wanderers and was transferred to the Blues for £5,000 in time to play against the legendary Moscow Dynamo later that year.

Early in the conflict, during the period which became known as the "Phoney War", West Ham decided to pay all their players thirty shillings a week whether they played or not, according to Jack Rollin in his weighty tome, *Soccer At War*.

"About twenty four of their players were in the Army and the club considered that they should not suffer financially for their patriotism".

At this time only friendly matches were being played and Jack noted that on October 14, 1939: "West Ham, doubtless inspired by their club's recent benevolence, waded into Charlton 9-2".

And in 1941-42 after the formation of the break-away London League that on November 1, "Harold Cothliff scored inside ten seconds in Reading's 3-2 win over West Ham". And added: "The Hammers also lost 5-0 to Crystal Palace on November 22 but because of a road accident had had to play pivot Jim Barrett in goal".

Jack, who was my editor when I worked as an office junior and trainee reporter at *Soccer Star Magazine* in the 60s, also noted: "In November 1940 West Ham went to Brentford and played with nine men for twenty minutes, expecting the other two to arrive. Only a tenth turned up, so Brentford loaned them another player to complete the side. The Hammers thanked them and promptly won 2-0. In January 1941, West Ham played one short throughout the first half at Millwall, knowing that a replacement was almost certain to arrive at the interval".

Research shows that Hammers won that one, too, by 3-1 with goals from Eddie Chapman, Stan Foxall and Sam Small and further underlined the fact that anything could happen in war-time soccer.

Len Goulden

Local derbies were abundant in the first post-war season of organised football as fans flocked back to watch the "People's Game" after years of being starved of top level entertainment.

Although the 1945-46 season retained a regional format and was of a temporary nature with no promotion or relegation issues at its conclusion, the quality of the teams competing in the Football Leagues of the South and North were of a noticeably higher standard than was provided throughout WWII.

Competing in the 22 club Football League South, Hammers were pitched against no less than seven other London clubs

Back row L-R: Corbett, Yeomanson, Walker R, Gregory, Forde, Banner.
Front row L-R: Woodgate, Parsons, Neary, Wood, Bainbridge.

in addition to Luton Town. Their London rivals were Arsenal, Brentford, Charlton, Chelsea, Fulham, Millwall and Spurs.

Many fixtures were scheduled on consecutive Saturdays to add spice to the proceedings.

West Ham kicked off the first peace-time season at Birmingham, now proudly bearing the City suffix for the first time. But the Blues were defeated 1-0 by Charlie Paynter's men in front of 30,000 spectators at St. Andrews thanks to a penalty from captain Charlie Bicknell.

The Hammers were then given a tremendous boost by being allocated the next four matches at the Boleyn Ground, which although roofless and badly battered, gladly welcomed 95,000 fans through the turnstiles over the four games.

Arsenal (1-1), Birmingham City (3-2) and Tottenham (1-1) were the first three visitors before the last of the quartet, Aston Villa, left London with the points after their 2-1 win.

Reporting the Monday evening match for the *Daily Chronicle* was ex-Arsenal, Sunderland and England star Charlie Buchan. He commented that "Villa"s old men lasted the game well, with Cummings, Callaghan and Starling always prominent. West Ham were more youthful, but had no forward, except occasionally Foreman, who could outwit the ripe experience of the defenders".

The photograph at the beginning of this chapter, showing George Foreman racing with a Villa defender in the actual match, clearly shows the extent of the damage caused to the West Stand by the V1 attack in August, 1944.

The team boarding the aircraft to play the British Army of the Rhine. L-R Fenton, Corbett, Wood, Walker C, Walker R, Billy Moore (Trainer) Medhurst.

The South Bank and the Chicken Run were in a similar state of disrepair to leave Upton Park hardy patrons literally without a roof over their heads – thanks to the fact that the Ministry, although funds were available, would not permit the club to carry out the work required with part-time labour and odd material.

The 23,000 crowd at the Villa match was four thousand short of the number who turned up for the previous Saturday's meeting with Spurs. The goals came in the first half, that man Foreman equalising Ronnie Burgess's early counter for the North Londoners. The 27,000 gate was the highest at Upton Park since 1939 – many of whom risked their necks by climbing girders that were relics of the blitzed stands.

Hammers had completed the double over the Brummies on September 1, when the in-form Foreman scored twice before winger Charlie Whitchurch scored the winner after converting Archie Macaulay's pass.

Among the match-day visitors was Col. Ivan Vasilev of the Soviet Air Force, who before the war had played for Moscow Dynamo. He was joined by 20,000 other "comrades" present to cheer the Hammers on!

Match-winner Whitchurch had scored seven times in nine outings the previous season and played regularly up until Christmas 1946, when he accepted an offer to join Spurs. The return of other professionals from the forces having made the club overstaffed. He later played for Southend United before emigrating to Canada in the early 50s. He died in 1977 in Michigan,

George Foreman glances a header wide in the 1-1 draw with Arsenal in August 1945. Hammers' goal was scored by Charlie Whitchurch and the Gunners' by Joe Mercer.

USA where he was involved in rocket research with General Motors.

An indication of the amount of personnel West Ham had in the armed forces can be appreciated by the line-up which faced Leicester City in a League South fixture at Upton Park on December 1, 1945.

In addition to Flt.-Lt. Ken Wright, who was awarded the DFC, and fellow RAF man Charlie Walker, who was reserved a particularly warm return to the Boleyn after serving an extended tour of duty in the Far East, Hammers could also boast seven men from Army units in their team to face the Foxes. They were: Sgt. Harry Medhurst, BSM Norman Corbett, Paratrooper Dick Walker, CSM Ted Fenton, and Gunner Jack Wood.

But the high water mark of that first post-war season that returned to something approaching normality was, without doubt, the return of the FA Cup competition proper, after a six year absence.

The Third and Fourth rounds of the world's oldest cup competition were played over two legs in this transitionary campaign and Arsenal, with their pre-war dominance still fresh in the collective memory of football supporters all over the country, were the plum draw – and Hammers got them in the 1st leg at home.

Saturday, January 5, 1946 was a red letter day in Hammers history, but one the Gunners would want to forget. Against the stark background of Upton Park's still bomb-wrecked stands, it was the Arsenal who were blitzed. West Ham were four up at half-time and added two more in the second half in front of an incredulous crowd officially put at 35,000 but swelled by many more who climbed the flimsy barriers to gain entry. The *Stratford Express* headlined their report of the match: "Blitzkrieg at Upton Park" which expounded: "This first leg in the Third Round tie of the FA Cup between these old rivals at Upton park was without doubt the sensation of the day. The Arsenal were pulverised by a side that worked like a machine, with speed and accuracy allied with any amount of 'devil'. This Arsenal knew they were beaten at the end of half an hour. During that period the West Ham attack was devastating. Time after time it split the Arsenal defence wide open and scored four goals.

"The defenders had no answer to the Hammers' Blitzkrieg and although the home forwards lost some of their effectiveness in the second half, they were still the masters and added two further tallies". West Ham team on this great night with scorers in parentheses: Medhurst, Bicknell, Cater, Small, Walker, Fenton, Woodgate, Hall (2), Foreman (1), Wood (2) and Bainbridge (1).

The fact that the Gunners won the second leg 1-0 at White Hart Lane (they had their own bomb damage at Highbury) was academic. Hammers were in the Fourth Round against Chelsea and their former Star Lennie Goulden. But because of the state of the Upton Park ground, no doubt exacerbated by events at the Arsenal tie, the club decided to switch the first leg to Stamford Bridge where 62,726 gathered on the Saturday to watch Chelsea win 2-0.

The safety limit of 35,000 on the following Wednesday was reached very early in the afternoon, with thousands being locked out. The Blues had an early shock when their ex-Hammer Goulden collided with Irons' skipper, the redoubtable Charlie Bicknell and sustained a broken collar-bone that left the West Londoners a man short for the remaining 80 minutes. Almer Hall put Hammers ahead just before half-time, but despite laying siege to Blues' goal for the rest of the game, Chelsea's ten men held out.

Hammers were out, but once again the thrills and spills of the FA Cup had lit up their season and increased the club's bank balance.

Back in League South a new star was unearthed – Don Travis, a six foot sailor from Manchester, stationed in Edinburgh and with playing experience for Cowdenbeath and St. Mirren. He scored four times for the reserves in a trial against Chelsea's second string, signed pro and repeated the feat in his first team debut against Plymouth Argyle at the Boleyn. Remarkably, winger Woodgate got the other three goals in the 7-0 victory over the Pilgrims on February 16, 1946.

It had been a good season. The steely Irons had more than mixed it with clubs of First Division pedigree like Chelsea, Arsenal, Aston Villa and Wolves. The war was over, no longer were people waiting for the dreaded "doodlebug's" engine to cut out and the nerve shredding hiatus before they struck. The stoic dockers and all the other working class heroes of London's East End were once again hopeful for a brave new future… but still Upton Park had no roofs on its stands. As Charles Korr pointed out in his ground breaking work in *West Ham United: The Making of a Football Club,* published in 1986: "During the First World War, the landlord of the Boleyn Ground, the Archdiocese of Westminster, had been unsympathetic to West Ham's lost revenue and had dropped the rent only marginally. In 1939, however, the landlord took the initiative and made an interesting proposal to West Ham. The club could have the ground for a rent of £1 per annum and would be responsible for preparing the ground as a military training area. The forecourt provided space for drill manoeuvres, and other areas for shelters and practice ranges. West Ham accepted the terms, which also included a small fee to be paid to the Boleyn Social Club and an implied promise that favourable terms would be negotiated when the lease was renewed in four years".

After intense wrangling with the Borough of East Ham, the club were also able to secure a substantial reduction in the rates for Upton park, down from £1,350 to a peppercorn £200 per annum for the duration of the conflict. These welcome concessions helped the club conserve its meagre resources to refit and repair the ground after the war. Yet despite all their best efforts, all the club's attempts to obtain permission to carry out essential works were thwarted by government red tape. Preliminary work on the Boleyn Castle, which was also badly damaged, was allowed to start as early as December 1944 due to it having been listed in accordance with the Ancient Monuments Act of 1931, thus making it easier to obtain the necessary licence from the Ministry of Works to proceed with repairing the local landmark.

Appeals to commence work on the roofless Main Stand, South Bank and Chicken Run continued to fall on deaf ears, however, and it wasn't until the autumn of 1947 that the club were finally allowed to start repairs. Contracts were signed with Cearns Ltd., and by 1950 the club had paid out more than £165,000 to return the ground to its pre-war condition.

A NEW BEGINNING

Chapter 4

Before commencing the tumultuous, longest-ever season of 1946-47, which was afflicted by the worst winter of the century thus far, West Ham embarked on a pre-season tour to Switzerland; a country which had maintained neutrality throughout the war.

The trip was a resounding success and the party returned home in high spirits, having won six out of seven of their matches and drawn the other 2-2 with Zurich, boasting a goals-for total of 33; with only 7 conceded. They also came back with an amazing and amusing tale to tell relating to an incident which occurred prior to one of their matches. Apparently, everything was ready for kick-off when it was noticed there was no ball and the referee kept pointing skywards. The players thought he must have been crazy and waiting for it to rain footballs – and then it did. A plane dropped the match ball right in the middle of the pitch.

Suitably refreshed by their Swiss sojourn, it was Hammers' turn to be brought back down to earth on their return to "Austerity Britain", as they prepared to set off on the long train journey to Plymouth to face the Argyle in their first match in the Football League proper since 1939. The clerk of the weather was sending out mixed messages on that opening day of sunshine, thunder, lightning and floods, omens maybe of what lay ahead. West Ham's troubles began at Paddington Station, when faced with the arduous journey to the West Country on a buffet-less train with overflowing compartments and corridors, asked to be allowed on the platform first to avoid queuing, but were refused by the railway staff. Not surprisingly, West Ham lost to the Home Park Pilgrims, managed by West Ham 1923 FA Cup Final wing-half Jack Tresadern, 3-1; with only a goal from the club's practical joker, Jackie Wood, to show for their travels. Back at the Boleyn two days later a very healthy crowd of 28,000 (but only numerically, given the food shortages and other trials and tribulations they had had to endure) assembled to witness a cracking 3-2 win over Fulham with goals from Small and Macaulay (2), who would soon be on his way to then First Division Brentford. A week hence a near identical attendance gathered at the same venue, but on this occasion visitors Leicester City repeated their 2-0 victory at Upton Park in the last peace-time match played there on September 2, 1939. The Filberts also returned in early January 1947 to eliminate Irons from the Third Round of the FA Cup by dint of a 2-1 victory deemed very lucky by most observers. Early FA Cup exits in the Third and Fourth rounds would become the norm until the great run to a Sixth Round replay with Spurs in 1956. Meanwhile Irons were able to arrest a slide which saw them win just once in the first five matches of 1946-47 with an always welcome 3-1 win over arch-rivals Millwall on September 21, in front of the best gate of the season so far – 30,000 at a bulging Boleyn. An own goal by ex-Hammer Benny Fenton and two others by Dicky Dunn and Sammy Small ensured that the Lions remained at the foot of the Second Division table. A reflection of conditions in those days was illustrated by the fact that owing to the damaged state of Upton Park, the club were unable to reserve seats or issue season tickets; likewise, difficulty in obtaining paper prevented the club issuing a handbook – indeed, with permits required it was even a problem to obtain paper to print a programme. But even worse was to follow with the "winter freeze-up". It began in late January and by the 28th of that month weather observer Mr. T.W. Partis of Plaistow noted in his diary that the country was paralysed by 27 degrees of frost (–15°C) and an intense blizzard led to two inches of snow in just 15 minutes near his home. Even so, West Ham's scheduled Second Division fixture against Bradford Park Avenue still went ahead – just. A brief match report in a following programme commenting: "Until late in the week it looked as if the match would have to be postponed, but both teams overcame the difficult conditions; the 17,000 patrons got good value, and an enjoyable game resulted". Ken Bainbridge got Hammers' goal in a 1-1 draw against the Yorkshiremen who had a certain Ron Greenwood at centre-half. These were the days of the fuel crisis, power-cuts and food rationing with many clubs accepting clothes vouchers from supporters to buy much-needed playing kit. The programme for the match against Swansea Town on March 1 was printed on one side of a 7½ins x 5ins sheet by Helliar & Son which former programme editor Jack Helliar recalled: "Being 'worked off' on a treadle operated platen press", at their works in Barking Road. Despite the still icy conditions, there was a 21,000 crowd to see the game with the Swans which Hammers won 3-0. A contemporary press report included a favourable comment on a new signing from

Arthur Banner (5) gets up to a high ball at Park Avenue v Bradford.

Norman Corbett

Woodgate number 7, attacks the Coventry City goal.

Below: Terry Woodgate (left) again on the attack against Coventry.

Eddie Chapman bursts through the Plymouth defence, but Argyle's Keeper, Short, grabs the ball.

Queen's Park Rangers: "Frank Neary has played in two matches for the Hammers, and he has scored twice in each – not bad going. He seemed pretty sure-footed to me, and he must have been, judging from the way he tore in and crashed home his second goal with a first-time shot, without slipping up". After a brief thaw the snow returned with a vengeance, but still West Ham's home game with WBA went ahead on March 15, and this time big Frank, who was nicknamed "the brown bomber" went one better, bagging a hat-trick against the Baggies, in direct opposition to England international centre-half Harry Kinsell, who was later to join Hammers. To add to the acute fixture congestion, there was added difficulty in rearranging postponed matches due to a proposed ban on mid-week sporting events. A 2-1 win at the Boleyn against Sheffield Wednesday, who had ex-Hammer Joe Cockroft in their side and a 3-2 victory at Newcastle had left the Hammers optimistic of ending the season on a winning note for their last game of the season at Upton Park against third place Burnley who had former Hammer Reg Attwell at right-half, and were FA Cup runners-up, but the Turf Moor Club clinched promotion by inflicting West Ham's worst home defeat up to that time – 5-0.

The never ending season which began in a heatwave on Saturday, August 13, finally finished amid a deluge at Sheffield United's badly blitzed Bramall Lane on June 14. The Blades defeated those other proud wearers of red and white stripes, Stoke City, 2-1 to hand the First Division Championship title to Liverpool and West Ham's 1923 FA Cup Final captain George Kay, now manager of the Reds. Another team in red won the FA Cup – Charlton; but West Ham also had some silverware to show for their efforts when they defeated Walthamstow Avenue, and Spurs on their way to the final of the London Challenge Cup at neutral Highbury, where they beat Charlton Athletic 3-2 with two goals from Dick Dunn and one from winger Terry Woodgate. A newspaper report commented: "At half-time both teams took their refreshments on the field and then played on".

There was an interesting snippet in the season's final match programme versus Burnley which commented that manager Charlie Paynter and talent scout Ben Ives had spent nearly a fortnight in Ireland signing two new players – Eire international defender Johnny McGowan and forward or wing-half Tommy Moroney from Cork United. The pair were the first of an influx of imports who would cross the Irish Sea to make the Boleyn Ground a home from home during the late 40s and early 50s, but the transfer didn't go as smoothly as planned. In fact, there was more than a touch of farce about it. The duo arrived at Upton Park a week after the rest of the playing staff had started pre-season training because of "passage and passport" delays and turned up without their boots. Cork refused to post them on and they were forced to break in new ones. Despite some obvious discomfort, Moroney came through the annual public practice matches, in which the first team would take on the reserves as a curtain raiser for the new season, with flying colours, but his compatriot, McGowan, was not so fortunate. He suffered badly blistered feet, which prevented his expected first team debut and also injured a knee which necessitated two cartilage operations. He never did play in the first team, but played many times in the Football Combination side, whereas Moroney quickly made the first XI and was capped 12 times for his country whilst a Hammer. In 1948, following a recommendation from pre-war Hammers' centre-half Charlie Turner, Hammers again raided the Emerald Isle to sign wing-half Danny McGowan from Shelborne, who was no relation to Johnny. Six months later, West Ham went back to the Mardyke to sign Moroney's successor at Cork United,

West Ham v Plymouth, 1947
Ken Wright heads for goal.

Frank O'Farrell. Then in the summer of 1952, this time on the recommendation of Moroney, returned to Cork again to sign Noel Cantwell for £850. A paltry fee for the man who was destined to captain Hammers 1958 Second Division Championship side and be sold for £30,000 to Manchester United in 1960. Quite a profit. Others who joined the transfer trail to London's East End from the Republic were Fred Kearns from Shamrock Rovers and Johnny Carroll from Limerick, who were signed by Chief Scout Ives at the same time as Danny McGowan. Another who made the crossing was Evergreen United's Jackie Morley in 1955, but who failed to make the first XI. For those who may have wondered, there were three main reasons Hammers found Ireland such an attractive recruitment source. Firstly, the transfer fees required were small; secondly, the players were generally of a very high standard; but thirdly, and most important of all; they were exempt from National Service. So the club's forays into the transfer market targeting Ireland were yet another example of the West Ham board's well thought out policies to get value for money in what were extremely frugal times. Some might have called it penny-pinching, but as the new Chairman Reg Pratt reminded readers in a two-part article in the *Stratford Express* about the "Hammers' future" that "the club was still paying off some of the debentures for the 1924 construction (of the West Stand) and serious war damage had to be repaired". The board planned more changes for the comfort of the Boleyn Ground's spectators, but he could not go into detail until they knew it had the funds. On the playing front, between the years of 1946 and 1956, it was a matter of little and less, with regards to League success. The record for the ten year span being: 1946-47, 12th; 1947-48, 6th; 1948-49, 7th; 1949-50, 19th; 1950-51, 13th; 1951-52, 12th; 1952-53, 14th; 1953-54, 13th; 1954-55, 8th;

27.3.48: Plymouth Keeper, Short, saves from Eric Parsons. V Plymouth Argyle.

1955-56, 16th. A lot was going on behind the scenes, however. After a board meeting had been satisfactorily concluded on June 24, 1948, the Chairman, Mr. W.J. Cearns, reported that the manager, Charlie Paynter, had discussed with him the difficulty he was experiencing in carrying out his duties "owing to advancing age particularly in respect of managing the team regarding tactics, etc". Korr, p98. Then Paynter, under no pressure to resign his post, virtually rubber stamped the enrolment of his own successor when he suggested that former West Ham player Ted Fenton should be appointed as his assistant so he could "Learn the ropes" and be in position to take over the reins when he retired "in a couple of years time". Fenton had hit the headlines since leaving Hammers in 1946 to take over the role of player-manager of Southern League Colchester United and then guided the little Essex club to a Fifth Round FA Cup clash with Blackpool after dispatching Wrexham, Huddersfield Town and Bradford Park Avenue in the process. When he was offered the post to be manager at First Division West Bromwich Albion, Fenton first contacted his old mentor Paynter "for advice" before accepting the job. In his book, *At Home with the Hammers*, he gives the impression that he would have walked from Layer Road to East London to return to West Ham. Even though he would have been £5 a week better off at the Hawthorns. At a time when £5 was a princely sum and West Ham prided themselves in providing a daily lunch for twenty players to ensure that "no man goes without the food he needs", his sacrifice needed little explanation. Fenton, who at Colchester had helped to build his own office and was quoted as saying: "If you can find me houses for the players, I can get you

1947: Tommy Moroney, Norman Corbett, Danny McGowan.

the best team in the world", had, by working miracles on less than a shoestring, all the credentials that West Ham were looking for. To Fenton, compared to Colchester, Upton Park must have seemed like a palace, blitzed and bombed out stands regardless. Maybe even in those austere days he could see the potential for the Boleyn Ground to become the magnificent stadium it was when West Ham left in 2016.

In his book published in 1960 he expounded: "I want to make West Ham a glamour club. I want to make Upton Park London's jewel of the East. If the ideas dreamed up by myself and the directors come true, Upton Park will not only be the pride of dockland, but also the social meeting place for football fans from the more snob areas of London. Our main aim is to see Upton Park with a stadium to equal any. At the moment we are restricted on space. Our ground will take only 38,000. Before too long those days will be gone forever. Now we plan another double-decker stand like the present stand, and covering all round the ground. Then we will be able to house 50,000 people in the dry".

Although every aspect of Upton Park has been rebuilt since Fenton's futuristic envision of 1960, and the Boleyn Ground has been improved out of all recognition as I write in 2015, Ted's dream remained unfulfilled by a single criteria: capacity. Hence the move to pastures new for 2016-17.

But back to the harsh realities of post-war Britain and the East End in particular, where, in not too distant Hornchurch, there had been a bus strike on VE Day. Rationing, which would continue into the 50s, meant there were shortages of almost everything, especially

1947: Fred Kearns, Ken Bainbridge, Eric Parsons.

anything which began with "B", like beer, bacon, bananas and bread. Ironically, Winston Churchill, who had won the war in most minds, proceeded to lose the election in a landslide to Labour's Clement Attlee. At the microcosm which was the Boleyn Ground, beerless, but not cheerless, life went on. After serving his two year "apprenticeship", Fenton was officially appointed as only the third manager in the club's 50-year history in July 1950, when the legend who was Charlie Paynter finally retired. A richly deserved testimonial match followed against Arsenal on September 18, for the grand old man who most referred to as simply "Mr. West Ham". Arsenal were fitting opponents as they had provided the opposition (as the then Woolwich Arsenal) on November 12, 1906 when Charlie had been given the honour of being the first West Ham recipient of a benefit match. Perhaps tellingly, as when a young right winger, he'd had his promising career ended while playing against the Gunners in a London League reserve game at Plumstead in 1902. More than 18,000 spectators assembled at Charlie's beloved Boleyn for the game with FA Cup holders Arsenal who brought the FA Cup with them to bring added lustre to a gala occasion. His team gave him a winning send off, winning 3-1 with goals from Gerry Gazzard, Stan Johns and Robinson. The esteem in which Paynter was held throughout the game was reflected by the number of dignitaries present. As he sat watching from the director's box flanked on one side by the President of the Football League, Arthur Drewry and on the other, Stanley Rous, Secretary of the FA, his stature, although small by nature, could have been in little doubt. In the after-match boardroom ceremony he was joined by Viscount Alexander, politicians,

1947: Steve Forde, Jackie Wood, Dick Walker.

local football officials and the biggest star of the era, Vera Lynn. Also present were many of his "Boys", the West Ham players who performed under his tutelage over the years. Among those who turned up for their old boss were: Jack Morton, Vic Watson, Joe Cockroft, Jim Collins, Tommy Hodgson, Dick Leafe, Herman Conway, Ted Fenton, Dave Mangnall, Ted Hufton, Len Young, Stan Foxall, Len Goulden and Dick Walker who made a speech and presented Charlie with a special gift from them all. Frank O'Farrell, who was always knocking on Charlie's door, made his first team bow that night.

With FA Cup success strangely absent during Hammers first ten post-war seasons, the money to pay for the rebuilding of Upton Park and future improvements had to come from somewhere and it was found from a source extremely unpopular among the club's supporters – by selling players. Much of it from the sale of three "wonder wingers", Eric Parsons (£22,500 to Chelsea in 1950); Tommy Southren (to Aston Villa for £10,000 in 1954); and Harry Hooper (£25,000 to Wolves in 1956). Add a further sum of £10,000 which took "Young" Jim Barrett to Nottingham Forest in 1954 and the club had brought in £77,500 for four players who had cost just the nominal £10 signing-on fee each. Some business.

The first to go, Eric "Rabbit" Parsons, was the subject of an interview I conducted on behalf of *Hammers News Magazine* for the Vintage Claret series in February, 1996. In it he revealed how he came to join West Ham as a 15-year old before the war. "I actually joined the ground staff in 1938", he told me. "I impressed Charlie Paynter a year previously when I represented Worthing Boys against West Ham Boys in the sixth round of the English Schools Shield at

1947: Eric Armstrong, Ernie Devlin, Almeric Hall.

Upton Park.

"We lost 1-0, but it was considered a major triumph getting that far. After the match I was taken down to the boiler room at Upton Park by one of the club's scouts, Syd Gibson, and hoodwinked into signing amateur forms for Hammers. Syd put a form in front of me and said: 'sign here'. I said I'd better ask my teacher, but he said the teacher had already given his permission, so I signed. When I saw the schoolmaster, he told me he didn't know anything about it! I'd really had the wool pulled over my eyes, but was glad to be associated with West Ham".

But in Europe the first rumblings of war were being heard and would soon result in all out conflict to put an end to football in all but an ersatz war-time form for the best part of seven years. "I remember when war was declared and league football was abandoned after just three matches of the 1939-40 season. I left my digs in Henniker Gardens, East Ham and got the 2.30 p.m. train back to Worthing from Victoria.

"Most of the West Ham playing staff had already enlisted to the Essex Regiment Territorials, but, at only 17, I was too young to join up". Eric's chance to do his bit for King and Country soon came, however, when he received his call-up papers in 1942. "After six weeks with the Infantry Training Regiment at Congleton in Cheshire, learning Morse Code and to drive Ack Ack vehicles, I was posted to near my home with the 93rd Light AA Regiment RA at Middleton Manor in Sussex", he recalled.

"I well remember the time a few days before our regiment embarked on D36, which meant

1947: Don Wade, Derek Jackman, Ron Cater.

Ernie Gregory punches clear with Jack Yeomanson and Dick Walker in attendance.

Eddie Chapman challenges Spurs' Keeper Ted Ditchburn in 1947.

36 days after D-Day, to join the invasion force at Normandy, when we pitched camp on a bomb site at Canning Town under canvass. I took the opportunity to pop into Upton Park, but if my memory serves me correctly, only trainer Billy Moore was at the ground".

Eric had previously scored on his debut for Hammers' senior side in the 3-2 Boleyn win over Fulham in a League South fixture on April 1, 1944. A few months later he was part of the Allied advance attempting to extend the bridgehead at Normandy.

"When the war ended, West Ham came out to Germany to play the British Army of the Rhine to help raise the morale of the troops after a long, hard war", he continued. "It felt strange for me playing against all my old buddies for the army side in the match, which was staged at an RAF base at a place called Sella.

"Charlie Paynter and Archie Macaulay greeted me before the match but my allegiance to the Hammers was forgotten for 90 minutes. We had a useful side which included Leslie Compton of Arsenal and England, Eddie Bailey of Spurs and England and Billy Steel of Derby, Dundee and Scotland fame". Cheered on by 10,000 troops, the army defeated Hammers 4-2 with Eric starring for the khaki boys. After making 151 league and cup appearances for Irons, he moved across London to join fellow ex-Hammers Len Goulden and Harry Medhurst at Stamford Bridge, but revealed: "The truth is I never wanted to leave West Ham. But I fell out with the club over a benefit payment which I believed was due to me after having been a professional with the club since 1943. In those days, players were entitled to £500 benefit payment after five years' service, but the directors said I didn't qualify because I'd served in Germany between 1944 and '47, while they were happy to pay out to West Ham's home-based servicemen.

West Ham United 1949-50: Ernie Devlin, Norman Corbett, Steve Forde, Ernie Gregory, Tommy Moroney, Dick Walker. Front row, left to right: Eric Parsons, Gerry Gazzard, Bill Robinson, Danny McGowan, Ken Bainbridge.

"This obviously wasn't right and left a bitter taste, but it's all a long time ago now. Anyway, I received the payment when I joined Chelsea. The background to that deal was that the new manager, Ted Fenton, pulled me aside one day and said: 'Both Chelsea and Wolves want you'. It was no contest, because Chelsea were so handy for my Worthing home. But, as I say, I didn't want to leave West Ham, I was happy there. Personally, I think the club needed the money – £22,500 was a lot of cash in those days".

Young Jim Barrett, who sadly passed away at the age of 83 in October, 2014, continued a family tradition when he made his debut for West Ham at Blackburn Rovers in April 1950, following in the footsteps of his father, the great Jim Barrett who played for the Hammers 1st team between 1925 and 1945. When I interviewed him following his appearance as a guest of the club at a Sportsman's Evening staged as part of the club's centenary celebrations, "Young" Jim told me: "It was great to see so many of my old team mates after all these years. Harry Hooper, for instance, I hadn't seen since I left Birmingham City in 1960. It was also nice to see people like Frank O'Farrell, Noel Cantwell and John Bond, although I'd been at West Ham quite a while before they came on the scene.

"I actually joined the ground staff in August 1944 as a 14-year-old and I remember starting work on a Monday morning but being sent home at dinner time on my first day because a 'doodle-bug' had exploded on the south west corner of the pitch, causing terrible damage to that part of the ground. It was so bad that the team had to play their war-time matches away from home for four months and I had to delay my working life.

"I was the only youngster on the ground staff at the time and me and groundsman 'Dapper' Dan Woodards had to clean and maintain the whole of the ground on our own. But sweeping the terraces often had its rewards by way of finding the odd 10/- or £1 note. In fact, I often found more than I earned as a humble ground staff lad. I well remember the thrill of meeting the big name West Ham players as they returned home to Upton Park on leave or after being de-mobbed at the end of the war.

"There were big names like England internationals Len Goulden, Jackie Morton and Ted Fenton, in addition to other big name pre-war stars like Reg Atwell, goalkeeper Herman Conway, Dick Walker and Joe Cockroft, who returned briefly before joining Sheffield Wednesday. As a wide-eyed teenager I was in awe of all of them, but in those days it was the senior pros who taught the youngsters, sometimes nursing them through matches. There were no real coaches as such, let alone Schools of Excellence".

The transfer of Harry Hooper, so fondly remembered by Jimmy Barrett and a special guest at the West Ham versus Burnley match last season (2015-16), provoked a level of uproar, bitterness and resentment among the rank and file of West Ham supporters not seen since the departure of Syd Puddefoot to Falkirk in 1922.

But when I had the privilege of interviewing Harry for *Hammers News Magazine* in October, 1994, he told me the real reason behind his controversial move. "The truth is I never wanted to leave West Ham. My time at Upton Park was the happiest of my career. We had a great bunch of players and a fantastic set of fans – especially those in the

'Chicken Run'. There was a unique atmosphere about the place and Ted Fenton was slowly getting a championship winning team together – and most importantly of all, we were playing good attacking football to entertain the fans.

"No way did I want to go, nor did I have any inkling that a move was on the cards until Ted came to me after training one day and said that Stan Cullis wanted to meet me at Euston Station to talk about a transfer to Molineux. I explained to Ted that I didn't want to go, but he said there was nothing he could do – the club needed the money because the school in Castle Street wanted their land back, which was then serving as the main entrance to the ground on Green Street. The money received from Wolves paid for the current main entrance which was completed in time for the club's promotion to Division One in 1958". So Harry's transfer was intrinsically tied up to the history of the Boleyn Ground. But we are getting ahead of ourselves…

In March 1951, Ted Fenton got a tip-off from his brother Benny, then playing for First Division Charlton Athletic, that an unknown reserve team centre-half named Malcolm Allison "wanted away" from the Valley to play first team football on a regular basis. On his brother's recommendation, Fenton shelled out £7,000 to bring the 23-year-old "rookie" to Upton Park to replace the legendary Dick Walker. Having escaped a training régime in SE7 that he described as "rubbish", Big Mal explained to me the situation he found on joining the Hammers when I interviewed him in August, 1995: "When I signed for West Ham in 1951, the training 'facilities' were diabolical. There was a patch of ground behind the West Stand in front of the old Boleyn Castle where we'd stage practice matches and do laps round an old dirt track. We used to have to run in and out of a copse of trees. It was impossible for the trainer to keep his eyes on all players. If he was alert he might have spotted cigarette smoke filtering through the trees. Or we'd go over to Wanstead Flats and put coats down for goalposts and work out there.

"On other occasions we'd train on the pitch at the old gas works at East Ham. It was laughable really. Although he was a shrewd operator in the transfer market, Fenton rarely got involved in training matters, so it was left to Billy Moore and Harry Hooper Senior who, with all due respect to them, weren't really qualified for the job. In the end I took charge of training myself. Conscientious pros like Jimmy Andrews, John Bond, Mal Musgrove, Frank O'Farrell, Noel Cantwell and Dave Sexton, who all became managers, would volunteer for my training sessions back at Upton Park in the afternoons.

"The groundsman, 'Dapper' Dan Woodards used to hate the sight of me, because we trained on the pitch and we were always at loggerheads. Two nights a week we would hold training sessions at the ground for youngsters, which is how players like Bobby Moore, Geoff Hurst, Tony Scott and John Cartwright came to the club". And so the seeds for the famous Academy of Football were sown and the tactical blueprint which propelled the club into the First Division in 1958, established.

Big Mal's recollections of his run-ins with groundsman Woodards struck a chord and reminded me that the man who gave Mal his reference for his introduction to West Ham

04.02.50: Wade in tussle with QPR's Powell.

24.02.51: Dick Walker v Queen's Park Rangers. D 3-3.

The Boleyn Ground circa 1952.

– Benny Fenton – also came under the scrutiny of the protector of the Upton Park greensward, as he explained to me in an interview in *Hammers News Magazine* in February 1997: "When I joined the groundstaff and my older brother Ted at West Ham in 1935, I was paid the princely sum of 30/- a week and expected to take on a multitude of menial tasks to keep the Boleyn Ground spick and span.

"My daily routine started at 7.30 a.m. and included dusting, brushing and ironing the club's billiard table, cleaning and sweeping the gym and then washing down the bathrooms and two slipper baths. Other chores were cleaning the dressing rooms and any brasswork that needed doing before embarking on the major task of the day – sweeping the terraces. But I would rarely be allowed onto the playing pitch, which was constantly under the eagle-eye of groundsman and former West Ham player, 'Dapper' Dan Woodards".

When he was manager of Colchester United in the 50s, Benny Fenton again came to brother Ted's aid by selling him winger Mike Grice for £10,000 in an attempt to replace the departed Hooper. But the original 'Arry boy was a hard act to follow, as Mike explained in 1996: "Harry was an idol at West Ham and it took me a while to get on the right side of the Upton Park fans, who I must say I found the fairest in the country. But if you were having a bad spell they let you know it – especially those in the Chicken Run! Myself and my opposite winger Mal Musgrove used to dread playing in front of them if we were out of form. In fact, we used to love away matches!

"But when the Hammers fans get behind the team, as they invariably did, they were the most supportive and passionate in the country. The players used to love it when they swayed and

MAY THE NEW SEASON BRING

U MANY THRILLS LIKE THIS

Capturing the concentration and tension of our greatest game, our picture heralds another season's excitement. May 1953-54 bring skill and sportsmanship for the pleasure of all of you.

The scene shown will revive memories. It is from Blackpool's third round F.A. Cup-tie at West Ham in 1952. Players racing for the ball are Wright, Gregory and Allison, of West Ham, Mortensen, of Blackpool, Parker, of West Ham, and Brown, of Blackpool.

sung 'Bubbles' – it's a song that still brings a lump to my throat when I hear them singing it in televised games. It really is that special to me".

Ken Tucker, who sometimes played on the opposite flank to Grice, once took the expression "local boy" to its extreme when, according to one Hammers fan I met while researching this book, he was still serving behind the counter of the confectionery shop he ran in the Barking Road just 15 minutes from kick-off – explaining: "This is my busiest day of the week!" Before dashing off to play already in his playing kit. Poplar born Ken, who was said to be the only West Ham player to own a car at the time, transferred to Notts County in March, 1957, after falling out with boss Fenton.

Grice, meanwhile, went on to make a major contribution to the 1958 Second Division Championship winning triumph, playing in 29 games and was an ever present on the team's return to the top flight in 1958-59. It was all a far cry from the dawn of the decade when only the 23 goals of centre-forward Bill Robinson had saved the club from an ignominious fall into the old Third Division South in 1949-50. Signed from Charlton Athletic in January 1949, he won an FA Cup winners medal with the Robins in 1947, and was appointed the full time organiser of the club's first-ever youth section when he retired from playing at the end of 1952-53. He was qualified enough for the role after scoring 60 times in 100 games in the claret and blue. When Robinson left the club to take over as manager of Hartlepool United, Ted Fenton invited Jim Barrett to return to Upton Park in 1960 in a coaching capacity. Jim takes up the story in Tim Crane's interview with him in *Ex Magazine* in 2012: "I had

Derek Parker, George Wright, George Taylor, Malcolm Allison, Bert Hawkins, Frank O'Farrell, Terry Woodgate, Jimmy Barrett, Harry Kinsell, Gerry Gazzard, Tommy Moroney.

26.09.53: v. Birmingham, lost 1-2. Ernie Gregory challenged by Kinsey. Frank O'Farrell (6).

West Ham 'keeper Ernie Gregory lies face down in the mud after deflecting a shot into his own net during a third-round cup tie against WBA in 1953.

been transferred from Forest (105 games and 64 goals) to Pat Beasley's Birmingham City (10 games and 4 goals) but I wasn't enjoying it and after one particular game with West Ham I got talking to Ted. He asked if I'd be interested in looking after the 'A' team following the departure of Bill. So I packed my bags and headed back south".

Jim also shed further light on his earlier days at West Ham when he continued in the same article: "I loved my time working as part of the team that looked after the ground. I worked with a couple of ex-West Ham players who pulled on the shirt before the war… Dan Woodards, a lovely man and a really good groundsman, and David Baillie, who was a painter. I was really lucky to have those old players around me. I used to find more money than I earned. I was getting something like a pound a week, but found plenty of old pennies and tanners that got stuck under the turnstile counter. The club also ensured we got free access to the local Odeon and cafés.

"One thing that sticks in my mind is how all the players used to come back in the close-season to help get the pitch in shape. They didn't have to do it, but they did. We used to flatten the mud on the pitch by pulling a huge piece of tin weighted down by wood. The pitch had to be flat because if it froze you could still play but if it was lumpy the ice would make it too jagged and unplayable. The tin was actually the old Bovril advert at the ground".

At the tail end of another mediocre season on April 16, 1953, the gloom of Hammers' campaign was literally "lit up" by the most significant post-war event at the Boleyn Ground thus far. It was part of the most exciting development in football: the introduction of floodlit

Above: Harry Hooper single-handedly takes on the Huddersfield Town defence at a muddy Boleyn in '54.

Below: One of AC Milan's 6 goals in the floodlight friendly rout at Upton Park.

WEST HAM UNITED
FOOTBALL COMPANY LIMITED

TUESDAY, 14th DECEMBER, 1954 at 7.30 p.m.
FLOODLIGHT MATCH
WEST HAM UNITED
versus
MILAN A.C. (Italy)

Our photograph shows an incident from the West Ham United v Wacker (Austria) match on Oct. 19th, 1954. From left to right the Hammers' players in the photograph are Kinsell, Hooper, Foan, O'Farrell, Dick and Sexton. The ball can be seen as a white speck just below the grand-stand facia in the centre of the photograph.
Photo—N. Quick.

OFFICIAL 3D PROGRAMME

WEST HAM UNITED
FOOTBALL COMPANY LIMITED

TUESDAY, 19th OCTOBER, 1954 at 7.30 p.m.
FLOODLIGHT MATCH
WEST HAM UNITED
versus
S.C. WACKER (Austria)

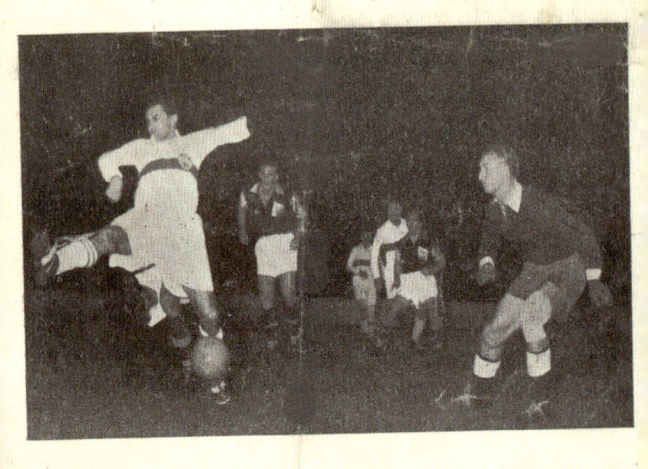

OFFICIAL 3D PROGRAMME

WEST HAM UNITED
FOOTBALL COMPANY LIMITED

TUESDAY, 5th OCTOBER, 1954 at 7.30 p.m.
FLOODLIGHT MATCH
WEST HAM UNITED v. V.F.B. STUTTGART

V.F.B. STUTTGART
Schlienz, Bogelein, Steimle, Buhler, Hinterstocker, Retter, Kronebitter, Krieger, Waldner, Barufka, Baitinger

OFFICIAL 3D PROGRAMME

WEST HAM UNITED
FOOTBALL COMPANY LIMITED

TUESDAY, 6th APRIL, 1954 at 7.30 p.m.
WEST HAM UNITED
versus
SERVETTE (Switzerland)
FLOODLIGHT FRIENDLY

OFFICIAL 3D PROGRAMME

WEST HAM UNITED
FOOTBALL COMPANY LIMITED

TUESDAY, 22nd MARCH, 1955 at 7.30 p.m.

FLOODLIGHT MATCH

WEST HAM UNITED
versus
HOLLAND SPORTS CLUB (Rotterdam)

OFFICIAL 3D PROGRAMME

WEST HAM UNITED
FOOTBALL COMPANY LIMITED

MONDAY 18th NOVEMBER 1957 at 7.30 p.m.

West Ham United v LKS Lodz (Poland)

L.K.S. LODZ
Grzywocz   Janczyk   Szczepanski   Stusio   Baran   Szczurzynski
Jezierski   Wieteski   Soprek   Szymborski   Kowalec

OFFICIAL 3D PROGRAMME

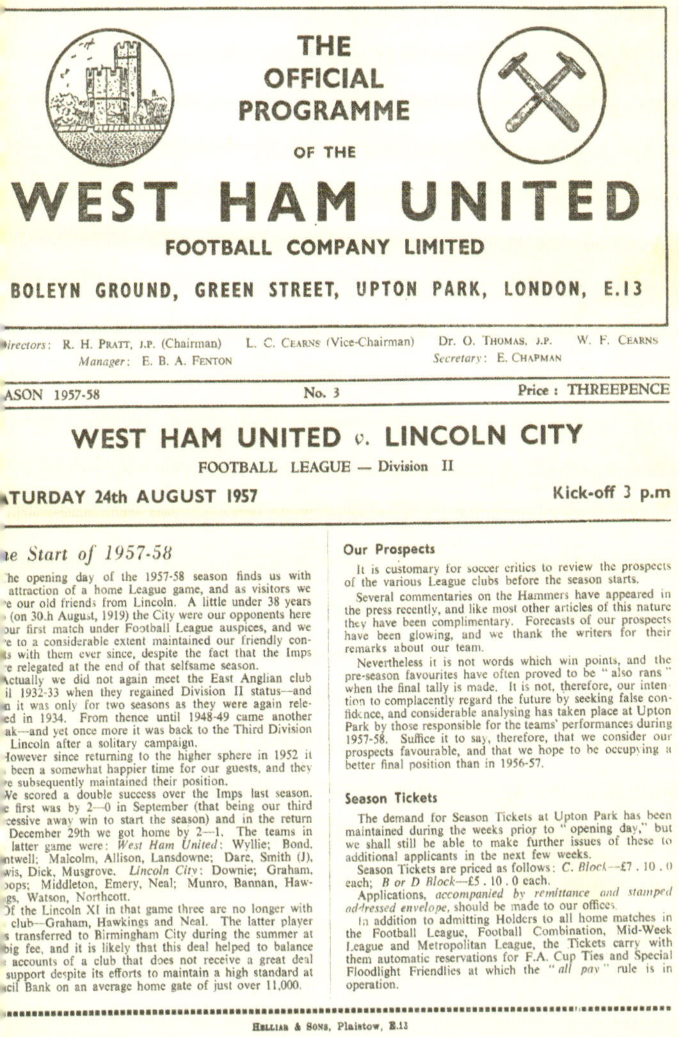

THE OFFICIAL PROGRAMME OF THE WEST HAM UNITED FOOTBALL COMPANY LIMITED
BOLEYN GROUND, GREEN STREET, UPTON PARK, LONDON, E.13

Directors: R. H. PRATT, J.P. (Chairman)   L. C. CEARNS (Vice-Chairman)   Dr. O. THOMAS, J.P.   W. F. CEARNS
Manager: E. B. A. FENTON   Secretary: E. CHAPMAN

SEASON 1957-58   No. 3   Price: THREEPENCE

WEST HAM UNITED v. LINCOLN CITY
FOOTBALL LEAGUE — Division II

SATURDAY 24th AUGUST 1957   Kick-off 3 p.m.

The Start of 1957-58

The opening day of the 1957-58 season finds us with the attraction of a home League game, and as visitors we have our old friends from Lincoln. A little under 38 years ago (on 30.h August, 1919) the City were our opponents here in our first match under Football League auspices, and we were to a considerable extent maintained our friendly contacts with them ever since, despite the fact that the Imps were relegated at the end of that selfsame season.

Actually we did not again meet the East Anglian club until 1932-33 when they regained Division II status—and then it was only for two seasons as they were again relegated in 1934. From thence until 1948-49 came another break—and yet once more it was back to the Third Division for Lincoln after a solitary campaign.

However since returning to the higher sphere in 1952 it has been a somewhat happier time for our guests, and they have subsequently maintained their position.

We scored a double success over the Imps last season. The first was by 2—0 in September (that being our third successive away win to start the season) and in the return on December 29th we got home by 2—1. The teams in the latter game were: *West Ham United:* Wyllie; Bond, Cantwell; Malcolm, Allison, Lansdowne; Dare, Smith (J), Dick, Musgrove. *Lincoln City:* Downie; Graham, Troops; Middleton, Emery, Neal; Munro, Bannan, Hawkes, Watson, Northcott.

Of the Lincoln XI in that game three are no longer with the club—Graham, Hawkings and Neal. The latter player transferred to Birmingham City during the summer at a big fee, and it is likely that this deal helped to balance the accounts of a club that does not receive a great deal of support despite its efforts to maintain a high standard at Sincil Bank on an average home gate of just over 11,000.

Our Prospects

It is customary for soccer critics to review the prospects of the various League clubs before the season starts.

Several commentaries on the Hammers have appeared in the press recently, and like most other articles of this nature they have been complimentary. Forecasts of our prospects have been glowing, and we thank the writers for their remarks about our team.

Nevertheless it is not words which win points, and the pre-season favourites have often proved to be "also rans" when the final tally is made. It is not, therefore, our intention to complacently regard the future by seeking false confidence, and considerable analysing has taken place at Upton Park by those responsible for the teams' performances during 1957-58. Suffice it to say, therefore, that we consider our prospects favourable, and that we hope to be occupying a better final position than in 1956-57.

Season Tickets

The demand for Season Tickets at Upton Park has been maintained during the weeks prior to "opening day," but we shall still be able to make further issues of these to additional applicants in the next few weeks.

Season Tickets are priced as follows: *C. Block*—£7 . 10 . 0 each; *B or D Block*—£5 . 10 . 0 each.

Applications, accompanied by remittance and stamped addressed envelope, should be made to our offices.

In addition to admitting Holders to all home matches in the Football League, Football Combination, Mid-Week League and Metropolitan League, the Tickets carry with them automatic reservations for F.A. Cup Ties and Special Floodlight Friendlies at which the "all pay" rule is in operation.

HELLIAR & SONS, Plaistow, E.13

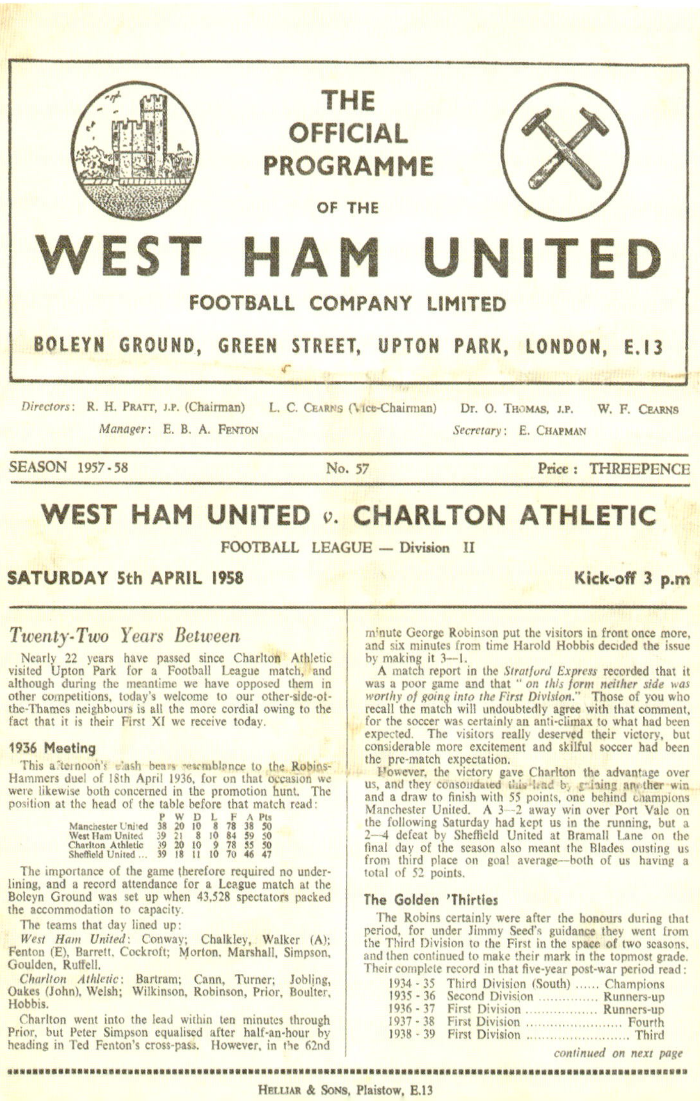

THE OFFICIAL PROGRAMME OF THE WEST HAM UNITED FOOTBALL COMPANY LIMITED
BOLEYN GROUND, GREEN STREET, UPTON PARK, LONDON, E.13

Directors: R. H. PRATT, J.P. (Chairman)   L. C. CEARNS (Vice-Chairman)   Dr. O. THOMAS, J.P.   W. F. CEARNS
Manager: E. B. A. FENTON   Secretary: E. CHAPMAN

SEASON 1957-58   No. 57   Price: THREEPENCE

WEST HAM UNITED v. CHARLTON ATHLETIC
FOOTBALL LEAGUE — Division II

SATURDAY 5th APRIL 1958   Kick-off 3 p.m.

Twenty-Two Years Between

Nearly 22 years have passed since Charlton Athletic visited Upton Park for a Football League match, and although during the meantime we have opposed them in other competitions, today's welcome to our other-side-of-the-Thames neighbours is all the more cordial owing to the fact that it is their First XI we receive today.

1936 Meeting

This afternoon's clash bears resemblance to the Robins-Hammers duel of 18th April 1936, for on that occasion we were likewise both concerned in the promotion hunt. The position at the head of the table before that match read:

	P	W	D	L	F	A	Pts
Manchester United	38	20	10	8	78	38	50
West Ham United	39	21	8	10	84	59	50
Charlton Athletic	39	20	10	9	78	55	50
Sheffield United	39	18	11	10	70	46	47

The importance of the game therefore required no underlining, and a record attendance for a League match at the Boleyn Ground was set up when 43,528 spectators packed the accommodation to capacity.

The teams that day lined up:

West Ham United: Conway; Chalkley, Walker (A); Fenton (E), Barrett, Cockroft, Morton, Marshall, Simpson, Goulden, Ruffell.

Charlton Athletic: Bartram; Cann, Turner; Jobling, Oakes (John), Welsh; Wilkinson, Robinson, Prior, Boulter, Hobbis.

Charlton went into the lead within ten minutes through Prior, but Peter Simpson equalised after half-an-hour by heading in Ted Fenton's cross-pass. However, in the 62nd minute George Robinson put the visitors in front once more, and six minutes from time Harold Hobbis decided the issue by making it 3—1.

A match report in the *Stratford Express* recorded that it was a poor game and that "on this form neither side was worthy of going into the First Division." Those of you who recall the match will undoubtedly agree with that comment, for the soccer was certainly an anti-climax to what had been expected. The visitors really deserved their victory, but considerable more excitement and skilful soccer had been the pre-match expectation.

However, the victory gave Charlton the advantage over us, and they consolidated this lead by gaining another win and a draw to finish with 55 points, one behind champions Manchester United. A 3—2 away win over Port Vale on the following Saturday had kept us in the running, but a 2—4 defeat by Sheffield United at Bramall Lane on the final day of the season also meant the Blades ousting us from third place on goal average—both of us having a total of 52 points.

The Golden 'Thirties

The Robins certainly were after the honours during that period, for under Jimmy Seed's guidance they went from the Third Division to the First in the space of two seasons, and then continued to make their mark in the topmost grade. Their complete record in that five-year post-war period read:

1934 - 35   Third Division (South) ...... Champions
1935 - 36   Second Division .... Runners-up
1936 - 37   First Division .... Runners-up
1937 - 38   First Division .... Fourth
1938 - 39   First Division .... Third

continued on next page

HELLIAR & SONS, Plaistow, E.13

Terry Matthews   Jimmy Andrews

matches, which would revolutionise the sport. Spurs were the visitors that historic spring evening and Hammers deservedly defeated their illustrious First Division opponents by 2-1 with goals from Jimmy Barrett and Tommy Dixon in front of 25,000 dazzled fans. For the record, the West Ham team that lined up in fluorescent shirts that night were: Gregory, Wright, Kinsell, Parker, Allison, Bing, Southren, Barrett, Dixon, Andrews and Hooper. The floodlights, which were not the tall pylon types of later years, were installed by W.J. Cearns at a cost of £5,100 and were mounted at intervals on top of the Chicken Run, two corners of the South Bank roof and under the roof of the West Stand. The following Monday, April 20, another healthy crowd assembled under the Boleyn bulbs and witnessed a thrilling 3-3 draw with St. Mirren. When 27,000 turned up for another extravaganza under the lights against First Division Sunderland on October 5, 1953, it was obvious the East End was well up for this new floodlight lark. Especially as their favourites out-dazzled the Wearsiders (who played in fluorescent pink shirts) with goals from Sexton and Dixon to win 2-0. Two weeks later, on October 19, when mighty Hearts, who were to finish the season as runners-up in the Scottish First Division, were humbled by an amazing 7-0, with Andrews (2), Sexton (2), Gazzard, Parker and Stroud getting the goals – the general footballing public at large were beginning to sit up and take notice of this new-fangled football by floodlight thing.

By the time the Buddies, as St. Mirren were nicknamed, made a return visit to east London the following spring for a second tilt at Hammers in another "floodlight friendly", the club

Jim Barrett Jnr.

Jim Barrett Snr.

Below: Johnny Dick is thwarted by Fulham's custodian, Ian Black.

Above, all eyes are on the ball as Robb scores Tottenham Hotspur's second goal in the first Cup-tie against West Ham, at White Hart Lane. Left, a picture of despair is Gregory, West Ham goalkeeper, as he sees the ball go in from a Harmer penalty.

THESE SHOTS MADE THE CROWD ROAR

Below, a determined Tottenham raid is ended when Gregory leaps out and up to push the ball away.

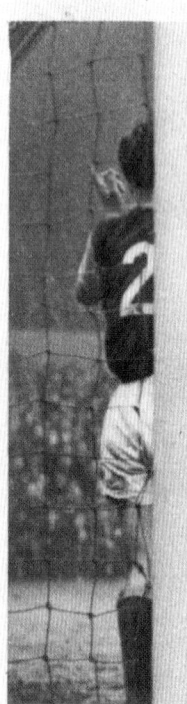

Someone's going to hit the ground—hard. It's Smith, of the Spurs.

Left, Gregory again leaps to foil a Tottenham rush. Below, another view of the Robb goal, with exultant Spurs throwing their arms up in glee—and Gregory looking as though he can't believe it.

Left, Reynolds, Spurs' goalkeeper, tips a shot from Dick over the bar. Above, six white-shirted Spurs are foiled by Gregory.

John Dick in the promotion decider v. Liverpool 19.4.58
He is foiled by Liverpool 'keeper Doug Rudham.

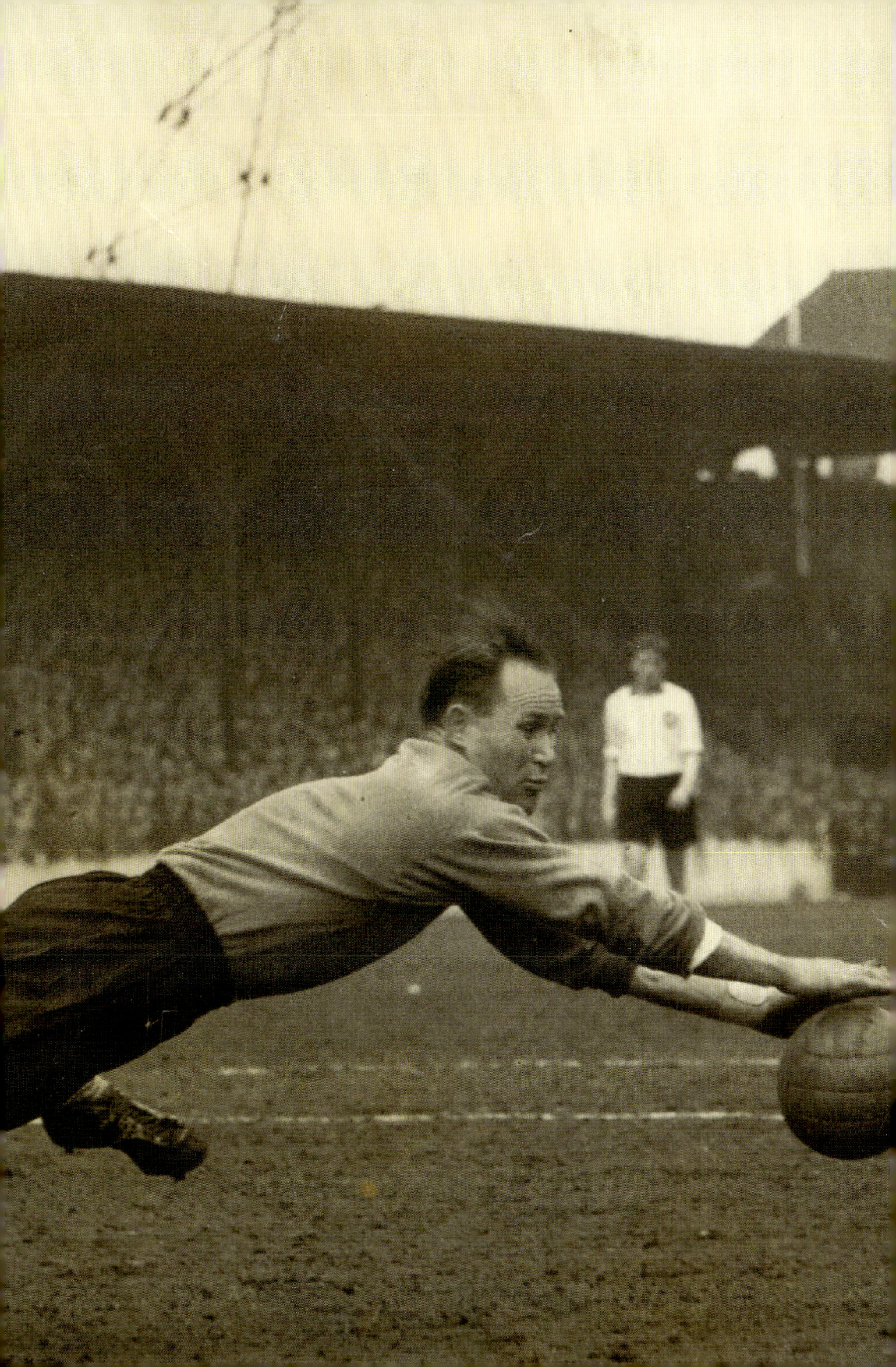

had all but paid for their new asset in full. This time the Scots returned home to Love Street licking their wounds after a 3-1 defeat through yet more goals from Dixon (2) and Parker. The attendance a very respectable 17,000. Another two crowds of 20,000 plus versus Servette of Switzerland (5-1, Dick, Arnott 3, and Barrett) and Olaria of Brazil which finished 0-0, before the season's end left the Hammers more than pleased with their 18-month experiment with "football by floodlight" which left them undefeated after seven games and with an extremely healthy profit in the bank. Their bill from the London Electricity Board was a lot higher though. But one thing was certain: football under lights was here to stay.

There was an unusual occurrence at Upton Park on January 2, 1954. Leading visitors Stoke City by 4 goals to 1, through tallies by Johnny Dick (2) and Tommy Dixon (2), the match was abandoned due to fog in the 83rd minute, which rolled in over the old uncovered North Bank, robbing Hammers of two certain points. Worse still, when the match was replayed on April 12, Stoke earned a 2-2 draw with Hooper and Dick scoring for West Ham. One wonders, in retrospect, why the floodlights weren't switched on!

A stalwart West Ham fan who has a vivid memory of Hammers since WWII is Bert Wilson, a great friend of former club physio, Rob Jenkins. He reminisced about those days with me last summer: "I used to live in the pre-fabs at Wanstead Flats and first supported the Irons during the worst winter in living memory of 1946-47. Me dad used to take me on the trolley bus from the Crooked Billet to the Boleyn Tavern to see my heroes.

"Old-time stars like Ernie Gregory, Dickie Walker, Terry Woodgate and Eric Parsons were my favourites then. I was there in '47 when 'Rabbit' scored two brilliant goals when we beat Barnsley 4-0 and also when Jack Yeomanson scored his only goal for the club with a shot from the halfway line against Plymouth in '48 when we won 3-0.

"I also recall when we were given a real footballing lesson in the finer arts of the game when we lost for the first time under the lights by 6-0 to AC Milan. Then there was the uproar when Harry Hooper was sold to the famous Wolves, after we'd got to the Sixth Round of the cup. But it was all forgotten when we won the Second Division in '58 with new stars like Allison, Bond, Cantwell and Dick".

Great memories from a grand old man, who is claret and blue through and through.

Bert was spot on with his recollection of the Milan match. It was indeed a salutary lesson handed out by the star-studded Italians in front of a record 35,000 crowd for a floodlit friendly at Upton Park. A mark which still stands today.

A fair proportion of the capacity crowd was made up of the Italian population of London and probably further afield as the gates were closed well before kick-off and the "House Full" notices went up. Among the visiting line-up were a truly international cast of stars including two Swedes (Gunnar Nordahl and Nils Liedholm), a Dane (Leschley Soerenson), an Uruguayan (Alberto Schiaffino), an Argentinian (Eduardo Rigagni) and several natural Italians, who had all won honours at various national levels.

After being fortunate not to concede an early goal, AC went ahead following an own goal from Ken Brown and Ken's direct opponent Nordahl made it 2-0 just before the interval. Following

Below: The Huddersfield 'keeper saves from Vic Keeble as Town's famous full-back Ray Wilson looks on.

the break, the Milanese put on an exhibition of truly brilliant football capped by further goals by Rigagni, Nordahl again, Soerenson and another own goal this time by Noel Cantwell to complete the rout. The technical and tactical superiority of the Italians combined with their high levels of fitness were not lost on those present on an unforgettable night. Like the Hungarian's comprehensive dismantling of England at Wembley the previous year, the Italians devastating display left a lasting impression on all serious students of the game, not least Messrs Allison, Cantwell and Bond who, after all, had felt its full effect. They say every cloud has a silver lining and it might have been more than coincidence that West Ham lost just two of their next fourteen Second Division matches of which they won nine. Lessons had been learned. No doubt the players' unofficial meetings in Cassettari's Café in the Barking Road after training were even more animated than usual during this period, as they manoeuvred the salt and pepper pots on the formica table tops to represent players in the famous red and black striped shirts and discussed ways to score and prevent goals as Phil Cassettari poured the tea. The trio they called the ABC of West Ham – Allison, Bond and Cantwell would often be joined by other radical reformers in West Ham's ranks like Malcolm Musgrove, Frank O'Farrell, Jimmy Andrews and Dave Sexton.

Sexton, in particular, had been inspired by the march of the Magnificent Magyars and their game changing 6-3 defeat of England in '53 combined with the further confirmation of their

Arsenal's Jack Kelsey saves from Dick, 1959.

Andy Smillie and Malcolm Musgrove on attack v. Huddersfield Town in F.A. Cup tie. January 1960.

(Above) Phil Woosnam coming out for his first game v. Arsenal, November 8, 1958, as Ron Greenwood watches.

total supremacy following the 7-1 victory in Budapest six months later. But although he didn't play against AC Milan on that dark, deep December night in 1954, lit only by the brilliance of the Milanese all-stars and the Upton Park floodlights, the Italian's performance also impressed him greatly as he watched the carnage unfold from his vantage point in the West Stand. So impressed, in fact, that as a fledgling coach a decade later, he funded his own pilgrimage to witness an AC-Inter Milan derby clash at first hand. Little surprise then, with such dedication, the Cassettari Clan all went on to be top managers in their own right, inspired as they were by the brilliance of Puskas, Hidegkuti, Nordahl and Schiaffino *et al*, and out of unmitigated disaster the seeds of the Academy were sown.

If the Milan match represented the defining moment in the collective consciousness of the nascent Academy and indeed, even the catalyst for their very existence, the visit of Holland Sports Club of Rotterdam for another floodlit friendly at Upton Park three months later, seemed very small beer by comparison. But the match, on March 22, 1955 came with quite a caveat: it was the first-ever match to be televised "Live" from Upton Park.

Unfortunately, the prospect of having the second-half beamed into their living rooms, kept a lot of fans at home and the attendance down to a disappointing 10,600. The low turn-out was a major factor in the club's decision not to stage any more "Live" TV from Upton Park. The result, too, was disappointing. A very rare 0-0 stalemate for such matches bearing in mind earlier 7-0 and 8-2 wins over Hearts and SC Simmering respectively. The Hammers team which took the

MALCOLM ALLISON
West Ham United

Vic Keeble on attack v. Liverpool 19.4.58, but the Red's 'keeper Doug Rudham saves in the crucial promotion battle at a packed Upton Park which ended 1-1.

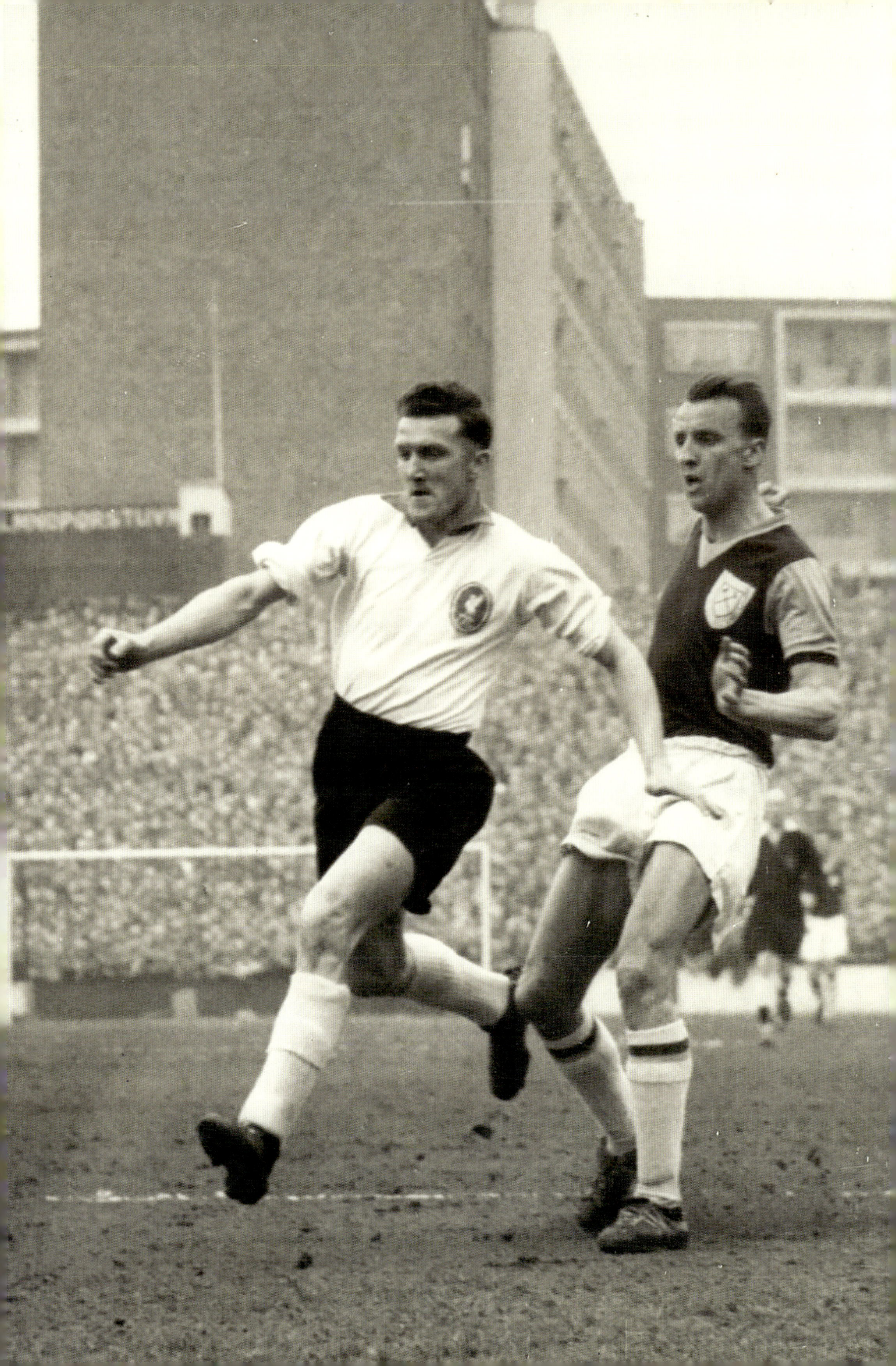

Always something cheery brewing at the home of the happy Hammers, a[nd] this time it's the after-training cup of tea. "Come and get it!" sin[gs] out Trainer Bill Moore, and the thirsty West Ham warriors line up. (Left [to] right): Malcolm, Dixon, Musgrove, Chiswick, Cantwell and Allison.

field on this historic occasion was: Taylor, Wright, Cantwell, Malcolm, Allison, O'Farrell, Foan, Bennett, Sexton, Moore (Brian), and Musgrove.

Ironically, the man who would have been most likely to have prevented the game with the Dutch visitors ending goal-less – Johnny Dick – was actually in Holland representing the Football Combination against a Netherlands Select side in a match to take place in Rotterdam the next day. Also missing was crowd favourite Harry Hooper, selected for England B versus Germany B at Hillsborough the following day.

In a Second Division fixture the previous month there had been another disappointing attendance at Upton Park when an all-time low crowd of just 4,373 turned up for the match with Doncaster Rovers on February 24, 1955. But on this occasion the low turn-out had nothing to do with "Live" TV and all to do with atrocious weather conditions. An extract from the match report in the next home programme recorded: "Snow covered the major portion of the pitch, and with further snowfalls during the game, the playing surface churned up into ankle deep mud that made close passing very hazardous. Consequently many good moves broke down, and it was left to a penalty area slip up to bring about the only goal of the match scored by Walker for Rovers.

At this point it might be a good idea to quote in verbatim, the contemporary match report under the headline: "WEST HAM'S 45 SECONDS OF DESPAIR. West Ham 0, Doncaster Rovers 1".

"Forty-five miserable seconds in the biting cold and swirling snow against Doncaster on

When in doubt ask one who knows. . . . Still at Upton Park is Dick Walker (left), former West Ham centre-half, who is here seen passing on some good advice to "Football Monthly" contributor, inside-left Johnnie Dick.

Thursday last altered West Ham's promotion chances from that of 'reasonably rosy' to 'outside'. In those 45 seconds, West Ham should have taken a goal lead. Instead they found themselves a goal down – and lost two valuable points at home – their first league defeat there since August 30th.

"Saga of the seconds followed a Hooper corner when inside-right Les Bennett headed forward. It looked a certain goal but the ball swerved away to strike a post, and while Bennett was still shaking his head in despair, Doncaster goal-keeper Hardwick took the kick.

"The ball caught West Ham's defence spread-eagled, and reached outside-left Geoff Walker. As Taylor came out to collect his long kick, centre-forward Jimmy Walker nipped in, dribbled round Taylor and shot into an empty net.

Doncaster's poised and purposeful combination held out until the end, but the home side's attack must bear the full brunt of criticism for the defeat, After a confident start, they slowly deteriorated into pretty-pretty football against a strong visiting defence.

Too often, golden chances were wasted by the tendency to make that one pass too many. In that respect, all the forwards fall down. Hooper, although having the measure of Graham, seldom centred direct into the goalmouth. While the rest of the line waited patiently for his cross, Hooper held his own dribbling act, while hugging the goal-line.

"Bennett lacked speed on the heavy going while Sexton, apart from one or two good midfield moves, could make little headway against Williams. It was left to Dick and Musgrove for the direct power but although Musgrove did attempt a direct effort or two, the only shot of note

The West Ham team that played Bury at Gigg Lane in 1956. Back row L-R: Bond, Malcolm, Allison, Wyllie, Pyke, Cantwell. Front row L-R: Musgrove, Parker, Lewis, Dick, Tucker.

that deserved a goal – apart from Bennett's header – was by right-half Andy Malcolm in the first half.

"(Attendance 4,500 – lowest since the war)".

"*West Ham*: Taylor, Wright, Cantwell, Malcolm, Allison, O'Farrell, Hooper, Bennett, Sexton, Dick, Musgrove.

"*Doncaster Rovers*: Hardwick, Makepeace, Graham, Hunt, Williams, Herbert, Mooney, Tindill, Walker J, Jeffrey, Walker G".

I wonder what that match reporter thought when West Ham, amazingly, went on to win their next six consecutive Second Division fixtures to put their promotion bid back on track. However, true to tradition, they then only managed to gain two points in their last seven matches to again fade from the picture.

Hammers again struggled to make a serious bid for promotion in the 1955-56 season, but enjoyed a considerable silver-lining with a tremendous run to the quarter-finals of the FA Cup, at which stage they were finally eliminated in an Upton Park replay by Spurs.

The first seven Second Division fixtures at Upton Park had seen just over 133,000 fans come through the turnstiles, but the enduring drawing power of the FA Cup competition was emphasised yet again when 130,000 paid to watch the four FA Cup ties against Preston (5-2), Cardiff (2-1), Blackburn (0-0) and Spurs (1-2).

There's no doubt that by performing so well against top flight opposition the Hammers had sent out a clear message to the First Division: "We'll be joining you soon!"

Further excitement should have ensued following the announcement that the Second Division fixture against Bury at Upton Park on March 19, 1956, would be the first Football League match to be played at Upton Park by floodlight. Inexplicably, in the event only 14,300 turned up to watch. Had the novelty worn off?

Those present were rewarded by an exciting encounter though, which saw their favourites prevail with a 3-2 victory over the Shakers with goals from Hooper, Billy Dare, and Dick. Bury were floodlight pioneers in their own right, having been the first club in the North West to install them. So humble Gigg Lane stole the march on local rivals Manchester United and City, just as West Ham had on all their London rivals with the exception of Arsenal.

Despite West Ham's win on this historic night, the main talking point post-match was one of Bury's goals scored by their centre-half Norman Neilson which a report in the next match programme described: "Neilson took a huge kick from about ten yards inside his own half which Gregory could only help into his own net".

Our great goalkeeping legend wouldn't have been happy about this one. Could he have been blinded by the lights?

At this time (1955-56), FL matches under floodlights could only be staged if both teams were in agreement, but football by night was given a huge boost with the advent of a brand new competition reserved solely for willing participants, the Southern Floodlight Cup. Although regarded as a first team tournament, it was certainly no money-spinner, but it was fitting that West Ham, as floodlight pioneers, should win the inaugural competition by defeating Aldershot in the first-ever final 2-1 with goals from Tucker and Dare. Yet only 5,000 witnessed Hammers skipper Allison lift the cup at an eerily empty Upton Park.

Earlier in the year, on October 26, 1955, Wembley had hosted its first floodlit match when London defeated Frankfurt 3-2 after being 0-2 behind, in the inaugural Inter Cities Fairs Cup Competition – four years after West Ham had lit up Upton Park against Spurs in '53.

Long after the dust had settled on the 1955-56 season the *Playfair Football Annual* for 1956-57 raised some highly perceptive and thought provoking points in their review of Hammers performances during that campaign on which they commented: "At no time threatening to make an upward bid, and not always free from anxiety about the future, West Ham United did raise an unusual query. Was their play better suited to the First Division than the Second? The cup-tie returns raised it. Preston North End and Cardiff City were beaten, and following a win at Blackburn, West Ham should definitely have won on the Tottenham Hotspur ground and gone on to the semi-final. Football for which opponents often expressed admiration was played in many League games and the assurance now given is that the emphasis will be on goal-getting. Whether this end will be achieved without Harry Hooper seems doubtful. This winger was sold to Wolves late in the season to help pay for ground alterations in process".

It was a season which saw another B. Moore come briefly to the fore. This was not Bobby, but Brian Moore, a ball-playing inside-forward signed from Distillery after being discarded by Glentoran, in February 1955, for a fee of £4,500. His promising FL career was tragically cut short when he received an eye injury playing against Middlesbrough at Ayresome Park on Boxing Day 1955. He and team mate Geoff Hallas, who had received a similar injury, were both granted a joint testimonial match after being forced to retire from top class football. There was a happy postscript for Brian however, as he later joined Cambridge United in the Eastern Counties League and as West Ham were running away with the Second Division title he helped

West Ham 1957-58 Brown, Allison, Bond, Gregory, Cantwell, Malcolm. Front row (L-R) Grice, Smith, Dare, Dick, Musgrove

himself to a record 49 league goals as the "U's" finished runners-up to Spurs "A" to gain an invitation to join the Southern League. Inspired by his mentor and hero, the great Wilf Mannion, he also scored another 19 times in other competitions – not bad for a player blind in one eye.

In the West Ham fashion, Irons won their first three away games of 1956-57 in convincing fashion, but gained just one point from the first three at home. The highest attendance of the season, 36,500 turned up at Upton Park for the visit of local rivals Leyton Orient on February 16, 1957 following a run of six straight wins with the O's visit making it seven thanks to goals from Bill Lansdowne and Eddie Lewis securing a 2-1 victory. But that's as good as it got as the promotion bid fizzled out and Hammers finished eighth in the table.

It was left to the youth team to fulfill any hopes of bringing silverware to Upton Park as 15,000 turned up to witness the first leg of the FA Youth Cup Final on May 2, 1957, against Manchester United. And what a team it was, lining up: Brian Goymer, Joe Kirkup, Albert Howe, Clive Lewis, Roy Walker, John Lyall, Clive Rowlands, John Smith, George Fenn, John Cartwright and Terry McDonald. Up against a rampant United XI which included David Gaskell in goal, Nobby Lawton, Alex Dawson and Mark "Pancho" Pearson in attack for the "Busby Babes", it was the young Hammers who scored first in the 22nd minute through Cartwright, but Dawson equalised in the 35th minute. Further goals by Lawton in the 50th minute and Reg Hunter fives minutes later made it 3-1 for the young Reds. Fenn's penalty conversion gave hope for the second leg of the final at Old Trafford five days later, but United's class showed as they scored five times without reply to win the trophy for the fifth successive year. There was some consolation however, as Bill Robinson's young charges won the Southern Junior Floodlight Cup. Another good omen was mention of "One of our Colts – Bobby Moore – played at Stamford Bridge last Monday evening for London versus Glasgow Boys: Bobby showed up very well at centre-half", ran the report in West Ham's official programme.

West Ham's prospects for the 1957-58 season were generally predicted to be good with many so-called experts forecasting that this could be Hammer's year.

But a preview of the season in the match programme for the opening Second Division fixture versus Lincoln City at Upton Park sounded a cautionary note as it commented: "Several commentaries on the Hammers have appeared in the press recently, and like most other articles of this nature, they have been complimentary. Forecasts of our prospects have been glowing, and we thank the writers for their remarks about our team.

"Nevertheless, it is not words which win points, and the pre-season favourites have often proved to be 'also-rans' when the final tally is made. Suffice to say, therefore, that we consider our prospects favourable and that we hope to be occupying a better final position than in 1956-57".

The refusal of the writer to be over optimistic seemed well founded when, after twelve games, the much fancied wearers of the claret and blue had only accrued the same amount of points and were occupying a distinctly ordinary position in mid table.

Then manager Fenton produced a master stroke when he signed centre-forward Vic Keeble for £10,000 from First Division Newcastle United.

It was the second time the astute Fenton had signed the robust, bustling goalscorer, having secured his services for League newcomers Colchester United from the local King George Youth Club in 1950.

Ted remembered how his 23 goals in 46 games had helped the little Essex club to establish themselves in the old Third Division South before he moved on to Newcastle for £15,000 in February 1952.

When Vic arrived at Upton Park the club arranged a private practice match to test his fitness which was watched from the sidelines by former West Ham and England centre-half legend "Big Jim" Barrett. When Vic headed home an unstoppable header with immense power from a fair way out he was said to shout out: "Cor, blimey! What have we found here? We'll win the League easy!"

It was a prophetic prediction from Jim, who'd played against all the best number nines including Dixie Dean, Ted Drake and Tommy Lawton, because 29 league games and 19 goals from their new recruit later, the Hammers were back in the First Division as Second Division Champions after an absence of 26 years.

When I interviewed Vic for *Hammers News* in September 1994, I asked him how that West Ham side compared against the Newcastle side which won the FA Cup in 1955.

"We ran them close. We also had a strong pool of players that year, and finished sixth in

Back row L-R: Andy Malcolm, Ken Brown, John Bond, Ernie Gregory, Noel Cantwell, Bill Lansdowne.
Front row L-R: Mike Grice, Johnny Smith, Vic Keeble, Johnny Dick, Malcolm Musgrove.

Andy Nelson

Billy Dare

Billy Neville

Brian Rhodes

Eddie Lewis

Mick Newman

George Wright

Malcolm Allison

Doug Wragg

Fred Cooper

West Ham team 1956. Back row (l-r) Cantwell, Gregory, Allison, Malcolm, Wright, Lansdowne. Front row (l-r) Grice, Smith, Dare, Dick, Musgrove.

our first season in Division One. I'll never forget the reception we got from the fans at King's Cross station when we returned from clinching the title with a 3-1 win at Middlesbrough in the last match. They lifted captain Noel Cantwell on their shoulders and gave us a real hero's welcome.

"Johnny Dick and I really hit it off that season, we had an almost telepathic understanding and were great mates off the pitch. I think I got 24 league and cup goals and John got 23. It was the last time West Ham got more than 100 goals in a season. And we carried on where we'd left off in our first season back in the top flight. John bagging 27 goals and me 20.

"They were great days with Canters, Andy Malcolm, Ken Brown and, of course, Bondy, who was a Colchester lad, like me. I remember going back for a match at Newcastle when they made me captain for the day. Which was the done thing in those days. But the lads hung back as I led the team out and there I was running out in front of 40,000 Geordies with Ken Brown and co. laughing their heads off in the tunnel!"

The late Ted Fenton gave an amusing account of the events leading up to his signing of Vic from the North-Easterners.

"I got Keeble in October 1957 and his scoring partnership with John Dick played a major part in our promotion. I originally signed Vic as a schoolboy when I was at Colchester. He then moved to Newcastle and I considered him to be just the man we needed at West Ham to

The great Stanley Matthews (centre) almost scores for Blackpool in the 3rd round meeting at Upton Park which Hammers won 5-2. The players l-r are Gregory, Wright, Charnley and Bond.

Malcolm Pyke seems to be orchestrating as Jimmy Hill forces a fine save from Gregory in Hammers goal. Fulham won this Hammers tie 3-2 at the Boleyn.

Jackson almost scores for Stockport in the previous round watched anxiously by (l-r) Bond, Brown and Malcolm.

clinch the title. Newcastle's directors knew I was going there to watch him, but Vic, who had been having a rough time, didn't.

"Before the match I ran into the Newcastle skipper, Jimmy Scoular, and asked him to tell Vic I was there. The message must have got through, for in the first half Vic ran around like a bloody lunatic and scored two goals. Two Newcastle directors sitting in front of me were having a hell of a row. It was one of those 'we can't let him go' efforts.

"I nipped down to the dressing rooms at half-time, knocked on the window and Vic popped his head out. 'All right, Ted?' he said with a laugh. 'Great' I said, 'but for heavens sake ease up now!"

Vic chuckled as I recounted the tale and with his rich Colchester burr still evident, replied: "Yes, that's pretty well an accurate account of what happened. I think the match was against Leeds United". If it was against Leeds, it must have been a reserve match, as my research shows that Vic had only scored one First Division goal for the Magpies up to that stage of the 1957-58 season.

But West Ham's eventual success that never-to-be-forgotten season was not just down to the goalscoring exploits of Keeble and Dick. The whole team played their part, and none more so than the quick-silver forward Billy Dare, whose 11 vital goals in the 12 games prior to Keeble's arrival had been paramount in keeping the Irons in contention for promotion as he ran through opposing defences like mercury. Also right-half Johnny Smith deserves a lot of credit.

The defence also earned many plaudits with Gregory rock steady in goal, as was tough as teak ever-present Andy Malcolm at right-half. Left back John Bond and centre-half Ken Brown had only missed two games between them with the former weighing in with a priceless 8 league goals. His partner, Eire international and skipper Noel Cantwell also mustered four goals in his 33 league appearances to add to the 101 goals total – the highest in the club's 112 year history so far. Eight of these came in the record-breaking 8-0 home win over Rotherham United on March 8, 1958 when Dick hit four, Keeble two and rising star Johnny Smith also scored a brace against the mesmerised Millers. Left-winger Mal Musgrove, who didn't score against the hapless Yorkshiremen, but did so on nine other occasions during his 39 outings that record-breaking campaign, also made a major input with his lightning dashes down the flank and deadly crosses. As did Mike Grice on the other wing, while Micky Newman, Bill Neville, Eddie Lewis, Malcolm Pyke, Bill Landsdowne and Andy Nelson were also mentioned in dispatches.

As if the League action wasn't enough, the FA Cup, too, added even more drama to a momentus nine months of non-stop excitement that had the Boleyn bulging at the seams. Three home ties versus Blackpool (5-1, Keeble 3, Dick 2), Stockport County (3-2, Eddie Lewis 2, Keeble) and Fulham (2-3, Grice and Bond) saw 107,500 fans come through the overworked turnstiles to fill the grand old ground to its rafters. The Fulham game in particular was a real see-saw affair played out in an atmosphere of almost unbearable tension and drama before the 37,500 crowd in the best traditions of a typical London "derby".

Joe Hulme, the ex-Arsenal winger, writing in the *Sunday People*, described the spectacle:

West Ham United Reserves, 1953-4. Winners - Football Combination Cup and Football Combination (Division 1)
H. Hooper (Trainer), A. Noakes, G. Wright, W, Nelson, G.Taylor, K. Brown, F. Kearns, A. Blackburn, D. Bing,
T. Southern, A. Foan, Mr R.H. Pratt (Chairman), F. O'Farrell, K. Tucker.
The following players (not in the photograph) also won medals. J. Barrett, J. Bond, P. Chiswick, G. Gazzard,
H. Hooper, H. Kinsell, A. Malcolm, D. McGowan, D. Parker.

Harry's Boys: Double Champions!

Another unusual father and son pairing at the Boleyn Ground was that of Reserve Team trainer Harry Hooper senior and his son also Harry, who could operate with equal efficiency on either wing.

Harry junior was a member of his dad's Reserve XI which won the Football Combination and also the Combination Cup in 1952-53 to complete a very rare "Double". In fact, I can't recall any West Ham XI completing any such feat before of after, making Harry senior's feat unique in the club's history.

Harry the elder was born in Nelson, Lancashire in 1910, and joined his local team in 1928. He moved to the Blades in 1930 and won an FA Cup runners-up medal with them in 1936 when they lost to Arsenal at Wembley, 1-0. Ted Drake got the goal. Still in the Second Division, the men from the red half of the Steel City were finally promoted in 1938-39 with Harry captaining the team from wing-half. After 269 outings in League and Cup for the Bramall Lane outfit, he was transferred to Hartlepool United after WWII and made a further 67 appearances there before joining West Ham as a trainer in 1949.

Luckily for Hammers, he brought his son with him, whose story has been well covered elsewhere in this history. After eight years at the Boleyn, during which time he'd brought players of the calibre of Ken Brown, John Bond, Frank O'Farrell, Noel Cantwell and, of course, his own son through to the First Team. He left to take up the managerial reins at Third Division North Halifax Town in 1957. While at the Shay, he did much to revitalise a struggling team and left them on a better footing when he departed in 1962.

"A real treat… the game, the crowd – a bunch of Londoners, I can't say more – and 19-year-old Tony Macedo who kept goal for Fulham". Joe went on to describe Macedo's performance as "The finest piece of goalkeeping at the Boleyn Ground since the days of Ted Hufton", which he crowned eight minutes from time by saving Ken Brown's header, that seemed certain to earn a replay. The Hammers got off to a flying start when Grice scored after just 90 seconds, but in the twelfth minute Roy Dwight, long before anyone knew he was Elton John's cousin, equalised. Eleven minutes after half-time Jimmy Hill contributed his share to the "Match of the Day" with a first-time left-footer, only for Cantwell to make the score even again from the penalty spot in the 65th minute, to add to the drama, this was twice-taken as one of the home players had encroached into the penalty area when the first shot found the net. The decider arrived in the 75th minute when Johnny Haynes for once lost his "Shadow" – Andy Malcolm – and converted Tosh Chamberlain's pass.

Although bitterly disappointed to lose one of the greatest cup-ties ever to be staged at Upton Park, Hammers exit may have been a blessing in disguise as they went on to win their next four Second Division matches culminating in the 8-0 demolition of Rotherham, while Fulham, who were also involved in the promotion hunt, became increasingly embroiled in FA Cup action. While they eventually went out in a semi-final replay meeting with Manchester United at neutral Highbury and fell between the classic "two stools", West Ham went on to achieve their true aim of reaching the promised land of the First Division.

The crucial Easter fixtures held the key to promotion when Notts County were defeated 3-1 at Upton Park on Good Friday by two goals from John Bond and an og to send the 30,000 crowd home in an optimistic mood. The next day an almost identical crowd saw a 0-0 stalemate with promotion rivals Charlton Athletic, again at the Boleyn, which kept both clubs' promotion hopes alive.

A 0-1 defeat at Meadow Lane in the return at Notts County was the only blemish as Hammers stepped up a gear to record a comprehensive 3-0 win over Cardiff City at Ninian Park through goals by Dick (2) and Malcolm. Then came the crunch game before a crowd of 37,750 against promotion hopefuls Liverpool in E13. On a never-to-be-forgotten night when the 'Upton Park Roar' was said to have been born, Bond scored a vital equaliser from a free kick to earn a 1-1 draw and another precious point.

In the final game against Middlesborough at Ayresome Park, goals from Musgrove, Dick and Keeble clinched the Second Division Championship in style.

But having realised the ambition they strove 19 seasons to achieve, in addition to the seven lost to the war, would Upton Park be ready to accommodate the increased numbers clamouring to witness their return to the top table of English football?

COVER STARS

TOPICAL TIMES, WEEK ENDING FEBRUARY 20, 1937.

| THE BIG CUP-TIES WEIGHED UP BY FUSE, THE DEMON, AND JOCK RUTHERFORD | 4 PANEL PORTRAITS OF FOOTBALL STARS FREE |

TOPICAL TIMES

NO. 901. [REGISTERED AS A NEWSPAPER AT G.P.O.] WEEK ENDING FEBRUARY 20, 1937. PRICE 2D.

WEST HAM F.C., 1936-37

Back Row (left to right)—Fenton, Bicknell, Weare, Walker (R.), Walker (A.), and Cockroft.
Front Row—Foxall, Marshall, Simpson, Goulden, and Morton.

NOV. 18th – 24th, 1949   SIXPENCE

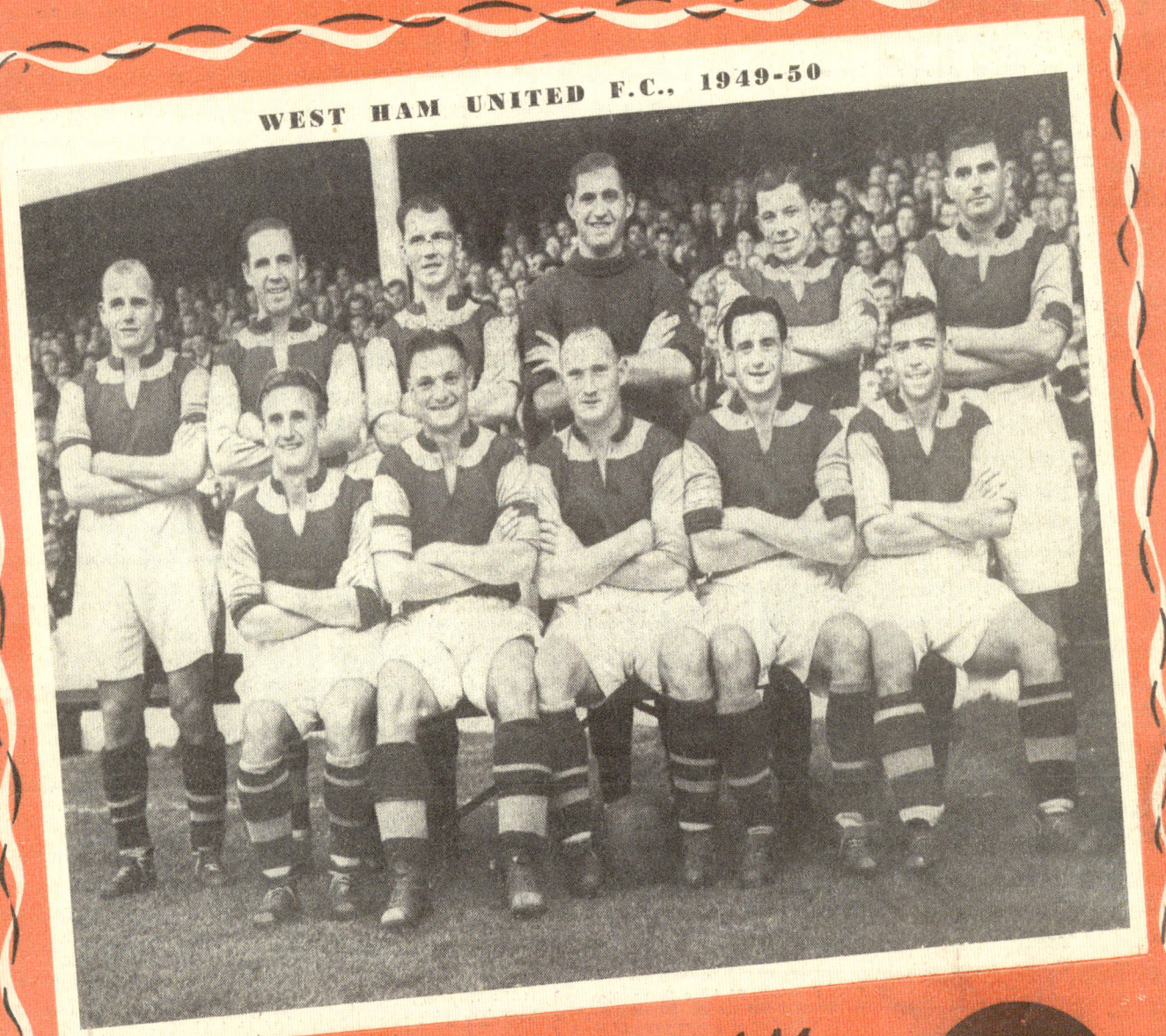

SPORT

WEST HAM UNITED F.C., 1949-50

WONDERFUL COLOURED TEAM PORTRAITS FOR EVERY READER...

Details INSIDE

APRIL 18th, 1953

Soccer Star, April 18th, 1953

THE NATIONAL SOCCER WEEKLY

Raich Carter's Soccer Star

6

THE ANGLO'S A SCOT!
— see Lee Norris's Soccertale, on Page 5, featuring Billy Liddell

Can you name our cover boys above! First three correct answers received will each win three glossy photos.

WE NAPPED LINCOLN & NATIONAL WINNERS

SPORT

Vol. 15, No. 273   SIXPENCE   APRIL 3—APRIL 9, 1953

WEST HAM UNITED F.C., 1953

Back row: D. Parker, G. Wright, E. Gregory, M. Allison, H. Kinsell, F. O'Farrell. Front row: T. Southren, J. Barrett, F. Kearns, T. Moroney, J. Andrews.

EASTER BIG RACE WINNERS
Selected By "Systex" and Major Wynne

20 PAGES OF HOLIDAY READING

SPORT

Vol. 16, No. 311   SIXPENCE   24th—30th DECEMBER, 1953

WEST HAM UNITED F.C., 1953-54

Back row: T. Woodgate, D. Parker, G. Wright, E. Gregory, H. Kinsell, T. Dixon, M. Allison. Front row: T. Southren, D. Sexton, F. O'Farrell, J. Andrews, H. Hooper.

A Merry Christmas To You All

"SPORT EXPRESS," 4—10 November, 1955

SPORT EXPRESS

17. No. 408   6d.   4-10 November, 1955

★ Another Major Wynne Coup ★
RETRIAL 18-1 WAS WINNING NAP
Now Turn To Page 14

WEST HAM UNITED F.C., 1955-56

Back row: D. Sexton, J. Bond, E. Gregory, M. Allison, N. Cantwell, P. O'Farrell. Front row: M. Musgrove, H. Hooper, W. Dare, J. Dick, K. Tucker.

Britain's Finest Soccer Service
Every Football League Line-up

EMPIRE NEWS
and Sunday Chronicle

THE TWO-IN-ONE
FOOTBALL ANNUAL
1959-60

Star Writers
- GEORGE SWINDIN
- BILLY WALKER
- ALBERT QUIXALL

All Codes Covered
400 PAGES

2/6

Edited by DAVID JACK and MALCOLM GUNN

Soccer STAR

THE NATIONAL WEEKLY   **9**D.

No. 39   ★   JUNE 23rd, 1956

He's a bundle of energy

LOOKING confident in this kick during a recent practice spell at West Ham is Frank O'Farrell, United's versatile wing-half, who came to London club from Cork United.

Nothing much was heard of him for two seasons—he had to wait that for his League début—but now this five-feet-nine-inch bundle of energy is a regular favourite with the supporters at Upton Park. Note the -book stance—youngsters could copy Frank's style with success.

THE OFFICIAL **F.A.** YEAR BOOK No 6
1953-54
2/6 NET

AN OFFICIAL PUBLICATION OF THE FOOTBALL ASSOCIATION

Pssst! WANNA BUY A STADIUM? see page 3

★   INSIDE YOU WILL FIND, ALL THE LATEST CLOSE SEASON GOSSIP, SOCCANDRA, SWAP SECTION, PEN FRIENDS, CONTINENTAL NEWS   ★

SPORT EXPRESS, February 28, 1957

Sport
EXPRESS

6D.

THE INDEPENDENT SPORTS JOURNAL

"Soccer Star" Vol. 7 No. 2, October 4, 1958

SOCCER STAR 9d.
The only Soccer Weekly

WEST HAM Pride and joy of London town are the Hammers (seen in the team group picture below). They have really shown they are more than a match for the best the senior division can offer. Picture shows, left to right: (Back row): Ken Brown, Johnnie Bond, Ernie Gregory, Noel Cantwell, Bill Lansdowne, John Dick. (Front row): Mike Grice, Andy Malcolm, Billy Dare, Malcolm Musgrove and Johnny Smith.
(Photo: Thompson's).

Line-ups • Photos
Overseas News

raise funds for your CLUB

LEGAL FUND RAISERS FOR BONAFIDE CLUBS. FOOTBALL, CRICKET, GREYHOUNDS, JOCKEYS, LETTER DOUBLES, CLOAKROOM TICKETS, DRAW TICKETS, STOPWATCH CARDS, PROBLEM NAME CARDS, TOMBOLA.

Send for Price List to:
R.J.R. Printing Supplies (TU)
P.O. Box No. 80, 339 TAMWORTH LANE, MITCHAM, SURREY (POL 2937)

SOCCER STAR, March 19, 1960   VOL. 8   NO. 26   ONE SHILL

★ **DEREK REEVES**
Personal pictures on pages 2-3

★ *Week-end Survey—6-7*
★ *All the Line-ups—8-9*

SOCCER STAR

WEST HAM: Left to right (back): M. Grice, N. Dwyer, K. Brown. (Centre): J. Cartwright, J. Kirkup, J. Bond, J. Dick, B. Moore, A. Malcolm. (Front): P. Woosnam, A. Smillie, N. Cantwell, V. Keeble, M. Musgrove. (R.1).

Raise FUNDS for your CLUB

THE SPECIAL R.J.R. FUND RAISERS HAVE COME TO THE AID OF MANY SPORTING ORGANISATIONS, BIG AND SMALL. OUR PERSONAL SERVICE FOR BONAFIDE CLUBS IS LEGAL. IT INCLUDES: FOOTBALL, CRICKET, GREYHOUNDS, JOCKEYS, LETTER DOUBLES, CLOAKROOM TICKETS, DRAW TICKETS, STOPWATCH CARDS, PROBLEM NAME CARDS, TOMBOLA. Send for Price List to:

R.J.R. Printing Supplies (TU)   P.O BOX NO 80, 339 TAMWORTH LANE, MITCHAM, SURREY   (POL. 2937)

Charles Buchan's FOOTBALL MONTHLY

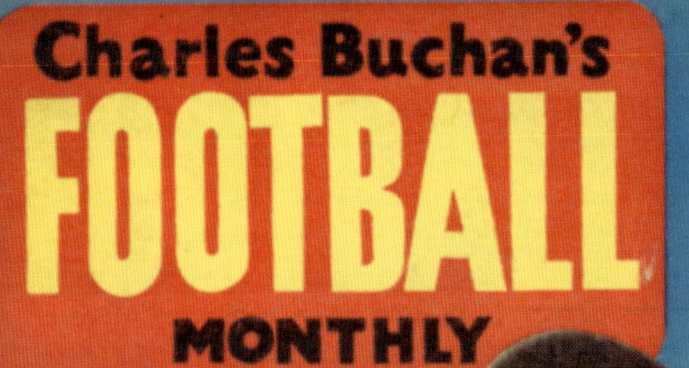

FEBRUARY, 1961
Overseas Price 2/-
Forces Overseas 1/6

1/6

PHIL WOOSNAM
West Ham and Wales

JIMMY McILROY
Burnley and N. Ireland

JOHNNY HAYNES
Fulham and England

JIMMY GREAVES
Chelsea and England

Are these Stars REALLY Giants?
—asks BILLY WALKER

THE WORLD'S GREATEST SOCCER MAGAZINE

SOCCER STAR, August 19, 1961.   VOL. 9. NO. 48.   ONE SHIL

★ Two teams on the cover every week

SOCCER STAR

WEST HAM L. to r. (back): Brown, Hurst, Kirkup, Leslie, Rhodes, Lyall, Bond, Moore. (Middle): Malcolm, Brett, Boyce, Dick, Sealey, Crawford. (Front): Woosnam, Musgrove. (P.A.I.)

Raise FUNDS for your CLUB
BY SELLING SPECIAL R.J.R. TICKETS (CRIMPED AND PRINTED) FOR FOOTBALL, CRICKET, GREYHOUNDS, JOCKEYS, LETTER DOUBLES ('USELESS EUSTACE', TEMPLE-GATE, etc.). SUNDRIES: CLOAKROOM TICKETS, DRAW TICKETS, STOPWATCH CARDS, PROBLEM NAME CARDS, TOMBOLA, CLUB STATIONERY. Send for price list to:

R.J.R. Printing Supplies (TU)   P.O. BOX NO 80, 339 TAMWORTH LANE, MITCHAM, SURREY   (POL 2937)

SOCCER STAR, *December 23, 1961* ONE SHILLING

SOCCER STAR

VOL. 10 No. 14

Compliments of the season to all our readers

Raise FUNDS for your CLUB
BY SELLING SPECIAL R.J.R. TICKETS (CRIMPED AND PRINTED) FOR FOOTBALL, CRICKET, GREYHOUNDS, JOCKEYS, LETTER DOUBLES ('USELESS EUSTACE', TEMPLEGATE, etc.). SUNDRIES: CLOAKROOM TICKETS, DRAW TICKETS, STOPWATCH CARDS, PROBLEM NAME CARDS, TOMBOLA, CLUB STATIONERY. Send for price list to:

R.J.R. Printing Supplies (TU)   P.O. BOX NO 88, 339 TAMWORTH LANE, MITCHAM, SURREY   (POL 2937)

SOCCER STAR, June 29, 1963   VOL. 11 No. 41   ONE SHILLING

SOCCER STAR

Raise FUNDS for your CLUB!

By selling special R.J.R. Tickets (crimped and printed) for FOOTBALL — CRICKET — GREYHOUNDS JOCKEYS — LETTER DOUBLES ('USELESS EUSTACE', TEMPLEGATE, etc.)

Sundries: CLOAKROOM TICKETS — DRAW TICKETS — STOPWATCH CARDS — PROBLEM NAME CARDS — TOMBOLA — CLUB STATIONERY, etc.

Send for price list to: **R.J.R. PRINTING SUPPLIES (TU)**   P.O. Box 80, 339 Tamworth Lane, MITCHAM, SURREY.   POL 293

SOCCER STAR, February 22, 1964   VOL. 12   No. 23   ONE SHILLING

SOCCER STAR

Raise FUNDS for your CLUB !

By selling special R.J.R. Tickets (crimped and printed) for POOTBALL — CRICKET — GREYHOUNDS JOCKEYS — LETTER DOUBLES ('USELESS EUSTACE', TEMPLEGATE, etc.)

Sundries: CLOAKROOM TICKETS — DRAW TICKETS — STOPWATCH CARDS — PROBLEM NAME CARDS — TOMBOLA — CLUB STATIONERY, etc.

Send for price list to: **R.J.R. PRINTING SUPPLIES (TU)** P.O. Box 80, 339 Tamworth Lane, MITCHAM, SURREY.   POL. 2937

WORLD SPORTS

MAY 1964

two shillings

JOHNNY BYRNE
West Ham and England

SPECIAL
F.A. CUP FINAL
EDITION

SOCCER STAR, *December 4, 1964* VOL. 13 No. 12 ONE SHILLING

SOCCER STAR

UNITED WILL SOON UNLOAD
(p.3)

Departures can be expected from Old Trafford in the near future, including some international players of repute. Tom Jagger reports on the developments.

BURNLEY LAD CATCHES EYE
(p.17)

Maurice Weedon writes about Turf Moor "wonder boy" John Price, the latest in a succession of outstanding wingers with the club.

UPS AND DOWNS FOR CHARLIE
(p.11)

It's been a season of mixed fortune for Sunderland centre-half Charlie Hurley. Our North-East expert Bill Nelson talks about the "big fellow" this week.

FRONT COVER PICTURE

Evasive action taken by West Ham United's Ron Boyce as he leaps over the diving Villa goalkeeper Geoff Sidebottom. The ball is under the 'keeper's chest. (P.A.1.)

Raise FUNDS for your CLUB!

By selling special R.J.R. Tickets (crimped and printed) for FOOTBALL — CRICKET — GREYHOUNDS — JOCKEYS — LETTER DOUBLES ('USELESS EUSTACE', TEMPLEGATE, etc.) Sundries, CLOAKROOM TICKETS — DRAW TICKETS — STOPWATCH CARDS — PROBLEM NAME CARDS — TOMBOLA — CLUB STATIONERY, etc.

Send for price list to: **R.J.R. PRINTING SUPPLIES (TU)** P.O. Box 80, 339 Tamworth Lane, MITCHAM, SURREY. POL 2937

CHARLES BUCHAN'S
SOCCER GIFT BOOK

THE WORLD'S
GREATEST FOOTBALL
ANNUAL
1964-65

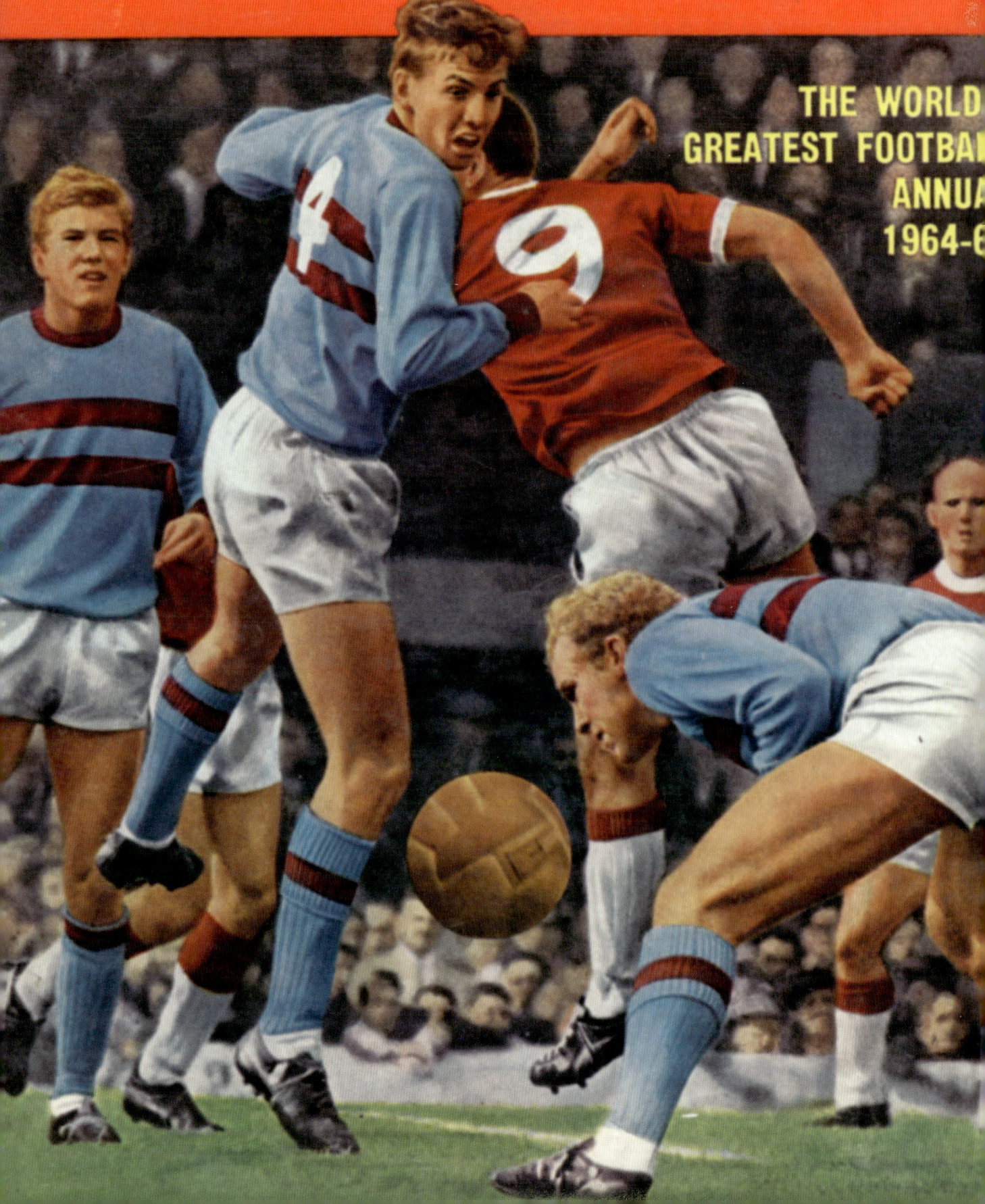

WORLD SOCCER

JULY 1965

TWO SHILLINGS and SIXPENCE

Styled for Action!!!

Bukta

Bukta Football and Rugby outfits are obtainable from all good sports dealers and outfitters.
Ask for copy of the Bukta true colour "1001" choice football catalogue. In case of difficulty write to:
SALES PROMOTION MANAGER, BUKTA, STOCKPORT, CHESHIRE.

WORLD SOCCER

OCTOBER 1965   TWO SHILLINGS and SIXPENCE

Styled for Action !!!

Bukta Football and Rugby outfits are obtainable from all good sports dealers and outfitters.
Ask for copy of the Bukta true colour "1001" choice football catalogue.
In case of difficulty write to:
SALES PROMOTION MANAGER, BUKTA, STOCKPORT, CHESHIRE.

SOCCER STAR, February 11, 1966   VOL. 14 No. 22

SOCCER STAR

ONE SHILLING and THREEPENCE

Inside

- *World Cup seats are a sell-out—page 3*
- *Closed circuit and Soccer—page 24*
- *Line-ups, news, gossip, pix.*

WEST HAM UNITED F.C.
Back row left to right: John Bond (now Torquay), Ken Brown, Martin Peters, Joe Kirkup, Jim Standen, Brian Dear, Eddie Bovington, Jack Burkett, Bobby Moore. Front: Peter Brabrook, Alan Sealey, Ron Boyce, Johnny Byrne, Geoff Hurst, Tony Scott (now Villa), John Sissons.
(M.P.I.)

Raise FUNDS for your CLUB!

By selling special R.J.R. Tickets (crimped and printed) for FOOTBALL — CRICKET — GREYHOUNDS JOCKEYS — LETTER DOUBLES ('USEFUL EUSTACE', TEMPLEGATE, etc.)

Sundries: CLOAKROOM TICKETS — DRAW TICKETS — STOPWATCH CARDS — PROBLEM NAME CARDS — TOMBOLA — CLUB STATIONERY, etc.

Send for price list to **R.J.R. PRINTING SUPPLIES (TU)**   P.O. Box 80, 339 Tamworth Lane, MITCHAM, SURREY.   POL 2937

The Inspirational Irishman leads out the Hammers at Upton Park.

Paddy is caught on the hop as the team runs out before he can give the signal to the Leyton Silver Band to play the Post Horn Gallop, as was the normal match day practice. Note the cigarette in his left hand, which he hasn't had time to roll.

Back at the Top
Chapter 5

An indication of the fervour, anticipation and excitement which precipitated the visit of First Division Champions Wolverhampton Wanderers to Upton Park for West Ham's first home game back in the top flight was illustrated some five hours before the match when the first queues began to form for that historic Monday evening kick-off of August 25, 1958.

When trainer Billy Moore entered at 2 p.m. he saw a Hammers fan by the Grand Stand turnstile. The would-be "first-man-in" shouted "I've been waiting 26 years for this, Bill!" It was a long while to wait, but proved to be well worth it as the Hammers – buoyed by their opening day 2-1 win at Portsmouth – set about the Wolves with a savagery usually associated with that particular beast. Albeit with a fair amount of skill and finesse thrown in. To Johnny Dick went the honour of scoring the first First Division goal at Upton Park for over a quarter of a century when he right footed the ball past Finlayson after Musgrove had hared down the wing and crossed to Keeble who found his colleague in the open. The second came from a 25-yard drive from Johnny Smith after Andy Malcolm had split the constantly under-pressure visiting defence with an along-the ground, slide-rule pass. But, it could have been more as the woodwork was struck three times and on several occasions only inspired goalkeeping by Finlayson stood between Hammers attack and a rout as shots rained down on his goal from all angles – something the famous Wolves were very unfamiliar with.

Yet they were gracious in defeat. One of the Molineux club's directors commenting "You have a fine team here. They deserved to win and we have no complaints". But what meant most was when England and Wolves captain Billy Wright entered the home dressing room to congratulate the Hammers on their performance and said: "Thanks for the game lads, and thanks for the 'runaround' – at least it proved we're fit". What Wolves' disciplinarian boss, Stan Cullis said is not recorded! What was recorded was the official attendance figure of 37,485, of which number every man, woman and child would remember that night under the Boleyn Ground lights when the Champions of England were run ragged by newly promoted West Ham.

During the summer of 1958, there was an application list of 10,000 for new season tickets. As only 2,000 were available, 8,000 were obviously unsuccessful with their application. It was

08.11.58: 0-0 v Arsenal: Tommy Docherty, John Dick, Jack Kelsey, Phil Woosnam, Evans and Wills.

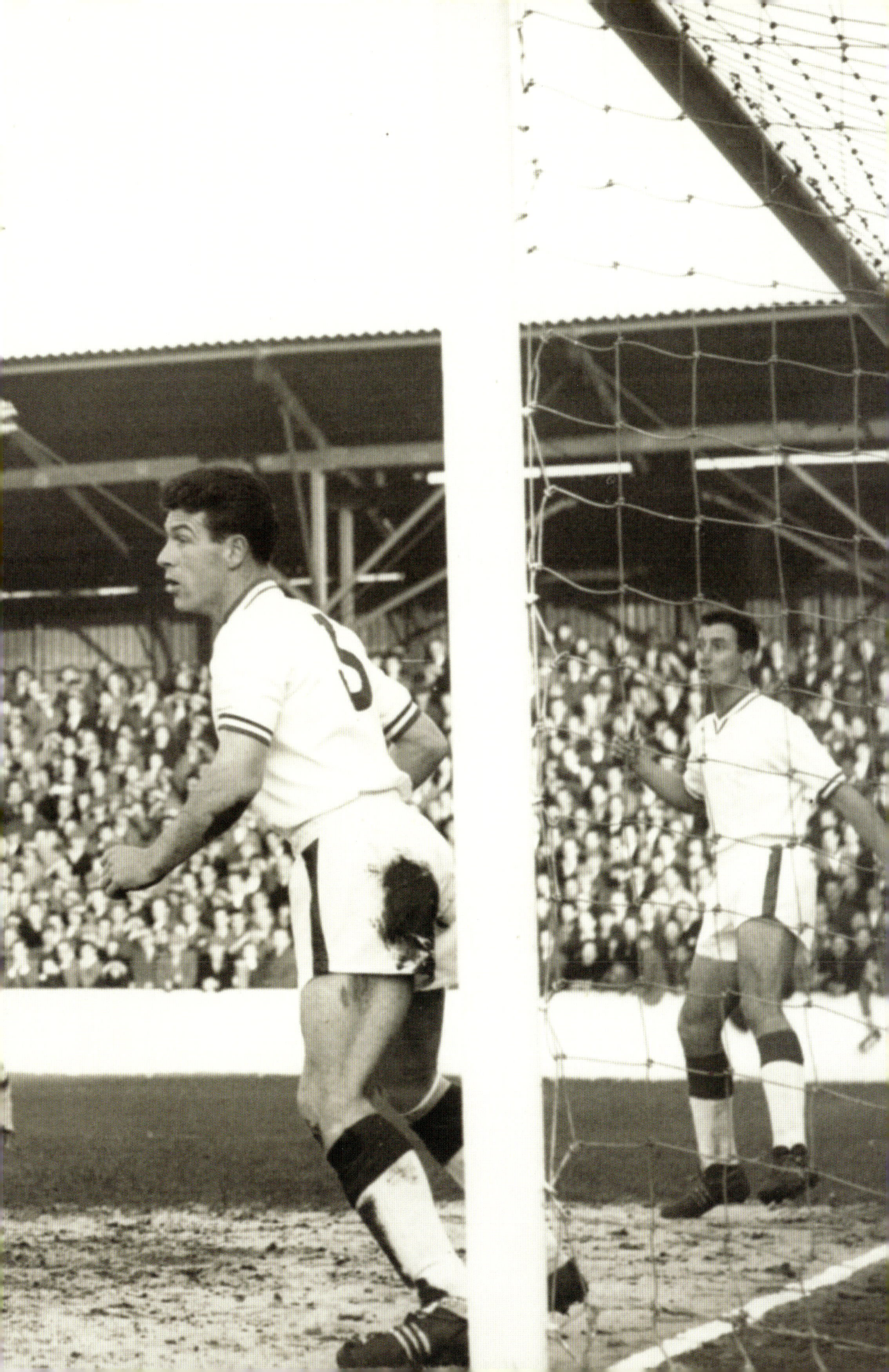

the first time in living memory that all requests for season tickets were over subscribed and it was patently obvious that Upton Park was simply not big enough to accommodate all those who wished to attend the big matches. That said, only 30,000 turned up for the next match against Aston Villa at the Boleyn to witness their favourites chalk up the kind of winning margin they had threatened against the men in old gold when they thrashed the equally famous men from Villa Park by the stupendous score of 7-2. It was a result that sent shock waves throughout the game, such was its magnitude.

The official programme for the Football Combination fixture with Luton Town on the following Saturday at the Boleyn Ground carried a report that succinctly summed up the Hammers biggest ever winning margin over the Midlands giants.

"John Smith had shown the way things were likely to go when he hit an upright soon after the start and as he also rattled the bar in the second half he was undoubtedly the unluckiest player of the afternoon. But the Midlanders could hardly hope to keep their goal intact in the face of an onslaught such as was perpetuated by an XI which outclassed them in fitness and in skill – so well illustrated when Malcolm Musgrove netted twice in three minutes, firstly with a solo run and then with a first-timer from a faulty clearance.

"From then on, everyone except Ernie Gregory joined in the upfield surge from time to time and it was impossible for the opposition to prevent shots from all angles. Bill Lansdowne and Vic Keeble made it 4-0 by half-time and despite a deceptive 'easing off' just after the resumption, we soon turned on the heat to score three goals to the Villa's two in the last 16 minutes – Johnny Dick netting two and Keeble another".

Next up, after a 4-1 reverse at "bogey-side" Luton Town had brought the high-flying Hammers down to earth with a bump, were Manchester United on September 8, 1958; a date that would become embedded into the consciousness of the majority of the 35,672 crowd who had managed to gain entry into another "night-of-nights" under the Upton Park lights. And not just because of the 3-2 victory over Matt Busby's Babes, for although not listed in the programme, at number 6 in the West Ham line-up was a certain Robert Moore, later to make the shirt his own property for West Ham and England and his name a legend around the globe.

He was, of course, Bobby Moore.

As United had defeated Blackburn Rovers 6-1 two days earlier, they might have expected to take a couple of points back to Old Trafford, but instead found themselves 3-0 down after an hour's play through goals from Dick, Smith and Musgrove in another scintillating performance. Although the Red Devils pulled a couple back, the Hammers held on comfortably to claim another massive scalp.

And as a report in a subsequent programme noted: "The selection of Bobby Moore at left-half proved justified by a display which foreshadows a grand future for a 17-year-old called upon to make his debut against one of Europe's leading sides".

Under the heading Accommodation Problems and Remedies in the Official Programme for the Manchester United game, the club attempted to address a situation that they knew was an inevitability of the rise in status.

Vic Keeble, whose goals helped Hammers back to the top.

It began: "The increased attendances at Upton Park this season have, as expected, brought some problems and we feel that it is only fair to our patrons to clarify one or two points.

"The huge interest caused by the visit of Wolverhampton Wanderers a fortnight ago meant that queues began to form outside the ground some four to five hours before the kick-off. This did not cause great difficulty in Priory Road and Castle Street, but it brought considerable confusion in the forecourt in Green Street owing to the confined space being fully occupied by spectators who wished to gain admission to the West Stand and Enclosure. In consequence, our gatemen were hindered in making their way to our office entrance, especially as their efforts to push their way through were understandably misinterpreted by those who were queuing! This brought inevitable delays in opening the turnstiles to all parts of the ground, and we can only express our regrets and apologies at the inconvenience thus caused. However, this has been remedied by the reorganisation of police arrangements and administration, and we trust that such incidents will not occur in future".

The article concluded: "Obviously, the completion of our new entrance in Green Street will help to overcome many of these difficulties and we are pleased to say that the plans for this are now finally settled and await only planning consent before work can proceed. When consent has been obtained, we shall publish a diagram showing the effects and advantages of this

Woosnam and Dick (10) attack the Chelsea goal in 1959.

long-awaited innovation".

In other words, it was organised chaos, and the discomfort of the fans can only be imagined as they struggled to gain a foothold on the packed terraces and stands – especially at the Arsenal match on November 8, when a season's best crowd of 38,250 crammed themselves in to see Phil Woosnam make his debut against the Gunners in a 0-0 stalemate after the "House Full" notices again went up 45 minutes before kick-off.

Altogether there had been eight home attendances of 30,000 or over during the season and, it looked as if the club had been caught "on the hop" as very little had been done to improve the Boleyn Ground since winning promotion. But perversely, there had been some surprisingly low crowds too. Like the 23,500 for Leicester, 22,022 for Leeds United, 21,500 for Preston North End and only 23,500 for the 5-1 victory over Manchester City which saw Dick 2, Grice 2 and Cantwell get the goals to secure a sixth place finish for the First Division new boys.

The two goals that Dick put past City's famous German goalkeeper Bert Trautman enabled him to overhaul by one goal his 26-in-a-season post-war Hammers' FL goalscoring record which he had previously shared with Bill Robinson, who was now Assistant Manager having previously been in charge of youth development.

Before the curtain was finally drawn on the 1958-59 season, Bill had the chance to study the fruits of his labour as the Hammers youth team entertained Blackburn Rovers in the first leg of the FA Youth Cup Final at Upton Park. No less than ten of the youngsters eventually

Noel Cantwell passes back to Noel Dwyer v. Luton Town. Circa 1959.

progressed to first XI football, but couldn't overcome the Blackburn lads on this occasion as the match before a 14,000 crowd ended 1-1 with Andy Smillie scoring the Hammers goal. The young Irons were pipped in the second leg at Ewood Park, 1-0 in extra time before a massive gathering of 28,000 against a strong Rovers side who had eliminated Manchester United in the semi-finals and boasted future England internationals Fred Pickering and Keith Newton among their ranks. So the last chance of any silverware for the season was gone as the first team squad prepared to embark on their continental tour to Holland, Belgium and Germany. One of Hammers opponents, Borussia Dortmund, would make a dramatic appearance at Upton Park seven years hence, as we shall see. But for now would have to be content with their 3-1 "friendly" victory over their future European Cup Winners' Cup rivals.

On July 29, 1959, the West Ham United boardroom hosted a very special event: the 80th birthday celebration of "Mr West Ham" himself – former player, trainer, manager, secretary and now ambassador-at-large, the legendary Charlie Paynter.

Organised by the West Ham United Old Players' Association headed by former Hammer Alex Anderson in conjunction with the club, it made for a memorable evening of nostalgia for "C.W.P."

Among the former players present were: Percy Allen, Alex Anderson, Jim Barrett (Snr), Tommy Caldwell, George Carter, Eddie Chapman, Jim Collins, Ted Collins, Herman Conway, Norman Corbett, Stan Earle, Stan Foxall, Viv Gibbins, Len Goulden, Tommy Hodgson,

Above: Noel Cantwell and Paddy. (Above right) Ron Greenwood leads out Brentford at Boleyn, 10.4.48.

Ted Hufton, Jimmy Ruffell, Danny Shea, Jack Tresadern, Albert Walker, Vic Watson and Tommy Yews.

Also present were the Chairman, Reg Pratt, who welcomed Charlie on behalf of the club and handed over telegrams of congratulations (including one each from the Football Association and Football League), Frank Cearns, Jack Helliar, Trevor Smith of the *Ilford Recorder* and several representatives from Fleet Street. It was a gathering that further underlined the enduring affection and esteem with which the great man was held in after 59 years' service to West Ham United and the wider world of football.

In that wider world, several major topics were being discussed in earnest prior to the commencement of the 1959-60 season by players, fans, commentators and administrators alike.

The issues up for debate included floodlights, the need for substitutes, the lifting of the maximum wage and the effect of the ever growing threat of televised matches.

On the latter subject, West Ham United's Secretary and former player, Eddie Chapman, had expressed his views on the matter via the pages of *The Official FA Yearbook of 1958-59*.

Perhaps mindful of his own club's ill-fated experiment of allowing the second-half of their floodlit friendly match with Dutch side Holland Sports to be broadcast live from Upton Park, which subsequently kept the attendance down to 10,600, Eddie didn't pull any punches in his article which began in feisty fashion: "One of the most controversial aspects fast gaining momentum is the question of television in respect to live broadcasting of matches. This problem arises at a time when the majority of Football League clubs are facing a continuation of falling gates, a further increase in players' wages and increased expenses on ground maintenance.

"We have had enough proof that TV has drastically interfered with the patronage at our theatres and cinemas, but what have the television authorities suggested to subsidise the loss of revenue? The difficulties seem insurmountable and what a bleak outlook confronts any attempt at a serious discussion of the televising of live football matches.

"Let the agreement reached for the relaying of film extracts for later showing continue and even be extended, but live televiewing of Saturday afternoon matches – no, never!"

The TV companies had also set up the cameras at Upton Park on Saturday evening February 2, 1957 when West Ham had taken the opportunity to stage the England versus Luxembourg Youth International while the first team were playing away at Barnsley.

On this occasion, only 5,500 fans turned up despite the presence of a pair of Hammers being in the England line-up, future Hammers' manager supreme, John Lyall and later England coach Johnny Cartwright, who helped towards the 7-1 victory in the match that was televised that night. The armchair viewers saw little Luxembourg take a shock early lead with a slick headed goal but then the Young Lions take control with a certain young man by the name of Jimmy Greaves helping himself to four goals. The pen-pictures in the match programme had this to say about John Lyall: "The third member of an entirely new half-back line. A former Ilford schoolboy, he is at present a member of the office staff at Upton Park. Well-built, he has also played at full-back, but is a goalscoring type with a powerful drive".

With the benefit of hindsight, it is easy to understand the reticence of clubs to embrace the TV companies at that time, but the introduction of substitutes should have been a "no-brainer", if only such a phrase had existed in those days which seemed so fearful of change. Even to the extent of putting the game's most precious commodities – the players – in danger of most grievous injuries.

Reflecting on a Second Division fixture between West Ham United and Leeds United which took place at Upton Park on Saturday, September 20, 1952, in the Hammers' History page in a West Ham programme some 30 years hence, the match resumé just about summed up the ludicrous situation that existed in those days: "As the 'substitute rule' was still a long way off, the Hammers had to play with depleted forces after the first minute against Leeds United.

"Jimmy Barrett Jnr. bruised a thigh muscle in our first attack and was slowed up for the rest of the game; then Terry Woodgate pulled a calf-muscle in the 20th minute – leaving him a 'passenger' for most of the remaining period.

"It affected our team-work, and a couple of defensive errors permitted Ray Iggleden and Arthur Tyrer to score for the visitors. This made the opposition over-confident and they did not particularly bother to mark Woodgate. However, the Hammers' winger made the most of his

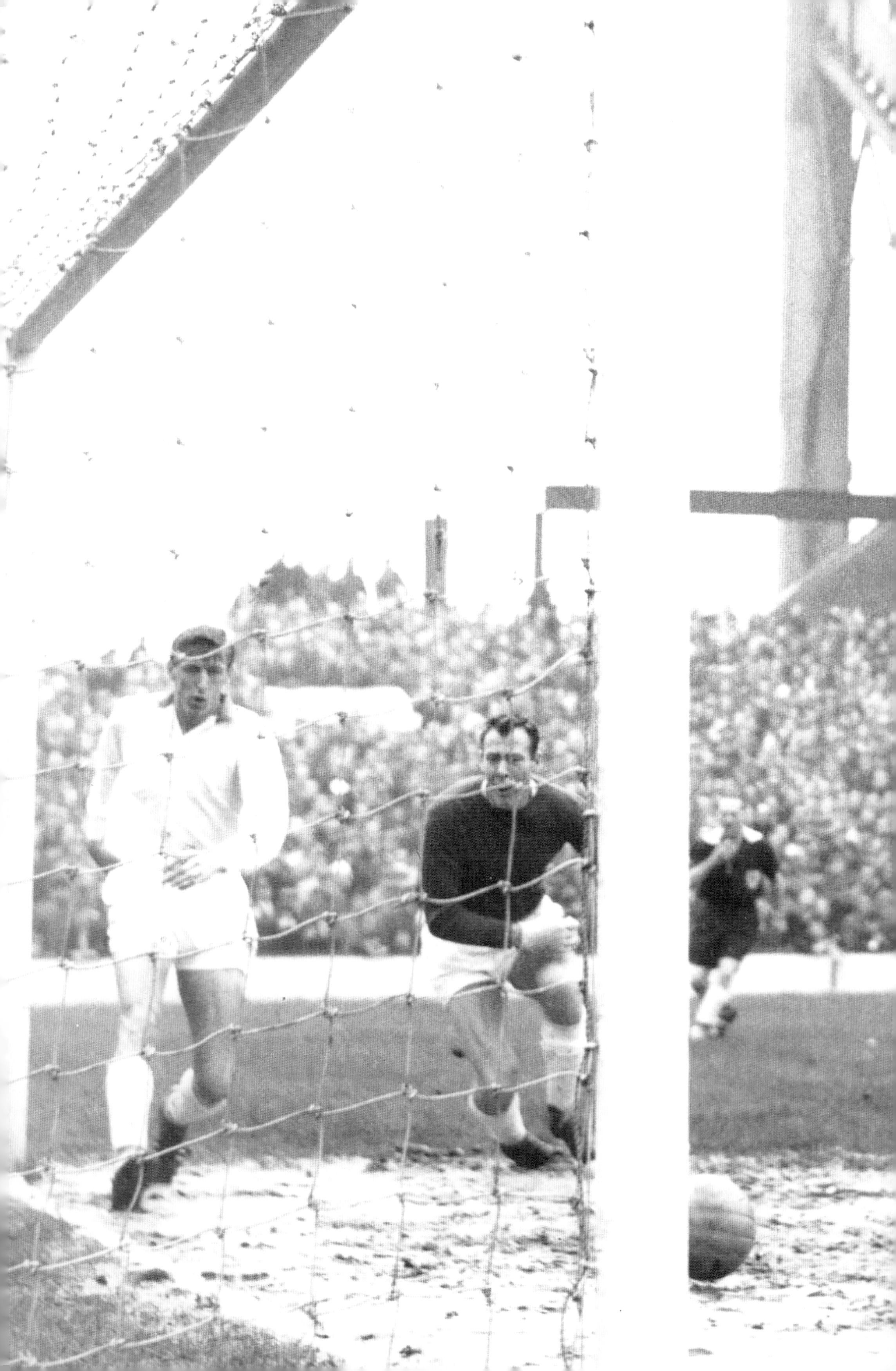

05.11.60: Dave Dunmore scores West Ham's 1st goal. Keeper Jack Kelsey, defenders McCullouch and Sneddon look on. v Arsenal. W 6-0.

chance to put Tommy Moroney away with a through ball, and the inside-left netted his second goal of the game to earn a point in a 2-2 draw".

Although West Ham's ten men escaped with a draw on this occasion, teams with one man or more affected by injury invariably struggled to salvage anything out of a game, as a host of losing FA Cup finalists between the years of 1957 and 1961 would readily testify.

Yet despite their "showpiece" game being ruined as a serious contest on a yearly basis, the old men of the Football Association dithered at Lancaster Gate, heads remaining in the proverbial sand.

The Football League, too, remained in the "dark ages" as the carnage raged unabated on a weekly basis until substitutes were finally allowed for the 1965-66 season. Ironically, West Ham's first substitution was against Leeds United at Upton Park when Peter Bennett replaced Jack Burkett in the 53rd minute of the First Division clash on August 28, 1965. Drawing 1-1 at the time of the substitution, the Hammers went on to win 2-1 with a Geoff Hurst strike in the 83rd minute.

As for the battle to abolish the archaic maximum wage, that was being ably fought by the man whose goal helped to eliminate the Hammers from the FA Cup in that Upton Park thriller in the promotion season of 1957-58 – PFA Chairman, Jimmy Hill – and would be implemented soon. And the man who scored the winner in that same game – Johnny Haynes – would become the country's first £100-a-week footballer.

With regards to floodlights, it was easier to count the major clubs who didn't have them installed than those that did on the eve of the 1959-60 season.

But it was almost "old hat" at Upton Park as Hammers could be justly proud to be recognised as floodlight pioneers; with only Arsenal switching on before the less fashionable, but no less ambitious, East Enders.

With just the Essex Professional Cup to show for their efforts in 1958-59, West Ham began their second season back in the First Division in fine fettle and won three out of the first four league fixtures, defeating Leicester City 3-0 in the season's opening game at Upton Park,

Moore robs the maestro.

Champions elect, Burnley 3-1 at Turf Moor and Preston North End 2-1 at the Boleyn having secured a 1-1 draw at Deepdale in the second match of the season. The great Tom Finney, who would retire at the end of the season, played in both games for North End, as did ex-Hammers' skipper Frank O'Farrell.

On September 5, a largely shirt-sleeved crowd of 28,000 assembled at Upton Park in the late summer sunshine optimistic in the knowledge that if their favourites could prevail over visitors Leeds United and Blackburn Rovers faltered at Ewood Park against Sheffield Wednesday, the Hammers would dislodge the Lancastrians from the top of the First Division table.

But on this occasion it was the Yorkshiremen, with a young Jack Charlton at centre-half and Don Revie at centre-forward, who would demonstrate how to overcome the disadvantage of playing with a man short. Yet when Phil Woosnam and Mike Grice carved out the opening for a typical Vic Keeble headed goal after 14 minutes, it looked like it could be the first of many; a possibility further enhanced when the visitors incurred the loss of right-half Peter McConnell with a torn thigh muscle after half an hour's play. Leeds, however, had other ideas and when George Meek was adjudged to have been fouled three minutes before the interval, soldier Chris Crowe stepped up to equalise from the spot.

Within five minutes of the resumption, Leeds scored again as Crowe headed home this time as Ernie Gregory came out to intercept. A spirited rearguard action from then on enabled the Elland Road outfit to repel all Hammers' efforts to gain the spoils of victory and the "ten men" the appreciation they undoubtedly deserved from the sporting Upton Park crowd. Had the crowd realised this would be one-club legend Ernie Gregory's last first team game, the cheers would have been for him, too.

His replacement, Ireland international Noel Dwyer, seemed a complex character by comparison; who could blow hot and cold from week to week. Rumours of a more sinister side to his nature would surface later in this season, as we shall see.

But for now these were heady days at Upton Park as the team quickly shook off the Leeds defeat to head the First Division table in mid-November by dint of a tremendous 3-1

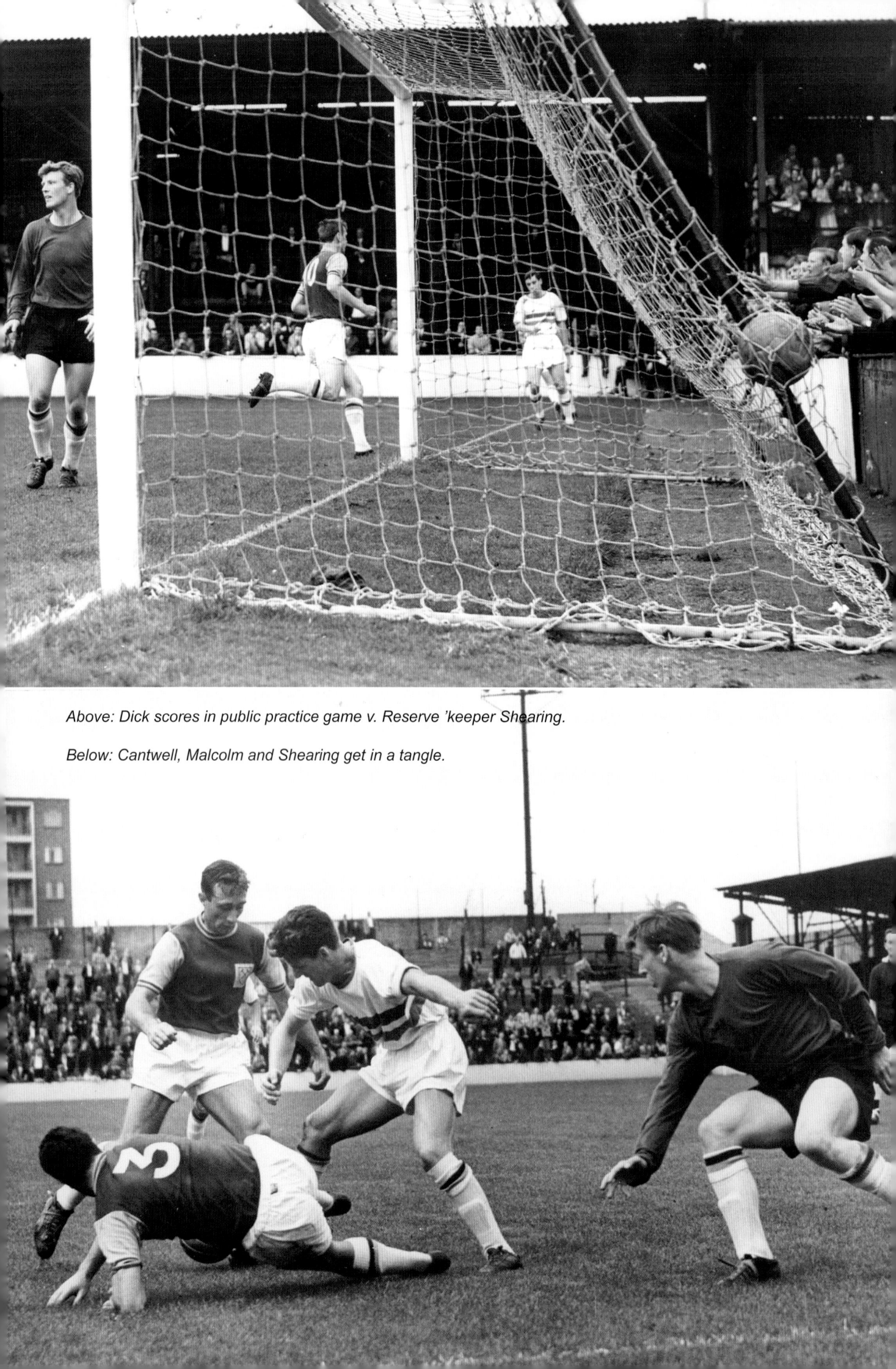

Above: Dick scores in public practice game v. Reserve 'keeper Shearing.

Below: Cantwell, Malcolm and Shearing get in a tangle.

victory at Arsenal.

With West Ham scoring for fun during this "purple patch", there was high jinks during an easy 6-1 victory over Third Division Reading in the third round of the Southern Floodlight Cup at Upton Park.

After "new boy" Harry Obeney had hit four goals and Andy Smillie and Mike Grice had made the score 6-0, goalkeeper Dwyer added to the entertainment when he opted to take a penalty awarded against the Biscuitmen for hands. His shot was saved by his opposite number Dave Meeson, however, and the would-be goalscorer was forced to make an undignified and hasty retreat back to his own goal as the uproarious laughter of the sparse 5,400 crowd echoed around the rafters of an incredulous Upton Park which hadn't experienced a scene like it since the days of George Kitchen.

Not to be outdone in the penalty missing stakes, the Colts in the South East Counties League managed to miss three against Bexleyheath & Welling Colts at the Town Ground, but still claimed their first win of the season with a 3-1 victory by courtesy of Roger Hugo (2) and Brian "Stag" Dear. Using his utmost discretion, as always, programme editor Jack Helliar deemed the unsuccessful trio should remain nameless. If anyone could reveal their identity now, they would surely be deserving of the title of the "World's Greatest Anorak!"

Despite a "where did that come from?" club record equalling 7-0 defeat at Sheffield Wednesday on November 28, which toppled the Hammers from the unfamiliar summit of

Walker (A), Chapman and St Pier coach youngsters, Dear, Charles, Beesley, Presland, Bickles, Boyce, Woodley, Hugo, Casky and Peters. 1960.

the First Division in spectacular fashion, with almost half the season gone, most at Upton Park were happy with the way the campaign had panned out thus far.

Albeit with some growing reservations concerning the "Jekyll and Hyde" form of goalkeeper Noel Dwyer, about whom one report from Sheffield claimed: "The man who took the biggest sucker punch of all was Eire international, Noel Dwyer". Adding: "Dwyer just couldn't take or punch the ball clear as it came across from the wings. He was beaten through rank bad judgement".

In a welcome diversion, the hunt for league points was interspersed by two visitors from the continent for the still popular "floodlight friendly" exhibition matches in the form of FC Austria and the more well known Czech Army side, Dukla Prague.

Against the Viennese side before an appreciative 22,500 crowd on a fine early October evening, the Hammers could count themselves unlucky to have been restricted to the two second-half goals from Woosnam and Dick which clinched a deserved 2-0 victory.

This was FC Austria's second visit to Upton Park as they were Hammers' guests during the course of a European tour in 1935. The match, on December 2, that year, resulted in a narrow 2-1 victory for Irons. Jim Barrett scored one of the goals, while the other went down as an "own goal". On this, their most recent visit, the Austrian's goalkeeper Herbert Gartner, played a proverbial "blinder". This was his second appearance at the Boleyn, as he turned out for SK Rapid in November 1955 and put up a fine performance then in helping his club to a 1-1 draw.

Back row, left to right: Greenwood, Kirkup, Lyall, Lansdowne, Leslie, Bond, Brown, Tindall, Moore, Chapman.
Middle row: Peters, Bovington, Scott, Woosnam, Byrne, Hurst, Musgrove, Burkett
Front row: Sealey, Boyce, Crawford, Dear. 1961.

Unfortunately, the clerk of the weather was not so kind for the visit of Dukla the following month when persistent rain before kick-off kept the crowd down to 10,300 to watch a side which included half-a-dozen Czech internationals, three of whom would go on to represent their country in the 3-1 World Cup Final defeat to Brazil in 1962 in Chile – Novak, Pluskal and Masopust, who opened the scoring. The same three players also opposed the Hammers in the two-leg final of the American Challenge Cup in 1963 at Soldier's Field Chicago and Randalls Island, New York; which the Czechs won 2-1 on aggregate.

But back to a rainy night in London's East End where the visitors confused their hosts by altering the numbers of their players from those listed in the programme. The match, nevertheless, turned out to be an interesting one for the fans who braved the elements to compare the similarities of style between the two sides.

Hammers, who led at half-time through a penalty converted by skipper Noel Cantwell, also fielded a player who would feature in Chile – Bobby Moore – who was lapping up new lessons playing against such different opposition. No one, it seems, begrudged Dukla their equaliser in what was an entertaining evening. Neither did anyone know who scored it, due to all those number and positional changes!

A welcome glint of silver was added to the Upton Park trophy cabinet when the Colts won the Southern Junior Floodlight Cup for the third time in succession when they defeated Chelsea Colts in the delayed 1958-59 Final at Stamford Bridge on Wednesday,

Upton Park, 1950s.

Back row, L-R: Trainer, Billy Moore, Malcolm, Brown, Gregory, Cantwell, Lansdowne, Pyke, Fenton. Front row L-R: Grice, Smith, Keeble, Dick, Musgrove. 1958.

October 14, by a 1-0 margin.

Hammers all professional side lined up at the Bridge: Peter Reader, Harry Cripps, Jack Burkett, Eddie Bovington, Bobby Moore, Geoff Hurst, Derek Woodley, Johnny Cartwright, Mick Beesley, Andy Smillie and Tony Scott. Andy Smillie got the goal in the 15th minute when he converted a penalty for hands to clinch a unique "hat-trick".

Six of the side had already been "blooded" in the first team and, quite remarkably, all went on to feature in the Football League. With that level of progression, there's always a team behind the team and the key men in the background consisted of Chief Scout and star-finder extraordinaire, Wally St. Pier, Youth Section organiser Bill Robinson, ably assisted by Stan Wilcockson, Frank Wilkins and Tom Russell.

But back among the senior pros, things were starting to go awry.

Although the first team had bounced back in commendable fashion by trouncing Nottingham Forest 4-1 at the Boleyn a week after the debacle at Hillsborough, where goalkeeper Noel Dwyer had picked the ball out of the back of his net seven times, the next away game at Blackburn Rovers would provide further trauma.

Going into the game at Ewood Park two weeks before Christmas joint second in the First Division table on 27 points with Tottenham, just a point behind leaders Preston North End in the almost unthinkable position of having League Champions Wolves, Champions-elect Burnley, Manchester United and Arsenal all below them; West Ham again capitulated in spectacular fashion against a rampant Rovers for whom Derek Dougan helped himself to four of the Lancastrian's goals in their 6-2 win.

After seeing out the 50s with a hard fought 3-1 home win over Birmingham City, thanks to goals from Musgrove (2) and Ronnie Brett in a match which saw former fan's favourite Harry Hooper and Dick both booked, the Hammers kicked off the 60s with another mauling from northern opposition by losing 5-2 at the Boleyn to the eventual Champions Burnley and would win just three more matches all season, none away. It would represent the worst second half of a campaign until 2014-15.

Yet when the dust had finally settled on all the disastrous debacles of this winter of discontent, despite the repercussions of the 7-0 defeat at Hillsborough which started the rot, the 6-2 defeat at Blackburn, the 5-3 loss at home to Burnley, the 5-0 deficit at Wolves, the 5-3 reversal at Old Trafford and notwithstanding the 5-1 FA Cup annihilation at home to Denis Law inspired Second Division Huddersfield Town.

One defeat stood out above them all and caused more ill-feeling, conjecture and damaging rumour to surround any match in the proud 120 year history of West Ham United and its forebears, Thames Ironworks FC.

The game in question was the First Division fixture with Newcastle United at Upton Park on Saturday, February 20, 1960. Prior to kick-off the Hammers were three places above the Novocastrians in ninth spot in the table on 31 points, with a game in hand. The Magpies had gained two points less than their opponents at this stage, so it was all to play for.

As the match report noted in the *Official Programme* for the following Saturday's Football Combination fixture versus Portsmouth reserves: "Our First Team lost the opportunity of moving into sixth place in the table last Saturday, a 3-5 defeat at the hands of Newcastle United pushing them down to the lowest place in the top half of the table". The report continued: "As far as the Hammers were concerned, it was indeed a game of fluctuating fortunes and what might have been" and provoked many an argument for fans and commentators alike among the 27,000 attendance.

"The Magpies went off to a 3-0 lead after 27 minutes, two of them from along-the-ground shots that went just inside the post; at that stage it appeared certain that they would coast to victory, and indeed they scored again only to be brought back to take a free-kick awarded before the shot was taken. Then came a transformation and a terrific Hammers' rally that brought two goals and a tremendous save by the visiting goalkeeper in the space of a minute; when we made it 3-3 four minutes after the interval it was once more anybody's game".

"Heavy rain at this stage made the going even heavier, and it would not have been surprising if the referee had decided to abandon the game. However, he did not do so, and it was the Northerner's ability to adapt themselves more readily to the conditions that brought two further goals and victory; Newcastle's fourth was undoubtedly the best of the match, and George Eastham earned much commendations for the manner in which he beat four men before hitting home with his left foot from about 12 yards". The report concluded: "A most entertaining game despite our disappointment at defeat".

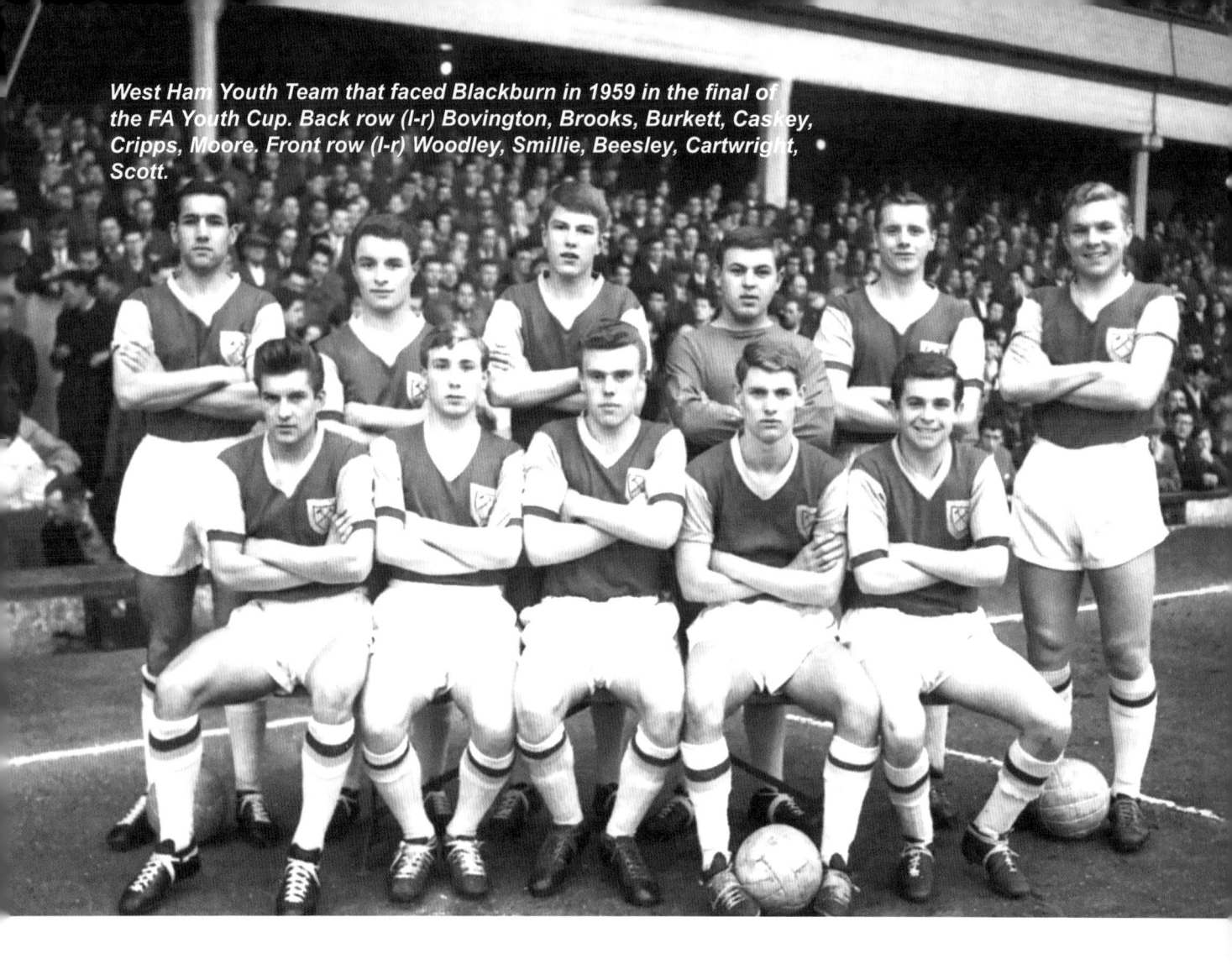

West Ham Youth Team that faced Blackburn in 1959 in the final of the FA Youth Cup. Back row (l-r) Bovington, Brooks, Burkett, Caskey, Cripps, Moore. Front row (l-r) Woodley, Smillie, Beesley, Cartwright, Scott.

What the report didn't mention was that Welsh international Phil Woosnam, who had orchestrated West Ham's fight back, was, to quote another report: "Apoplectic with rage", about the manner of the defeat and that one of the club's directors was so incensed he had stormed out of Upton Park in fury after the game.

In his book, *At Home With The Hammers*, which was published shortly afterwards, manager Ted Fenton had this to say after addressing the mauling at Hillsborough:

"A crowning blow, too, was the insinuation that a West Ham game had been 'rigged'. We went under 3-5 to Newcastle United, and some bookmakers who had to pay out complained of the amount of money that went on Newcastle and Grimsby (who played at Brentford that day) at the last minute.

"The inference was clear-cut. Yet I decided, with the full co-operation of my board, to take no steps about the whole disgusting affair. We decided to let it blow over as quickly as possible, and when the bookies stopped squealing at their losses and paid out, we thought we were right".

Ted continued: "They say, though, that a certain amount of mud sticks. Footballers are clean-living, clean-minded fellows. It's a slur to suggest *without proof* that such a thing as 'rigging' goes on. I was particularly distressed as, in all my years at Upton Park, I have never come across the slightest sign of anything of this nature".

But, despite Fenton's protestations, the rumours continued and goalkeeper Noel Dwyer, who

West Ham's Welsh international inside right Phil Woosnam who was appointed club captain following Noel Cantwell's transfer to Manchester United in December 1960.

West Ham United's Ireland international goalkeeper, Noel Dwyer, lets the first goal in during the controversial 5-3 defeat to Newcastle United at Upton Park in February 1960. There were claims that the match was part of a betting scam, but nothing was ever proved. On the left, Noel Cantwell.

had been held largely to blame in the press for the 7-0 hammering at Sheffield Wednesday, was again in the spotlight.

Against Newcastle, it was noted in John Helliar and Clive Leatherdale's book, *West Ham United: The Elite Era* that, "Dwyer goes from bad to worse, pushing Hughes' shot over his head into the net, then diving too late for Ivor Allchurch's trickled shot".

Whatever happened that day, it would be naïve to assume only one player was involved and unfair for only one player to bear the brunt of, let's remember, unproven accusations. Best then, to leave the events of that sodden February day of 57 years ago enveloped in the mists of time, to remain forever more, an unsavoury mystery of the past.

At this stage of the game, beleaguered manager Fenton could have done worse than to check on the form of veteran goalie Ernie Gregory, who was still earning his corn with some eye-catching performances in the Metropolitan League for the "A" Team. Young Brian Rhodes had stepped in admirably for the discarded Dwyer, but with the benefit of hindsight, wouldn't "Ernie, the Elder" have been a better option considering his vast experience?

Anyway, Ernie was still throwing himself around like a youngster in the third team who had won through to the Final of the Metropolitan League Professional Cup thanks to Ernie's heroics in the semi-final against Luton Town at Upton Park on March 28, 1960.

The team that lined up against the Hatters is worth a look at as it read: Gregory, Harry Cripps, Jack Burkett, Eddie Bovington, Martin Peters, David Hills, Derek Woodley, R. Boyce, Norman Bleanch, Andy Smillie and B. Dear. And as a report in a subsequent programme recorded:

"The star of this game was veteran goalkeeper Ernie Gregory who made several top rate saves from a dangerous forward line led by the experienced Mike Tracy. However, the whole team deserves credit for the 2-1 victory against a heavier built side, and there was no doubt that they had the edge in a hard-fought game which provided a high standard of play despite the rainy weather which made conditions unpleasant.

"Johnny Cartwright put Derek Woodley away in the ninth minute and our right-winger cut in and shot the ball into the roof of the net on the run. A defensive lapse let the Hatters in a minute before the interval, but seven minutes after the restart Woodley made another solo dash and ended with a shot that the opposing 'keeper could only parry and Andy Smillie followed up to net the rebound".

As you might have noticed, Johnny Cartwright is not listed in the starting line up, so as there were no subs in those days, maybe he was a last minute replacement. An "Anorak of the Year" award awaits anyone who can solve this one.

No less than nine of the 10 players who stood in front of Ernie on that Monday evening under the Boleyn bulbs graduated to play in the Football League, the only exception being David Hills, who joined Southern League Margate that close season where he teamed up with fellow ex-Hammers, Albert Foan and Fred Kearns under another former Hammer, manager Almer Hall.

You may have realised that four of the side which disposed of the Hatters went on to play in Hammers greatest triumph, the 2-0 victory over TSV 1860 Munich in the 1965 European Cup Winners' Cup Final at Wembley – Jack Burkett, Martin Peters, Ronnie Boyce and Brian Dear, and also that the latter two were listed in the line-up versus Luton by initials only, as they were still on amateur forms.

Incidentally, Ronnie Boyce tells a funny story about those days when he asked Ernie what the team was. Knowing that young Ronnie wanted to know if he'd been picked, Ernie replied: "Spinks, Stinks, Pen and Ink, Freeman, Hardy, Willis".

West Ham had a mountain to climb when they lost the first leg of the Final 4-1 against Chelsea after fielding seven amateurs at Stamford Bridge with young Frank Caskey in goal. But their own man-mountain Ernie Gregory would be back for the second-leg having announced that he would retire after having served the club since 1936.

West Ham selected a strong XI for the second-leg staged at Upton Park by floodlight on Monday, May 2, 1960 and lined up for what would be goalkeeping legend Gregory's last game: Gregory, Kirkup, Burkett, Bovington, Lansdowne, Obeney, Woodley, Cartwright, Brett, Hills, Dear.

Against all the odds, goals from Ron Brett (2), Cartwright and Woodley made sure he bade a winning farewell as the Hammers defeated the "Young Pensioners" 4-0 to take the Cup 5-4 on aggregate. Although he didn't play in the second-leg, it was Norman Bleanch's goal at Stamford Bridge that proved critical.

Also crucial was another inspiring display by the veteran Ernie, who signed off with a Cup Winners medal and a clean sheet to boot. He was appointed trainer of "his boys" in the close

A superb action shot from the promotion battle with rivals Liverpool in April 1958. John Dick challenges Reds' South African born goalkeeper Doug Rudham. The 1-1 draw earned Hammers a vital point towards their winning of the 1958 Second Division Championship.

season to begin another extended career.

But before this fitting finale for one of the club's greatest servants, the first XI, too, had enjoyed a brighter interlude with a "floodlight friendly" against Brazilian champions Fluminense.

Able to call upon nine full Brazilian internationals and one Paraguayian, reserve 'keeper Gonzalez, their coach, Zeze Moreira, was in charge of the national side in the early 50s.

Having won the Rio de Janeiro State Championship a record 17 times, it was not surprising that a crowd of 24,158 filed through the Upton Park turnstiles to witness first hand, soccer with a samba beat. They were not to be disappointed.

Freed from the shackles of the quest for points, Hammers matched the brilliant Brazilians with a performance which was reminiscent of their early season displays which took them to the top of the First Division.

When right-half Edmilson put the visitors ahead in the eleventh minute, it proved to be just the opening shot of a nine-goal thriller in which the Hammers seemed determined not to be outshone.

Dave Dunmore's equaliser in the 30th minute seemed to be the signal for the home side to step up a gear and when winger Mal Musgrove put Hammers 3-1 ahead with two headed goals in the space of five minutes, the result of prodigious leaps from long range passes from Bond and Grice in the 33rd and 38th minutes, it seemed Hammers might be on for a clear cut victory.

But Fluminense weren't champions for nothing and by the 64th minute of the second-half they were 3-4 ahead with stunning strikes from Jair in the 52nd minute and Escurinho 60 seconds later to leave Edmilson to put the boys from Brazil ahead again from a free kick. Not to be outdone, Bond levelled the scores in the 67th minute when he converted Cantwell's pass from an indirect free-kick and then Cantwell soared high to connect with Grice's corner after forcing his way past four defenders to make the final score 5-4 on the 72nd minute.

It was a remarkable result, given that 48 hours earlier the Hammers had lost 3-1 at already relegated Luton Town and would finish the 1959-60 season just four points away from that fate themselves.

The Silver Sixties
Chapter 6

Had some contemporary soothsayer or clairvoyant suggested to manager Ted Fenton on the eve of the 1960-61 season that the Upton Park playing staff already possessed three players who would go on to provide the nucleus of an England team to win the World Cup just six years hence, it's easy to imagine the mirth and ridicule such a seemingly far-fetched prediction would have provoked.

Yet two of this so far largely anonymous trio, Bobby Moore and Geoff Hurst, had already appeared in the first team and the third, Martin Peters, had signed apprentice professional forms. But under pressure boss Fenton would be long gone by the time this unlikely scenario became reality, so best we put away the crystal ball for now.

Certainly, no crystal ball was required to ascertain the retained list of players for the new season; it was printed in black and white in the official programme for the first game of the campaign against Aston Villa on Monday evening August 22, 1960 and comprised: Michael Beesley, Norman Bleanch, John Bond, Eddie Bovington, Ron Boyce, Ron Brett, Ken Brown, Jack Burkett, Noel Cantwell, John Cartwright, Harry Cripps, John Dick, Dave Dunmore, Mike Grice, Geoff Hurst, Joe Kirkup, Bill Lansdowne, John Lyall, Andy Malcolm, Bobby Moore, Malcolm Musgrove, Harry Obeney, Peter Reader, Brian Rhodes, Tony Scott, Peter Shearing, Andy Smillie, Derek Woodley and Phil Woosnam.

In addition, seven apprentice pros were listed: David Bickles, John Charles, Brian Dear, Alan Dickie, Reg Le Surf, Martin Peters and John Starkey, of whom Bickles, Charles, Dear, Le Surf and Peters had been members of the successful Youth Section which travelled to Holland to participate in a tournament to celebrate the Golden Jubilee of the Ensched Football Club, in addition to Hurst, Boyce, Beesley, Burkett, Michael Brooks, Frank Caskey, Dave Cunningham, Roger Hugo, Paddy O'Mahoney and Derek Woodley.

Accompanied by officials Wally St. Pier, Eddie Chapman and Albert Walker the party returned home triumphant after defeating Heracles, 2-1 (Boyce 2), Blau Wit, 4-1 (Beesley, Boyce, Hugo and Peters), Willem II, 2-1 (Dear 2) and Aarhus of Denmark 2-1 (Hurst 2) in the Final.

Other news in the programme was that following the death of Mr. Harold Longman, Mr. Roland G. Brandon had accepted the club's invitation to make up the fourth member of the Board of Directors to join current incumbents R. H. Pratt (Chairman), L. C. Cearns (Vice Chairman) and W. F. Cearns. It was also announced that Chairman R. H. Pratt had been appointed as Chairman of the Football Combination after serving on the committee of the reserve team's competition for many years at their headquarters in the Barking Road. Also announced was the retirement of First Team trainer Billy Moore who played at inside-left in the 1923 FA Cup Final side against Bolton Wanderers and the departure of Harry Butler, who joined the Upton Park ranks on a part-time basis in 1940 prior to being promoted to the post of Assistant Trainer in 1945. After taking charge of the "A" Team for many years he left to take up the position of Trainer at Millwall. Taking his place was Ernie Gregory who finally hung up his gloves after inspiring his teammates to that Metropolitan League Professional Cup triumph over Chelsea the previous May.

Another sad departure from the playing side was that of popular centre-forward Vic Keeble, whose goals had been greatly instrumental in propelling the Hammers into the First Division in 1958. Vic was forced to retire on medical grounds due to persistent back trouble. Controversial Eire international goalkeeper Noel Dwyer also left the club during close-season when he joined Swansea Town. But, as we shall see later, he would make a spectacular return. Also departing was promising young professional David Hills, who had left for Margate FC under the managership of ex-Hammer Almer Hall to join fellow former wearers of the claret and blue, Albert Foan, Fred Kearns and Alan Blackburn. Former Hammer's winger Ken Tucker was a visitor to the Villa match and declared that he would now only be a spectator at matches as he had decided to "hang up his boots" after ending his playing career at Margate the previous season. Ken, incidentally, was the "Guest of Honour" at my book launch for *Who's Who of West Ham* published in November 2005 to celebrate 100 years at the Boleyn Ground and the oldest

An unusual shot of West Ham winger Malcolm Musgrove attacking the Stoke City goal in the FA Cup third round, wearing an unfamiliar change shirt which is usually worn away from home.

Hammers Scottish International marksman Jackie Dick takes on the defences of Ipswich Town (top) and Blackburn Rovers (below). 1962.

attendee at 80 years of age. He thoroughly enjoyed himself and mischievously recounted a tale of once hurling a boot at Ted Fenton's head after falling out with his former boss.

In another incident recalled by that great West Ham fan and a pal of this scribe, Terry Connelly, of when he saw Ken driving down the Barking Road after a match at Upton Park when that eccentric character known as "Monty", who used to parade around the pitch before games playing a bugle in full army dress, caused Ken to break suddenly by obstructing his car and then began berating him. Until, that was, an irate Kenny got out of his motor to confront the "Old Soldier" and he realised who he was. "Monty" was then full of remorse and began bowing to his Hammers hero to make a grovelling apology.

Hammers, by the way, won that game against the Villa 5-2, with goals from Woosnam, Dunmore, Dick, Bond and Musgrove after losing the first match of the 1960-61 season 4-2 against FA Cup winners and First Division runners-up Wolves at Molineux.

Back at Upton Park was "Young Jim" Barrett, following successful spells with Nottingham Forest and Birmingham City where he had played with another Hammers legend, winger Harry Hooper. Jim was recalled to join the coaching staff after his playing career was curtailed by an injury sustained playing for Brum in the Fairs Cup semi-final against Union St. Gilloise.

A further addition to the back-room staff at the Boleyn Ground was made by the appointment of Bill Jenkins as the club's physiotherapist-trainer. Bill, an East Ham resident, was selected over a large number of applicants due to his previous experience with top amateur clubs Clapton FC and Walthamstow Avenue. He soon became a popular figure and a character in his own right at Upton Park.

A major talking point at the start of the season was manager Ted Fenton's decision, fully backed by his players, to adopt the revolutionary four-two-four system. The formation was used by the Brazilian side Fluminense against the Hammers at Upton Park at the end of the previous campaign and even though they won an exhilarating contest 5-4, the Rio De Janeiro club's interpretation of the system caught the imagination of the "thinkers" among the Boleyn Boy's ranks like messrs. Bond, Cantwell, Musgrove and Woosnam.

So the team fully embraced the experimental system. But it only seemed to work in home games, as results at Upton Park against Villa (5-2), Bolton (2-1), Manchester United (2-1), Blackpool (3-3), Blackburn (3-2), Birmingham (4-3), Preston (5-2) and, incredibly, Arsenal (6-0), amply underlined. But it was a different kettle of fish away as Hammers had to wait until November 12 for their first (and only) away win of the season against Manchester City at Maine Road.

An anonymous scribe in the *Football Champions Book* of 1961 claimed to know where West Ham were going wrong, as he outlined in an in-depth feature into the subject:

"The symbols 4.2.4 were introduced into British football last season (1960-61). West Ham started it by an open avowal of the tactical system which has been prevalent on the continent for some years and which international players like Phil Woosnam and Noel Cantwell had noted in matches against foreign teams.

"The trouble with 4.2.4 was that the symbols were endowed with a mystical quality. Clubs adopted the system and thought that should be the end of their worries, forgetting that it is the players who make the system work. West Ham adopted 4.2.4 at the beginning of last season after spending the month's pre-season training in perfecting the drill. But they made elementary mistakes which made the plan a failure. A typical line-up featured:

BRIAN RHODES
1

JOHN BOND   KEN BROWN   NOEL CANTWELL   BOBBY MOORE
2   5   3   6

ANDY MALCOLM
4

PHIL WOOSNAM
8

MIKE GRICE   DAVE DUNMORE   JOHN DICK   MAL MUSGROVE
7   9   10   11

"Andy Malcolm has a biting tackle, shadows tenaciously the most elusive opponent and does not excel in passing. He was made the linking wing-half. Noel Cantwell is the finest attacking full-back in the game. He was made a purely defensive unit. Bobby Moore excels as an aggressive wing-half, as he showed when captain of Young England. He was made to

Woosnam tries against Sheffield United

That great character Monty is led away by Police at the South Bank End.

Harry Obeney scores against Everton, despite the attentions of the Toffee's wing-half Jimmy Gabriel and goalkeeper Albert Dunlop.

'police' the outside-right. The midfield players should be on opposite sides of the field in order to obtain balance. Phil Woosnam and Andy Malcolm were both on the right flank.

"It would have been a happier line-up to make Malcolm stay deep alongside Brown, give Moore the licence of the attacking wing-half and allow Cantwell to remain at left-back. There would have been better balance and full use of the individuals' qualities.

"The departure of Cantwell to Manchester United broke up the defence, but even before then West Ham had abandoned 4.2.4 because the playing results were not good enough. A Pity. It was not the system that was wrong, but the way West Ham put it into execution".

So there.

But the main man behind the plan, inside forward Phil Woosnam, put forward his own views on it all via the pages of Charles Buchan's *Soccer Gift Book* in 1962, commenting:

"During the early part of season 1960-61, I was destined to play a key role in West Ham United's 4-2-4 plan which caused much comment in the press and which achieved some success, despite its detractors. The 4-2-4 Formation, employed by West Ham's manager Ted Fenton, was based on the successful plan adopted by the Brazilian World Cup winning team in Sweden in 1958.

"West Ham were not the only team to try this scheme in English football – but most of the attention seemed to be focussed on Upton Park – largely, I felt, because we were a leading

A panoramic view taken from the top of the North Bank of a match with West Bromwich Albion, before the cover was put on in 1961.

First Division club. In this plan, I, as inside-right, was required to patrol the mid-field area, with right-half Andy Malcolm. Bobby Moore, our left-half, spent most of his time up on attack, and so did John Dick, our big Scottish international goal-getter, who formed a two-pronged spearhead with centre-forward Dave Dunmore.

"In practice, Andy Malcolm always played behind me so that our rearguard consisted of John Bond, Malcolm, Ken Brown and Noel Cantwell. When we were forced on defence, Andy and I would play well back to reinforce our big defenders and help to form a strong barrier concentrated in front of goal. When on attack, I would go up to support Moore, Andy stayed back to maintain the four man defence.

"Well, 4-2-4 proved to have certain weaknesses. At times there were too many gaps left in midfield when opponents broke quickly away from a defensive position. One by one, the clubs discarded it and eventually we abandoned it at West Ham after several results had gone against us.

"But I believed then, as I still do, that there is a future for 4-2-4. I think this was borne out later in 1960 when Walter Winterbottom, the England team manager, decided to base his tactics along these lines, with marked success".

With or without 4.2.4, by Christmas Hammers had risen to 7th in the First Division table by defeating champions Wolves 5-0 in East London with goals from Musgrove, Dick, Dunmore (2)

WILL THAT BOY GET OFF THE PITCH!

Just as all's fair in love and war and gaining entry into Upton Park when the gates are locked, the same rules applied when collecting autographs.

The general consensus was: "Get them to sign by fair means or foul", and we usually succeeded. Many youngsters would track down visiting teams at their hotel or hang around railway stations, but me and my mate Tommo would operate at the ground before and after matches and also the training ground at Chadwell Heath.

But nowhere was out of bounds – not even the playing pitch. For a mischievous 13-year old, rules were meant to be broken.

I still recall the events of an experimental Friday night game in April 1962 when Birmingham City were the visitors to Upton Park.

I was standing by the players' tunnel in the West Enclosure when a few of the Brum boys came out to inspect the pitch. Then, in a moment of aberration, I jumped over the boundary wall and was on the sacred greensward. I got winger Mike Helliwell to sign my scrapbook and then followed his opposite flankman Bertie Auld down the tunnel and he signed too, uttering darkly as he did so: "You'll get me shot" in his abrasive Glaswegian accent. That's when the announcer piped up with "Will that boy get off the pitch", over the tannoy system.

The match itself was an exciting affair. When the visitor's right-back Stan Lynn was injured after just two minutes and reduced to a virtual passenger on the wing, it seemed the odds were stacked against them. This was not the case, however, as the battling Brummies stuck resolutely to the task of getting something out of the game. When Jimmy Bloomfield equalised Mal Musgrove's 30 yard rocket-shot which put the Hammers ahead in the 55th minute, in the 59th, it was "game on". Sixty seconds later Lynn, of all people, put the Blues ahead. Upton Park was stunned into silence.

Luckily, Musgrove was on hand to restore the equilibrium with another of his long range thunder-bolts 15 minutes from time to temporarily silence the boo-boys who had been on his back all season.

The following season I was at the Boleyn when our courageous goalkeeper Lawrie Leslie broke a leg repelling a Bolton Wanderers attack. Bolton won 1-2 after Peters went in goal.

After the match a lot of the home fans were in an ugly mood and were waiting for their team coach to leave afterwards.

I always used to try and get into the players' car park before and after matches to get signatures. A commissionaire used to guard the gate and a game of cat and mouse between us had developed over the months. He was as hell-bent on keeping me out as I was to get in.

Often there would be an impasse, but on this occasion, with a baying mob waiting to give Bolton a traditional Upton Park send-off, my adversary was distracted from his post long enough for me to slip through unnoticed.

The Bolton team coach was right in front of me – empty. I slipped on board and hid at the back waiting for my prey.

They arrived amid a barrage of boos, jeers and missiles and seemed to be relieved to get on board. They were certainly surprised to see me emerging from between the seats clutching my precious scrapbook with pen in hand.

Even so, they good-naturedly signed the pictures in the Bolton section of the scrapbook and I remember centre-half Bryan Edwards – who played over 500 games for the Trotters between 1950 and 1964, commenting as he signed: "They're sick because we beat them".

There were some famous names on board including a very young Francis Lee, and England internationals Eddie Hopkinson and Freddie Hill – who later joined Malcolm Allison at Manchester City along with Lee.

So the Wanderers left Upton Park with a verbose and vitriolic diatribe of abuse ringing in their ears as their coach, on which I'd been an uninvited guest just minutes earlier, gingerly made its way out of the old school gates and out into Green Street under the watchful eyes of a police escort.

JOHNNY BYRNE
West Ham and England

Johnny Dick heads towards the Spurs goal at White Hart Lane at Christmas 1960.

and Moore. Although it would be a high water-mark, as once they left the bear pit which was Upton Park, like a fine vintage claret – they didn't travel well and were in freefall by the time the festive season was over and the last of the wine poured; once again becoming fodder for those old music hall comedians' jibes of "coming down with the Xmas decorations".

Knocked out of the FA Cup in a Third Round replay at Stoke City, come season's end they would finish two places lower than they had the previous campaign (16th), with two points less (36) and again, just four points away from relegation.

But by this time a new man was at the helm who would change the course of the club's history… Ron Greenwood.

Welcome the outsider.

Unlike his three predecessors, Syd King, Charlie Paynter and Ted Fenton, Greenwood was not a former Hammers player, in fact, he was from another claret and blue stronghold, Burnley in Lancashire.

Before we delve too deeply into his background, let's try to shed some light on the events surrounding the departure of the man he replaced, promotion winning boss Ted Fenton.

As we have already indicated, the 1960-61 campaign was a poor one from the playing point of view for the club with, true to tradition, a sharp decline in form from Christmas onwards when just three victories were recorded against, ten before the festive season.

Despite hopes being raised by a 4-0 home win versus Everton on February 11, 1961 when Harry Obeney (2), Dick and Musgrove got the goals, by the time of the visit to struggling

Preston North End exactly a month later, the Hammers had incurred another two defeats and couldn't afford to lose at Deepdale. But they did, 4-0 to a North End outfit who included ex-Hammer Frank O'Farrell at left-half. Fenton's position, which had already been under scrutiny, was now under the microscope.

The following Monday a practice match had been arranged for the West Ham First XI to play the full England team in preparation for their next series of international games. The game was played behind locked doors, with only representatives of the press and England and Hammers officials being admitted.

According to the report in the following week's match programme versus Fulham, the team lined up: West Ham United: Rhodes, Kirkup, Bond, Malcolm, Brown, Hurst, Brett, Woosnam, Obeney, Dick, Musgrove.

England: Springett (Sheffield Wednesday), Armfield (Blackpool), McNeil (Middlesbrough), Robson (WBA), Swan (Sheffield Wednesday), Kay (Sheffield Wednesday), Brabrook (Chelsea), Greaves (Chelsea), Baker, J. (Hibs), Haynes (Fulham), Charlton, R. (Manchester United).

In his autobiography, Yours Sincerely, Ron Greenwood recalled the events at Upton Park that fateful evening.

"The first hint that my career was about to take an abrupt change in direction came in March 1961. England were playing West Germany in an Under-23 international at Tottenham on the Tuesday but, the night before, Walter Winterbottom took the senior squad to Upton Park for a practice match. That same evening, by sheer coincidence, Ted Fenton left West Ham, suddenly and without real explanation. All the press were there and the next morning the story was given royal treatment. I read the reports but did not feel involved.

"Next day we set off for the Under-23 match and Walter, who was sitting next to me on the coach, started talking about the game at Upton park the previous evening.

" 'West Ham beat us 1-0', he said 'and if you think Bobby Moore's a player you should see this chap Geoff Hurst. He scored this goal against us, from left-half. It was unbelievable. Almost from the half-way line!' Then, suddenly, he asked 'would you be interested in the job at West Ham?'

" 'I'm happy at Arsenal', I said. 'In any case, if they're going to sack people like they did last night, it's obviously not a happy club".

The events of the evening probably made up one of the most bizarre nights in the ground's 112 year history… the night a match was played in secret behind closed doors and behind the scenes the club's manager was sacked without any explanation. The shocked Fenton, who had no contract, was told simply to clear his desk and pack his bags by Chairman Reg Pratt.

Also in the eerie, empty atmosphere of a crowdless Upton Park, Geoff Hurst delivered an uncanny portent of an England event still five years hence with his "thunder-bolt" winning goal.

Yet what a lot a people don't realise is that it wasn't Ron Greenwood who first converted England's World Cup winner from left-half to inside-left, but the vanquished Ted Fenton. Who had played him in the number 10 shirt in the semi-final of the Southern Floodlight Cup against Arsenal at Highbury on April 5, 1960 when Hammers won 3-1 to reach the final.

But it wasn't Hurst that scored the goals, it was Musgrove and Cartwright (who scored twice) who grabbed the limelight in what was recognised as virtually a first team competition. Ironically, Cartwright's future lay in coaching, while his playing career ended in near obscurity with Southern League Wimbledon and then Bath City under Malcolm Allison, his mentor. While Hurst…

Although the club were initially blasé about the need to appoint a new boss quickly and quite happy to leave the board, assisted by skipper Phil Woosnam and the trainer Albert Walker, in charge of first team matters; another two defeats in the wake of Fenton's departure at home to Fulham (1-2) and at Blackburn (1-4) may have hastened their search. At any rate, just over two weeks after gaining an invaluable point in a 0-0 stalemate with Arsenal at Highbury, the Gunner's Assistant Manager was duly appointed full-time Manager-Coach of West Ham United to be solely in charge of the playing staff, on Tuesday, April 11, 1961.

Fenton, meanwhile, had been in the thick of a relegation dog-fight having taken over as boss of Third Division Southend United three weeks previously – giving the lie to West Ham's statement issued the day after the England trial match to the Press Association that: "For some time Mr. Fenton had been working under quite a strain and it was agreed that he should go on sick leave".

Greenwood's first match in charge was for the first of three successive draws, versus Manchester City on April 15, 1961 when new signing Alan Sealey scored his first goal for the club in the 1-1 draw at the Boleyn before a crowd of just under 18,000.

Canning Town born Sealey, who had been signed from Leyton Orient in a straight swap deal for Dave Dunmore by Chairman Pratt, would become one of Greenwood's first "converts" and make a major contribution to the history of West Ham United.

The next two matches of the "Greenwood Era" were against his home-town club Burnley under the Turf Moor lights on Tuesday, April 18 and Cardiff City at Ninian Park the following Saturday, the 22nd (my birthday!). The two fixtures provided the "new boy" the perfect opportunity to get to know his squad, because after the visit to Lancashire where Hammers gained a creditable 2-2 draw after being 2-0 down to the reigning First Division champions through a timely brace from left-winger Mal Musgrove (who was rapidly proving himself Hammer's best goal scoring winger since the days of Jimmy Ruffell) Wales were to play Spain at Ninian the next night in a vital World Cup qualifier. So having travelled north for the game against the Clarets, the squad stayed in Lancashire overnight and entrained to Cardiff the next morning. They then saw Phil Woosnam score Wales' goal in an unlucky 2-1 defeat to the Spaniards in the international on Wednesday and afterwards moved on to Porthcawl. After a pleasant couple of days at the seaside the party travelled back to Ninian for the match versus the Bluebirds on the Saturday where they collected another welcome point in a 1-1 draw thanks to a John Dick leveller from a Tony Scott cross in the 69th minute before returning to London the same evening.

The whole week was a typical Greenwood exercise, not only had the party returned home with two precious points which effectively staved off the threat of relegation, they had also improved their football knowledge by watching world class performers of the calibre of Alfredo

Above: Joe Kirkup clears in the 3-2 win v Nottingham Forest (Musgrove, Scott and Sealey) at Upton Park in September 1961.
Below: Wolves' Chris Crowe heads towards goal, policed by John Lyall.

BOBBY MOORE
West Ham United

Di Stefano, Del Sol and Luis Suarez at Ninian Park where there was a distinct contrast for the attendance figure for the international (45,000) and the First Division clash with the City (10,000). But now everyone connected with the club could look forward to the visit of outgoing champions Burnley at Upton Park in the last game of the season. I know I was. This was my belated 13th birthday present – my first ever visit to Upton Park. I went with my father George who worked at the railway yard in Stratford as a welder, he was really good at his job as many of his friends testified and later in life made me a wheelbarrow and a solid iron grill for my barbeque. He had supported Hammers from pre-war days and was born in Stratford – so this move would have been like going home for him, I suppose. I wish I'd have asked him to make me a solid iron replica of the club crest now, he could have done that easily.

Anyway, we stood together on the old North Bank, which was still uncovered then. I remember the ground wasn't packed and when I checked it up in John Northcutt's and Steve Marsh's *Complete Record*, the attendance was 18,761. The one being me, of course!

Behind us, set up high at the back of the terrace, was the old half-time scoreboard and in the right hand corner, a cage-like enclosure known as the boys pen. Although presumably girls were allowed in too.

To our immediate left was the oldest part of the ground which was affectionately known as the "Chicken Run" and ran the entire length of the east side of the pitch backing on to Priory Road. It was a low rudimentary structure constructed almost entirely of wood but supported by 20 steel girders spaced out at regular intervals from end to end and topped off with a corrugated iron roof on which three four-lamp mini floodlight pylons where precariously perched. The South Bank at the Castle Street end of the ground was covered and served by two ten-lamp floodlights mounted on both roof ends. The North Bank was served by the same number of lamps mounted on single 30ft poles. To our right was Upton Park's pièce de résistance, the magnificent West Stand, with 4,500 seats in the upper tier and room for 8,000 standing in the enclosure below.

Yet, even as I gazed around in awe on my first ever visit to what would become a second home, changes were afoot as outlined in the notes in the official programme lovingly put together by Jack Helliar from his family printing business in the Barking Road, E14.

Within an article headlined *Our Present and Future*, we were informed: "From the spectator's angle there will be definite improvements to the Boleyn Ground before the start of next season. We have already made the preliminary moves, and you will have noted that work has commenced on the twin tasks of covering the North Bank and installing a new floodlight system.

"A roof on the North Bank will bring it into line with the other end of the ground and the floodlights will in future be mounted on pylons on each corner of the enclosure. This is all part of a long-term policy, which we hope will finally result in the erection of a new structure to replace the East Enclosure (better known to Upton Park habituées as 'The Chicken Run!'."

There was more good news when readers were informed that prices of admission to matches at the Boleyn Ground for season 1961-62 would remain unchanged at: Season Tickets (West)

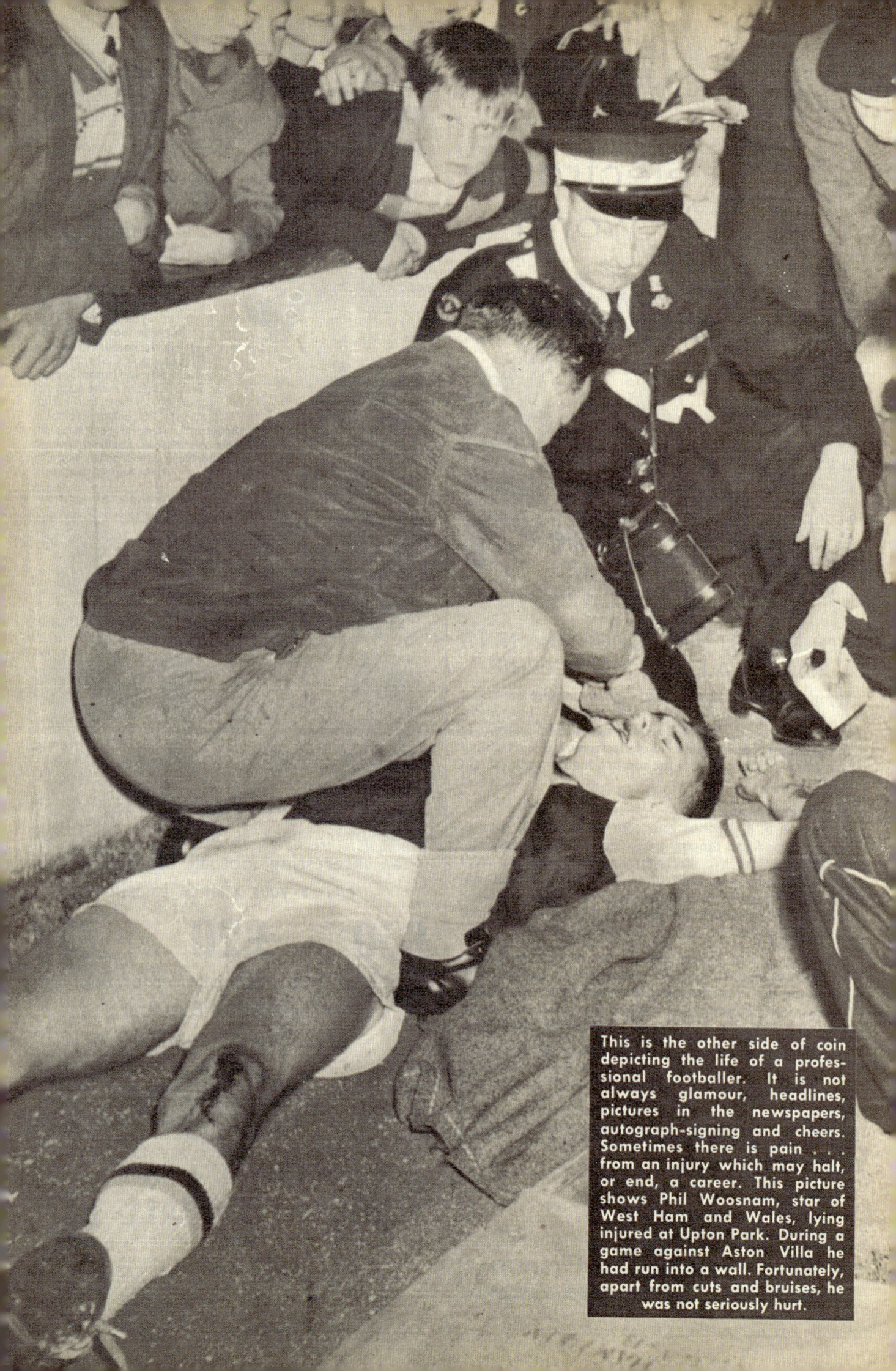

This is the other side of coin depicting the life of a professional footballer. It is not always glamour, headlines, pictures in the newspapers, autograph-signing and cheers. Sometimes there is pain... from an injury which may halt, or end, a career. This picture shows Phil Woosnam, star of West Ham and Wales, lying injured at Upton Park. During a game against Aston Villa he had run into a wall. Fortunately, apart from cuts and bruises, he was not seriously hurt.

£9.10s.0d, (East) £7.10s.0d. Ground: 2/-. East Terrace: 3/6. West Enclosure: 3/6. E Block: 5/-. B&D Blocks: 7/-. C Block: 8/6.

The access points to pay these (by today's comparisons) ludicrously modest sums were far easier to negotiate since the completion of the new main entrance on Green Street the previous summer, ensuring that the chaotic scenes of overcrowding around the turnstiles of the 1958-59 season were no longer a problem.

Upton Park was now served by forty six turnstiles at the following locations:

West Enclosure	4 turnstiles in Castle Street
	5 turnstiles in Green Street
North Bank	6 turnstiles in Priory Road
	5 turnstiles in Green Street
Grandstand (seats)	10 turnstiles in Green Street
Chicken Run	4 turnstiles in Priory Road
South Bank	12 turnstiles in Castle Street

The result on my first-ever visit to Upton Park which would become a regular pilgrimage? Burnley won 2-1, but no disgrace there, especially as skipper Phil Woosnam scored a fine goal to as least give us something to cheer on the day. More importantly though, I had noted the route from Gidea Park to Upton Park and had already decided to go to matches either on my own or with my pals the following 1961-62 season which seemed to hold so much promise in store for a wide-eyed 13 year-old… and what a fixture it gave us on the opening day – Manchester United at home!

Also, as promised. There was a brand new roof on what would become my spiritual home – the North Bank; and the towering new floodlights could be seen from miles around as the season was poised to get underway amid a wave of barely concealable anticipation and excitement. In addition, the club had raided the rich Scottish hunting grounds during the close season to buy new players and returned with two exciting new signings from over the border, Scottish international goalkeeper Lawrie Leslie from Airdrie and winger Ian Crawford from Hearts, who could play on either flank and had won every domestic honour possible at Tynecastle.

Meanwhile, new boss Greenwood seemed to be warming to life in London's East End despite having to give up the post of manager to the England Under 23s due to his full-time commitment to Hammers.

It's certainly the impression he gave in his autobiography, *Yours Sincerely*, when recalling: "West Ham, I discovered, was my sort of club. It belongs to its own patch in East London, a local club in the best sense, with a crowd that is second to none. The West Ham fans identify with the players and there is a genuine relationship between them; they all belong to the same family. No other club in London is quite like it.

"The club itself is well equipped and well administered, while Upton Park is compact but not small and has a style and atmosphere all its own. The old Chicken Run has now gone but, in my early days there, this popular area opposite the main stand somehow stood for West Ham. It was low and tatty, its steps were wooden and occasionally I would wander over and marvel that it never burnt down There was usually a lot of paper and rubbish underneath, and although we had a regular clear-out, there was always a chance that a cigarette or match carelessly thrown away would start a blaze. Sometimes we would find something smouldering, but the Chicken Run survived – and the sight and sound of the crowd in the old place letting rip with *I'm Forever Blowing Bubbles* always delighted me. I suppose the Chicken Run was a bit of an eyesore, but it was all part of the West Ham tradition – and tradition is, after all, the foundation of our game".

The Chicken Run and its inhabitants was indeed part and parcel of the unique Boleyn Ground scene, as were some of the more eccentric characters to be found around and about the place.

Two who spring to mind are Paddy, who was employed by the club as an odd-job man, and "Monty", a former soldier who some said suffered shell-shock in WWII.

Paddy would always be on duty at the mouth of the players' tunnel prior to kick-off, waiting to give the signal to the conductor of the Leyton Silver Band that the West Ham team were coming out so they could strike up their Post Horn Gallop signature tune as they ran on to the Upton Park pitch. Legend has it that Hammers' inspirational Irish international promotion skipper, Noel Cantwell, brought Paddy back to the Boleyn following one of his frequent visits back to the Emerald Isle to represent his country.

There was a rather fetching picture published in the *Official Programme* for the First Division match with Leeds United on December 6, 1958 accompanying the first in an occasional series titled: *Backstage at Upton Park*, featuring Paddy under the surname of O'Leary alongside Head Groundsman George Izatt and colleague Len Locke, who like his boss George, served in the RAF in the Middle East during WWII. As the article went on to explain: "Paddy's forte is 'general duties' and it is difficult to pin down his official capacity to any one task! However, he comes into the public eye more frequently than his two colleagues, and can usually be seen to be 'quick off the mark' when returning the ball on match days when the final whistle has blown!"

In his excellent book, *The Managers*, Tony McDonald gave further insight into Paddy's myriad of responsibilities while interviewing Ron Greenwood's son, Neil, for his late father's section in the book: "He (Mr. Greenwood) used to entertain the press after matches in his office at West Ham, sometimes till one in the morning. While Dad was chatting away to them for hours, I'd be off to see Paddy, the groundsman, in his little office near the players' tunnel where he kept a goldfish tank and a bottle of whisky. After most of the press had gone home, Dad and Paddy would go upstairs and then Dad would go behind the bar and serve drinks to whoever was left at the ground".

My own abiding memories of Paddy would be when visiting defenders would unceremoniously belt a ball right over the Chicken Run into Priory Road and Paddy would scamper off to retrieve it via the North-east corner of the ground.

As for Monty, he was very eccentric, bordering on mad. He used to wear an army uniform, or sometimes a grass skirt and march around the ground playing a bugle. Often he would run

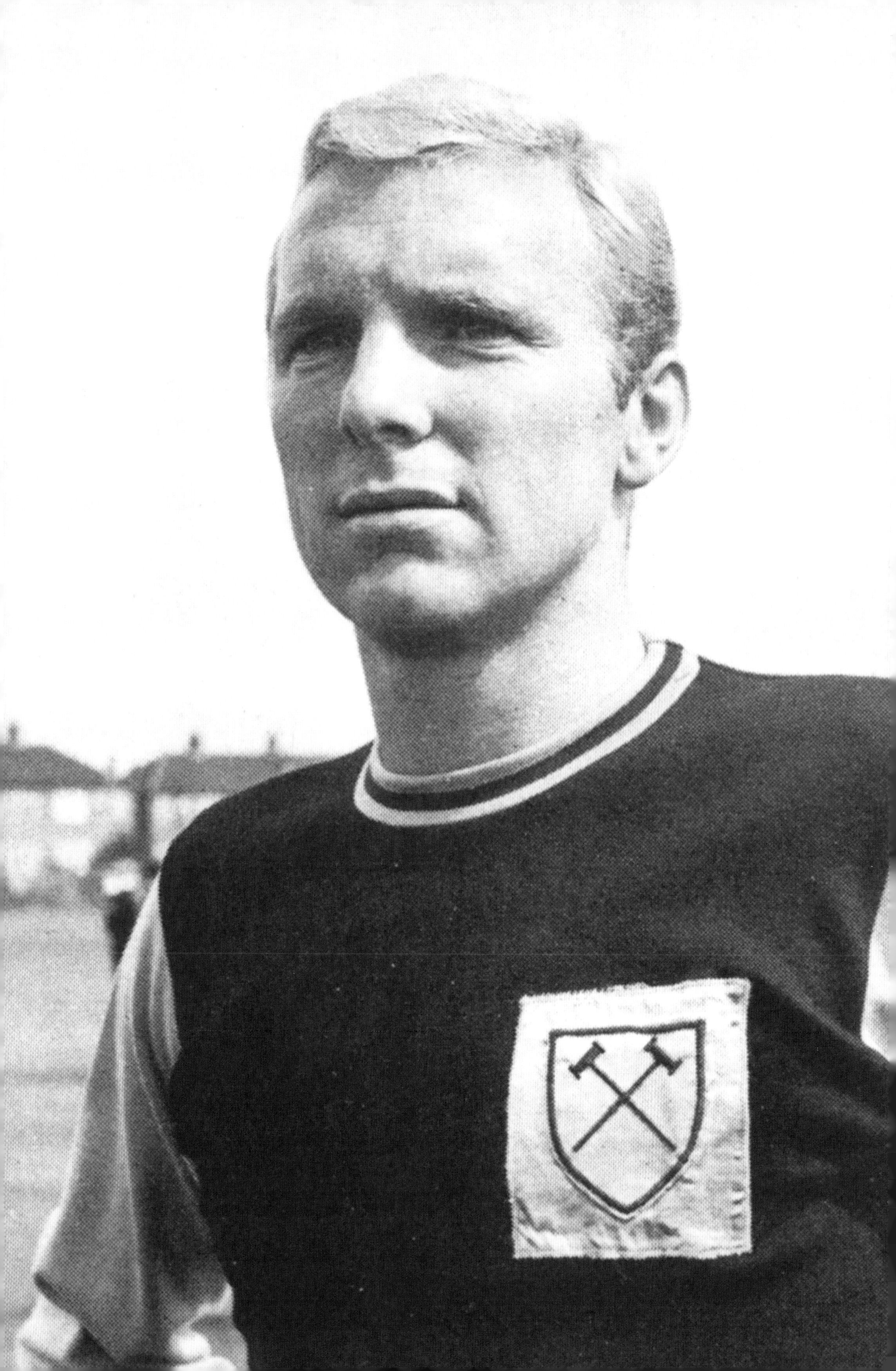

Roger Hunt scores for Liverpool in the match won by Hammers 2-1 at Anfield on September 14 1963.

on to the pitch to score an imaginary "goal", which he would celebrate with the fans. Often the police would bundle him off the field. But he kept the crowd amused – that's for sure.

Anyway, me, Monty and Paddy (who didn't need to pay an admission fee, of course) cheered the Hammers on along with 32,626 other mortal souls – United fans excepted – as good old Johnny Dick equalised Nobby Stiles' 18th minute opener when he tapped in Alan Sealey's pass eight minutes before half-time and that's the way it stayed. Unable to make it to Upton Park was the new messiah, Ron Greenwood, off with a bad head cold. Bless. But a familiar face who was on duty was Noel Cantwell, back at Upton Park for the first time since his record-breaking transfer to the "Busby Babes" ten months before. One wonders if Canters' return caused Paddy to suffer divided loyalties with all things considered. If so, a draw was definitely the right result.

Yet even as I am writing what are now my own personal memories of spectating at Upton Park, it has just dawned on me that I had attended the pre-season public trial match against Charlton Athletic on the previous Monday night under the new floodlights and North Bank roof. But the lights were not switched on – it was a 6.30 KO.

Me and my old mate Geoff (Tommo) Thompson helped swell the "gate" to a meagre 7,711 and the match report in the subsequent programme for the United match helped to fill in some long-forgotten details in my memory bank after a lapse of 54 years: "Last Monday's public practice match attracted a 7,711 attendance to Upton Park. We fielded our prospective First XI and Charlton made three changes at half-time in their provisional League line-up. The Athletic equalised through White (Ronnie) in the tenth minute after John Dick had put the Hammers in front (five minutes), but Phil Woosnam (15 mins.) and Alan Sealey (42 mins.) made it 3-1 before Kinsey (Brian) scored Charlton's second (43 mins.). Andy Malcolm equalised for the visitors with an 'own goal' seven minutes after the restart, but with six minutes to go Woosnam hit a hard shot with his left foot on the turn to bring us a 4-3 victory".

The same programme notes also informed us under the heading *Ground Improvements*: "The additional expenditure which we have incurred during the close-season has not been confined to players' wages and the signs of this will be readily seen by all here today; indeed they have been visible for the past few weeks to everyone in the vicinity of the Boleyn Ground for one can hardly miss the imposing sight of our new £15,000 floodlight system rising above the surrounding buildings!

"In addition we have covered the North Bank at a cost of £20,000. This will provide protection from the weather to the majority of the 11,000 spectators in that area and we can now claim to have accommodation for over 33,000 under cover, being one of the few clubs in the country

THE BATTLE OF UPTON PARK: Malcolm Musgrove and Ken Brown help to defuse a dangerous incident in the West Ham v Chelsea match at Upton Park in September 1961 as Lawrie Leslie is put on a stretcher after being injured in a collision with Bobby Tambling. West Ham still won the game with only 10 men.

with cover on all sides of the ground. We hope that these improvements will be reflected in increased attendances at the times when they will be used to maximum advantage".

Just four days after the opening match of that 1961-62 season against Manchester United, I became a fully-fledged West Ham United supporter when I went to my first away match with another life-long mate Geoff Brodie, who was a Spurs fan. The game was against the League and Cup "Double Winners" at White Hart Lane on one of those balmy August evenings that has remained long in the memory.

Although it's 54 years ago as I write, I've never forgotten West Ham's two goals that night which secured a 2-2 draw before a crowd of over 50,000. The first equaliser was scored by man-of-the-moment Phil Woosnam five minutes before half-time just as Spurs' new floodlights were switched on to gasps from the crowd. Woosie had signed a new contract seven hours before kick-off to finally end speculation of a big-money transfer to AC Milan. His goal, struck from 30 yards, was an unstoppable effort and further underlined his value to his team. The second equaliser, an equally spectacular long range strike from left-winger Mal Musgrove after Terry Dyson had again put Spurs ahead, seemed to be hit with even more venom.

So, after an unlucky 3-2 defeat against Wolves at Molineux the following Saturday, the stage was set for a quick return match two days later with "Super Spurs" when 36,348 eager fans crammed into Upton Park to witness another classic encounter, this time under the new Boleyn bulbs.

With over 11,000 spectators officially packed onto the North Bank terrace and many more youngsters admitted by gatemen "turning a blind eye" as they slid underneath the turnstiles, as was common practice in those days, conditions were decidedly uncomfortable on a hot, humid evening during which the St. John's Ambulance men were kept busy as several of the fans fainted in the heat. The decibel levels seemed to have doubled at this end of the ground since the introduction of the cavernous new roof and five minutes before half-time it was very nearly raised when Tony Scott put the Hammers in front after Spurs had survived wave after wave of home attacks.

West Ham's performance on this "night of nights" had Fleet Street's scribes reaching for superlatives like the *Daily Express* correspondent who under the heading: WONDERFUL WEST HAM CRUSH THE SPURS introed his report: "Real Madrid, Barcelona, Benfica, Milan… you can have the lot! In the heart of London's cockney land last night, West Ham licked skilful Spurs in one of the greatest club matches you could ever wish to see". And after

Fulham's Graham Leggatt scores for Fulham in the 2-0 defeat at Craven Cottage, despite a worthy effort by goalkeeper Lawrie Leslie to save.

Les Allen had equalised in the 64th minute continued: "Fourteen minutes from time, with the 36,348 crowd hushed to an eerie silence, West Ham goalkeeper Lawrie Leslie punted the ball out to his fellow Scottish international John Dick, just inside the centre-circle. The inside-left flicked the ball deftly on, and there, sprinting like a greyhound, was Alan Sealey, the 19-year-old centre-forward who was reared just a goal-kick from the ground. Two seconds later the ball lay still in the Spurs' net. West Ham, 2, Spurs 1". At this point, the home crowd began chanting: "We want six". Norman Giller in the *Daily Express* was equally as generous in his praise, enthusing: "This memorable match will be replayed in thousands of minds in the years to come". Mine included.

With typical modesty, new boss Greenwood directed all the kudos for the stunning victory to his players post match, pointing to the Hammers' euphoric dressing-room and telling Giller: "There are the boys who must take all the credit. They were wonderful". But there can be no doubt he was the architect of Spurs' first defeat since being crowned Double Winners. Setting his stall out perfectly with the irresistible mix of youth and experience at his disposal, he left his players in no doubt of future expectation levels. His charges didn't let him down and by the end of September were sitting proudly in second place in the First Division table behind leaders Burnley. Earlier that month though, Upton park witnessed its first post-war crowd trouble in the match with Chelsea, whom the home side still managed to defeat 2-1, despite at one stage being reduced to nine men following injuries to skipper Woosnam and crucially, goalkeeper

Leslie. Ahead 2-0 at the interval by dint of goals from Dick and the ever effective Musgrove, Chelsea pulled a goal back when Bobby Tambling chased a through ball at the South Bank end and in attempting to leap over the advancing Leslie caught the fearless custodian on the forehead with his studs, slicing open his scalp in the process. The ball broke to Barry Bridges who scored. The referee, Mr. L. Hamer of Bolton, who despite his name, allowed the goal to stand instead of awarding a foul which most supporting Hammers cause believed would have been the right decision in the circumstances as Leslie would take no further part in the game and would be replaced by Bobby Moore between the posts for the remainder of the match. As Woosie, as Welsh international Woosnam was popularly known, had already left the field for treatment following a crunching tackle by Chelsea's villain of the piece, the uncompromising Scottish international wing-half Tommy Docherty, the crowd were not over enamoured and a dozen or more from the Chicken Run and South Bank decided to invade the pitch to exact vengeance for what they saw as rank bad refereeing and plain dirty play by the opposition. Now these insurgents were nothing like those skinhead types who would follow later in the decade and blight the national sport for many years to come, they were big grown, rough as you like, men and looked like they had finished a shift at the nearby docks. They were not best pleased and for a time the situation looked decidedly ugly.

Fortunately, decisive action by a handful of stewards, the local constabulary and some of the players, particularly a very diplomatic Ken Brown, managed to calm the situation and usher them off before any real harm was done. Nevertheless, it was seen as a major incident and the press had a field day with one major newspaper calling for fences to be installed and even moats

Alan Sealey just fails to connect with his head against Nottingham Forest at Upton Park, as Peter Grummitt saves.

Lawrie Leslie punches the ball clear from the Arsenal attack at Highbury, policed by Ken Brown and John Bond.

to prevent a recurrence. Although the prompt intervention of the "peace-makers" prevented the situation escalating into a full-blown riot and saw the perpetrators unceremoniously frog-marched down the tunnel in less than ten minutes, more than one newspaper headlined the events as "The Battle of Upton Park".

Luckily, the Football Association chiefs remained unswayed by the sensational coverage and the only punishment handed out to the club later was a written warning regarding the future conduct of Upton Park's patrons. Fortunately no further action was forthcoming, but it was a close call.

As for the main protagonist, Docherty – who fouled throughout with a smile on his face – the Chelsea board must have been impressed with his performance because barely two weeks later they had sacked Ted Drake and appointed Docherty in the role of player-manager. One of his first signings was that of a reluctant Andy Malcolm to replace himself in the number four shirt, but it was to no avail, Chelsea were relegated to the Second Division at season's end, helped there by a stupendous long-range volley from Bobby Moore in the return fixture at Stamford Bridge which enabled Hammers to win 1-0 and complete their only "double" of the season.

Yet despite that somewhat lean statistic, the team performed well during Greenwood's first full season of tenure and could have gone top on Boxing Day but for a 3-2 defeat to Blackburn Rovers at the Boleyn. In the top six for most of the season, they eventually had to settle for

Moore watches as Ken Brown heads clear from Derek Doogan in the 1-1 draw with Aston Villa at the Boleyn.

a still respectable 8th place, but there was no sign of the great cup runs to come as Irons crashed out of the fledgling League Cup in the 2nd round when losing 3-1 at home to Aston Villa and then suffered a debilitating 3-0 defeat to Plymouth Argyle at Home Park, in the FA Cup Third Round. There was also an inauspicious first appearance for the destined triumvirate of Moore, Hurst and Peters in a 3-0 drubbing at relegated Cardiff City near season's end.

The following season, 1962-63, was again opened with a visit from Second Division Charlton Athletic for a pre-season practice match at Upton Park. The previous routine of staging a pair of encounters with the Club Colours versus The Whites (reserves) on consecutive Saturdays had been discontinued when the Football League gave permission for member clubs to stage friendly fixtures among themselves in 1961. The main reason for me being able to dredge the corners of my memory to recall this long-forgotten game with the Addicks, obstructed by the hazy details of maybe a thousand matches in between then and now, was because of an unpleasant experience I had when collecting autographs before and after the game. You see, then as now, autograph collecting was a very popular pastime and I had spent much of an indifferent summer lovingly putting together a scrapbook with pictures culled from the pages of *Charles Buchan's Football Monthly*, *Soccer Star* Magazine and football souvenir editions of the *London Evening News* and *Standard*.

Within its 300 odd pages, every team in the First Division had a section, as well as Leyton Orient who me and Tommo used to watch on alternate Saturdays. The idea was to get as many of these "signed" when the relevant teams visited Upton Park and, of course, there was an extra big section set aside for Hammers.

While players like Phil Woosnam and Bobby Moore were major targets for us "graphers", Charlton also had a fair sprinkling of stars, like that great South African Stuart Leary, who also excelled in his dual role as county cricketer for Kent, and the Scottish international full-back John Hewie.

It was during a scrimmage to get their signatures outside the players' entrance that I noticed someone tugging at my scrapbook. Now this wasn't a light tug, but someone hell-bent on stealing my pride and joy and expletives were exchanged to leave my assailant in no doubt that he would have a fight on his hands should he persist. The trouble was he looked a real "hard nut", a greaser type complete with bikers leather jacket and scowl to match. In a one-on-one he'd have made mincemeat of yours truly, after all I'm a writer, not a fighter.

The danger seemed to have passed, but when we finally made for home up a deserted Green Street, I noticed my greaser friend close behind – too close. Just as I was about to warn Tommo of the imminent danger, with impeccable timing he spotted a copy of *Charles Buchan's Football Monthly* in a newsagent's window and went to investigate until my frantic shouts alerted him to take flight.

By sheer luck, a number 58 bus was pulling away from the stop and with a record-breaking sprint we both managed to leap on board the back platform with the greaser a split second too

Bottle party at West Ham. Amid a clutter of bottles and litter, Hammers' goalkeeper Jim Standen lies injured during the Cup match with Everton.

late to grab the stanchion and haul himself on.

Predictable insults were exchanged as the would-be scrapbook thief receded further in the distance, my precious book clasped safely under my arm to remain a cherished possession to this day. And as for that *Charles Buchan's Football Monthly* that my life-long pal Tommo was so keen to see with near fateful consequences; I'm looking at a copy of that self same edition as I write. It was dated September 1962 and featured the late, great John White on the front cover, who was so sadly and prematurely lost to the game when struck by lightning while playing golf.

Hammers, incidentally, watched by only 5,000 again defeated the South Londoners by 2-1 thanks to goals from Ian Crawford and John Dick (his last as a Hammer) before embarking on their worst start to a season that anyone could remember.

Although I didn't appreciate it at the time, my parents did me a favour when they booked a family caravan holiday for the last week of August 1962, but I doubt if my father had much to do with the scheduling which meant that we would miss the home game with Spurs on August 25 and the away match at Leyton Orient on September 1. Having lost 3-1 at Villa on the opening day and 4-1 to Wolves under the Upton Park lights 24 hours later, I suppose the writing was on the wall for the Spurs game at the Boleyn, yet even so, it was hard to take in the magnitude of the 6-1 defeat to the Lilly Whites while sitting baking on a Cornish beach as news filtered through at agonising intervals via transistor radio of the debacle unfolding in East London; Lyall o.g. 10m., Medwin 14, Greaves 54, 58, Jones 62 and White 74. A token tally

In the same match, Everton's Alex Young gets in a shot which is blocked by Eddie Bovington (right) despite Jack Burkett's challenge.

Geoff Hurst scores against Fourth Division Workington Town in the sixth round of the Football League Cup, which is won 6-0. Byrne (right) watches.

from Woosnam (who else?) was scant consolation especially, as we were informed, Spurs should have scored another six. So the Hammers' fans who had chanted "We want six!" in the corresponding fixture almost exactly a year before, finally got them. Albeit, in the wrong net.

Some respite was forthcoming via the trusty transistor which relayed news of a creditable 0-0 draw in the mid-week against table topping Wolves at Molineux, enabling yours truly to enjoy the rest of my holiday while imagining myself as being the sixth member of The Famous Five as I rock-pooled and scoured the cliffs and coves in search of smuggler's caves. Well, I was only 14. It was back to earth with a bump though, as by the time the Penzance to Paddington express had steamed into London the following Saturday evening, the headlines in the *Star, News* and *Standard* football specials were there on the news stands to greet us; "Leyton Orient 2, West Ham 0". So this was what being a West Ham fan was all about. And, as if things couldn't get any worse, it was ex-Hammer Dave Dunmore who headed the O's first goal to really rub salt into the Irons' wounds.

Luckily, Greenwood managed to steady the ship and his decision to follow Fenton's lead of a few seasons earlier by switching Hurst to inside-left in place of the departed Dick (farewell old friend), this time paid dividends as he proved to be a revelation in an extended run in the side. The team responded by knocking in a few goals. Most notably in a 6-1 away win at Manchester City (Musgrove 2, Scott, Byrne, Peters and Hurst), a 4-0 victory at Blackburn (Hurst, Musgrove, Byrne and Peters), a 5-0 romp over Birmingham at Upton Park (Byrne 2, Hurst, Musgrove and Brown) and a 4-4 thriller with Spurs (Peters, Kirkup, Boyce and Scott) at

White Hart Lane, where they came back from being 2-0 down only to be denied victory by a last minute equaliser from Dave Mackay.

Hitting a rich vein of form over the festive period, when they were mostly known to falter, they again came back from a two goal deficit against Forest on a snow bound City Ground. This time duly getting the 4-3 scoreline, two days before welcoming in the New Year, thanks to goals from McKinlay o.g., Byrne and Brabrook (2). It would be their last First Division victory, or match for that matter, for over six weeks as the "Big Freeze" set in. When FL duty was eventually resumed on another snow covered surface at Sheffield United's Brammall Lane, the Hammers started where they had left off with another superb away win against the Blades by a 2-0 margin with a Hurst strike and a second half penalty from Byrne, resplendent in their "Lucky" light blue shirts with two claret hoops. Having already been involved in a 0-0 stalemate in the Third Round of the FA Cup with Fulham on a frozen Upton Park pitch that would have been deemed unplayable today, they went on to eliminate the Cottagers on yet another atrocious surface in the replay which ended in a blizzard, but a 2-1 victory courtesy of goals from Boyce and Byrne with another penalty.

I well remember the freezing conditions which prevailed during the first match under the Boleyn lights as I had been unexpectedly presented with a ticket for the West Stand by a lovely Harwood Avenue, Hornchurch neighbour named Jack White, who deemed it too cold to go himself. He was certainly right, because I have never been so cold at a game before or since and vowed I would never sit to watch a game again. The match was played with an orange ball throughout, as was the replay which, as I was still suffering from hypothermia, I didn't see.

Next up in the FA Cup were Second Division Swansea Town in a rescheduled 4th round tie under the lights at Upton Park, complete with "black sheep" Noel Dwyer in goal. Needless to say the Irishman had a "blinder" in holding Hammers to the solitary Boyce goal of the game in which he alone prevented a rout on a pitch which now resembled a sea of mud as the thaw had set in.

Such was the brilliance of Dwyer's goalkeeping masterclass, in a very uncharacteristic display of emotion, Bobby Moore ran the whole length of the field to congratulate his former team mate with any bad feelings about the Newcastle debacle obviously forgotten.

West Ham were now well on their way to their best FA Cup run since the glorious failure in the Sixth Round against Spurs in 1956, but it would come with an unsavoury caveat.

Champions-elect Everton were the visitors in the fifth round, but the match would be marred by the gamesmanship of the Liverpudlian players and the hooliganism of their supporters who had taken over a large part of the North Bank and were hell-bent on causing trouble. I knew because I was standing in amongst them on the packed North Bank right behind the goal. Although the match was played in an uncomfortable atmosphere throughout, the situation worsened in the second-half as West Ham began exerting more pressure on the Everton goal with the Blues defending the North Bank end. As I was standing just a few yards behind the goal net, I can particularly remember the intimidating tactics of Everton's red-headed England international left-half, Tony Kay. He persistently elbowed West Ham's Ronnie Boyce while awaiting the arrival of corner kicks and never missed an opportunity to get in a sly kick or dig. I'd witnessed Mr. Kay's (later jailed for match fixing) tactics at Leyton Orient earlier in the season when the O's played host to Kay's previous club, Sheffield Wednesday, and he and his team mates' rough house tactics sparked a pitch invasion by O's fans irate at the treatment meted out to their favourites. In the 59th minute of the game at Upton Park, the situation reached powder-keg proportions when West Ham were awarded a penalty for handball as Dennis Stevens tried to tackle Moore. A cascade of bottles and other missiles rained down from the North Bank terrace and they weren't being thrown by West Ham fans. It took four policemen to drag a protesting Everton fan off the pitch and it was some time before order was restored. When it was, Johnny Byrne coolly slotted the spot kick just inside keeper Gordon West's right-hand post, then further pandemonium broke out. More bottles were thrown and a police inspector was hit by a piece of concrete hurled from the North Bank.

So, for the second season in succession, there had been serious crowd disorder at Upton Park, but unlike in the Chelsea match, in this instance the problems were not exacerbated by poor refereeing or misbehaviour by West Ham supporters. On the contrary, had it not been for the unflappable demeanour of the international standard referee, Mr. Jim Finney (who at one stage called the two captains together to call for calm), and the tolerance shown by the Hammers fans and players in the face of extreme provocation, the situation could have escalated into a full scale riot. As it was, four Everton fans invaded the pitch and Jim Standen

The match with Burnley (below) was the author's first ever visit to the Boleyn Ground, but unfortunately he witnessed Burnley win 1-2

was pelted with glass bottles at the South Bank end, when yobs behind his goal vented their frustration as their dreams of Wembley slipped away.

As Maurice Smith reported the next day in the *Sunday People*: "We were asked by the police if we wanted to prosecute anyone". West Ham Secretary Eddie Chapman told me afterwards, "We have told them, no".

From my vantage point on the volatile North Bank, the person who should have been prosecuted was wearing an Everton shirt and had red hair. But what the hell, we were through to the sixth round!

West Ham were drawn away to face Liverpool at Anfield in the sixth round and for once the Blue half of this great football divided city were willing the Reds to win. It was a perverse kind of logic which Evertonians hoped would bring revenge of sorts.

The match, which was played on Grand National day, Saturday, March 20, 1963 is best summed up by two letters received by the club and which appeared on the *Official Programme* for the game with Ipswich Town on Good Friday, the first was headed:

FROM A LIVERPOOL SUPPORTER: "I would like to thank you and your team on giving us Kopites an excellent game and also what is more important, a great sporting exhibition. It was one of the nicest and cleanest games we have had at Anfield this season. Although I am glad we got through to the semi-final, I offer my regrets to you for being unlucky losers.

"Once more, thanks for your team's sportsmanship". Yours sincerely, Robert Jackson, 52 Seacome St., Liverpool".

FROM A HAMMERS SUPPORTER: "I am sure in writing these few lines I express the feelings of all the supporters that made the trip to Liverpool. We were really proud of our team and of the great performance they put on, the way they kept the 'Kop' in silent and nervous apprehension for a full 80 minutes was just great". F. Philpott, East Ham.

So although that great trio of stars, Johnny Dick, Mal Musgrove and Phil Woosnam had all departed to Brentford (£17,000), Leyton Orient (£11,000) and Aston Villa (£25,000) respectively, Greenwood's young team was shaping up nicely.

Incidentally, while West Ham were battling away at Anfield before losing 1-0 to a Roger Hunt goal in the 81st minute, a 66-1 outsider won the National at nearby Aintree – *Ayala*.

One wonders, as outsiders themselves, if any of the West Ham players had a punt on it. Johnny Byrne was known to like a bet, sometimes feigning injury during a game so that physio Bill Jenkins could tell him how a particular nag had got on as he treated his "injury". It's doubtful if he'd have tried any such stunt in a game as important as the Anfield showdown though. Or would he? Coincidentally, his namesake, Liverpool's Gerry Byrne saved a cert goal when he headed a lob from Sealey over the bar. Any despondency hanging around Upton Park following the FA Cup exit was soon lifted by the news that the club had accepted an invitation to be the English representatives in that summer's North American International Soccer League to be staged in New York, Chicago and Detroit. Before the Stateside extravaganza, however, everyone at Upton Park was given a further massive boost when the youth team won through to the Final of the FA Youth Cup competition.

Their achievement was all the more laudable owing to the quality of the opposition they overcame to get there. Following a 3-3 draw (Dryden 2 and Sissons) in the Second Round against Brighton & Hove Albion at the Goldstone Ground before the "Big Freeze" had set in, the young Hammers easily disposed of the Seagulls 6-1 in the delayed replay almost two months later thanks to goals from Britt (3), Sissons, Dryden and a superb solo effort from the largely unsung amateur, Terry Archer.

Next up were Bert Head's sparkling Swindon Town outfit featuring the brilliant Don Rogers at outside-left, but they too were swept aside by a 4-1 scoreline under the Boleyn lights with the usual suspects, Sissons (2), Britt and Dryden, providing the goals which sent the Railwaymen back down the tracks to Wiltshire empty-handed.

In the Fourth Round against Portsmouth at Fratton Park, the Hammers were trailing 1-0 at the interval, but rallied in the second half to take the tie by a 3-2 margin with goals from Dryden, Sissons and a 20-yarder from Bobby Howe. A crowd of 6,500 turned up at Upton Park to witness the Fifth Round clash with Aston Villa and the majority didn't leave disappointed as the Hammers again won through a hard-fought tie by four goals to two thanks to a brace a piece for Britt and Sissons. So it was on to the semi-final to face the young Wolves in their Molineux lair on Saturday, May 18, 1963. I was at Upton Park that day watching the first team replicate the 6-1 scoreline they had attained against Manchester City at Maine Road the previous September. The Boleyn pitch, which for so long had resembled a snow covered ice-

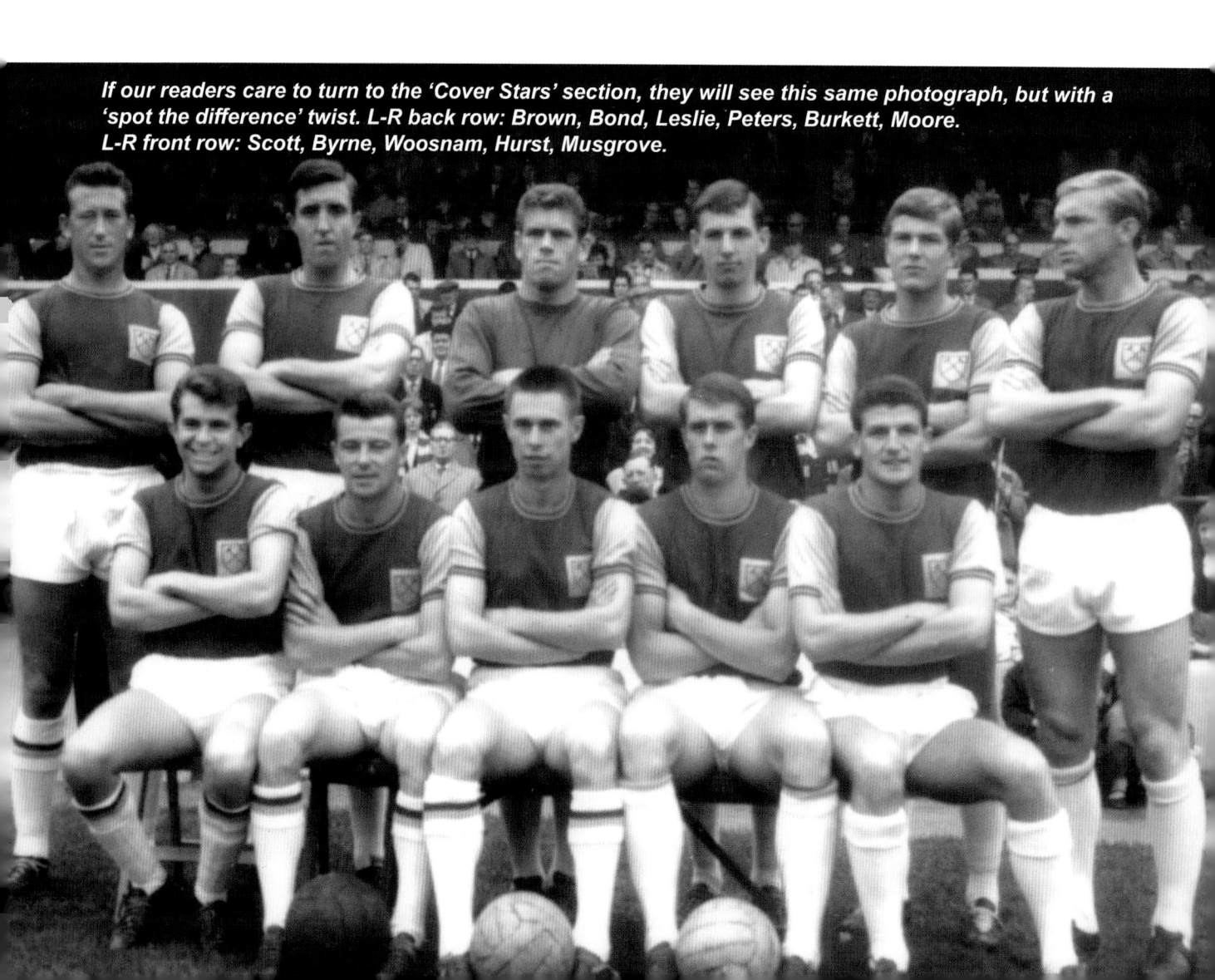

If our readers care to turn to the 'Cover Stars' section, they will see this same photograph, but with a 'spot the difference' twist. L-R back row: Brown, Bond, Leslie, Peters, Burkett, Moore. L-R front row: Scott, Byrne, Woosnam, Hurst, Musgrove.

rink, then a mud bath, was now a dust bowl. But the conditions didn't stop Hurst (2), Sealey (2), Boyce and Brabrook's goals consigning City to the Second Division. I was one of the crowd of only 16,600 witnessing the Mancunian's demise while keeping tabs on what was occurring at Wolves via the public address system. Good news! Our Colts had drawn with the Wolf Cubs, 2-2 to secure an Upton Park replay the following Tuesday courtesy of tallies by that man Britt again and Trevor Dawkins.

In his book entitled, *Harry – My Autobiography*, Harry Redknapp gave a fascinating insight into the build up to that match at Molineux:

"When we got to the semi-final, our opponents, Wolverhampton Wanderers, insisted on playing the game on a Saturday. Mr. Greenwood protested, but as it was an away fixture, he had no say. To our amazement, when we arrived to get the coach up to Molineux, there he was, getting on board with us. He chose a youth semi-final over a first-team fixture. Incredible".

So, with such support from the boss, you could be excused for thinking that the result of the replay was a foregone conclusion and West Ham duly got revenge for the 1954 FA Youth Cup semi-final defeat to the Wolves by winning 4-2. Once again the scorers' names had a familiar ring to them; Britt, Dryden, Sissons and one from Peter Bennett. So the stage was set for the final. Let Harry once again set the scene.

"The final was over two legs against Liverpool. Tommy Smith, who went on to be an Anfield legend and notorious hardman was their Captain. We lost the first leg away 3-1. The return was on the night of the FA Cup Final. I can't even tell you who won it that year, I was so wrapped up in our game. It was a full house at Upton Park and by half-time we were 2-1 down, losing 5-2 on aggregate. We came out in the second-half and terrorised them. We scored four goals and won 6-5 on aggregate". A notoriously bad loser, Liverpool's Manager Bill Shankly labelled the West Ham team "Animals", which given the club's reputation for being a soft touch as far as Northerners are concerned, it was probably the best compliment they could have had.

Martin Britt, who had scored what proved to be a vital goal at Anfield, scored a hat-trick, all with his head. Dryden and Dawkins scored the other two to complete the comeback and make it 6-5.

But that wasn't the end of the excitement as the Hammers had also reached the Final of the London Minor Cup and were due to meet Chelsea's Colts just two days after defeating Liverpool on Monday, May 27, under those overworked Boleyn bulbs. To reach the final, the same set of 12 players who'd won the FA Youth Cup had disposed of Millwall 7-1 in the First Round (Britt 4, Sissons 2, and Dryden), attendance 1,300; Spurs 5-0 in the Second Round (Britt 3, Charles and Sissons); and Fulham 9-2 in the Semi-Final (Britt 3, Bennett 2, Sissons 2, Dryden and Redknapp). The same line-up of Mackleworth, Burnett, Kitchener, Dawkins, Charles, Howe, Redknapp, Bennett, Britt, Sissons and Dryden played in every game with the exceptions of when Terry Archer replaced Bennett in the 6-1 win over Brighton in the FA Youth Cup and then Sissons in the London Minor Cup Final against Chelsea, whom the young Hammers defeated 2-0 (Britt and Howe) to complete a unique "double". All the LMC games were played under the advantage of being at Upton Park.

In his autobiography, Harry Redknapp gave his readers a revealing idea into what life was like in and around the famous old ground in those far off days and we make no excuse for reproducing further extracts here as he recalled:

"Ron (Greenwood) was another old-school character, like Bill Nicholson. The manager's door wasn't always open in those days. Even senior players wishing to see Ron had to make an appointment. And you had to be in the first team a good few years before you were on first name terms. Until that point, he was always Mr. Greenwood. As apprentice professionals, we had to do the chores. We trained in the morning and then returned to Upton Park to get the first team kit ready for the next day. The laundry would stink with sweat or be caked in dry mud, but you had to make sure it was washed, dried and rolled up ready for use. After that, we were free, but we were all young and football mad and would often go onto the forecourt for a kickabout. That was the beginning of what would be an outstanding West Ham youth team, although Ernie Gregory, the first team coach, saw us as more of a nuisance. He came out one day and moved us on, told us he had to get home, and we should go home, too. When Ron found out, he gave Ernie the most frightful bollocking. 'As long as they want to stay out there, as long as they are playing football, we'll stay here with them as long as they want', he said. He loved the fact that all his apprentices just wanted to play. We weren't going off down the snooker hall or into the bookmaker's, so what was wrong with that? He was a proper football man, Ron". And referring again to when the Hammers youngsters defeated their Liverpool counterparts he continued: "It's one of the only times I ever saw Tommy Smith beaten up: Martin Britt bashed him all over the place. Tommy was brave, but at 16 Martin was a man. I was knocking balls into him from one wing, John Sissons was flying down the other – at the end, Ron (Greenwood) was in tears. You've never seen a man so proud. He loved that his forecourt kids had won the Youth Cup. It meant as much to him as the FA Cup and that has stuck in my mind ever since".

In his next book titled: "*A Man Walks Onto a Pitch*" also published by Ebury Press a year later in 2014, Harry again returns to his footballing roots and those days of training on the Upton Park forecourt during that freezing winter of 1962-63:

"At West Ham we mucked in together and roughed it when we had to. I remember the terrible winter in 1963, clearing the snow off the forecourt of Upton Park with the rest of the players so we could train. Job done, we would play on it for two hours in silly little plimsoles, sliding everywhere. Even Bobby Moore trained on the forecourt at Upton Park. I remember as a junior we had to wait for the main group to finish, sitting inside looking through the steamed-up windows because all the training pitches were under snow".

Not surprisingly, the adverse weather conditions led to countless postponements and eventually a serious fixture pile-up. During the period we've just covered, the congestion was at its worst and those twelve players that served West Ham so well – let's call them the "Dirty Dozen" – were forced to play an astonishing six matches in nine days of which they won five and drew the other! The schedule was: Saturday, May 18, 1963 v. Wolves, semi-final FA Youth Cup. Tuesday, May 21, Wolves, replay. Thursday, May 23, Liverpool, 1st leg of FA Youth Cup Final. Friday, May 24 v. Chelsea (at Chadwell Heath) SEC League. Saturday, May 25,

Liverpool, FA Youth Cup Final 2nd leg. Monday, May 27, Chelsea, London Minor Cup Final. With the exception of the SEC match with Chelsea, all these matches were staged at Upton Park. Surely a record in itself?

Excuse me now as I need to back track a little – a month or so in fact. But it should all fit in rather nicely if you bear with me. This *is* a slightly wacky alternative history, after all. The reason for the rewind features around the First Division clash between our favourites and Nottingham Forest on Monday, April 22, 1963. I distinctly remember the game in question as it was my 15th birthday and I went along to the floodlight match with my life-long pal, Tommo and another very mischievous character we knew only by his surname – Herbert. When I perused the *Official Programme* recently, it stirred a few memories. Under a resumé of the Third team's performances in the Metropolitan League over Easter of that year, for instance, there was a short report on the "A" team's match with Guildford City Reserves at Chadwell Heath on Good Friday, April 12. The Hammers line-up consisted: Mackleworth, Burnett, Kitchener, Lansdowne, W. White, D. Wallace, Redknapp, J. Gadston, Barrett, Howe, and T. Archer. The players preceded by their christian name's initial were amateurs and the Barrett listed at centre-forward is, of course, the team's player-coach, Jim Barrett Junior whose family name looms large in the history of West Ham United FC. "Young" Jim, it seems, was determined to contribute further to that history as the programme notes explained: "Jimmy Barrett was the star on this occasion, as he netted four of our goals in a 5-1 victory, the other Hammers' tally

Jim Standen (below) making the kind of save that made him so popular at Upton Park, following his transfer from Luton Town.

A Surprise for Ivy!

Bill Town, a highly respected former East London publican, related an amusing tale to me when I told him I was working on this book.

Now residing in the historical market town of Romford, Bill ran a string of pubs during his career as a landlord and could count among them The Swan on Stratford Broadway, The Princess Alice at Forest Gate, the Tollgate Tavern at Chadwell Heath and the White Hart in Romford High Street (later better known as The Bitter End), where he was mine host for many years.

"When I was a barman at the Swan, there was a lovely lady called Ivy who ran the food bar. She also acted as a landlady to young West Ham players at her house in East Ham", Bill recalled over a pint in The Lamb in Romford Market, along with the landlord Tomasz (a Gornik fan), his good lady Melisia and yours truly.

"Bobby Moore, Tony Scott, Brian Dear, Andy Smillie, John Cartwright, Harry Cripps, Bobby Keetch and Eddie Bovington all used to knock about together so there was always a crowd round Ivy's visiting whoever was lodging there.

"One day, on Ivy's birthday, she left them 'holding the fort' while she went out to celebrate, leaving strict instructions of 'No parties while I'm gone!'

"When she returned many hours later, she heard very loud music when she turned into her road – coming from her house.

"Storming in, she was about to let rip when all the lads burst into a chorus of 'Happy Birthday'. They then informed the by now speechless Ivy that they'd had a whip round and bought the record-player for her", laughed Bill.

Around about the time of the 1966 World Cup Finals, Bill was working at the Tollgate, just across the road from Hammers' training ground off the London Road at Chadwell Heath.

"I got to know Bobby Moore very well as he became a regular visitor, popping in every day after training. It was always a pleasure to serve him and Johnny Byrne and a little later, Jimmy Greaves, too", Bill recalled fondly.

Another former Romford publican, Dave Campbell, actually played for West Ham's youth team in the late 50s.

"I was spotted by the Hammers' chief scout Wally St. Pier" Dave told me when he popped into the Lamb last summer.

"I was playing for a Dagenham side, Ballonian FC, when Wally gave me some games in the West Ham youth team. It was the same time that Roger Hugo signed.

"Wally told me that I had all the skills required to make the grade, but lacked the dedication needed. Which was a surprise to me because my main ambition was to be a professional footballer".

Dave later ran the Golden Lion public house in Romford and also The Ship at Gidea Park, two of the oldest pubs in the area. Another story Bill Town told me, was when West Ham's goalkeeper, Jim Standen, walked into the Tollgate at Chadwell Heath, with his two sons as he usually did on a Sunday. But this was a special Sunday, as it had just been announced that he had just topped the bowling averages for Champions Worcestershire CCC in 1964, when Bill cheekily shouted out to him, "when are you gonna learn to throw a ball Jim?". Another pub in London Road which was also very popular with the West Ham players was the Slaters Arms, Romford, which for many years was run by the late and much loved landlady Steph. The Slaters was often frequented by footballing icons such as Bobby Moore, Johnny Byrne, Brian Dear and Jimmy Greaves.

Owzat!

Jim Standen holds yet another ball.

West Ham's 'Wonder Winger' Johnny Sissons cracks across yet another centre from the left wing.

being notched by Harry Redknapp".

That brings us very neatly back to Harry's autobiography, *Always Managing*, in which he recalls those days of playing for the "A" team in the Met. League:

"Our coach was Jimmy Barrett – Young Jim, as he was known, because his father, also Jim, was a legendary centre-half with West Ham before the war. Young Jim was a midfielder and a hard man, like his dad. He looked after us when we played as West Ham's A-team in the Metropolitan League each Saturday. We'd be up against men's non-league teams like Chelmsford City or Bedford Town, and they didn't like 15-year-olds getting the beating of them. They would try to take lumps out of us, at which point Young Jim would put himself on and settle a few scores. No matter the size of the player, he would sort them out. There were more than a few who thought they had got away with giving some kid a lesson, only to find themselves visited by Jim. He never let a kicking go unpunished".

So there you have it – Young Jim Barrett in a nutshell, from the man who played with him and under him, all those years ago. Sadly, last year at Haverhill, Suffolk, Jim died and so did the ethos of a golden era.

As for that match with Forest, the programme for which reignited these memories, the Hammers laid on the perfect Birthday treat for Yours Truly, felling the Foresters with four goals from a triumvirate destined for a higher station: Moore, Hurst 2 and Peters. Ironically, Sir

The players ready to embark to the USA to take part in a North American Soccer League in the summer of 1963. Back row L-R: Scott, Hurst, Peters, Boyce, Burkett, Sealey, Bickles. Front row L-R: Leslie, Kirkup, Bill Jenkins, Lyall, Brown.

Geoff missed out on his first-ever hat-trick by fluffing the second of two penalties he took in the same amount of minutes. Even so, Tommo, Herbert and myself, a much humbler trio, but nevertheless one which had helped swell the "gate" to a modest 18,179, went home happy; perhaps too happy as we were in such high spirits we began larking about on the train taking us back to Gidea Park from Forest Gate. You know, swinging on the hand straps and general horse play. But our exuberance had been spotted by three stern looking young ladies who seemed like "grown ups" to us and informed us that they were in fact school teachers. They then demanded to know which schools we attended and our names and addresses. It didn't require rocket-science to know they weren't going to put us forward for a recommendation, but we kept up the high jinks and carried on regardless. Then, using our programmes to shield our faces behind, we began singing a song by American artist, Bobby Vee, called "The Night has a Thousand Eyes", which was a big hit at the time. When it was time for the chorus, we lowered our programmes and began moving our eyes from side to side while peeping over the top.

This didn't go down well at all and one of our new "teachers" was in such a rage she punched me square on the jaw. It was a good shot, too. Luckily, the train had now arrived at Gidea Park and we scrambled out of the doors and legged it at break-neck speed, but still singing and laughing. After all, it's not often that West Ham score four on your Birthday!

The West Ham party returned from their American adventure with praise for their performances ringing in their ears from all quarters as administrators, commentators, fans and opposition players waxed lyrical over their tactical nous and sportsmanlike displays while flying the flag for the British game.

After winning the six team league which comprised of Kilmarnock (Scotland), Mantova (Italy), Oro (Mexico), Valenciennes (France) and Preussen Munster (West Germany) to qualify for the two-leg Championship play-off v. Gornik (Poland) and then the American Challenge Cup Final against Dukla Prague (Czechoslovakia) also over two legs, some typical comments included: "West Ham did more in 90 minutes to boost soccer in this country than anything I have seen here" – Alec Cassidy, a leading soccer administrator in Detroit.

"West Ham are very, very good. I predict they will be a world-class team within two years". – Joseph Masopust, the great Dukla and Czechoslovakian wing-half. Ron Greenwood added: "Our second game against Dukla was the most perfect technical display I have seen from any British team I have been connected with. We played well and could so easily won the cup. In both games against Dukla our fine play created chances we did not take. Now we must think in terms of winning and not being runners-up. The team gained more experience in ten matches against teams from other nations than the average league player at home gains in 15 years".

Not to be outdone, the Youth team, too, enjoyed a successful summer, winning the International Youth Tournament staged at Augsburg, West Germany.

Pitted in Group 2 against Bayern Munich (West Germany), BK Copenhagen (Denmark) and Schwaben Augsburg (West Germany) in the eight team competition, the young Hammers were successful against their three opponents in order listed by margins of 3-0 (Britt, Bennett and Archer), 1-0 (Dawkins) and 2-0 (Britt and Bennett). This 100% success qualified them to meet Cannes (France) in the Final, whom they defeated 2-1 after extra-time (Britt and Bennett) to win yet another trophy.

All in all, then, hopes were high among all levels of the Upton Park playing staff on the eve of the 1963-64 season and the supporters, too, were optimistic about the team's prospects for the new campaign. Behind the scenes, the programme for the second home game of the season against Ipswich Town informed its readers how spectating would be more convenient this season: "We have carried out a number of improvements on the Boleyn Ground during the summer, and hope that these will be appreciated as part of our long-term plan in this part of our policy. Among the toilet facilities which have been improved are those under the South Bank terracing, whilst we have carried out considerable works at the rear of B and C Blocks in order to provide similar facilities for our Grand Stand patrons. We are to carry out the construction of similar toilets at the rear of D and E Blocks later, as although the present facilities at the end of the terracing are reasonable we feel that we would like to provide a higher standard throughout the whole of the Grand Stand. The improvements to the dressing-rooms which we mentioned in these columns at the end of last season have now been carried out, and we can claim that these are now as good as on any other ground in the country. The colour-scheme is in the club's claret-and-blue".

Starting off with two wins (an early "double" over Blackpool) and two draws, the players seemed to have responded to their plush new surrounds, but soon slumped to return one win in the next nine league games – a 2-1 win over Liverpool at Anfield which would be their last there until 2015-2016 season's 3-0 success under new manager Slavan Bilic.

Did the fans chant "We've got the best toilets and dressing-rooms in the land"? No, improvement was on hand, however, when three straight wins versus Everton, Manchester United (where Britt got the only goal) and WBA were followed by four consecutive draws. There was an unmitigated disaster on the horizon yet though, when top-of-the-table Blackburn Rovers inflicted West Ham's heaviest-ever defeat at the Boleyn Ground in all its 112-year history at that venue by the tune of 2-8 on Boxing Day 1963. Typically, two days later in the return at Ewood Park, the same XI with the exception of Eddie Bovington in for Peters, managed to redress the balance somewhat by winning 3-1 with a goal from Hurst and a brace from Byrne. But Bovington was the real match winner by keeping England international inside-forward Bryan Douglas, who'd orchestrated the Boxing Day massacre, quiet.

Six days before the Boxing Day debacle, I'd witnessed another "typical" West Ham performance at Ipswich Town, but this time of the worst kind. The match was played on a Friday evening, presumably not to clash with the last Saturday shopping opportunity before Christmas. Despite the switch, only 11,765 hardy souls braved the freezing conditions. This was my third visit to Portman Road in my two years of watching the Hammers and remained the only venue I'd seen them play outside of the Metropolis. Unlike my first visit when Town were First Division Champions-elect, they were rock bottom and would be relegated. When I took up my position in the enclosure, I found myself standing next to the architect of Town's back-to-back Second and First Division Championship successes of 1961 and '62, Jimmy Leadbetter. He looked like all the rest of what was a very rural looking home support, but that's what it was like in those days, in stark contrast to today when you would never find yourself next to a Premiership star in a million years. Anyway, it soon became apparent why Town were holding up the rest of the table as Hammers were two up after 57 minutes thanks to goals from Byrne (penalty) and Brabrook. As the result looked a foregone conclusion I decided to go back down under the stand to get myself a hot cup of Oxo and a hot-dog which I had been unable to do at half-time due to the hundreds of frozen fans who had the same idea. Now, though, the Tea Bar was almost empty apart from a few softies like myself who were trying to thaw out. Before I could take my first bite out of my hot-dog and a sip of Oxo, however, there was a huge roar from up above and much banging and stamping of feet. Town had obviously scored. Then I spotted a lad who, like me, was a former pupil of Hylands Secondary Modern School in Hornchurch by the name of Soames. I was about to say hello, when he asked me the most stupid question that has ever been put to me in my whole life to date, it was: "What are you doing here?" Before I could utter a suitable expletive-ridden reply, there was another huge explosion of sound from up above and this time it seemed the ceiling would fall in. The Town had scored again! Soames had dashed off upstairs, leaving me to ruminate in a state of shock. What an idiot, I thought, as I finished my sustenance and made to go back onto the paddock. But, as I reached the top of

Former West Ham goalkeeping hero Lawrie Leslie seems to be proving that anything that the man who replaced him in Hammers goal, Jim Standen, can do, he can do better as he makes a spectacular save in front of the North Bank to deny Geoff Hurst a goalscoring opportunity in the match played at Easter 1964, against Stoke City.

the stairs, I was almost blasted back down as another huge roar rent the freezing East Anglian air – they'd scored again! Now the crowd were singing, something about cattle and geese. It was time to get the train back to Romford, after all, there would be worse to come on Boxing Day. For Town, too, who would lose 10-1 to Fulham at Craven Cottage, but like us, would bounce back in the return game to win 4-2. As Greavesy said, "It's a funny old game". Almost ten years ago, When I was watching a game at Arsenal with my son, I saw Soames again. It looked like he was with his son, too. Having related the tale to my son before, I pointed him out to him and said "Do you think I should ask him what he's doing here?" But I resisted the temptation, after all, it must have been forty years ago, even then. Although he was injured and didn't play that night, Ipswich's centre-half and captain during their halcyon years was a former Hammer, Andy Nelson, who later became manager of Charlton Athletic. Well, my son Chris worked with a Dave Nelson, who it turned out was Andy's nephew. They are now good pals. Andy's brother, Bill, who also played for West Ham in the 50s, was a member of the XI which defeated Liverpool 2-1 at Anfield in September 1954 with goals from Dave Sexton and Harry Hooper. Thanks to the face saving victory at Blackburn, Hammers had managed to steady the ship in time for the FA Cup Third Round visit of Charlton Athletic on the first Saturday of the New Year which attracted a bumper crowd of 34,155 to Upton Park, many thousands of whom were from the other side of the water. A fair number of the vociferous Charlton contingent had colonised the North Bank and I can remember them singing along to the 45 by The Dave Clark Five which was a big hit at the time and interjecting the deafening chant of CHARLTON! Just before the oft repeated chorus of "*Glad All Over*".

It's a good job they got their singing in before the game because they had little to cheer about during or after as Hammers ran out 3-0 victors over their Second Division opponents with goals from Hurst, Byrne and Sissons to go through to the Fourth Round and another London derby with nearest neighbours, Leyton Orient. After a hiccup at Sheffield United where they lost 2-1 with just a Sissons goal to show for their efforts, the team then struck a rich vein of form. Thanks to Byrne's trademark goal, the "double" was completed over Liverpool (a feat unrepeated until 2015-16) in the 1-0 Upton Park victory, followed by a 2-2 draw at Villa Park (Hurst 2). Now performing like a team transformed, Spurs were put to the sword by the tune of 4-0 (Hurst, Sissons, Boyce and Byrne) before a packed crowd of 36,914 at an ecstatic Boleyn and it could have been more. Then Wolves were tamed 2-0 at Molineux (Hurst and Byrne) before League duties were concluded for a fabulous February with a 4-3 home win against Sheffield Wednesday after being 4-1 ahead (Byrne 3, 1 pen. and Hurst). Interspersed with the League action the team had also negotiated three more rounds of the FA Cup with victories over Orient, after a 1-1 draw at Brisbane Road (Brabrook), and then a 3-0 replay win (Hurst 2 and Byrne), versus Swindon, at the County Ground, 3-1 (Hurst 2, Byrne) and Burnley 3-2 (Byrne 2 and Sissons) in an all-ticket thriller before 36,651 in East London to qualify for the semi-finals for the first time since 1933.

Manchester United finally won the right to be Hammers' opponents in the showdown at Hillsborough after a protracted Sixth Round clash with Sunderland which went to two replays.

When the Red Devils won 2-0 in the League at Upton Park a week before the cup game with a weakened side, the bookies made them odds-on favourites to win through to Wembley.

So it was more in hope than expectation that my father, brother-in-law Chris (who was married to my sister, Val) and myself piled into an old Bedford van and set off for the long journey to the blue half of the "Steel City" of Sheffield and more precisely, Wednesday's Hillsborough home. It was the day that the "rains came"... and never seemed to stop coming. When we entered the ground via the Leppings Lane end we could see the pitch was a sodden morass and there was little shelter from the elements if, like us, your tickets were for standing only. But we spotted a small covered area nestling between the Leppings Lane Stand and the ground's "Jewel in the Crown", the magnificent cantilevered North Stand. It was from this vantage point that we incredulously witnessed one of the biggest FA Cup upsets of the post-war era unfold. At no stage did our heroes, again in their "lucky" sky blue shirts with the two claret hoops, resemble underdogs, in fact, it was Busby's boys who looked like the second-raters. But, tantalisingly, it was still 0-0 at half-time. With rain still hammering down relentlessly, the pitch resembled a quagmire as the teams emerged for the second-half, but the atrocious conditions were forgotten when Boyce, spotting Gaskell off his line, lofted the ball over him from outside the box in the 56th minute. Now the huge West Ham support were singing and dancing in the

Jim Standen makes the kind of safe catch that he made his trademark. Was with Worcestershire County Cricket Club, with whom he topped the bowling averages when they won the County Championship in 1964, to add to his Cup Final Winners' medal with West Ham the same year. The picture below was taken during the 4-0 thrashing of Spurs in February 1964.

rain as they sensed the way to Wembley was opening. Sure enough, seven minutes later, Boyce scored again from a short corner, the details of which I can remember clearly to this day. As Sissons prepared to take a corner over on the old Archibald Leitch Grand Stand side, Burkett made a move to receive it short, but Pat Crerand spotted what was going on and came over to cut it out, Sissons then acted as if he'd changed his mind, and Burkett retreated as Crerand went back into the centre. At the last moment, however, Sissons gestured for Burkett to come again and quickly played it to him short. Burkett then chipped the ball across and Boyce headed home from just outside the six-yard box. Pandemonium once more ensued as the rain-drenched West Ham players and fans went into wild celebration. Despite Denis Law pulling a goal back in the 78th minute, Captain Colossus, Bobby Moore's "killer" ball to Hurst two minutes later effectively finished the game off as the number 10 scored what would be considered almost a replica of his fourth goal in the World Cup Final two years later.

The two teams, who had been welcomed on the field by the Dagenham Girl Pipers, left it to the strains of "Bubbles", but only Greenwood's "Muddy Marvels" would have appreciated the send off. Yet even as its sweet refrain was fading on the damp Yorkshire air, Greenwood would have been aware of work still to be done with a League game at Leicester the following Wednesday, a London derby against Arsenal the next Saturday and then the return Second Leg of the Football League Cup semi-final versus Leicester at Upton Park to come just two days later, making a total of four games in nine days. Yes, Hammers had been staging a dual challenge in the two domestic cup competitions and had booked their passage into the second semi-final nine days before Christmas with a 6-0 Upton Park win over Fourth Division Workington Town at Upton Park (Byrne 3, Hurst, Boyce and Scott).

The Hammers had kicked off their run in the fledgling League Cup by luckily defeating neighbours Leyton Orient by 2-1 at the Boleyn (Scott and Byrne) in the Second Round before facing Aston Villa and ex-skipper Phil Woosnam in Round Three at Villa Park, who they defeated 2-0 (Bond and Britt). In the Fourth Round, playing without Moore who is on England duty, Hammers drew 3-3 at Swindon Town (Hurst, Brabrook and Boyce) before coasting the Upton Park replay 4-1 (Hurst, Brabrook, Byrne and Scott). If you think you're experiencing *déja vu*, don't worry, we drew both Orient and Swindon in the FA Cup.

The First Leg of the League Cup semi-final versus Leicester City on Wednesday, February 5, 1964 at Filbert Street was a thrilling affair, although when Ken Keyworth, Bobby Roberts and Mike Stringfellow put the Filberts 3-0 ahead after just 19 minutes, the tie looked over as a contest. Although Hurst reduced the arrears, when Frank McLintock made if 4-1 just after the break, the homesters lead again looked unassailable, but 20 minutes from the end Hurst latched on to Byrne's "chip" and again reduced the deficit. In the 82nd minute Sealey made it 4-3 from Moore's pass and in a furious final flurry, Byrne had his shot blocked on the goal-line. Phew!

So it was still "all to play for" in the Second Leg which drew a record crowd for a League Cup tie thus far to Upton Park, numbering 27,393; on Monday, February 24, 1964. The First Leg at Leicester had been classed as a "Thriller" by those who witnessed the exchanges, but the second tie reached new heights in the performances of both teams to win plaudits from fans, administrators and neutral observers alike. An England-class display from Gordon Banks kept the Hammers scoreless for the first time in 13 cup ties in this momentous season and goals from McLintock and Ian Gibson were enough to see the City qualify for the Final versus Stoke City. In a truly stirring cup-tie, Hammers had chances galore but couldn't, for once, score. But they contributed fully to a truly great exhibition of everything that is good in the game on an evening when their opponents, in an extraordinary display of sportsmanship, applauded them as they left the field. The West Ham fans, too, showing their innate sense of fair play, to a man stood and applauded the victorious Leicester City team to the rafters.

With Wembley looming, West Ham lose four out of their last five games, but in the last home game and penultimate match of the season, they enjoy a last hurrah by defeating ten-man Birmingham City, 5-0 with goals from Brabrook 2, Sissons, Hurst and Byrne, who would all play in the FA Cup Final against Preston North End the following month. In the *Official Programme* for the Brum game it is announced that admission prices for the 1964-65 season would be increased to:

North and South Bank..	4s.0d.
West Enclosure and East Terrace...........................	5s.0d.
E Block...	7s.0d.
B and D Blocks..	9s.0d.
C Block..	11s.0d.

The price of season tickets would remain the same at:
C Block: £12.0.0 each;
B and D Blocks: £10.0.0 each.

West Ham Youth team which swept the board in 1962-63. Standing L-R: Terry Needham, Martin Britt, Dennis Burnett, Colin Mackleworth, Billy Kitchener, Peter Bennett, Bobby Howe. Seated: Harry Redknapp, Trevor Dawkins, John Charles, John Sissons, John Dryden.

The excitement surrounding the forthcoming Wembley date notwithstanding, the curtain still hadn't finally closed on activities at Upton Park. Yet to be played were two important Youth team fixtures, against Chelsea Colts in the final of the Southern Junior Floodlight Cup on April 20 and Leyton Orient Colts on the 28th in the London Youth Cup Final; formerly the London Minor Cup of which Hammers were the holders, of course, but lost 2-3 (Howe and Britt) to the O's. There was also a big night planned for young John Lyall, who had been granted a Testimonial in which the West Ham first team would take on an XI billed as the All Stars on the 27th, and would include former team mates John Dick, Mal Musgrove, Andy Malcolm, Noel Cantwell and Lawrie Leslie. The fact that the match was staged just five days before "the big one" and 18,800 fans turned up to support Lyall, who'd had to retire prematurely due to injury, said a lot about West Ham's reputation as a family club who looked after their own. The result of the match was almost immaterial, but for the record was 5-0 (Hurst 4 and Redknapp) to West Ham on a wonderful evening which was a credit to all concerned and a memorable night for John. The incident I remember most about the game, despite the plethora of goals, was when Bobby Moore feigned injury and stayed grounded long enough to reduce the crowd to a hushed silence as they began to envisage playing the most important game in the club's history without the star man. Needless to say, he was soon up on his feet in jovial fashion as everyone breathed a huge sigh of relief as he sprinted away laughing.

Moore goes down with cramp in the titanic semi final battle with Manchester United at Hillsborough in 1964.

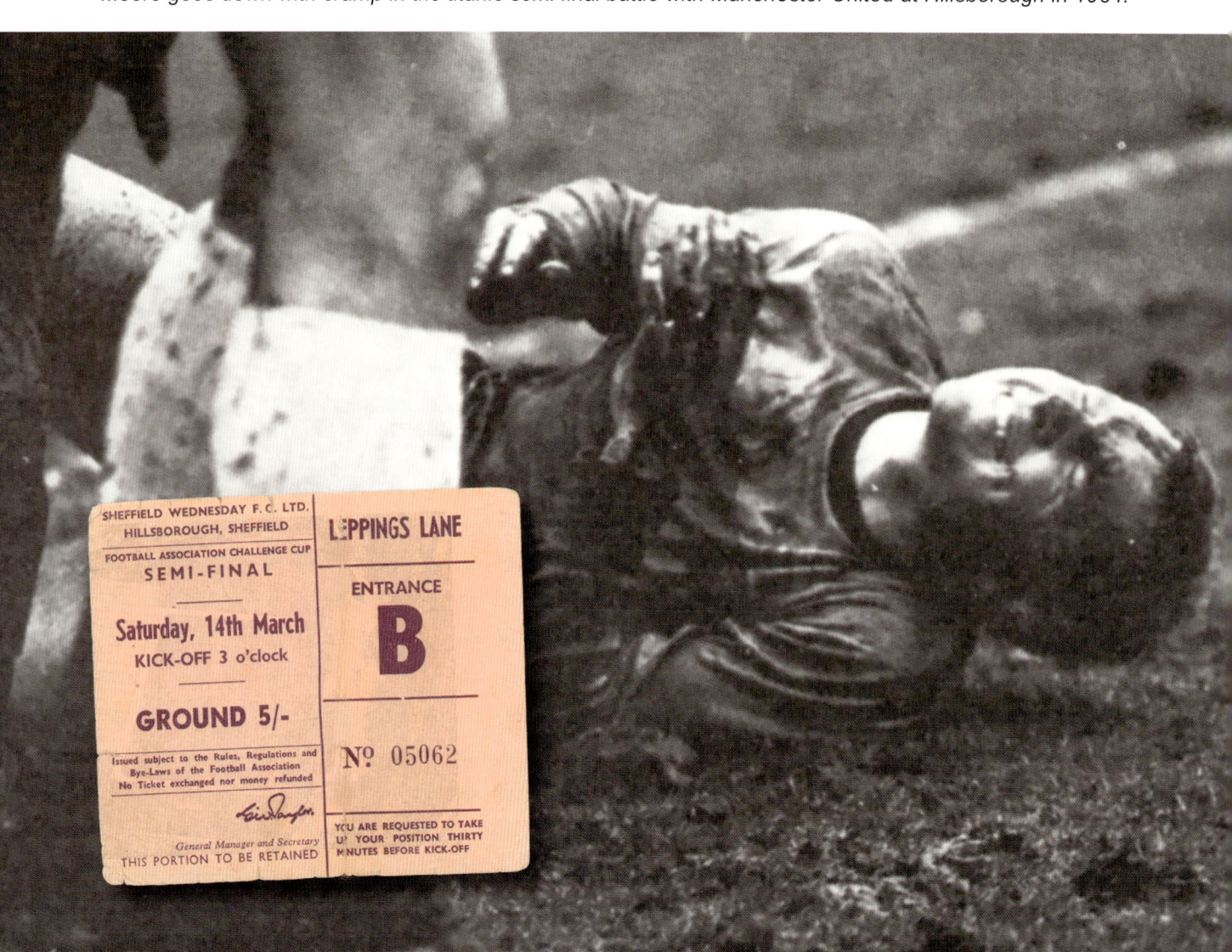

Back in the ever-more competitive world of youth team football, the Hammers Colts had managed to retain the services of no less than nine of the squad that had served them so well in 1962-63. They began their Southern Junior Floodlight Cup campaign with a sensational 10-1 win in front of a crowd of 3,300 at Upton Park on September 30, 1963, in the First Round against Southampton. The main tormentor of the shell-shocked Saints was right-winger Redknapp, who although not renowned for scoring many goals, scored three on this occasion and his opposite flankman, Johnny Sissons, also scored a hat-trick. Britt bagged a brace while Bennett and finally Dryden, two minutes from time, got the others. There was another big score in the Second Round against Queen's Park Rangers at Upton Park on December 2, as the Young Irons kept on the cup trail with a 5-0 win over the West Londoners, this time in front of a 3,500 attendance. Fielding the same team that had routed the Saints, on this occasion Sissons distinguished himself further by scoring four times with Britt getting the other. Having kicked off the defence of their London Youth Cup with a 6-1 victory over Brentford at Griffin Park the previous month, fielding newcomers Alan Herbage and Gadston in attack, the youngsters would soon be embroiled in a triple cup quest as they began their defence of the coveted FA Youth Cup. This they did with aplomb with a 3-0 victory against Fulham in front of a 2,200 Boleyn Ground gathering on December 18, by dint of goals from Bennett, Dryden and Redknapp. In the new year the young Iron Cubs continued in their hunt for more silverware unabated and seemed determined to emulate the achievements of the First Team by knocking near-neighbours Leyton Orient out of two separate cup competitions during 1963-64. Drawn against the O's in the Third Round at Brisbane Road on January 20, the same team that defeated Fulham lined up against Orient: Mackleworth, Needham, Kitchener, Dawkins, Andrew, Howe, Redknapp, Bennett, Britt, Sissons and Dryden. Watched by a bumper crowd of 5,600, which included a large contingent of Hammers' fans, a match report that appeared in the programme for the first team's FA Cup Fourth Round replay with the O's nine days later (29/1/'64) summed up the proceedings thus: "The Hammers eventually won by 5-2, after a game in which errors and mishaps were mixed with a spate of very good soccer from our team. During the course of overcoming a very robust opposition we were awarded two penalty-kicks (which we missed), conceded another penalty (which was converted) and had a goal given against us after the referee had apparently stopped play for an offside decision; Johnny Sissons had a personally eventful evening, scoring two goals, hitting the post once, having a penalty saved and then suffering a nose bleed after a collision! John Dryden (2) and Martin Britt completed our scoring – and we made further progress in our efforts to retain the trophy".

Young "Sisso", would be back at Brisbane Road five days later, playing in front of a crowd far greater than that which witnessed his heroics for the Youth Team as 34,345 were clicked through the turnstiles for the Fourth Round FA Cup tie to create a new ground record attendance which still stands to this day. But they had to squeeze 'em in – I know, I was there! Along with 8,500 other Hammers' fans who had managed to get their hands on a precious ticket. An extra 1,037 were in attendance for the Upton Park replay which finally witnessed the Hammers overcome an O's XI (thanks to a Hurst hat-trick) which included three members who had previously worn the claret and blue – Mal Musgrove, Dave Dunmore and Eddie Lewis. But back to the "Young Ones".

Of the squad who had won the FA Youth Cup so gloriously the previous campaign, Sissons, Britt and Charles had all played for the First Team and had all made their debut in the 0-1 reverse to Blackburn Rovers at Upton Park in May, 1963. Charles, was now over age, but both Sissons and Britt continued to support their young colleagues, sometimes, as we shall see, at the expense of playing for the First Team. Britt, in only his second senior outing, had covered himself in glory by scoring the only goal against Manchester United (26/10/'64) to give his team a rare victory at Old Trafford and further distinguished himself by scoring another two goals during a seven match run in the side in which he was on the losing side on only one occasion – when he scored in the 2-1 defeat at Birmingham City.

On February 10, 1964, Britt scored again, this time in the 62nd minute of the Fourth Round FA Youth Cup tie against Arsenal at Highbury after a throw-in from Sissons was met by a pass from Howe for the centre-forward to left foot the ball home from 10 yards. A needlessly conceded free-kick 8 minutes later led to the Young Gunners equalising however and three minutes from time David Jenkins headed the winner to send the Hammers fans in the 3,862 crowd home in a sombre mood. So the "Treble" was off, but the "Double" still very much on. As if to underline the fact, Hammers bounced back just seven days later by defeating Leyton Orient Colts in the semi-final of the SJFC by three goals to two, fielding the same XI that had lost at Highbury with the exception of Herbage for Sissons who was playing for the First Team at Wolves where they won 2-0 with a goal in each half from Hurst and Byrne. After building up

Sissons scores from an acute angle at the South Bank End, in the sixth round of the FA Cup against Burnley, as Hammers progress to the semi-final with a 3-2 victory.

Hurst scores West ham's third goal in the 3-1 fifth round victory at the County Ground, versus Swindon Town.

a two goal lead at Brisbane Road, both scored by Britt – the first a header from Dawkins' cross and the second with a strong shot on the turn – there were distinct feelings of *déja vu* as the O's fought back to level through strikes by Price and Lambert, with the match descending into a "blood and thunder" affair, typical of a London Derby clash. A saviour was at hand, however, in the form of left-winger Dryden, who finished off a four-man move to score a last-minute winner amid scenes of great excitement and set up a meeting with Chelsea, who had won at Portsmouth in the other semi-final, in the Final.

Played over two legs, the Hammers' "Young Dudes" lost the first game 2-0 against "The Doc's Ducklings" at Stamford Bridge on March 11, as a result of goals from Wilks and McCalliog. Sissons was left out due to the proximity of the FA Cup Semi-Final versus Manchester United at Hillsborough three days later and Herbage again deputised. This was not the case a week later though, as programme editor Jack Helliar's notes for the League Cup semi-final meeting with Leicester City succinctly explained:

"Exactly a week after their defeat at Stamford Bridge our Colts secured a resounding victory in another knock-out tournament; this time it was the London Youth Cup which occupied our attention, and the match which took place at Upton Park last Wednesday (18/3/'64) was a Second Round tie.

"Our youngsters' determination to atone for their previous set-back was underlined when both Martin Britt and John Sissons requested permission to play in this game, rather than to take a likely place in the First Team at Leicester (for a First Division fixture) the same evening. We were therefore able to field our recognised strongest line-up of: Mackleworth, Needham, Kitchener, Dawkins, Andrew, Howe, Redknapp, Bennett, Britt, Sissons, Dryden.

"Our opponents – Tottenham Hotspur Colts – must have deeply regretted this decision, because Britt scored a hat-trick and Sissons two goals in a 7-0 victory. It took 12 minutes for Britt to put us ahead, and another goal from the same player right on the interval virtually finished the Spurs. The North-Londoners attempted to keep a man tight on Sissons throughout the game, but he eluded him on many occasions and the second-half became something of a rout. Peter Bennett and John Dryden each got one goal, so Harry Redknapp was the only forward not to score; but our right-winger led the opposition a real dance, and he played a considerable part in laying on opportunities for his colleagues. It snowed almost throughout the 90 minutes play, and this unpleasant weather helped to keep the attendance down to a mere 1,500. We now play Arsenal in the Semi-Final, so will have the opportunity to avenge defeat in our FA Youth Cup Quarter-Final".

A very respectable crowd of 5,000 assembled at Upton Park on Monday evening, April 17, and duly witnessed the Hammers exact revenge of sorts over the Gunners, although it must be noted that the London Youth Cup was of lesser stature than the national FA Youth Cup competition. With Dryden unfit, Herbage deputised and fitted in well as Hammers took a 1-0 lead through, you've guessed it, Britt after ten minutes play. Although the Gunners levelled just before the break, Britt restored his team's lead with a trademark powerful header within a minute of the resumption and with 20 minutes left again used his head when he nodded the ball to Sissons who netted from close range to seal a 3-1 win and a passage to the Final against Leyton Orient at Upton Park on Tuesday, April 28.

Before the game, however, the young Hammers had another important fixture to contend – the Second Leg of the SJC Final versus Chelsea – again at Upton Park – on April 20.

A lot was riding on this game, call it London Pride, if you like. Chelsea, remember, were 2-0 ahead from the First Leg and wanted revenge for their 2-0 defeat to Hammers in the previous year's London Minor Cup Final. Behind the scenes too, there was a lot of rivalry. For years Chelsea's legendary Chief Scout, Jimmy Thompson, had been "working" West Ham's patch to poach highly rated prospects for the West Londoners who were known to offer inducements like TVs, fridges, washing machines and other household appliances to youngster's parents to get them to sign on at Stamford Bridge. They also offered higher wages, too.

The list of players Thompson was able to entice across to West London was long. Too long, and enough to make Hammers' chief representative, Wally St. Pier, weep. Among those who initially trained at Upton Park on Tuesday and Thursday evenings under the auspices of established pros like Noel Cantwell, John Bond, Malcolm Allison and Mal Musgrove were: Barry Bridges, Terry Venables, Allan and Ron Harris, Bert Murray, Ken Shellito and Mike Harrison. Jimmy Greaves and Peter Brabrook were also on the radar, but they, too, ended up in SW19.

So, you see, a lot of pride was at stake in that Final against Chelsea's Colts. As it turned out, this time it was the Blues turn to lift the Cup with a 3-1 victory. Britt's goal was scant consolation

ROOTES
SERVICE
BEST FOR CARS, VANS & TRUCKS
TEL: LAD 3232
Ladbroke Hall, Barlby Road, W.10

No. 25,601

World's Largest Evening Sale

The Even
and
LONDON TH

SPECIAL SOUVENIR PICTUR

ON THE W
ROAD

THE LINE UP

PRESTON NORTH END
(White shirts, dark blue shorts)

A. KELLY

G. ROSS   J. SMITH

N. LAWTON (Capt.)   T. SINGLETON   H. KENDALL

B. WILSON   A. ASHWORTH   A. DAWSON   A. SPAVIN   D. HOLDEN

Referee: A. Holland (Yorks)   (30)   Linesmen: S. Stoakes (Notts)   F. Bricknell (Devon)

J. SISSONS   G. HURST   J. BYRNE   R. BOYCE   P. BRABROOK

R. MOORE (Capt.)   K. BROWN   E. BOVINGTON

J. BURKETT   J. BOND

J. STANDEN

WEST HAM UTD.
(Claret and light blue shirts, white shorts)

g News

SOUVENIR PICTURE EDITION

The Finest Buy you'll ever make in FIRES or COOKERS
Cannon IS THE NAME

APRIL, 30 1964 — PRICE 3d.

OF THE FINALISTS
EMBLEY

THE FOOTBALL ASSOCIATION CHALLENGE CUP COMPETITION

FINAL TIE

PRESTON NORTH END v **WEST HAM UNITED**

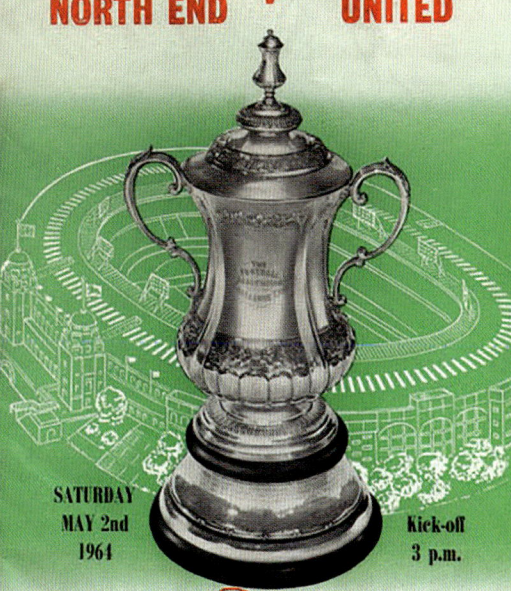

SATURDAY MAY 2nd 1964 — Kick-off 3 p.m.

WEMBLEY
OFFICIAL PROGRAMME . . . . ONE SHILLING

ashback to the first ever Wembley Cup Final in 1923 when West Ham were beaten 2-0 by Bolton. The crowd, officially given as 47, invaded the pitch after 25,000 had gained admittance without paying. The match was saved by the now famous police- on a white horse (marked by arrow) who gradually coaxed the crowd back over the touchline and allowed the game to 40 minutes late. Inset is The Earl of Harewood, the new President of the Football Association who will present the trophy.

West Ham — Are Worthy

against the aggregate score of 5-1.

Prestige apart, there was a surprising confirmation of just how valued the revenue from Youth Team fixtures were perceived by the parent club in the Chairman's Annual Report to shareholders of West Ham United FC given at the Annual General Meeting on February 11, 1964.

Partly published in advance of the actual meeting in the programme for Hammers' home FA Cup Fourth Round replay versus Leyton Orient on January 29, 1964, dealing with financial aspects of the 1962-63 season, and headed: Financial Facts and Figures, it revealed: "In keeping with the general trend, our average home gates fell from 25,731 to 23,425, but due to increased admission charges, and our successes in the FA Cup and FA Youth Cup, our net income showed an increase of £12,700". Proof that every £ was needed and appreciated. The report continued: "At the same time, however, our expenditure rose by £16,800, resulting in a loss in the Revenue Account of £461. Wages again rose by over £2,000 and represented 55.5% of our income".

"There is one other particular item in the Revenue Account to which we feel some reference should be made, and that is Ground Repairs of over £16,000. Much has been written in the

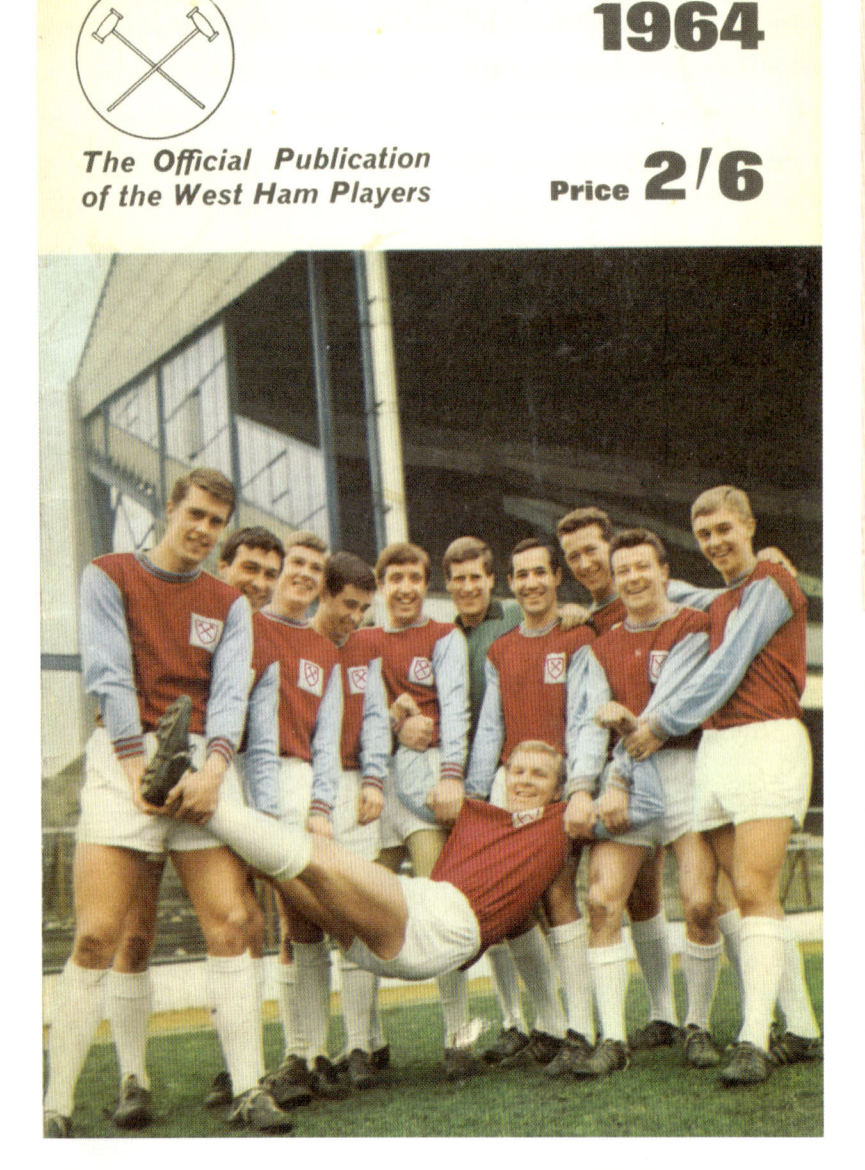

Left: The players official brochure for the 1964 Cup Final. Bobby Moore gets the bumps, held up by team mates. L-R: Geoff Hurst, Peter Brabrook, Jack Burkett, Ronnie Boyce, John Bond, Jim Standen, Eddie Bovington, Ken Brown, Budgie Byrne and Johnny Sissons. Against the backdrop of the West Stand.

Above: Self explanatory, but never the less, the Holy Grail of sought after football tickets, which the author was so desperate to get in his grubby little hands.

press about the need for clubs to provide more comfort for their patrons. There is still much muddled thinking however, as to how clubs are to meet the cost of these very desirable amenities. It is still not generally appreciated that there is no Income Tax relief for new capital expenditure. The only way therefore for clubs to meet these costs is out of taxed income and from the donations from Supporters Clubs 'Building Fund' schemes.

"No one can accuse this club of not making strenuous efforts to improve its amenities. Since 1958, the major items carried out include the vastly improved Main Entrance (£45,000), covering the North Bank (£14,000), new floodlights (£17,000) and new toilets for seat-holders (£5,000). This last item, by the way, was paid for out of the 'West Ham United Building Fund', which is sponsored by our Supporters Club. All this adds up to the fact that in the last five years we have spent around £100,000 on new work, repairs and general maintenance. In spite of this, there is still a very considerable programme mapped out for the future, which includes the complete re-terracing of the North Bank, the extension of the new toilets in the Grand Stand, improving seating, the addition of 'A' Block, and a new seating stand to replace the East Terrace. Given the right kind of support, these are the plans we hope to carry out".

History proved that this wasn't just wishful thinking by the West Ham hierarchy, as all these projects were duly realised and completed by the end of the 60s, facilitated by the swollen Upton Park coffers which the cup successes of the mid-part of the decade had generated.

Chronicled almost to the extent of "over-kill" in the plethora of books and various other media forms in the intervening 52 years, Hammers slightly fortuitous 3-2 Wembley victory over "Proud Preston" North End to at last deliver the FA Cup to an adoring East End public so long deprived of silverware, hardly needs further exposure here. Suffice to say, the goals that won it were all scored by former Youth Team players in Sissons, Hurst and Boyce, as if to further underline the importance of "home-grown" talent in an area that, since Syd King's day, had been rightly revered as a "hot-bed of football".

What is worth examining here is the paltry ticket allocation of just 15,000 to the supporters of the two 1964 finalists. Bearing in mind the capacity at Wembley then was 100,000, it doesn't take a genius to work out that the fans of the two teams involved would receive just 30% of the total ticket allocation. As West Ham's average home attendance was 24,616, the shortfall is clear to see. Having been present at all of the ties which led to Wembley in '64, with the exception of the Fifth Round clash with Third Division Swindon Town at the County Ground, I was one of many thousands of Hammers' fans searching for a precious ticket in the weeks leading up to the Wembley showpiece.

The club operated a voucher and lucky programme numbers scheme to give fans a chance of purchasing a ticket. I remember the winning number printed in the match programme versus Bolton Wanderers on April 4, was 435. I had 434... one digit away from a 17s.6d. seat ticket! I was also out of luck with the voucher I was given at the turnstiles, which, had it bore any one of a selection of 12 different numbers, I would have been entitled to buy a 7s.6d. standing ticket, that I would have much preferred to a seat.

So it was the case of carrying on the search for the Holy Grail of football tickets undeterred by a series of false hopes and "blind alleys". Despite working at the time for that "footballing bible", *Soccer Star* Magazine, as the office tea-boy and general go-fer. There was still no joy. One day while out on an errand in Chancery Lane, I decided to ask one of the newspaper vendors if they could help in my quest. "I've got a fiver". I told one, "He's got a fiver", he parroted. The next thing I felt someone tugging on my wallet in my back pocket.

"I'd forget about that if you know what's good for you", said my not so friendly newspaper seller, as I took his advice and retreated towards Fleet Street, thankful that I'd held on to my wallet and the precious fiver within with which I still hoped would be enough to tempt someone to part with a Cup Final ticket, which, it seemed, were rarer than a Bobby Moore own goal. Come Cup Final morning, I was still ticketless and resigned to watching the game on TV. Then a miracle happened. Still in bed, I heard something came through the letter-box. It was a letter addressed to me – something of a rarity in itself. When I opened it, out popped TWO CUP FINAL TICKETS! One a 17s.6d. seat, the other a 7s.6d. standing ticket.

They were sent by my late brother, Christopher, who was then stationed at RAF Sleaford in Lincolnshire, somehow, god only knows how, he'd managed to get them up there. As you can imagine, the Hogg household erupted like the Chicken Run celebrating a goal against Spurs. We were all going to Wembley!

The full squad: Physio Bill Jenkins, Joe Kirkup, Ken Brown, John Bond, Jim Standen, Martin Peters, Jack Burkett, Eddie Bovington, Bobby Moore. Front: Alan Sealey, Peter Brabrook, Ronnie Boyce, Budgie Byrne, Geoff Hurst, Johnny Sissons, Tony Scott.

Details of the game and my memories of it are hazy now, to say the least, after the passage of 52 years, but what I do vividly recall was after watching the post-match celebrations and shouting myself hoarse for the previous 90 minutes of fluctuating fortunes as the match swung one way and then the other until Boycie's header finally won it for his local team, was drinking a Coca Cola in the bowels of the famous old stadium. A Coke has never tasted that good to this day.

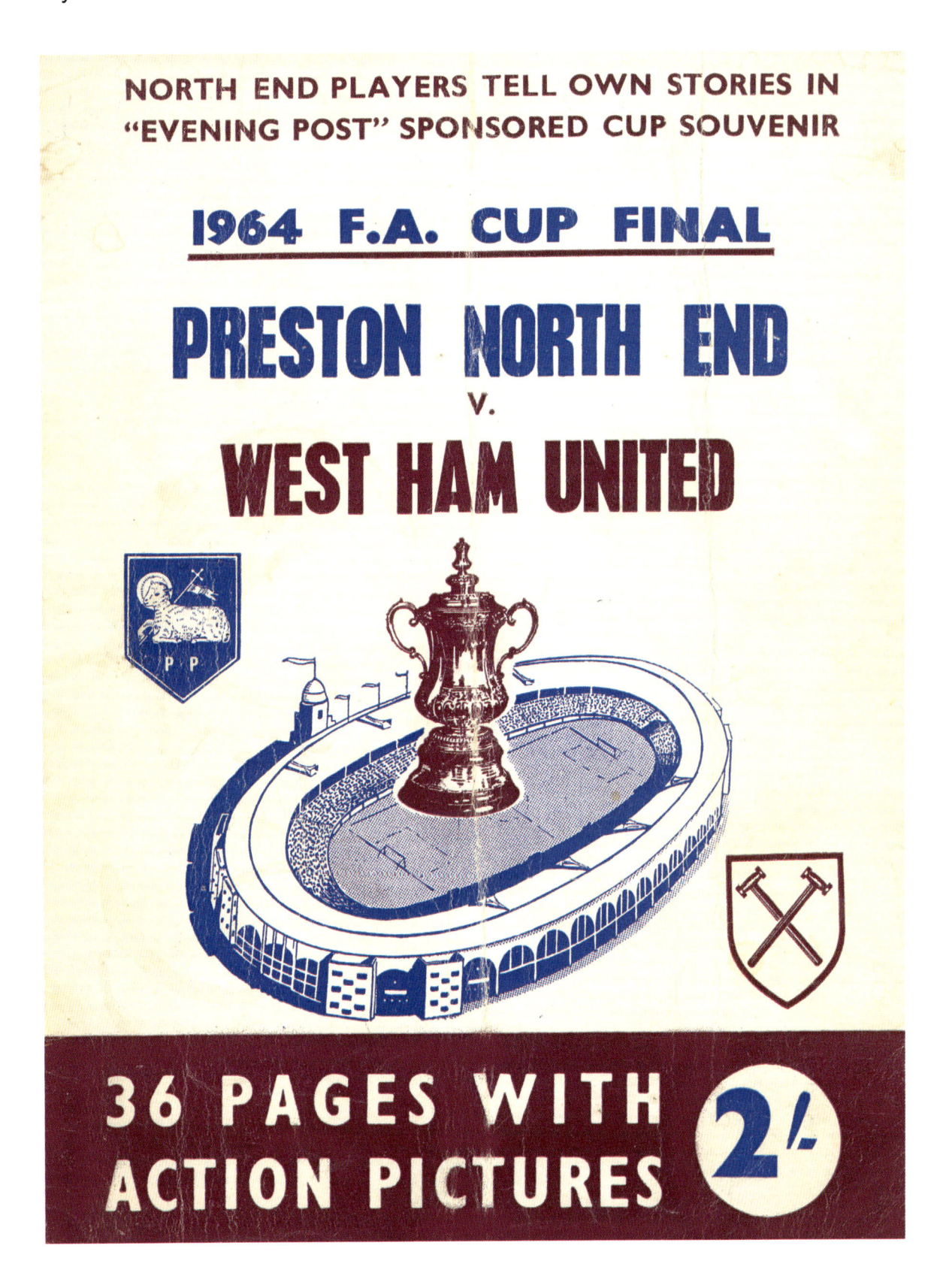

In less time than it takes to play the Cup Final

PENGUIN

will CLEAN & PRESS your clothes!

EAST HAM RECO__

NO. 3419

Registered as a Newspaper

and BARK__

THURSDAY

WEM__

HAMMER__
FINAL S__

COLOU__
FOUR
EXCLUSIV__
PICTU__
PLAYERS'

TO mark West Ham Uni__
in reaching the Football
Ham Recorder make wee__
London by producing this
Hammers. It includes a m__
ture of the West Ham team
End at Wembley on Satu__
the autographs of the 16-str__

Featured in these pages a__
the men who on Saturda__
will be striving to make t__
dream of a lifetime con__
true

NEWHAM
RDER
ECORDER
FIVEPENCE

3rd 1964

The Voice of East Ham

PENGUIN

AMERICAN CLEANERS
for
ONE-HOUR CLEANING
—at no extra cost!
264-266 Green Street
Upton Park
GOOD LUCK HAMMERS!

BLEY 1964

CUP
ARS

CIAL
OF
ORDER
ND
RAPHS

performance this year
ion Cup Final, the East
paper history in East
ur supplement on the
full-page souvenir pic-
ill meet Preston North
also reproductions of
Ham first-team squad.

MOORE THE
AGNIFICENT

Enter the Gladiators. Mooro leads out the team in the run up to Wembley, followed by Eddie 'The Bov' Bovington and Geoff Hurst.

FA CUP '64

WEST HAM UNITED V. PRESTON NORTH END, MAY 4

3/6

CUP FINAL SOUVENIR 1964

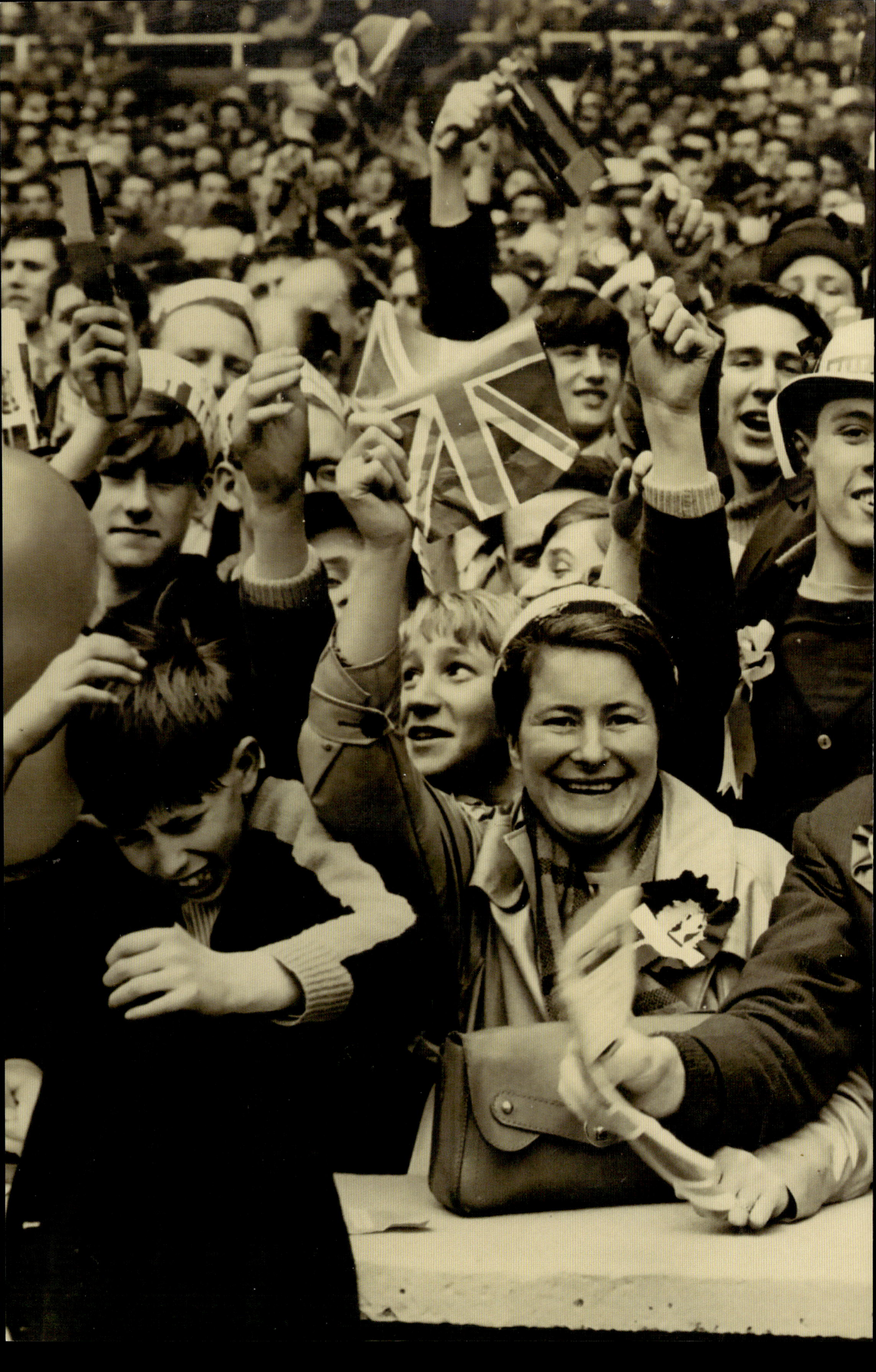

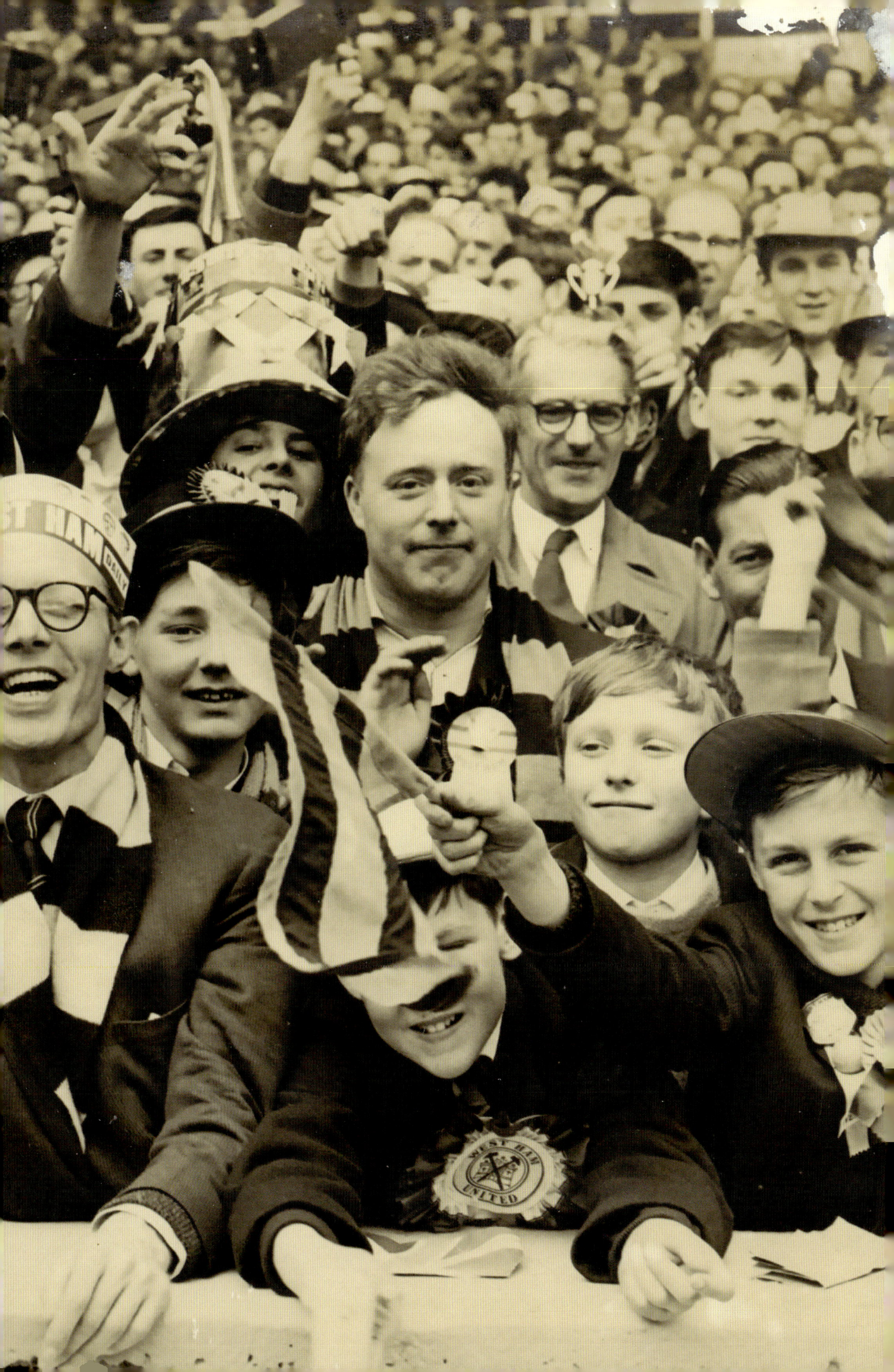
ST HAM
WEST HAM
UNITED

Above: The teams are led out by PNE Manager Jimmy Milne and his West Ham counterpart Ron Greenwood, followed by Skippers Nobby Lawton and Bobby Moore.

Below: Preston's winger Doug Holden capitalises on Jim Standen's fumble to put Proud Preston 1-0 ahead early on.

Top right: A delighted Holden wheels away as the ball is in the net with a disconsolate John Bond (right) and Alec Ashworth celebrating (number 8).

Below right: Sissons beats four Preston men to hammer the Hammers' equaliser not long after.

1-1

2-1

Top: Preston go ahead again through centre-forward Alex Dawson, who beats Ken Brown in the air to head home. Below: Another angle on Dawson's goal from behind the goal as the ball sails in, watched by Moore (6) Burkett (3) Bond and 'Keeper Standen.

2-2

Top: West Ham equalise in the second half to make it 2-2, when Hurst's header hits the underside of the bar and is helped over the line by goalkeeper Alan Kelly's attempt to save.
Below: Then the dramatic injury time winner by inside right Ronnie Boyce, who has headed home Peter Brabrook's centre to spark wild celebrations.

2-3

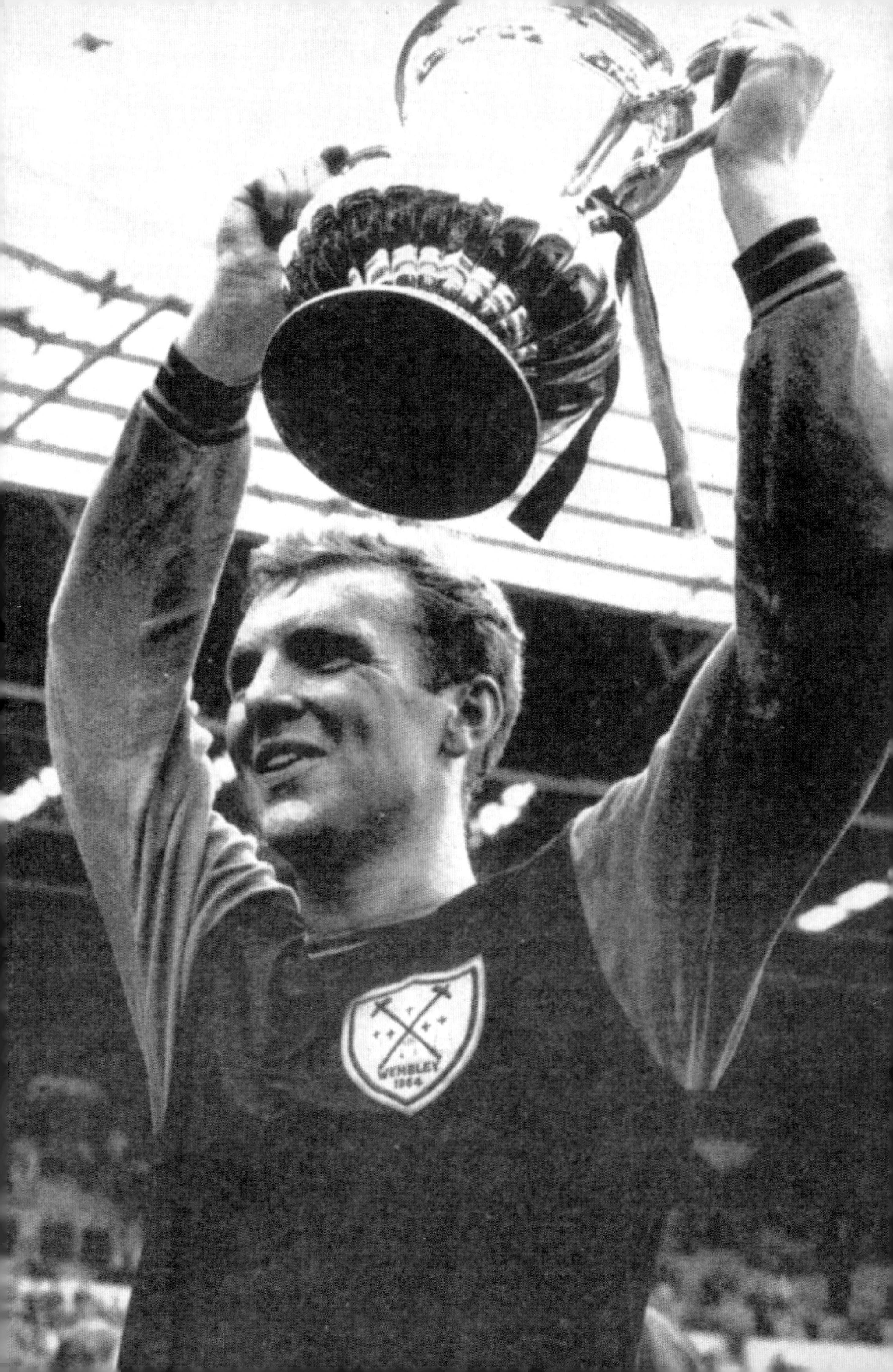
WEMBLEY
1964

Above left: Boyce runs behind the goal after his last gasp winner. Above right: Sissons consoles Kendall after the final whistle. Below left: West Ham's victory lap of honour begins with Burkett, Moore (with Cup) and Brabrook, taking the trophy to show their ecstatic fans. Below right: Johnny Byrne and Bobby Moore parade with a giant hammer.

Above, below and top right, the coach edges its way along the Barking Road, which is festooned with flags, bunting, banners and balloons. They were feted all the way to East Ham Town Hall, where they were turned away by the Police due to safety regulations, because of the magnitude of the excited crowds awaiting them.

Top: A rare colour photograph for that time, shows the coach decked out with the Hammers' crest.
Below: The Police's fears were well founded by the scenes outside the Town Hall. The scene was reminiscent of the 1923 Cup Final when that famous White Horse Billy, held the crowds back to allow the game to begin.

ROOTES
SERVICE
BEST FOR CARS, VANS & TRUCKS
TEL: LAD 3232
Ladbroke Hall, Barlby Road, W.10

No. 25,604

World's Largest Evening Sale

The Eve

a d

LONDON

Tumultuous G

WELCO

Well Done HAMMERS

ng News

WEST HAM SOUVENIR

Look smarter in... Plaza NYLONS

MAY 4 1964

PRICE 3d.

ing For The Hammers

ME HOME!

GO ON, MY SON!

There have been many noted pairings of father and sons playing for West Ham United over the club's long and illustrious history, but only one incidence of a son succeeding his father as a prominent member of the club's back-room staff – as was the case with physiotherapists Bill and Rob Jenkins.

Bill was in charge of the medical room during the halcyonic days of the 60s and Rob in the similarly successful times of the mid-70s and early 80s.

Bill senior was born in the Rhondda, at Tylerstown, which was where Jimmy Wilde, the famous British professional flyweight and World boxing champion, also hailed from.

Bill "Bomber" Jenkins was equally as tough, who, in his youth, used to win most of the mountain races in the Rhondda Valleys and was, according to his son, a "wonderful athlete".

A fiery character, there's an amusing tale of when he chased "Budgie" Byrne all round the ground after he'd played one of his mischievous tricks on the man supposed to be looking after his good health and fitness. Luckily for Budgie, Bill couldn't catch him – otherwise he would have been back on the treatment table.

Bill, from a family of twelve, seemed destined for the coal mines that were just about the only source of guaranteed employment in the Principality in those days and in fact, did work in that subterranean world for a spell, before deciding there was a better future outside of Wales and joined the Royal Army Medical Corps.

During his time in khaki he qualified as a physiotherapist and pharmacist and rose to the rank of Captain. After serving his country for 16 years, during which time he'd been "under canvas" in Egypt and South Africa, Bill joined Isthmian League Clapton FC who played at the Spotted Dog ground under the managership of ex-Hearts and West Ham wing-half, Norman Corbett.

Norman, a long-throw expert, was one of three famous footballing brothers who all played for West Ham – the other two being David, who played four Second Division matches in 1936 and Willie, who made 26 WWII guest appearances – a couple with brother Norman.

When Bill Jenkins made the short journey to continue his career with Walthamstow Avenue in 1960, young Rob, newly qualified as a physiotherapist like his father, succeeded him at Clapton FC. Then, when Bill senior moved up to the First Division with West Ham to take over from Billy Moore in 1961, Rob replaced him at Green Pond Road where, in his first season, the Avenue won the FA Amateur Cup at Wembley by defeating West Auckland 2-1 – with just ten fit men before a 45,000 crowd.

Not to be outdone, Bill found himself at Wembley twice with Hammers in 1964 and '65, of course. But by the latter year son Rob had joined him at the Boleyn Ground as Reserve Team Attendant.

By this time father and son had established a physio's clinic above Bobby Moore's sports shop in Green Street – the perfect location for such a venture, surely?

Then, in 1966, Bill and Rob decided to open their own clinic just a few doors down, where players from all over London continued to flock, as well as stars of stage and screen like Peter Ustinov and William Holden ("who thought the world of my Dad" according to Rob).

When Geoff Hurst picked up a hard-to-diagnose back injury, he turned to Rob and he remained one of his clients up until the clinic closed in 2016 amid a fanfare of publicity.

Following Bill senior's sad and sudden death on August 15, 1966, as he was preparing for the new season, the club also turned to Rob to fill his father's role, making him the youngest physio in football.

Many present and former players attended his funeral, including internationals Johnny Dick and Phil Woosnam, who he had continued to treat even although they were with other clubs. But Bill had left the Hammers' players in good hands – his son's.

Physio, Bill Jenkins Senior with the skipper and the Cup. Son Rob (inset).

West Ham's 'Lady of Letters' Secretary Pauline Moss, pictured (on the right) holding the F.A. Cup with a colleague in 1964. She went on to serve the club for 36 years under three of its most famous managers, Ten Fenton, Ron Greenwood and John Lyall. Others in the informal gathering left to right: George Izzatt, Bob Fixter, A. N. Other (behind), Club Secretary Eddie Chapman, Groundsman Bill Fossey (behind), Chief Scout Wally St Pier (behind), Ron Greenwood, Paddy (kneeling with lucky cat), Scout Arthur Bradshaw Lamb (behind), A. N. Other. The unknown little girl (kneeling) gives this photo a nice family look.

Europe Beckons

Chapter 7

Fresh from a mini-continental tour, the team were in high spirits and fine fettle for the start of the ground-breaking 1964-65 season. The nine-day visit to Austria and Germany between August 5 and 14 was staged as close as possible to the start of the season with the express purpose of preparing the team for the upcoming European Cup Winners Cup tournament, for which their Wembley win had automatically qualified them to contest.

Victories over FK Austria (3-0, Sissons, Byrne and Moore) and Graz AK (1-0, Byrne) were followed by a 1-0 defeat against stiffer opposition in FC Nuremburg, to sound a timely warning of the task ahead. The squad also got a taste of the tight travelling schedules ahead when the touring party left Germany on the Thursday morning (August 13) after the Nuremburg match, lunched at London Airport and then flew to Manchester. They stayed there until Saturday morning before embarking on the short journey to Liverpool by coach to play the Kopites at Anfield in the Charity Shield. The Hammers had joined the "Jet-Set!".

Fears expressed by a writer in the *Liverpool Echo*: "With Liverpool committed to a European Cup game on Monday and West Ham just returned from a Continental tour we may get less than an all-out effort..." proved to be unfounded as the two teams put on a four goal thriller for the 38,858 attendance, well worthy of the occasion. After "Smiler" Wallace had given Liverpool the lead following an uncharacteristic blunder by Moore with a low shot that crept in after hitting both uprights, the game quickly developed into a classic encounter with thrills and spills at both ends. Hammers first equaliser, a minute before the interval, was the result of a five-man move which ended with Byrne meeting Bovington's delicate chip with the grace of a ballet dancer, taking the ball chest-high on his right instep and neatly steering the ball wide of Lawrence in the Liverpool goal all in the same split-second move. As good old Trevor Smith noted in his *Recorder* match report: "It was a goal of such perfection, such timing, that it was greeted with an astonished silence". Centre-forward Byrne admitted to having a "voice" in Liverpool's second goal four minutes after the break, however, as he explained post-match: "I was coming up behind my namesake, Gerry Byrne, when Callaghan pushed the ball back to him. I shouted 'Shoot', hoping he would because I was certain that he could not score from that distance and position. It will go over, or Jim will pick it off, I thought. But it went in!" Under siege for most of the second period, Hurst, having already gone close, managed to save the game when he beat Byrne (G.) to the ball to score the leveller six minutes from time.

Having won the toss of a coin for the right to hold the handsome trophy for the first half of the season, a carnival-like atmosphere prevailed when it was paraded around the ground along with the FA Cup before the first home match of the season nine days later by the Youth Team against Manchester United under the Upton Park lights.

Coming so soon after the titanic semi-final battle at Hillsborough, it was inevitable that the "House Full" notices would go up with ten minutes to kick-off with 37,070 fans crammed inside. Safety issues were raised when hundreds of late-comers simply scaled the walls in their desperation to get in to see their favourites pit their wits against Charlton, Best and Law *et al*. The club were sufficiently worried to issue a warning post-match through Secretary Eddie Chapman who explained: "We closed our gates for the simple reason that the crowd inside had reached the safe figure. Anyone else getting in after that jeopardised not only their own safety, but also that of the spectators already in", he declared.

"We were able to accommodate the maximum possible number in everywhere on Monday except on the South Bank, where bad packing by fans forced us to close the gates before the limit was reached", said Eddie, who estimated that another 6,000 fans were locked out.

"I saw about a hundred gate-crash by getting over the walls and I think there must have been several hundred who got in this way, despite the best efforts of the MPF to repel the boarders. We have taken action to ensure that this will not happen again".

The Hammers' Secretary also warned fans about climbing up on stand and terracing roofing. Two small boys raised a gasp on Monday night when they scaled the North Bank roofing to retrieve a ball which ended up in the guttering after a David Herd shot had landed on the roof.

Eddie Presland   *Geoff Hurst*

After this considerable feat of daring and agility, the pair made off smartly with Hammers brand new ball!

"We realise that they got a good ball out of it, but it was an incredibly dangerous thing to do. The roofing is only of asbestos sheeting and the pair could easily have crashed through it onto the crowd below, or slipped over the edge", concluded Ed.

The vast majority of fans who did get in by fair means (or foul) were treated to a gala occasion which inspired Trevor Smith to intro his match report: "There never were such days at Upton Park!" Before going on to offer fair warning on the off-field events: "Star-loaded Manchester United, always a tremendous attraction at Upton Park, are the more so after last season's Homeric semi-final struggle. With even more fascinating games in the offing, however, it is clear that Hammers must take swift steps to ensure that their cramped ground does not become the scene of a tragedy through gate-crashing hundreds".

There was little danger, with the talent on display, that the extraordinary off-field events would overshadow those on it, though. A blistering opening spell of attacking play swept Hammers to a two-goal advantage after 19 minutes through Byrne and Sissons to send a packed Upton Park into raptures.

As the first-half closed with three home corners in succession, the crowd were prepared for a rout after the break, more so when United lost their "Enforcer", Maurice Setters, through injury in the 58th minute. Then as is often the way, despite this loss, United's ten men started to get the better of the exchanges and the majestic Law rose above Standen to head a neat goal, just as he had done at Hillsborough four months previously. But with 11 minutes left, the Hammers again regained control and the score was destined to finish a replica of the "Sheffield Shock" as Hurst added a third goal five minutes from time after the veteran Bond had beaten Best to the ball to set him up. The win gave Irons maximum points following their opening day 2-1 victory over Fulham at Craven Cottage. Yet, just four days later, they slumped to a 2-3 reverse against Nottingham Forest in the Friday floodlight fixture at Upton Park. Once again, off-field incidents were to the fore in the crowd of 26,760.

Traditionally one of West Ham's "bogey" sides, the Hammers looked like they might reverse this trend when, despite being overrun by an enterprising Forest performance in the opening stages, they were awarded a dubious penalty in the 14th minute. As Trevor Smith in the *Recorder* reported: "West Ham greeted the decision with a barely concealed air of mystified delight... Forest with outraged anger. Ex-Arsenal man Johnny Barnwell went so far as to hand Mr. Burtenshaw a shove which, in any other situation, would only mean an invitation to fisticuffs.

"The referee, however, ignored the invite – and also his rulebook – so the indignant Barnwell glowered at his heels as he placed the ball on the penalty spot. John Byrne duly slotted the ball past Grummitt to maintain his goal-a-game record and give the Hammers the lead.

"Before the game could restart, stewards behind Grummitt's goal called the referee's attention to something which had been thrown on the pitch near the edge of the penalty box to the left of the North Bank goal. Mr. Burtenshaw brought the missile, which could be clearly seen as broken glass, to the tunnel and police went out to patrol behind the goal, where it seemed a

Martin Peters

group of Forest fans had followed Barnwell's example by attempting to start what is known in police court jargon as a 'fracas'."

But Saturday morning headlines in the national papers screamed "West Ham Riot" and angered club officials including manager Greenwood who commented later: "It was obviously not one of our supporters – why would they protest because we scored from a penalty? But to describe the incident which was all over in a minute, as a riot is just absurd, and does not help the public image of the game at all".

Rather than hinder Forest, however, the incident seemed to encourage their cause as Barnwell levelled just before half-time and then put the Trent men ahead in the 58th minute.

Although Hammers equalised through Sissons, left-winger Alan Hinton scored what proved to be the winner in the 73rd minute to make it Forest's night.

I was standing on the North Bank that evening and there was nothing going on that endorsed the sensationalised headlines in the newspapers the next day to my knowledge.

Two further 3-1 away defeats, to Manchester United and Stoke City respectively, forced Greenwood to make changes as he dropped Brown and Brabrook for the visit of Wolves, but, as he said: "It could have been almost anyone – somebody had to be hurt". Bringing in Peters for Brown and Sealey for Brabrook, the changes had the desired effect as toothless Wolves were tamed 5-0 with Hurst (2), Byrne, Sissons and Skipper Moore scoring the goals to stop the rot and set in motion a steady improvement which saw the team rise to a high-water mark of

4th position in the First Division table two weeks before Christmas. By that stage Hammers had also reached the quarter-finals of the European Cup Winners Cup by defeating La Gantoise of Belgium and Sparta Prague of Czechoslovakia, 2-1 and 3-2 respectively on aggregate.

For reasons best known to themselves, the club decided to make the return home leg against the Belgian part-timers an all-ticket affair which kept the gate down to 24,000. For the record, the increased admission prices were:

    Grand Stand: C Block.................................... 20s.0d.
    Grand Stand: B, D and E Blocks.................... 15s.0d.
    East Terrace and West Enclosure................... 7s.6d.
    North and South Banks.................................. 6s.0d.

It would be nice to say that the fans got value for money, but they had to endure a less than entertaining introduction to European football as the Buffalos of Ghent went home with a 1-1 draw courtesy of a Peters own goal. Although Byrne's leveller just before half-time put them through, the Hammers fans booed and slow-hand-clapped the performance throughout the game. So Boyce's headed goal from a corner at the Stade Jules Otten in the first leg proved crucial. The Belgian minnows from the "City of Flowers" and celebrating their Centenary Year, were the only team applauded off the field at the end of a dismal 90 minutes for the watching Upton Park faithful – 500 of whom followed the team to Ghent – who'd had to pay extra for the privilege.

Between the disappointing performance against the Belgians and the next Cup Winners Cup tie against Sparta, the Hammers hit an irresistible vein of form to have the Boleyn Ground's habitués singing their praises again. Yours truly among them. November was a particularly good month, which after a 1-1 draw with Blackburn Rovers on the 7th, yielded three straight victories against Arsenal at Highbury 3-0 (Hurst, Byrne and Peters), Leeds United 3-1 (Kirkup, Byrne and Peters) and Chelsea at the Bridge 3-0 (Sealey, Peters and Hurst). While the first team were drubbing Arsenal in North London, the reserves – not to be outdone – thrashed the Gunners second-string 7-2 at Upton Park. The Hammers second XI lined up: Dickie, Kirkup, Presland, Dawkins, Bickles, Charles, Redknapp, Bennett, Britt, Dear and Scott. And as the programme notes in the match versus Leeds duly recorded:

"The Gunners went ahead with an early goal and we had a rather unhappy opening ten minutes before settling down to give a brilliant exhibition. Trevor Dawkins paved the way to our equaliser which was netted by Martin Britt and then Dear put us in front with a shot over the keeper's head as he was falling. Arsenal got back into the game to draw level, but we went in at the interval 3-2 ahead thanks to a somewhat fortuitous penalty duly converted by Dear. That more or less finished Arsenal, as the second-half was very much 'one-way-traffic'. Dear completed his hat-trick to round off a great afternoon's work, with Tony Scott (2) and Harry Redknapp also finding the net to make the final tally 7-2 in our favour.

"Thus the only forward not to score was Peter Bennett, but he could take consolation from the fact that a tremendous header by him rebounded from the bar to give Scott one of his goals". The win kept Iron's reserves top of the Football Combination table above

Johnny Byrne in action against Sparta Prague.

Peterborough United in second.

Interspersed with their fine pre-Christmas First Division form, were Hammers two ECWC ties with crack Czechs Sparta Prague, against whom the team finally proved their European credentials. Drawn at home first, Hammers (without Bobby Moore who was hospitalised due to testicular cancer) huffed and puffed against the defensive-minded Czechs in the first half, but finally breached their "Iron Curtain" after the break.

The East Europeans packed their defence with nine men – sometimes ten – and did not stand on ceremony, inflicting a catalogue of gruesome fouls on Byrne, Sissons, Peters and Hurst before they eventually cracked under relentless pressure in the 59th minute. From yet another free-kick, the ball was cleared to full-back Bond, the West Ham special agent with a licence to score, who struck a thunderous first-time left-foot volley from all of 25 yards high into the North Bank end goal. In an effort to waste time, the harassed Czechs kicked the ball over the roof of the Chicken Run four times, but goalkeeper Kramerius, who had saved his side time and time again, was finally beaten again in the 82nd minute when Sealey, who had his first effort blocked, slammed in the rebound from close in. But would two goals be enough? wondered the 27,590 hoarse-throated fans who'd witnessed their team's wonderful win.

They got the answer soon enough when Sissons put West Ham 3-0 ahead on aggregate after just 14 minutes of the return leg at the National Stadium in Prague to stifle the chant of "Sparta,

Ronnie Boyce

John Sissons

Sparta" as 45,000 Czech fans were silenced by the discipline, determination and, above all, the bravery of Hammers' all-English team as they triumphed over some savage tackling and indifferent decisions by the Bulgarian referee to reach the quarter-finals, despite losing the tie 2-1. On the team's victorious return to Blighty they went straight into a First Division clash with West London rivals, Fulham, just three days later at Upton Park, who they defeated 2-0 (Byrne 2) to secure a season's high-water mark position of fourth in the First Division table. The XI showed but one change from the team that triumphed in Prague, Brabrook for Sealey, lining up: Standen (who crucially saved a penalty against the Czechs), Bond, Burkett, Bovington, Brown, Peters, Brabrook, Boyce, Byrne, Hurst and Sissons.

The reserves, meanwhile, were still topping the Football Combination table under the auspices of coach Ernie Gregory, but the bubble had burst for the Youth Team after three years of unprecedented success.

An article by Trevor Smith (who else?) gave a fair indication of what was going on among the Upton Park youth ranks earlier in the season: "A crowd of almost 3,000 spectators were at Upton Park on Monday evening (28/9/'64) to see Hammers Colts in action against Crystal Palace in a Southern Junior Floodlit Cup first round replay match. Hammers won 2-1. But manager Ron Greenwood was not at all happy about the fans attitude towards his youngsters, many of whom left school only this summer. 'If the fans are going to watch these games, they must be ready to give these very young, inexperienced players a fair chance', said Greenwood on Tuesday.

"The West Ham chief was angry at the noisy reaction of some of the crowd on Monday when Hammers struggled to win against an average Palace team.

"Said Greenwood: 'Those fans who groaned and jeered when mistakes were made, were quite obviously judging our present youth line-up on the teams we have had in the past two or three seasons. This is quite unfair. Our current side is in its first year, half of the players were still at school only a matter of weeks ago and they are at the very beginning of learning their profession. The crowd must appreciate this. They must show the tolerance the position justifies and realise that this youth team football goes in three year cycles and that therefore a side in its first season as a team has a lot to learn'.

"He added: 'Our lads will almost certainly get a beating from some clubs whose team is largely made up of players in their last season as Youths. Players who in fact are really mature. This is how it ought to be, too, if anyone is to learn anything'.

"West Ham's own highly successful Youth Team reached the end of its three year life-span last season (1963-64), only goalkeeper Colin Mackleworth and winger Harry Redknapp from that squad are still eligible to play in youth soccer. But three seasons of phenomenal success have educated Upton Park fans into expecting great things from youth matches – as shown by Monday's attendance of 2,900. Now these enthusiastic West Ham followers must readjust their expectations if their support is to be of value to Hammers' new youngsters".

Greenwood was certainly right to predict that the club's new crop of youngsters would "get some beatings", as they tumbled out in the early rounds of the LFA Cup, 0-3 to Spurs; the SJFC 1-5, also to Spurs; the FA Youth Cup, 0-7 to Arsenal and the London Youth Cup, 1-2 to Millwall.

Prior to the commencement of the 1964-65 season some changes had been made in the behind-the-scenes administration of the Youth Section. The decision of Tom Russell to accept a lecturing appointment in Uganda left a staff vacancy, as Tom had been official-in-charge of our Youth Section team which competed in the South East Counties League. Fortunately a ready replacement was at hand, as the retirement of John Lyall from playing made him available to take over the post. As a qualified FA coach, John was able to assist in that field as well as supplementing the office staff, having served in the office as part of his groundstaff duties prior to becoming a full pro in May 1957, so he was no stranger to the job.

In addition to ably assisting Chief Representative Wally St. Pier in their special duties with the Youth Section, Tom was largely instrumental in bringing Bobby Moore to West Ham as a 16-year-old in 1956.

At around the time young Bobby was preparing to leave the Tom Hood School in Leytonstone, East London, he received a message to go to see a sportsmaster of a Hackney school – Tom Russell. When they made the meet the conversation went along the lines of: "Hello Bobby, I've seen you play in schools matches quite a lot and I think West Ham would be prepared to give you coaching. Are you interested?" To quote from his book, *My Story by Bobby Moore,* he replied "Interested, I was over the moon. Just as it seemed I was being passed over in favour of all the brilliant youngsters in schools football in East London. My big moment had come".

WEST HAM UNITED

LIGA DEPORTIVA ALAJEULENSE
ERNIE GREGORY TESTIMONIAL MATCH
MONDAY 10th OCTOBER 1960 at 7.30 p.m.

No. 16

OFFICIAL PROGRAMME 6ᵈ

Helliar & Sons, Plaistow, E.13

WEST HAM UNITED

FLUMINENSE
(RIO DE JANEIRO — BRAZIL)
MONDAY 25th APRIL 1960 at 7.30 p.m.

No. 53

OFFICIAL PROGRAMME 6ᵈ

WEST HAM UNITED

LIVERPOOL Colts
FOOTBALL ASSOCIATION YOUTH CUP
FINAL : SECOND LEG
SATURDAY 25th MAY 1963 at 7.30 p.m.

No. 57

OFFICIAL PROGRAMME 6ᵈ

Helliar & Sons, London, E.13

WEST HAM UNITED

BOLEYN GROUND : LONDON E.13

No. 23

OLYMPIAKOS
EUROPEAN CUP WINNERS CUP
First Round : First Leg
WEDNESDAY 24th NOVEMBER 1965 at 7.30 p.m.

OFFICIAL PROGRAMME 6ᵈ

WEST HAM UNITED
BOLEYN GROUND : LONDON E.13

No. 42

REAL ZARAGOZA CLUB DEPORTIVO
EUROPEAN CUP WINNERS CUP
Semi-Final : First Leg
WEDNESDAY 7th APRIL at 7.30 p.m.

OFFICIAL PROGRAMME 6d

WEST HAM UNITED
BOLEYN GROUND : LONDON E.13

No. 45

1 F.C. MAGDEBURG
EUROPEAN CUP WINNERS CUP
Second Round : First Leg
WEDNESDAY 2nd MARCH 1966 at 7.30 p.m.

OFFICIAL PROGRAMME 6d

WEST HAM UNITED
BOLEYN GROUND : LONDON E.13

No. 47

WEST BROMWICH ALBION
FOOTBALL LEAGUE CUP : FINAL (First Leg)
WEDNESDAY 9th MARCH 1966 at 7.30 p.m.

OFFICIAL PROGRAMME 6d

WEST HAM UNITED
BOLEYN GROUND : LONDON E.13

No. 53

BVB 09 BORUSSIA DORTMUND
EUROPEAN CUP WINNERS CUP   Semi-Final : First Leg
TUESDAY 5th APRIL 1966 at 7.30 p.m.

OFFICIAL PROGRAMME 6d

So had West Ham's, but they took their time in fully signing him up. Moore began his football career playing for South Park Boys, in the Ilford League. His first honour was captaining Barking Primary School to winning the Crisp Shield in 1951. He then progressed as part of both the Leyton Schools team and Essex Boys. A local scout attached to West Ham by the name of Jack Turner was alerted to Moore's talent by the said sportsmaster, Tom Russell, and sent in a report: "Looked fairly useful, but wouldn't set the world on fire". Which is exactly what he went on to do, of course. Moore, in any event, was invited to attend West Ham under their new youth policy for training on Tuesday and Thursday evenings at the Boleyn Ground under the tuition of some pros like Malcolm Allison, Noel Cantwell, John Bond and Malcolm Musgrove. In August 1956 he signed amateur forms for Hammers and in October made his debut for West Ham Colts against QPR. The rest, as they say, is history. So West Ham United FC and England have a lot to thank that Hackney sports teacher for.

As for the club's 1964 class of young hopefuls, they did eventually settle down to form a useful unit and comfortably secure a top half position in the South Eastern Counties League table with newcomers like Barry Simmons, Trevor Hartley, Frank Lampard (Snr.), Roger Cross and Trevor Brooking to the fore.

In the absence of any further positive news on the start date for work to commence on the proposed new extension to the West Stand, there was a snippet to brighten the mid-winter gloom when it was announced in the local press that a new feature was set to be in place for the home match with Stoke City at Upton Park on Saturday, January 1, 1965 on the Cearns-built structure... A magnificent red neon sign bearing the name West Ham United FC in two foot-high letters on the front of the West Stand over the forecourt entrance to the ground facing Green Street. Said Secretary Eddie Chapman: "This is something several other clubs have already. We intend that the sign should be alight whenever we play here". And why not? We deserved to have our name in lights. We were the FA Cup holders, after all. The new innovation didn't prove a lucky omen though, Stoke won 1-0.

Talking of the FA Cup, I have good reason to remember West Ham's first defence of the famous old trophy against Birmingham City in the Third Round of the competition on January 2, 1965 at Upton Park. I can particularly recall the match because I only saw half of it. I was so late getting to the ground, I had to forsake my usual position on the North Bank, only managing to gain admittance in the South Bank – at half-time! I can't remember exactly why I was so late, but I have an idea it was because I'd overslept. Possibly because of a hangover, as I'd just discovered beer at the time. Certainly my favourites played as though they were the "worse for wear" as they were 2-0 down until Johnny Byrne reduced the deficit four minutes before the break and at least ten minutes before I'd managed to get through the turnstiles.

This was the first time I'd ever stood on the South Bank and the first thing I noticed was a distinct lack of atmosphere compared to the North Bank. I put this down to the fact that the roof only extended half way over the terrace and despite the obvious lack of protection this gave its inhabitants in wet weather, the acoustics were nowhere near as loud as they were on the cavernous North Bank. Here the noise seemed to escape upwards instead of creating all around sound. The decibels seemed to be only half the volume of those at the other end of the ground. Of more importance, however, was the fact that we were 2-1 in arrears and, according to the spectators around me, had been totally outplayed in the first-half by City's slickers.

Even as the Blues' fans bellowed out yet another rendition of the Brummies' FA Cup anthem: "*Keep Right on to the End of the Road*". I wondered if they had tumbled Hammers' secret ploy, which was common knowledge, but never talked about at Upton Park. You see, during this era the team used to much prefer kicking into the North Bank in the second-half. To do this they had to first ensure they were the first team out on the pitch before the game and head towards the North Bank to kick in. If West Ham won the toss, they would always elect to defend that end in the first-half. If they lost the toss, the away team would invariably decide to stay put to defend the South Bank end during the first-half, unwittingly buying into West Ham's *modus operandi*. I breathed a sigh of relief as the Hammers turned to the right to defend the South Bank as they came out of the tunnel to commence the second-half and try to pull the game out of the bag. It was Upton Park's best kept secret that the players were convinced that the North Bank, like the Kop was to Liverpool, was worth a goal if the chips were down. And they certainly were on this occasion, two one down, in fact.

There was also an added omen, because when West Ham defeated the then just Birmingham FC in the Sixth Round at Upton Park in 1933, they'd kicked into the North Bank (then uncovered) in the second-half and created the shock of the season when winning 4-0, despite the fact that the Hammers were then a Second Division club and their opponents were in the First.

It certainly seemed that the omens were on Irons' side again as they started the second-half like a team transformed.

As Trevor Smith reported in the *Ilford Recorder*: "For five frantic minutes after the restart, Birmingham were on the rack. Their much-publicised defensive plan was literally torn up and flung in their faces as West Ham turned on a supercharged display of attacking soccer.

"All five forwards engaged in a furious, baffling bout of diversionary running and switching that left hapless Birmingham vainly attempting to compute through which of the numerous gaps the final thrust was coming. Ironically, the equaliser after 50 minutes was right out of the 'Traditional English Football Handbook'. The spectacular flying Sealey tore hell-for-leather down his wing after a gem of a Boyce pass, rounded full-back Green, rammed in a taking low cross – and there was the burly Hurst bursting past Hennessey and in front of Schofield to snap home a goal in the complete striking leader fashion. Tom Lawton never did it better than this one. Pandemonium followed as Hurst turned away, combining a restraining

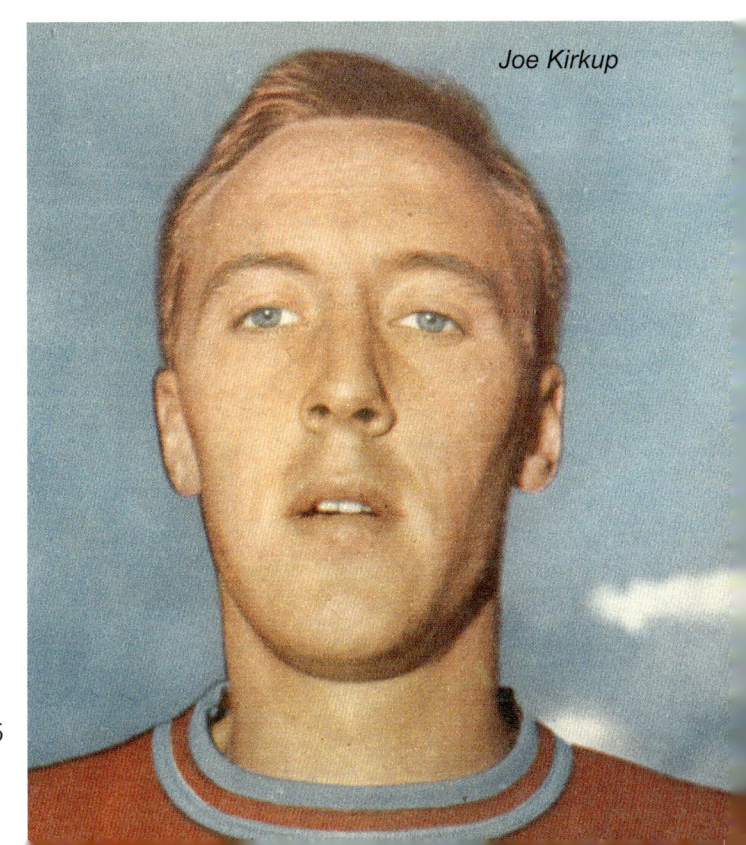

Joe Kirkup

Enter the Gladiators (2): Moore emerges from the Upton Park tunnel followed by Johnny Byrne and Eddie Bovington, who looks full of intent. In the players' pen are Brian Dear (clapping), Eddie Presland (above), Tony Scott, Martin Britt, Bobby Howe, Peter Bennett, Trevor Dawkins and John Dryden (to the right), John Lyall (leaning on newspaper).

leap with the triumphant clenched fist gladiatorial salute. Quite, quite clearly nothing in the world could save Birmingham now.

"The *coup de grâce* came soon after. Tony Scott, surely back to stay after this classic exhibition of tactical skill, stranded the giant Lynn on rather less than a tanner to send Byrne dancing away on the left. Byrne, in turn, dribbled past a defender, drew the defence, and cut back a low centre accurately to the waiting boot of Hurst, who belted it high into goal with awesome power.

"After this, the marvel was that Birmingham survived further goals until the last minute. Hurst, played clear through by Byrne and Sissons, miscued with only Schofield to beat.

"The final score was placed more in perspective when Byrne pivoted and fired in a hot one which Schofield could only push away to Sissons who hammered his first shot against Schofield's brave dive and then nonchalantly crashed the second chance home". Thanks, Trevor.

When West Ham drew Chelsea in the Fourth Round at Upton Park the powers-that-be immediately decided to make the tie all ticket and reduced their official safety limit from 38,500 to 37,000. "We'd rather play safe than be greedy", explained Secretary Eddie Chapman. He also revealed that the club was to make a full allocation to all 5,000 members of their thriving Supporters Club. "With Chelsea so near we felt that many of their fans would be here in the queues, so we have made sure that all of their members would get priority", said Ed.

As it was, fans queued overnight to make sure of a ticket, but many were left disappointed, leaving West Ham lamenting the relative smallness of their ground and boss Greenwood to declare: "We could sell this tie to 60,000 fans if we had room".

Going to the game on the back of a 3-2 defeat at Spurs (Byrne and Sissons) and a 3-2 home win over Burnley (Boyce, Bond and Byrne), the Hammers were the bookies favourites by dint

The long road to Wembley

Say it with flowers. Above left: Ken Brown leads the team out for 'The Battle of Prague'. Above: Bond and Peters clear their lines. Below: Under seige, the Hammers survive the second half to go through to the next stage.

Alan Sealey takes on Arsenal's Bill McCullough watched by George Armstrong.

of their 3-0 win at Stamford Bridge in November, when they knocked the Blues off the top of the First Division. But this was the FA Cup.

That game certainly was a lesson in tactics for Chelsea's chasers. At the end, the Blue's young Scottish defender, Eddie McCreadie spontaneously clapped Hammers off the field. "You've given us a real lesson" he said to the astonished West Ham players.

When asked could Hammers do it again? Ron Greenwood replied: "We were surprised Chelsea did not tumble what we were doing. Maybe they still haven't". But would not comment further.

Having been preceded by a perfectly observed minutes' silence for Great Britain's inspirational war-time leader and former Prime Minister, Sir Winston Churchill, the match began in a somewhat sombre mood with both teams wearing black armbands to show their respects to a man who had helped to save these Isles from Nazi tyranny. But within ten minutes Chelsea had scored what would prove to be the only goal of the game.

As ever, we'll let that doyen among football reporters, Trevor Smith, explain how it happened in the contemporary match report in the following weeks' edition of the *Ilford Recorder*: "Ken Brown, rushing to reinforce Kirkup's policing of a Tambling burst into the middle, was pulled up for obstruction. It was a debatable decision, since Kirkup had already turned upfield in possession but referee Smith probably felt stern action like this would stop any chance of a rough-house. From the free-kick Tambling blasted in a shot which was deflected and Standen did well to change course in mid-air and palm it round off an upright. The corner was cleared away into touch. From the throw-in another half-clearance led to a Murray shot. Standen dived to cover the near post – and was down there at full-length as the ball hit a defender and whipped away across the prostrate goalkeeper's body. Heroically, Standen stuck up a knee to deflect the shot out of goal. Bridges, Brown and Tambling fused together in a fight to get a touch. The latter won, and Chelsea were ahead".

Ken Brown claimed: "I wasn't conscious of moving back as I saw the ball hit Jim's legs. It came out in a high arc and I thought 'I can get this'. There were two Chelsea forwards with me and there was only about six inches in it at the death. If I had size 14 feet I reckon I'd have touched it before Bobby Tambling – that's how near a thing it was. I was sick".

And Standen's view: "I saw this shot coming in after the throw-in and dived to my near post. I'm certain I would have held it, but the ball hit somebody, Eddie Bov' I think, and was deflected across me. I was already down then, but I stuck my knee up and was well pleased when I diverted the ball out again. It could have gone anywhere... over the bar, round the post, or even in the goal. I was delighted when it went out. I jumped up, but before I could move further, Bobby Tambling had rushed in and toed it in".

So there you have it, the complete anatomy of the goal that knocked West Ham out of the cup 52 years ago.

How West Ham could have done with a Churchillian speech at half-time. Maybe they got one, but it was destined not to be West Ham's day as they lost their grip on the trophy.

Martin Britt (9) hammers home a header in the 4-2 victory over Sheffield Wednesday.

One man who did give a speech after the game was Chelsea's boss Tommy Docherty, who said: "Some teams you can come to and play your own game without any worry. You can't do that with West Ham. We like meeting West Ham for this reason, because it means you always learn something from the game. It was typical of cup-tie football. West Ham had more of the early play, but we got the goal from a double deflection. That's what you expect in cup football". Chelsea had tumbled.

But the chastened Hammers still had plenty to play for with the upcoming ECWC quarter-final with Lausanne foremost in their minds. Before the victorious visit to Switzerland, where Hammers scored a precious 2-1 win with goals from Dear and Byrne, there was a sad decline in League form however, with six defeats out of the next seven First Division games. Relegation form.

Thankfully, help was at hand with the introduction of a burly figure from the reserves – Brian "Stag" Dear. In the last ten League matches he scored the same amount of goals, including an incredible five goal haul in the space of 20 minutes either side of half-time against West Bromwich Albion on Good Friday at Upton Park. The quickest-ever nap hand scored in a First Division fixture.

It was only right and proper that Stag's goal fest was against Albion, as their own W. G. "Ginger" Richardson had scored four times in five minutes against the Hammers at Upton Park on November 7, 1931. A feat, like Brian's, that is still recorded in the *Guinness Book of Records*. But we are getting ahead of ourselves. Before Stag's Good Friday goal glut, Hammers still had to overcome Swiss minnows Lausanne in the second-leg at Upton Park and then the Star-studded Spanish Cup winners Real Zaragoza in the first leg of the resultant semi-final at the same venue.

That both were dispatched by a one goal margin in close run encounters gave further evidence of Dear's burgeoning talent as he hammered the final decisive tally in the 4-3 (Tacchella o.g., Dear 2, Peters) victory over the Swiss in the 89th minute and then the first in the 2-1 (Dear, Byrne) win over the Spaniards before a packed crowd of 35,000.

The 30,000 odd Cockneys who gathered at Upton Park expecting their favourites return clash versus Lausanne to be a formality received a big shock – to such an extent that they were sportingly applauding the gallant Swiss at the final whistle. Although progressing to the semies on an aggregate of 6-7, the Hammers could hardly have anticipated the sheer determination of the "Lausanne Lambs" who turned out to be lions in a thrilling, roller-coaster tie.

In-control Irons could have changed ends with a five goal lead – but the Swiss defenders employed all means, woodwork, legs, bodies and feet to prevent West Ham scoring. Then, with eight minutes of this frustrating first-half left, Lausanne broke away to score through Dutch international Kerkhoffs and drew level on aggregate. Unluckily for them, full-back Tacchella deflected a dangerous cross from Sealey into his own net and in the very last minute of this half Dear gave his side a 4-2 aggregate lead after Kunzi had dived bravely to parry another Sealey cross. With these two goals in their locker, Hammers looked to be cruising to victory, but, again, the Swiss retaliated and left winger Hertig took advantage of a defensive mix-up to bring the men from Lake Geneva back into the match.

After struggling to regain their earlier form, Hammers scored again in the 60th minute when Peters headed home a Sealey corner. But still the visitors came back and with ten minutes left the fighting Swiss were rewarded when Eschmann executed a fantastic overhead kick to beat Standen. With just two minutes of this pulsating contest to go, however, Dear struck again – finally knocking the stuffing out of Lausanne when he converted a Hurst pass.

Before the eagerly awaited clash with Zaragoza, Hammers got "in the mood" with successive First Division victories – a 2-1 home win against Arsenal (Hurst 82, Byrne pen 87) and a 3-2 victory over Aston Villa at Villa Park (Hurst 50, Byrne 58, Dear 63) after being 0-2 down at the break. Then they lost at Leeds 2-1 (Dear 66).

Hopes were still high for the visit of the Spanish though, whose forward line was dubbed "El Magnifico". Two goals ahead after 27 minutes, Hammers were well in control. It was that man Dear again who stunned Zaragoza after only nine minutes. Santos put a high lob against the home bar but Hurst cleared to Sissons, who raced down his wing before crossing with pinpoint accuracy to Dear who was running into the angle of the six-yard box at the far post to give Yarza no chance with a superb diving header at the North Bank end. Fifteen minutes later Hammers shocked Zaragoza again with another goal out of the blue. Moore cleared cleverly to find – of all people – centre-half Ken Brown racing down the right wing – Brown eluded a defender and his centre was swept on by Sissons to Byrne who flashed a beautiful shot on the turn wide of

Bobby Moore leads out the team for the titanic battle with TSV 1860 Munich in the ECWC Final at Wembley.

Bobby Moore exchanges pennants with his Munich counterpart, centre-forward Rudi Brunnenmeier.

Yarza into the net. Zaragoza were rocking and showed it with a succession of nasty fouls – and minutes later Peters almost made it 3-0, but his header was stopped on the line by Reija.

In the 55th minute, however, after much pressing by the Spaniards, right-winger Canario hit an upright and seconds later he beat Moore and saw his shot bounce off Standen's body into the net. As the minutes ticked away the crowd began slow-hand-clapping West Ham – but this gesture hardly did justice to another wonderful evening under the Upton Park lights or the skills of the hard, but extremely talented Spaniards. By winning their last four games Hammers managed to finish the domestic season occupying a respectable enough ninth position in the First Division table. Blackpool were defeated 2-1 at Upton Park in the final league game of the campaign thanks to Dear's 14th goal in 13 matches and one from a less likely quarter – long-serving centre-half Ken Brown who equalised Moir's earlier strike for the Tangerines with a powerful header from Sissons' cross in front of the North Bank. Only the second he would ever score. Watched by a crowd of 22,762 to bring the season's average attendance figure to 25,808, the game was quickly forgotten as all thoughts were now focused on the return with Zaragoza in Spain five days later, apart from an amusing incident when the patrons of the Chicken Run good humouredly serenaded a heavily bearded police sergeant with a splendid rendition of "I'm Henry the Eighth, I am" as he bravely if somewhat foolishly patrolled the length of their patch!

It's doubtful if there has ever been a performance by and English side on foreign soil to match the courage and determination displayed by gallant West Ham United in Zaragoza on the evening of April 28, 1965, which even eclipsed the heroics of Prague four months earlier.

Looking on with pride in the 28,000 crowd at the Estudio de la Romareda was a small 350 plus contingent of Hammers' fans who paid £75 per head for the privilege. They travelled with the West Ham United Supporters Club under the auspices of Secretary Syd Russell who had held the post for the previous 17 years on charter flights with the British Eagle airline and certainly got their money's worth on this historic night in the club's history.

It was the Hammers magnificent defence – brilliantly marshalled by the blonde colossus Bobby Moore – which took the honours for an unlikely victory and quick-silver Sissons who netted the 54th minute equaliser.

As the *Ilford Recorder* duly reported: "It was the mercurial Sissons, racing sweetly through the middle for a finely-judged forward pass from Brian Dear, who squeezed home the vital goal to give Hammers a 3-2 aggregate victory. During the first half, however, West Ham had Moore to thank, for when Zaragoza launched their heart-stopping assaults, it was only Moore who kept Hammers' heads above water.

"It was one-way traffic, with Zaragoza throwing everything into attack and West Ham defending resolutely – but after 27 minutes Standen brilliantly saved a header from Marvelino. He could only turn the ball to Lapetra, and the winger put the Spaniards level on aggregate.

"The small, faithful band of spectators now thought that the dam must surely burst, but the Hammers clung on to their toe-hold – although they received a fortunate escape when Lapetra blazed over the top in the 79th minute. 'Then came Sissons' sudden, dramatic equaliser and Zaragoza were visibly stunned for a few minutes. They soon regained their composure, however,

Alan Sealey flies through the air with the greatest of ease, but, unfortunately handles the ball instead of heading it home.

and Dutch referee Leo Horn twice ignored Spanish appeals for penalties". West Ham United: Standen, Kirkup, Burkett, Peters, Brown, Moore, Sealey, Boyce, Hurst, Dear, Sissons.

Now all the "Over the moon" Hammers team and fans had to do was await the winners of the other semi-final play-off in Zurich between Turino (Italy) and TSV 1860 Munich to discover their opponents in the Final at Wembley on the historic evening of Wednesday, May 19, 1965. The fact that Munich defeated Turino 2-0 was of little consequence to Hammers fans – with confidence "flying so high" even the prospect of facing Real Madrid wouldn't have daunted them. All anyone was interested in now was being at Wembley as the clamour for tickets began.

Although it is over 50 years ago now, I can recall that tickets were far more readily available than for the previous year's FA Cup Final between West Ham and Preston North End.

With West Ham's paltry allocation of just 15,000 tickets and something like 60,000 East Londoners clamouring for them, West Ham's then Club Secretary Eddie Chapman, obviously found himself in an impossible situation.

Interviewed six days before the West Ham versus Munich final in the *Ilford Recorder*, Eddie revealed: "We were given a much bigger allocation this time". But tantalisingly did not reveal what that allocation was. But went on to add: "We expected something like a maximum attendance of 75,000 for the Cup Winners' Cup Final, but it seems that the game has caught the public's imagination.

"Wembley told us earlier in the week that they had sold out their remaining tickets. They asked us to return any of our allocation that are unsold... but from the requests we've had already, it is pretty obvious we will not have any to send back". He concluded.

Last year in the final season at the Boleyn, I met up with an old pal of mine who I hadn't seen since those days, Jeff Cardy, who used to contribute to *Over Land and Sea*. He reminded me that I got his ticket for the final and also for three other pals of mine, Geoff Thompson, Geoff Brodie and Mike Berry, who all, like me, lived at Ardleigh Green in those days. Then the coin dropped. I remembered that I'd seen an advert in a travel agents window offering tickets for sale. So I collected the money from them at the old British Railway Club in Helen Road, Gidea Park and we all went to the match together. I think They were 7/6d each. And what a night it was. I particularly remember thinking how I'd never seen so many West Ham fans together in one place. Everywhere was awash with claret and blue. I recall, too, how friendly the German fans were and swapping pennants, badges and flags with them. I believe 9,000 travelled over from Germany. I reckon West Ham's allocation was about 50,000. But a lot more would have got tickets like I did and on the black market.

So I was one of the lucky 100,000 who duly turned up at Wembley to witness a textbook performance from two teams which has probably influenced every coaching manual published in the intervening 52 years.

We all know West Ham ultimately won 2-0 to send the East End into raptures that night of nights and all the football purists among the many millions who witnessed the spectacle around the world on TV, too.

We all know Alan Sealey's two goals ensured him immortality in football folklore, so what's the point in rewriting the same match report for the umpteenth time here, hoping for another angle, a new slant, when its all been done before. But what of the architect of this unlikely triumph, master coach Ron Greenwood. That could be interesting.

When I was working for *Hammers News Magazine* as its advertising sales manager and historical writer, the editor, Kirk Blows, asked me to make Ron Greenwood the subject of the popular monthly feature "Vintage Claret", which I had penned every month since January 1993.

As it was a month before the 1998 World Cup was due to commence and both Frank Lampard and Rio Ferdinand were in the running to go, I thought this was a good opportunity for me and the magazine, as I had always harboured ambitions to interview the great man. But I was also sceptical as I'd heard he no longer gave interviews.

As soon as he picked up the phone at his Brighton home, I realised that my fears were well founded. "No, no I no longer give interviews", he interjected my request.

"But Ron", I replied. "Can I just ask you one question?" "Well, it seems like you are going to anyway", he replied.

Didn't the great Dukla Prague and Czechoslovakian wing-half Josef Masopust, tip Hammers to win a major European competition "within the next two years" after his side had defeated

Early action involving Sissons (right) and Petar Radenkovic (left), Munich's Yugoslavian goalkeeper.

West Ham 2-1 on aggregate in the Final of the North American Challenge Cup in New York in 1963? I ventured.

Silence and then begrudging laughter from the other end of the line.

"Yes, he was spot on with his prediction. We defeated TSV Munich 1860 in the European Cup Winners' Cup Final 2-0 at Wembley two years later!" He exclaimed, clearly warming to the subject.

The interview I then proceeded to conduct with Mr. Greenwood duly appeared in the *Hammers News Magazine* dated April 1998 and as it is the last interview he ever granted, we reproduce in verbatim here:

"Former West Ham and England manager Ron Greenwood, the tactical genius who put the Hammers on the map both at home and abroad, and guided his country to the 1982 World Cup Finals in Spain, has a message for current English boss Glen Hoddle prior to the team's departure to the 1998 World Cup Finals in France.

"He's got to be his own man and ignore the media and public who'll try and pick his squad for him. He's got to stand by his own beliefs, as I'm sure he will. No one knows the strengths and weaknesses of the players at his disposal better than himself".

What about Rio Ferdinand? Isn't there a direct parallel between his possible call-up and the late selection of Bobby Moore by Walter Winterbottom for the 1962 World Cup Finals in Chile?

"That's what I mean, I don't want to be quoted saying who Glen should be taking to France, I'm out of it all now. Besides, anything I say could be blown up out of all proportion by the national newspapers.

"Bobby was older when he was picked in 1962 after my recommendation to Walter Winterbottom. Maybe Glenn will take a chance and take young Ferdinand out there and maybe he won't risk it. It is his decision entirely!

"I've seen Ferdinand and his young colleague Frank Lampard Jnr. a couple of times this season and was very impressed with both of them. They have superb natural talent and could make it at the highest level. But it's a pity that they haven't got a really senior pro to help them on the field – someone like Trevor Brooking, Billy Bonds or Alvin Martin to encourage them and point out any errors.

"As long as they show 100% commitment and enthusiasm for their country at whatever level

Bobby Moore lifts the trophy with (L-R) Kirkup, Sealey, Peters, Hurst, Boyce, Sissons and Dear.

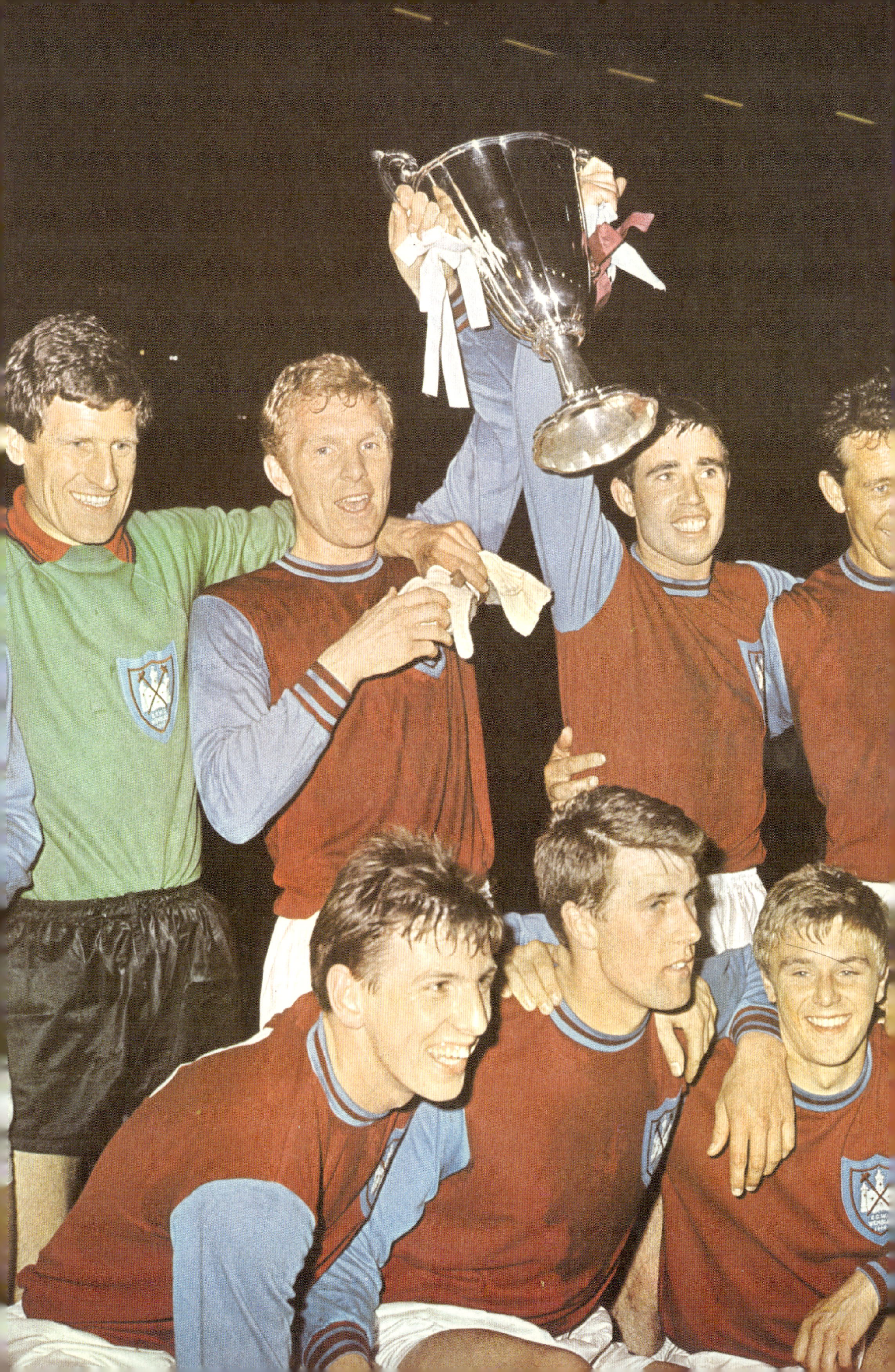

they've been chosen, they'll get their chance in the full side.

"Look at Geoff Hurst. He was patient in 1966 and when Jimmy Greaves picked up an injury he came in with dramatic results".

It's a shame that West Ham are not as well represented at England international level as they were in the mid-sixties, I ventured, when Moore, Hurst, Martin Peters and Johnny Byrne were an integral part of the set-up.

"Yes, well I'd brought all of those players through at either England Youth, or Under-23 level when I managed both of those representative sides in the late '50s and early '60s".

If Byrne, who Ron tagged the "English Di Stefano" in reference to the great Argentinian forward who also starred for Spain and Real Madrid, hadn't got injured against Scotland at Wembley in 1965, West Ham might have had four players in the 1966 World Cup winning side, I suggested.

"Football's full of 'Ifs', but, yes, Budgie was unfortunate in that respect, he could have played a role. But the final was still very much a West Ham thing".

Ron broke the world transfer record to bring Budgie to West Ham for £65,000 in 1962, but that couldn't happen now (1998), could it?

"No, that's why it's so important that the club continue to develop home-grown talent and bring through players of the calibre of Lampard and Ferdinand, as I'm sure Harry Redknapp and Frank Lampard Snr. will.

"In the wake of the Bosman ruling, there's so much skulduggery now with players' agents making money the main criteria. Today it's all about making money. But good luck to the players if they can get it. I only wish the lads under me could have earned more."

What was the secret of his success in making West Ham a renowned force in the 60s by winning the FA Cup in 1964 and the ECWC a year later?

"To be fair, Ted Fenton had done a good job in getting the club into the First Division in 1958 and I inherited a lot of good players off of him.

"Most importantly, they were all eager to learn and appreciated the advice that was passed onto me by Walter Winterbottom – 'Look outside your own back yard to widen your horizons'."

In addition to Johnny Byrne, Ron also signed winger Peter Brabrook, who had played for England in the 1958 World Cup finals in Sweden. Transferred in a protracted £33,000 deal from Chelsea, he completed Ron's successful playing squad.

Was the decision to compete in the International Soccer League in the States in the summer of 1963 against top class continental opposition like Dukla Prague, Górnik, and Recife of Brazil a major stepping stone to success?

"Yes, we learned more that summer than we would have done in five European campaigns about how the game was evolving around the world".

Looking back, Ron's efforts as national manager to win World Cup glory in Spain '82 compared better than some more recent attempts and he remained philosophical 16 years after the event.

Badly hampered by injuries to two of his key players, Kevin Keegan and Trevor Brooking – the latter's two unforgettable goals against Hungary in Budapest doing so much to put England on track for Spanish qualification – Ron's England nevertheless returned home undefeated having

NEWHAM RECORDER
and BARKING RECORDER

EAST HAM

NO. 3475
Registered as a Newspaper

THURSDAY MAY 20th 1965

FIVEPENCE
The Voice of East Ham

TENNIS & CRICKET
Complete range of equipment and clothing by all leading manufacturers.
The Ajax Sports Co. Ltd.
291-3 High Road, Ilford
Telephone Ajax at ILF 0604

PENGUIN AMERICAN
1 HOUR CLEANING
LEY STREET, OPPOSITE
STATE PARADE, BA

| Win £300 this week— see page 6 | POLICEMAN ON MURDER CHARGE —PAGE THREE | Bandits miss £15,000 in pay day snatch —PAGE SEVEN | Gravedigger goes mod. to mohican —PAGE TEN |

LAST NIGH
HAMME
MATCH

SEALEY'S GOALS WIN CUP

'Europe' triumph

By TREVOR SMITH

WEMBLEY, Wednesday

HAMMERS have done it! Before a delirious capacity crowd here tonight they have become only the second British club to put their name on the European Cup Winners Cup. Fantastic scenes followed their 2-0 win over Munich 1860.

The West Ham players raced around the vast stadium proudly bearing the handsome trophy.

On the terraces there was a swaying mass of claret and blue flags, streamers and banners. Skipper Bobby Moore, the superb captain - general of a great victory, seized the cup and flung it high in the air in undisguised delight.

A wide smile

Young East Ham - born Brian Dear found a Munich blue and white flag from somewhere, and ran and ran and ran, waving it wildly like a man possessed. Ken Brown bore a huge wooden hammer painted claret and blue.

And the man all East London will today hail as a hero, Alan Sealey, contented himself with a smile as wide as the Thames at Woolwich.

For it was Sealey, married to a local girl just four days ago, who lifted West Ham to this new, highest pinnacle with a heart-stopping two-goals-in-two-minutes burst in the second half.

Before this sensational moment the game had shifted and fluctuated swiftly as the well-drilled Germans fought a splendidly conceived campaign and refused to panic as Hammers fluffed their chances.

But even clever, gallant Munich had no counter to Sealey's searing two minutes —and in the final reckoning were lucky to get away so lightly.

West Ham opened purposefully and in the first minute Alan Sealey was only stopped breaking through on the German left by a blatant foul.

The free kick, however, went straight into the arms of the Munich goalkeeper Radenkovic. Within a minute Radenkovic lay injured after colliding with Brian Dear as the West Ham man headed over from a Hurst cross.

Both sides were playing at half pace as they tried to feel out weaknesses. The first real chance came to West Ham after nine minutes when Dear got through on the right and left Sissons

● See back page

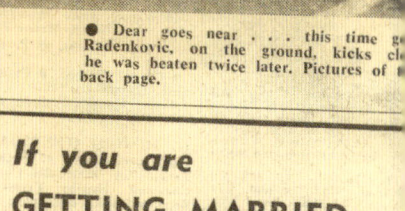

● Sealey, the two-goal hero, tussles with the Munich left-back, Wagner.

● Dear goes near... this time Radenkovic, on the ground, kicks cle he was beaten twice later. Pictures o back page.

Protesting tenants start a row in the council chamber

By DENNIS GORDON

THERE were angry scenes in Newham Council chamber on Tuesday when irate council tenants shouted protests about rent increases which had just been aprroved by the Council.

The Mayor, Cllr. Terence McMillan, three times threatened to expel people from the public gallery to maintain order.

When the meeting was closed people in the gallery shouted abuse at councillors. Other tenants button - holed councillors as they left the Chamber and told them personally of their complaints. A large crowd gathered outside the Town Hall protesting to coun-

formed Newham Council Tenants' Association presented the mayor with a petition protesting about the increases.

Members of the Tenants' Association were responsible for heckling the council, Mr. Ray Offley of Plaistow, one of the organisers told me: "We have not finished yet. The next step will be to picket the housing committee with posters.

"So far most of our members are in West Ham but our activities are snowballing and we expect dissatisfied East Ham tenants will join us soon."

Also protesting at the meeting

crescent, East Ham, showered councillors with leaflets saying "Stop the Civic Centre —cut the rates —save our £2 million."

Notification of the rent increases—due to come into effect at the end of this month—were sent to the council's 22,000 tenants by post. They were also informed how a rebate system would work.

No increases will be more than 7s. 6d. a week and rents in areas scheduled for redevelopment will not go up at

facts of the scheme. Some did not know of the rebate scheme which allowed rent cuts for people in difficult circumstances.

There was little discussion in council about the proposals. Chairman of the housing committee, Cllr. E. S. C. Kebbel said he "very much regretted" the necessity to increase rents.

He revealed that subsidies of nearly £1½ million were made to Housing Accounts and this placed a very heavy burden on all citizens.

Because of this "the council

If you are GETTING MARRIED THIS SUMME

May we help you with your furnishing problems as CURTAINS, HOUSEHOLD LINENS (blankets, sh pillow cases, towels, etc.), WEDDING GIFTS.

If you will require TERYLENE NET, BROCA VELVETS, or GAY PRINTS for your curtains we be pleased of the opportunity to show you our sele in the furnishing department where you are welcom browse through the stock, either by yourselves or the help of one of our assistants. They will give yo advantage of their experience and knowledge as reg colours and if you have your measurements, how m yards you need.

OUR MAKING-UP SERVICE FOR CURTAINS CARRIED OUT BY EXPERTS. IT CAN SAVE Y HOURS OF WORK WHEN YOU ARE PRESSED TIME. YOU WILL BE SURPRISED HOW INEXPENS IT IS TO HAVE YOUR CURTAINS MADE.

QUILTS, BEDSPREADS, BLANKETS, SHEETS, etc. well over 50 years FAIRHEADS have maintained a rep tion for household linen which is second to none as rega value-for-money and quality. We do not pretend cannot buy "something" at a lower price. But when is setting up home one does not require just "somethin When it comes to BLANKETS, SHEETS, etc., they m be of attractive appearance but they must also be capa of giving you years of use. Our HOUSEHOLD LINE are selected with both these factors in mind. Our bu realises that the appearance of the merchandise mu appeal to you, but it is up to him to see it is back up by sound, dependable quality.

WEDDING GIFTS. Today most young couples prepa a list of presents they would like (it saves getting cruets). Very often this list contains such useful item as TOWELS, TABLECLOTHS, etc. We have a section our LINEN DEPARTMENT especially dressed out w suggestions of this type. Many are in attractive presen tion boxes and prices are over such a wide range tha whether you want to buy a small gift for an acquaintan or one for a near relative, you are bound to find attractive gift at the price you want to pay.

IT'S EASY TO PARK WHEN YOU SHOP AT FAIRHEADS
The multi-storied car park (6d. for 1 hour, 1/- for 4 hours), for 500 cars is immediately behind our store. If you request it our staff will deliver the goods direct to your car

G. J. FAIRHEAD Ltd

conceded just one goal. Drawn in Group Four against France, Czechoslovakia and Kuwait, England beat the French 3-1, the Czechs 2-0 and Kuwait 1-0 to progress to the second round where they were pitched against old enemies and hosts Spain in Group B.

England took on the Germans first in front of 75,000 fans in the magnificent Bernabau Stadium. In a tight, negative encounter, England finished happy with a 0-0 draw. But when the Germans beat Spain 3-1, it left England requiring victory by two clear goals to qualify for the semi-finals.

Ron faced a dilemma over whether to play the nearly fit Brooking and Keegan from the start against the Spaniards or leave them on the bench for use if needed.

Both had been injured and had not yet played any part in the tournament, yet both were potential match winners. It was thought that either player could only last a maximum of 30 minutes, so Ron opted to leave them on the bench.

Ironically, when both were brought on in the 63rd minute with the game at 0-0, the pair missed chances they would surely have scored if fully fit and the match ended goalless. England were out.

"At the end of the day, I had to think of the welfare of the players concerned. Both had been injured and could have suffered permanent damage if I had played them for 90 minutes."

Before the World Cup, Ron had selected three other West Ham players for England in addition to Brooking. Alvin Martin, Alan Devonshire and Paul Goddard were awarded caps and Billy Bonds was twice selected only having to miss out because of injury.

"It probably helped their cause that I was England manager", Ron laughed, "But I don't think any of them let me down, do you?" No, I replied, and Ron never let us down either.

So ended the last ever interview given by Ron Greenwood, the man who transformed a team of also-rans into winners within the space of just two glorious years in the "Silver Sixties".

"And what became of Alan Sealey", the man whose two goals sealed his manager's greatest ever triumph? Well, although he did play another four first team games in the 1966-67 season, he never scored another goal for West Ham after failing to fully recover from a freak training ground accident in August 1965, when he broke a leg during an impromptu game of cricket, just three months after his greatest moment.

It happened when he dashed to retrieve a ball hit by a team mate and ran into a form bench. The next time I saw Alan play after that wondrous night at Wembley was in August 1969 – for my local team Romford against King's Lynn in the Southern League at their Brooklands ground in front of a few hundred fans. Alan scored one of Boro's goals in a 2-1 victory over the Linnets. Another ex-Hammer, Harry Obeney, scored Romford's other goal that day for a welcome win, but there was no disguising how far the name Alan Sealey had slipped down football's ladder in four short years.

Yet in a newspaper feature on Hammers reaching the FA Cup Final in 1980, when asked about his two Wembley winners against Munich, he replied simply: "No sooner done than it's forgotten. It's all fish and chip paper in the morning". But West Ham manager Ron Greenwood was more forthcoming, saying "This was our greatest game, a tremendous advertisement for British football". And added: "I was delighted that Alan was the match-winner. He was a really bubbly character.".

DAILY EX

No. 20,206   THURSDAY MAY 20 1965

Forever blowing bubbl

EAST END GOES WILD AT HAMMERS' CUP VIC

NIGHT OF

PRESS

Weather: Sunny but cool

Price 4d.

—AND THEY SING OUTSIDE THE BOLEYN PUBLIC HOUSE

GLORY

The Queen plays host

From COLIN LAWSON and ARTHUR CHESWORTH

BONN, Wednesday.

IN silvered splendour tonight the Queen gave a banquet to German leaders in a palace poised 1,000ft. above the Rhine.

Wagner never had it so good: this was spectacle on a breathtaking scale.

Four and a half tons of silver and china brought from London gleamed on the tables, backgrounded by tiers of roses and carnations on pink-white marble walls.

The Queen wore yet another stunning dress, Chantilly lace encrusted with pearls and diamonds, set off by necklace and tiara of sapphires and diamonds, and ...with a sash of a...

...ORKS

...ong the banks ...ift river, tens ...of Germans ...atch a display ...ft to dazzle

...he magnificence ...ueen's Petersberg ...ere was a link ...undane affairs. ...as the lobster ...was served, an ...an ante-room ...a portable TV ...ned in to Euro-...sion for the West Ham v. ...unich match at Wembley. ...aide's task was to ...ep football fan Chancellor

PAGE TWO, COL. SIX

EUROPEAN CUP WINNERS' CUP

FINAL TIE

TSV MÜNCHEN 1860
v
WEST HAM UNITED

EMPIRE STADIUM · WEMBLEY
EUROPEAN CUP WINNERS CUP
FINAL TIE
Wednesday May 19, 1965
KICK-OFF 7.30 p.m.
YOU ARE ADVISED TO TAKE UP YOUR POSITION BY 7 P.M.
CHAIRMAN, WEMBLEY STADIUM LTD.
7/6
WEST ENCLOSURE
ENTER TURNSTILE G
ENTRANCE 64
STANDING
TO BE RETAINED (See Plan & Conditions on back)

EMPIRE STADIUM · WEMBLEY
EUROPEAN CUP WINNERS CUP
FINAL TIE
Wednesday May 19, 1965
KICK-OFF 7.30 p.m.
YOU ARE ADVISED TO TAKE UP YOUR POSITION BY 7 P.M.
CHAIRMAN, WEMBLEY STADIUM LTD.
25/-
SOUTH TERRACE
ENTER A
ENTRANCE 32 RIGHT
ROW 15
SEAT 86
TO BE RETAINED (See Plan & Conditions on back)

MAY 19th 1965   **WEMBLEY**   Kick-off 7.30 p.m.
OFFICIAL PROGRAMME   ONE SHILLING

On the last occasion I ever had the pleasure of meeting Alan, at me and my old pal Tony McDonald's *Who's Who of West Ham* book launch in December 1994, two years before his untimely death, I reminded Alan of his old white Ford Anglia car in which he often used to give Ron a lift. "Yeah", he replied, "It seems a long time ago now". But Alan never considered his display against Munich as a career best, plumping instead for his contribution to a 1-1 draw with Burnley at Upton Park on October 7, 1963. Having witnessed Alan's performance at first-hand as a spectator at that Monday night floodlit encounter with the then redoubtable Lancastrians, I have to agree with Alan's choice.

He scored Hammers goal and ripped Burnley's defence apart that night with a never-to-be-forgotten display of wing-craft so rarely seen in today's game. Ron Greenwood was of the same opinion, as Alan later recounted: "I remember sitting outside Ron's office the next day. I overheard him talking to the former England manager Walter Winterbottom and telling him he'd just witnessed the best display of off the ball running he'd ever seen. When I realised he was referring to my performance against Burnley it was a very proud moment".

Although he was dogged by ill-health later in life, Alan helped out at Chadwell Heath when Harry Redknapp was manager. Alan's favourite phrase when coaching the youngsters was "Let it run" meaning let the ball do the work, a little like Trevor Brooking used to do when he dropped his shoulder and let the ball run. Shortly before he slipped into a coma in hospital they were the last words he said.

As I said in the four page special *Hammers News* tribute to Alan which I penned in 1996 following his death, I would have liked to have told Alan that not all newspapers the morning after the Wembley triumph over Munich ended as fish and chip paper – many are the prized possessions of West Ham fans, including this scribe. The story of Alan Sealey, the man whose two goals made West Ham front page news that marvellous May morning in 1965 and a household name all over Europe, will run and run.

1966 and all that

Chapter 8

> "If you are an Anvil
> hold you Still
> If you are a Hammer
> Strike your fill"
>
> - Old German proverb.

With the cash from successive Wembley wins behind them, Upton Park was a hive of activity during the close-season of 1965 when, at long last, work started to extend the upper-tier of the West Stand closer to the south east corner of the ground and partially close the gap that had existed since the stand was built in 1925.

Incredibly, the work had been held in abeyance for 40 years as blocks B, C, D and E awaited the missing piece in the jig-saw, A, to turn up.

When the work was completed it enabled the extension of the club offices to include new administration facilities and an enlargement of the counting-house to monitor match day attendances in addition to increasing capacity by another 600 extra seats. The completion of A Block made additional space on the top terrace at the back of the stand enabling a new office suite which included that area and the former offices. This was completed the next close-season. Apart from the enlarged accommodation for full-time staff, a new counting-house (for admission staff) and a tea-room for players' wives (who were allocated seats in A Block) were also installed. The old seating in B Block was also removed as part of the revamp and new tip-up seats (similar to those in A Block) installed. It was also proposed in due course to upgrade all the other blocks in similar fashion. The Board Room was also extended by incorporating the office formerly used by manager Ron Greenwood.

The press too, were looked after by moving the area set aside for them to the front of D Block, giving the writers and commentators their best view of any of the London grounds.

Commendably, spaces were also found there for the Hospital's "network" broadcasters and the BBC for direct match broadcasts.

All this was in addition to the re-concreting of both the North and South banks during that hectic close-season of 1965.

Board Room minutes from the AGM of February 15, 1966 gave another fascinating glimpse of what went on off the field as well as on at that tumultuous time:

"Our last report to you was one of great success. Fortunate indeed is the Chairman who can present a subsequent report of even greater success, for season 1964-65 was without doubt the most successful ever.

"Our performances in the European Cup Winners' Cup, culminating in a most memorable final before a 'full-house' Wembley, earned for us a niche in the annals of soccer.

"For it was not only the winning of one of Europe's major prizes at the first attempt, but the manner of it, that gave us so much satisfaction. The BBC TV award for 'The Team of the Year' and the UNESCO gold medallion for sportsmanship, will be permanent reminders. Once again we pay tribute to the genius of our manager, Mr. Ron Greenwood, and to the tremendous efforts of all the players involved.

"The ECW Cup Competition is well known to be a 'money-spinner'. The financial arrangements are that the home team keeps all its own receipts and pays all its own expenses, which are naturally very heavy. Our own actual receipts amounted to £66,476 (including £21,000 from the Wembley final!), whilst our expenses came to £26,018 leaving us with a net balance of £40,458. This almost equalled the drop in receipts from the FA Cup and FL cups of £41,639. That was the 'jam', but it is also encouraging to know that our league gate receipts, which are our 'bread-and-butter', showed an increase of £22,349. You will also notice a big increase of

Back row (L-R) Peters, Brown, Kirkup, Burnett, Standen, Dickie, Charles, Bovington, Burkett, Moore.
Front row (L-R) Sealey, Brabrook, Britt, Bloomfield, Byrne, Hurst, Sissons, Dear. 1965-66.

£3,523 in Broadcast fees. Of this, the largest item was the £2,796 we received as our share of the Eurovision TV fee for the Final at Wembley. To save time, I do not intend to deal in detail with the remainder of the Revenue Account, but shall of course be pleased to answer any particular points on which you desire clarification.

"On the Balance Sheet you will have noticed the increase of £32,802 on Freehold Buildings (Ground). This is almost entirely the cost of erecting 'A' Block to the Grandstand, and we would like to place on record our appreciation of the efforts of our contractors of completing a technically very difficult structural operation in such excellent time and fashion. It is a long-awaited dream come true, and it is greatly appreciated by our patrons.

"It is worthy of note that the sum of £15,000 has been donated by the Building Development Fund towards the cost of this capital work, and our sincere thanks are given to all concerned in this splendid effort.

"Again we take this opportunity of expressing our warmest thanks to our team of workers and our many voluntary helpers, for their loyal and unstinting efforts".

So that was the end result of off-field activities during the summer of 1965, but on-field results were not so good as the club, far from putting their feet up following the stunning Wembley triumph, instead embarked on their busiest-ever close season programme.

Succinctly as ever, programme editor and club PRO, Jack Helliar, summed up the summer's activities in the official programme for the first match of the 1965-66 season versus Sunderland on the evening of Monday, August 23: "In the four months which have passed since the previous issue of our official journal, our First XI has played a dozen or so matches at venues in Spain, the Republic of Ireland, North America and Germany – as well as in England. Our fortunes have fluctuated considerably, for we have plumbed the depths as well as reaching the heights; our experiences have been enthralling and disappointing in turn, but from it all we have learned a great deal".

A week before the Wembley win on May 12, the Hammers visited Dublin to play in a benefit match on behalf of Tom Farrell and Tony Byrne of Shamrock Rovers. The game attracted an attendance of over 10,000 to Dalymount Park, where a cleanly contested duel ended in a 3-1 victory for West Ham. So for the second time in a year, Irons preceded a Wembley Cup Final win with a testimonial match.

So, rather than take it easy as they may well have felt entitled to do following their Wembley heroics, the Hammers' close season was hectic to say the least. Indeed, as the programme notes for the first home match of 1965-66 against Sunderland duly noted: "It was one of the heaviest close-season competitive programmes of any club".

First up was a return visit Stateside to compete in the North American Soccer League which Hammers won in 1963. Hammers began their campaign, after a short sojourn for holidays, on Friday June 18 versus New Yorkers at Randalls Island. Fielding their cup winning side Hammers held the upper hand in a scoreless first half only to concede an own goal a minute after the interval and went further behind when Kosmidis made it 2-0 in the 66th minute. Although Boyce pulled one back, the New Yorkers held on to win 2-1. To complete a bad start, Joe Kirkup was injured and played no further part during the tour.

Bond replaced him during the next match two days later against Hammers' Wembley opponents, Munich 1860 and Bovington took over Peters' right half position who replaced Boyce at inside-right. The Munich side had five changes from their Wembley line-up. Following a good start Peters headed past Radenkovic in the third minute, but Munich levelled through Luttrop after ten minutes play. Sealey came out in place of Bond for the second-half and he was again the hero of the hour when he headed the winner nine minutes from the end. This match was also at Randalls Island. Following a very welcome ten day break the still upbeat Hammers party continued their schedule with a meeting with Brazilian side Portugesa on July 1 at the Shea Stadium (where the Beatles would play their last major live show in 1966). Having missed a host of chances unlucky Irons found themselves 0-2 down after 18 minutes through goals by Dida and Mattar against the run of play before Dear (32) and Tony Scott (42) converted Bovington's pass to level the score, but then Frade made it 3-2 to the South Americans on the stroke of half-time.

After Mattar scored again in the 53rd minute, Boyce kept the Hammers in contention when he scored from Sealey's pass. However, Dida got another in the 73rd minute and Mattar completed his hat-trick to make the final count 3-6 in Portugesa's favour at Randalls Island.

In the return match against New Yorkers. Hammers had conceded the game before half-time when goals from Horst (5, 17) and Neubauer (28) virtually wrapped it up for the home team.

Although Hurst (57) pulled one back and Boyce had a goal disallowed near the end, Hammers were well beaten.

With Johnny Byrne back in action for the first time in nine weeks since he was injured playing for England versus Scotland in early April for the game with Italian side Varese on July 8, hopes were still high in the Hammers camp that they could save the tournament.

Undeservedly trailing in the 16th minute when Marcolini headed home, the team rallied to score twice via a 30-yard drive by Eddie Bovington and Ken Brown's fine header from Moore's centre. Alas, Boatti levelled the score at 2-2 just before the break and that's how it finished with the thermometer registering 85 degrees. Incidentally, it was a unique occurrence for Brown and the "Bov" to get on the scoresheet together, having only scored two goals each in the whole of their careers. With just pride to play for in the last game against Portugesa on July 13, there was precious little of that in evidence in another abject display and a 2-0 defeat. The fact that Byrne was again injured and replaced by Bovington at half-time certainly didn't help matters but the team were struggling and already 2-0 down by then after Mattar had scored both goals (10, 29) to take his tally to five against the Hammers in two games and the Brazilians to an easy win at Randalls Island.

There was little time to rue the demise of a second American dream, however, as after a brief spell off-duty the players resumed training on July 26 and departed the following week for a three match tour in Germany.

Byrne missed the trip due to the cracked ankle-bone he sustained against Portugesa which necessitated a long spell of treatment. Two promising teenagers were included in the touring party though, Dennis Burnett and Harry Redknapp and both did well on their First XI debuts.

The team against FVP Stuttgart lined up in front of a 25,000 attendance at the Neckar Stadium on August 3: Standen, Kirkup, Burkett, Peters, Bovington, Moore, Sealey (Redknapp), Boyce, Hurst, Bennett (Dear), Sissons.

The Germans went ahead through centre-forward Hans-Otto Peters after 20 minutes play, but although the team fought hard until the final whistle, an equaliser could not be found.

Another 25,000 crowd turned up at the Wald Stadium for Hammers next match against Eintracht Frankfurt four days later. After Dear had a goal disallowed in the 23rd minute, attack-minded Hammers had to wait until three minutes from half-time to take the lead when Sissons crossed for Peters to head in after the half-back had run 30 yards to make the connection.

Lothar Schamer equalised from 20 yards on the hour, but a nice left-wing move with seven minutes left on the clock ended with Sealey making the final score 2-1 in the tourists favour. Team: Dickie, Burnett, Burkett, Peters, Brown, Moore, Redknapp (Sealey), Boyce, Hurst (Bennett), Dear (Bovington), Sissons.

In the final match of the tour the Hammers once again met their now old friends TSV Munich 1860 at Sechziger Stadium before a massive 40,000 crowd who were hoping the Lions could exact some revenge for their two previous defeats earlier in the summer. After Irons had twice hit the woodwork, Kuppers scored for TSV after 15 minutes and from then on Hammers' attack was thwarted by some magnificent goalkeeping from Radenkovic until Peters won a loose ball to score from 18 yards for the leveller.

Brian James in the *Daily Mail* summed it up rather nicely when he concluded his report: "It was nice to be with an English team applauded from the pitch – for their manners as well as their method". Team: Standen, Kirkup, Burkett, Peters, Bovington, Moore, Sealey, Boyce, Hurst, Bennett, Sissons.

On Saturday, August 14 the same XI were in action at the Crystal Palace Recreational Centre against Crystal Palace FC. Palace took the lead early in the game through Keith Smith but thanks to a headed goal almost on the stroke of half-time by Geoff Hurst, it was all square at the break. Hurst got the winner in the last minute from the penalty spot to seal a 2-1 victory.

The 1965-66 season was barely 90 seconds old when West Bromwich Albion knocked Hammers proudly worn European crown wildly askew as winger Clive Clark put them ahead at the Hawthorns after a defensive mix-up.

With four players out injured; Sealey, Dear, Brown and Byrne, Bovington looked anything but a centre-half with young Peter Bennett, making his second appearance in the first team, looking out of his depth, it was no surprise when Jeff Astle scored a second on 38 minutes and Clark added a third in the penultimate minute after a 35 yard dash before taking the ball round Bovington and Standen twice apiece then casually netting.

Meanwhile, back at Upton Park in front of a 2,900 crowd, the sorely missed Byrne was orchestrating the 9-0 massacre of Shrewsbury Town's reserves. All of the West Ham forward line got on the scoresheet with Byrne, John Dryden and Redknapp notching two goals each and Martin Britt and Bobby Howe getting one each. The other tally was an own goal. The standout was crowd favourite Redknapp's second in the 77th minute when his first-timer from around the 30-yard mark swerved into the top corner for a spectacular goal. Byrne also signalled his return to competitive soccer with well taken efforts.

Not to be outdone, the Youth team incredibly also scored nine in the South-East Counties Division I clash with Charlton Athletic Colts at Chadwell Heath.

This match was played in the morning, so the opening honours of the 1965-66 campaign went to the Youth XI which annihilated a Charlton team containing six apprentices by 9-1 after leading only 2-0 at the interval.

Keith Millar (who later joined John Bond at Bournemouth) celebrated his first outing in this competition with four goals and was backed by a fine performance by his team mates. Roger Cross also netted a hat-trick. Alf Moss and Ray Tucker completed the scoring. Team: Death, M. Warren, Glozier, Brooking, P. Heffer (capt.), L. Stockley, S, Shaw, K, Millar, A. Moss, Cross, R. Tucker. Death, Heffer, Millar, Cross (Roger) and, of course, a certain Trevor Brooking all went on to play for the first team.

Then in the afternoon of that Saturday, August 21, the West Ham United Junior Team completed a "double" over Charlton in the Division II Cup at Chadwell Heath with a 3-0 victory in the club's first venture in Division II of the South East Counties League as the Under-17s made a notable start to the season. A Vince May strike and an own goal put the young Hammers 2-0 up at the interval with Peter Camp completing the scoring in the second half. Team: I. Mcquire, G, Shaw,

K. Radley, G. Robinson, R. Jarman, B. Hales, V. May, P. Camp, J. Bean, M. Lyons, R. Gell.

At the same time that all this was taking place, the 'A' Team didn't let the club down either by defeating Dunstable Town over at their Brewers Hill Road ground by 4-1. Despite making allowances for the comparatively below-standard opposition, The Hammers Third Team could be pleased with the performance of the fielded team which was somewhat light in experience. After missing some chances early on, the youngsters settled down to go 2-0 up by half-time and carried on the good work in the second period. Two goals from Paul Clements, one from Barry Simmons and yet another "own goal" completed the convincing victory which left just the first team with egg on their faces. Team: Mackleworth, Lampard, Kitchener, P. Deadman, Andrew (Capt.), James, T. Clements, P. Clements, Simmons, Smith, Hartley.

The opening day debacle was soon forgotten, however, as two days later a bumper 34,500 festival-mood crowd eagerly awaited their favourite's and visiting Sunderland to emerge from the Upton Park tunnel to a deafening roar with many eyes on the Wearsider's £90,000 new signing, "Slim Jim" Baxter from Glasgow Rangers.

Although welcoming Johnny Byrne for his first full appearance through injury since the previous April, West Ham were forced to field three reserves, Dickie, Bickles and Redknapp, who was making his League debut, due to further additions to their list of absentees which now included Standen and Brabrook.

It was a humid sultry evening under the Boleyn Bulbs, I know, I was there and as Bill Deacon's report in the *Ilford Recorder* informed his readers the excited Upton Park patrons didn't have to wait long for a goal: "Against a continual roar that would have done Wembley proud, West Ham's initial thrust paid off – in fact, it almost gave them two goals.

"A corner on the left (at the North Bank end) kept up the pressure and Peters came thundering up from the centre-circle to meet Sisson's centre and head it inches over the bar. A minute later the right-half made no mistake from Redknapp's corner. As the ball swung away from Sunderland's mass of goal-line defenders and into an open space Peters raced 20 yards to send in a perfect header which flew over the gaping Sunderland players and into the top corner, well out of goalkeeper Sandy McLaughlan's reach".

Hammers manager, Ron Greenwood afterwards commented: "We have been perfecting that move, with either Kenny Brown or Martin going up. But it was very well taken and a replica of the one he scored against Frankfurt this summer, from Sisson's corner.

"I thought he was very unlucky with the first effort. Both were the result of brilliant anticipation which is the essence of good football and which makes Martin such a fine player".

Leeds United were the next visitors to the Boleyn the following Saturday and once again, filling in for Trevor Smith as the *Recorder*'s West Ham reporter was their reserve, Bill Deacon, who had this to say about the clash with the Yorkshiremen: "The champagne bubbles of the previous Monday, against Sunderland, quickly burst, but drops of the stuff fell at infrequent intervals to whet our palates. The visitors deserved their 12th minute lead through Peacock, but in the end West Ham won deservedly – thanks to a brilliant goal by Geoff Hurst 12 minutes from the end.

"With typical aggressiveness and tenacity, Hurst somehow battled through crunching tackles by Cooper, Charlton, Bell and Hunter in the space of three yards to leave Sprake helpless".

West Ham equalised through Peters who slammed the ball home after Sprake had dropped it while being challenged by Moore and Kirkup two minutes before the interval, which as Bill explained in his report, was enlivened by fist fights on the North Bank: "The interval was made entertaining by a couple of fights which had the crowd swaying and policemen leaping athletically over the barrier to stop the fun and haul away two youths for disposal outside the ground".

Meanwhile, manager Ron Greenwood, who covered thousands of miles the previous season on the spying missions which played a vital part in his club's European Cup Winners' Cup triumph, was set to begin his travels again even though, as holders, they were given a bye until the second round.

On this occasion, Ron was preparing to take off, literally, on the relatively short trip across the Irish Sea. His destination Northern Ireland and the object of his journey to watch Coleraine in action against the crack Russian team Dynamo Kiev, in a 1st Round 1st Leg ECWC tie,

"It's a sixteen to one chance, of course, that we shall be drawn against the winners in the next round – but it's a good opportunity to see the Russians", commented Mr. Greenwood before leaving for the next league match at Sunderland (1/9/1965. Lost 2-1, scorer Hurst). From Roker Park the Hammers' boss was scheduled to travel to Northern Ireland and then to fly back directly to Leeds to rejoin his team for their league game at Brammall Lane the next Saturday (4/9/1965, lost 5-3, Hurst, Kirkup, Byrne). With Jack Burkett joining the ever-increasing injury list after the Leeds game, Eddie Presland deputised at both Sunderland and Sheffield prompting Greenwood to comment wryly: "Every cloud has a silver lining and at least these injuries mean a chance for some of our youngsters".

While all this was going on came the news that Hammers signed another two players to the full pro ranks to bring the professional staff up to its recognised full complement of 61. The newcomers were Keith Millar, who the previous season was with Walthamstow Avenue and Paul Heffer who was promoted from the amateur ranks.

Little did we know at the time how much West Ham would need those 61 pros during that 1965-66 season which was destined to witness the First XI contesting 62 first class competitive matches over its nine month duration. The most thus far and still a record intact as this book goes to press.

Neither was it appreciated that the club faced its biggest crisis on the playing side since manager Ron Greenwood's stewardship began in 1961.

It soon became apparent, however, that after the team's defeats at Sunderland and Sheffield United, a crisis of gargantuan proportions was indeed looming when those reverses were followed by two disastrous successive home defeats to Liverpool (1-5) and Leicester City (2-5) in the space of five days.

As the West Ham party prepared to travel north to Liverpool for a return First Division match more in hope than expectation against Shankly's rampant Reds (15/9/65) at their Anfield fortress, manager Greenwood denied that the club faced a crisis so soon after annexing one of Europe's most sought-after prizes, in an interview in that day's *Ilford Recorder*.

With Budgie Byrne, Peter Brabrook and Ken Brown missing from the 17 man squad that left Euston and Jim Standen now officially listed as unfit following the ankle knock he received at the Hawthorns, Greenwood had this to say: "Jim will not play in the first team again until both he and us are satisfied that the ankle is better. He is on the table now and he will stay there until he is fully fit".

Under the headline TIME FOR FAITH NOT PANIC the article, presumably penned by Trevor Smith, informed its readers that the following squad left for Liverpool: Dickie, Kirkup, Burnett, Peters, Moore, Bovington, Charles, Redknapp, Bennett, Hurst, Boyce, Sissons and Scott.

The squad was minus a recognised centre-half, but before he left Upton Park, the manager refused to be drawn on who would fill that position, but with a throw-away line claimed: "Ron Boyce could even wear the number five shirt". He also had to decide who to play at outside-left, Sissons or Scott, who had performed so well when drafted in for the previous two games. But one point upon which Mr. Greenwood would – and did – speak emphatically was his refusal to make wholesale panic changes following the 15-goals-in-three-games shock Hammers had suffered:

"Some of our players have lost faith in themselves for the moment. But I haven't lost faith in them. The best way I can show this is by not making panic changes. All players go through these spells at some time. I remember I did and when people lost faith in me I just got worse", he declared. But as for a crisis: "It's serious and I am worried... but these players are too good not to get over a bad start like this", he affirmed.

Then at 9.10 p.m. that Wednesday evening as teleprinters began to chatter the result from Anfield and the London football reporters sent their reports back to their Fleet Street offices, the air-waves were strangely muted... there was no news of a massacre, just Liverpool 1, West Ham United 1. Greenwood's faith in his team had paid off. In front of a 44,397 home crowd baying for claret and blue blood, the Hammers had set up an uncharacteristic "Iron Curtain" style defence to stop the rot and even took the lead through Hurst in the 37th minute to silence the Kop. Although Geoff Strong headed a second-half leveller, that's the way it ended and the "crisis that never was" was over. Team: Dickie, Kirkup, Burkett, Bovington, Charles, Moore, Bennett, Peters, Hurst, Boyce, Sissons.

Greenwood was vindicated further when the same team went to an eerily quiet Ewood Park in front of just 10,000 fans the following Saturday and sent Blackburn Rovers to the foot of the First Division table by winning 2-1, thanks to a brace from Peters.

Quieter still was the Stonecross Road ground at Hatfield in Hertfordshire where winger Tony Scott was playing his final game and scoring his last goals for West Ham in the "A" Team against Hatfield Town on the same day that the first team beat Blackburn.

Seldom can the ruthlessness of team selection have been more starkly illustrated than when Greenwood wrestled with the problem of whether to play Sissons or Scott against Liverpool at Anfield. He plumped for Sissons, prompting Scott to hand in a transfer request.

Scotty, as he was popularly known by the fans and his team-mates, was with the club for seven years and made 97 First Team appearances, explained his decision:

Moore, resplendent in West Ham's classic away shirt, blocks Law's attempt to centre at Old Trafford.

"When I was dropped for the Liverpool game last week it was quite clear to me that there is no future for me at West Ham now. It was a blow after playing what I thought were two good games in the first team, but with Johnny Sissons in front of me I have little chance of getting regular first team football which is what I want".

He didn't have long to wait.

On the same day that Greenwood swooped to sign midfielder Jimmy Bloomfield from his former club Brentford as cover for the now injured Boyce, Scotty signed for First Division pacemakers Aston Villa for a £16,000 fee and where he resumed his right-wing partnership with ex-Hammers' captain Phil Woosnam.

Happily there was no bitterness, when likeable Tony left. He even dropped in to say a personal thanks for everything to boss Greenwood.

On a sourer note, Greenwood flayed so called "supporters" who sullied West Ham's good name during the 3-0 defeat to Fulham at Craven Cottage by tearing down flags, throwing objects onto the pitch and assaulting a programme seller.

"These people are not supporters. They merely come hoping to get in on the success our players achieved in the last two seasons – and when things go wrong, resort to this kind of behaviour. They are just hooligans and we would be much better off without them. Fortunately, they are not typical of our fans and you can be sure they will not be around for long if success doesn't come. I was disgusted to see so-called fans behaving like that at Fulham wearing our colours. We do not want 'support' of this kind", he raged.

Worse was to follow seven days later when the Hammers decided to resume their early season fetish for conceding five goals at the City Ground, Nottingham, to a rampant Forest without reply.

Blameless, however, was goalkeeper Jim Standen, back in the team for the first time since that five goals conceded in three consecutive games sequence. Not so was new signing Jimmy Bloomfield and left-back Joe Kirkup. It was patently obvious that the former was no longer First Division class and the usually reliable Joe was culpable for the first goal after he'd committed the cardinal sin of passing the ball across and in front of his own goal which was picked up by an amazed Frank Wignall who gleefully scored.

In a sad footnote there was an explanation on *that* goal from a despondent Kirkup: "It was just a bad pass".

Meanwhile there was better news to report from the Junior section on an exciting new prospect with a familiar name – Charlie Williams.

In true "Roy of the Rovers" fashion the young Jamaican wrote for and got a trial with Hammers young Colts, scoring five goals in the specially arranged trial match.

He was given further opportunities after his sensational nap hand and scored another two goals in a 4-2 Chadwell Heath victory over Spurs Colts in a SECL Division I clash. This performance earned the dusky centre-forward promotion to the team to face Brighton the following Monday night at Upton Park in the 1st round of the London Youth Cup which was won 1-0 through a solitary goal from the Hammers new prospect. Ironically, Charlie turned up before the game nursing an injured wrist and minus his boots, not expecting to play.

Coach John Lyall saved the day by rushing the youngster to his nearby home to grab his boots and race back to the ground in time for him to play.

This was lucky for the crowd, who at once took the imaginative West Indian to their hearts with cries of "Come on Pele!" and cheered his well-taken winning goal to the rafters after he'd pulled down Brooking's cross and hammered the ball home in the 40th minute to inspire one scribe to predict "a future star in the Johnny Byrne mould".

The Reserves, too, helped to lift the gloom with two wins in four days. As the first team were capitulating on Trentside, they defeated Ipswich 4-0 at Upton Park thanks to a hat-trick from centre-forward Martin Britt, who was recovering from the knee injury that would eventually end his career, with the last tally coming from Bobby Howe.

Next up were Swindon Town at the County Ground where a 20-yard cross-shot from the eager-for-action Brian Dear late in the second half gave the second string their well earned 1-0 win as Tony Smith was injured in the first half and little more than a passenger from then on. Team versus Ipswich: Dickie, Burnett, Presland, Dawkins, Brown, James, Dryden, Smith, Britt, Howe, Sissons. Versus Swindon: Dickie, Bond, Presland, Dawkins, Andrew, Howe, Redknapp, Bloomfield, Dear, Smith, Dryden. Incidentally, this was one of veteran John "Muffin" Bond's last games in a West Ham shirt, as he transferred to Torquay United shortly afterwards.

In the issue of the *Ilford Recorder* dated 14/10/1965, alongside the unpalatable report on the match at Nottingham, there were several snippets of interest.

The man behind Hammers' Ground Development Fund, Jim Handscombe, reported another £500 winner. Jim also revealed that West Ham used £15,000 of the £18,000 the pool had brought in since its inception two years previously on the extension to the West Stand at Upton Park. Genial Jim also appealed for more agents to help him promote the highly valuable scheme from his office at the ground on match days. On a sadder note, fans were also informed of the death of Les "Greaser" Robinson who scored two goals in 19 games for the league side in the early 20s. Although by no means a regular, the inside-forward often top scored for the reserves and had the honour of scoring their 100th goal in the London Combination in 1923-24, he also enjoyed the reputation of being something of a comedian. Les joined the Boleyn ranks from Dagenham side Stirling Athletic and later joined Northampton.

Not for the first time, the much-maligned Football League Cup competition provided a welcome diversion for the Hammers league woes in the first half of 1965-66.

Drawn away to Third Division Bristol Rovers in the 2nd round at Eastville, Hammers appearance drew a bumper 18,354 crowd to the Pirates' homely enclosure. To a man they were not disappointed with the entertainment on offer either, although maybe a tad by the final 3-3 scoreline, as many neutral observers deemed them unlucky not to win a thrilling encounter. It looked all over approaching half-time, however, with West Ham coasting by courtesy of strikes by Hurst (2) and the returned from injury, Byrne.

But former Gunner Johnny Petts hit a cracker from 25 yards to add to John Brown's early equaliser to make it 2-3 at the break. Roared on by their best "gate" of the season, Rovers second-half onslaught pinned Hammers back on defence and speedy inside man Bobby Jones gave Moore a torrid time, laying on the equaliser for his right-wing partner Harold Jarman after 55 minutes. Despite constant home pressure on Irons' reargaurd the game ended 3-3 with the East Londoners relieved to hang on.

Despite the five star rating which was awarded to the game at Eastville by the *Daily Express*, only 13,160 attended the Wednesday night replay at Upton Park eight days later, including a fair contingent from Bristol's blue half. Or should we say quarter(s)? Even so, the two teams again

Ken Brown shakes hands with an Olympiakos opponent before the 2-2 draw in the second leg in Greece.

laid on an attacking thriller which the Hammers, minus Moore, just edged 3-2 with goals from Byrne (2) and cohort Hurst.

With Rovers boss Bert Tann, the ex-West Ham schoolboy star returning to his old stamping ground, the Bristolians gave the Hammers a big fright after trailing 2-0 at half-time. But Rovers hit back in double quick time after the interval with goals from Johnny Petts and Barry Jones in the 52nd and 57th minutes. After several more scares for the home side and extra-time looming, Hurst set up Byrne after a cross field run. Bernard Hall, in Rovers goal, dived to grab his cross, but "twinkle toes" Byrne got there first and cleverly pulled the ball out of the reach of the grounded custodian. Hammers had rode their luck again in a competition that was rapidly becoming a graveyard for those First Division clubs interested enough to enter.

Next up, in what many considered to be the "Cinderella Cup", were another Third Division club, Mansfield Town on a Wednesday night under the Upton Park lights. Occupying 14th place in the Division III table the Stags had a sprinkling of former First Division stars among their ranks including Albert Scanlon (Man. Utd.), Albert Cheeseborough (Leicester City), Colin Nelson (Sunderland) and Bill Curry (Newcastle Utd.).

Having lost 5-0 at Town's near neighbours Forest the previous Saturday, the Hammers were in no mood to show the Field Mill men any benevolence and were firmly in control from the outset. Even so, they were only 1-0 up at the interval thanks to a Hurst strike on 19 minutes following a Bovington-Peters move down the right flank. Struggling to find a way through the opposition's offside trap, the frustrated Irons' forwards had to wait until nine minutes into the second half to score again when Brabrook made amends for an earlier miss when he hammered his shot home off the bar when Hurst's effort was charged down and Britt missed the rebound.

Hammers gave the scoreline a more realistic look in the last eight minutes when young full-back Dennis Burnett notched his first senior goal with a brilliant left foot drive and Hurst added a fourth following a typical West Ham free kick which resulted in Hurst stepping over the ball, Bovington touching it to Peters who flicked it through the wall into the path of Hurst who did the rest. It was almost as if the Boleyn Boys had suddenly remembered that the League Cup now provided a new gateway to Europe – the winners gaining entry to the Inter City Fairs Cup – and some of their old spark and urgency was ignited again. Also the team had succeeded in not conceding a goal for the first time thus far and were through to the fourth round.

But Hammers had bigger fish to fry, The next day they learned they would meet top Greek side Olympiakos Piraeus in the first defence of the ECWC trophy won the previous May. But before that the team badly needed to get back on track in the First Division places with a formidable Sheffield Wednesday side the next up at Upton Park where West Ham had failed to win any of their last six league games... but a saviour was at hand in the form of a burly figure from the reserves.

Enter, Martin Britt.

With Byrne and Dear still not recovered from injury, Greenwood had little option other than to pitch the big, awkward number nine in against the Owls to face the equally cumbersome Wednesday centre-half, Vic Mobley.

Right from the start West Ham's attacking theories were based on the assumption that the deceptively mobile Britt would be able to dish out more than he took from the giant Mobley... and so it proved. For despite being 1-2 down at the interval and making the home fans suffer as usual after out-playing the visitors from the Steel City for most of the half, Britt's two second-half goals in front of a rapturous North Bank ensured a 4-2 victory and fully vindicated Greenwood's gamble. Sissons and Peters got the other two.

All this was achieved in the aftermath of boss Ron's uncharacteristic decision to grant several of his players permission to spend the Thursday evening before the game in a pub.

The pub in question was the Wheatsheaf at High Ongar which had been taken over by former manager Ted Fenton as *mine host*. With his charges scoring eight goals in four days, maybe Ron should have booked a weekly visit.

Dear and Byrne though were still suffering injury scares in their battle for full fitness. Great characters both, Stag (recently back after a broken ankle) limped off in the second string's London Challenge Cup tie with Brentford after a blow on the same ankle. He returned later but finally went off for good 15 minutes from time in the 1-1 draw at the Boleyn. The Bees went ahead through former Hammer Joe Gadston after 59 minutes and, with Dear off, looked likely winners. But the homesters earned a Griffin Park replay when Eddie Presland lobbed home after being set up by Bobby Howe. Tuesday's (19/10/1965) news on Dear from physio Bill Jenkins allayed major fears, however as he explained: "It was nothing serious to do with Brian's previous injury. He merely got a kick on the back of the same ankle and should be back by the weekend". But that evening in the replay it was Budgie's turn to cause concern that the Upton Park "Injury Hoodoo" had struck again. The game was only the second he had played in since a two week lay-off, ordered by Greenwood to help the mercurial forward to recover peak form and fitness impaired by a series of injuries dating from the previous season's cartilage operation. Byrne was showing signs of recapturing his old skill and fire against the West Londoners, until 15 minutes from time when he suddenly twisted the ankle he broke during the American Summer Tournament. This time it was boss Greenwood who headlined in many newspapers: "This was sheer irresponsibility. If the facts had been checked first it would have been clear that another break or fracture was very unlikely. An x-ray proved that there is nothing wrong. Johnny is expected to be fit enough to play this weekend, although he is not yet ready to be considered for a first team place again" he declared. The replay ended badly for Hammers. After taking a first-half lead when Peter Bennett scored from a Howe free kick, they were taken to extra time by Brentford, who then snatched the winner in the first period. West Ham: Dickie, Bond, Presland, Dawkins, Bickles, Howe, Redknapp, Bennett, Byrne, Dear, Dryden.

Next on the road were First Division new boys Northampton Town who had battled their way up from Division Four in record time and who would descend just as rapidly – still winless at the end of October. True to tradition, West Ham gifted the Cobblers their first victory with a lack-lustre performance at the County Ground. After Town Skipper Theo Foley had sent Standen the wrong way with a 29th minute penalty, it took veteran centre-half Ken Brown to show Irons shot-shy attack how to score with a thumping header – only his fourth, and last goal of his West Ham service. Ken was not on hand to prevent his namesake Ken Leek from back-heading the winner with ten minutes remaining to provoke a pitch invasion at the end and the unusual occurrence of Moore refusing to shake Foley's hand.

Back at the Boleyn the reserves were suffering too, going down 0-4 to Arsenal in front of a crowd of almost 5,000. Johnny Byrne, in his first game after his two-week lay-off, was rarely in the picture against his old adversary, Ian Ure, with little going right for a home attack in which only young Trevor Hartley impressed.

As it turned out, Byrne – Greenwood's ace in the pack – was still far from match fitness and top form. Almost a month away in fact. It wasn't until 20/11/65 that he finally shrugged off his injury woes to turn on a five star (and goal) performance in another Football Combination London derby against his old team Crystal Palace and win a place in the line-up to face Olympiakos in the ECWC.

As the first team were unluckily surrendering their proud record of remaining undefeated at Highbury since 1931, when going down 3-2. Budgie was happily banging in five goals in the second string's 6-1 demolition of Palace. Flushed with success over his nap hand and jubilant about his first team recall, Budgie was as chirpy as ever afterwards.

"I'm delighted, I feel on top of the world again. Naturally, I was feeling a little bit tired after the game, but I really enjoyed it", he said.

The reward of many weeks of hard training, often on his own, under the exacting eye of reserve team trainer Ernie Gregory, Johnny continued: "One of my main tasks was to get my weight down and Ernie was a great help, it was a relief to see my luck change". There was praise in return from Gregory to Byrne: "Johnny played really well, all his five goals were well taken, but the fourth was a real peach.

"He passed to Dear and took the return to crack the ball in from 25 yards". This was the goal that also gave Byrne to most satisfaction as he added: "I think it was probably one of the best I have ever scored".

Although Budgie stole the show, coach Ernie was quick to emphasise it was a team effort, commenting: "Although Byrne stole the limelight, the rest of the team played extremely well. It was one of the best performances of our season".

Palace scored first, but Byrne equalised when he brought the ball down well. His second was laid on by Dryden and the third came from a penalty. Then came that great fourth goal and the fifth was from a header. John Dryden added the sixth. West Ham: Dickie, Bond, Presland, Dawkins, Bickles, Howe, Redknapp, Smith, Byrne, Dear, Dryden.

Over in North London at rain sodden Highbury, Hammers could count themselves unfortunate not to add the Gunners to the scalp gained in the previous week's 2-1 victory over Chelsea at the Boleyn when Peters played a "worldy" in front of Alf Ramsey and scored the decisive goal. He scored again in London N5, but too late to prevent the narrow defeat.

Then at last came the long-awaited first defence of the Cup Winners' Cup trophy against Olympiakos of Greece at a mud-bound Upton Park (24/11/1965).

It was no contest, however, as West Ham – on the attack from the opening minute to the last

– cracked in four goals without reply to make the tie as painfully one-sided as the Cassius Clay-Floyd Patterson mis-match of the previous night.

The knock-out blows were administered by Hurst, in the 23rd and 43rd minutes – the first with a rocket shot from a fine Sisson's cross and the second following a Brabrook run and cross to the far post, Byrne, fully vindicating his selection following his long lay-off, with a flicked shot which deceived acrobatic keeper Fronimidis in the 56th minute and finally, Brabrook, who headed home Charles' cross in the 73rd.

To be fair to the graceless Greeks, who kicked anyone in claret and blue throughout, they were disrupted by injuries when losing inside-right Sideris with a pulled muscle after 30 minutes – seconds before Hurst's first goal – and ten minutes from the end when left-back Pavidis limped off to leave them with 9 men and a mountain to climb for the return in Athens.

So the Hammers had found their long lost goalscoring form just in the nick of time and continued in the same vein for the visit of Everton the following Saturday, winning 3-0 with goals from Sissons (2) and Brabrook.

The revival in the team's fortunes encouraged striker Hurst to give an upbeat interview in the *Recorder* newspaper and the normally reticent Greenwood to make a prophetic prediction by claiming: "There is not a manager in the First Division who would not willingly give at least £50,000 for him" and adding Nostradamus-like: "In my opinion he could easily get into England's World Cup team".

Spookily, the Soviet ref for the return leg against Olympiakos is none other than Bahramov, the linesman who would flag Hurst's second goal *bona fide* in the World Cup Final against West Germany. But West Ham neither received or expected any favours from him as they entered the fray at the Karaiskakis Stadium to an incredible barrage of sound created by 42,000 partisan Greek fanatics as they tried to unnerve their guests.

Smoke-bombs, hurled from the terraces of the dockside ground, exploded with thunder-clap intensity as West Ham came out onto the pitch before the start to test the tension in a shrewd ploy by boss Greenwood.

Flares blazed on the running-track, rockets zoomed out at the players and it was impossible to hear anything above the din.

This set the scene. The Hammers entered it armed with four goals and a growing experience won on foreign fields. If they had been found wanting in either, they would surely have perished under the sheer passion, intensity and brutal tactics of their kamikaze-style opponents.

Before the match was 20 minutes old, Peters was carried off, blood streaming from his right leg after a violent tackle by tough right-half Polychroniou, who blatantly went over the ball. Yet the official gave a free-kick the other way. The injury to Peters was greeted by cheers from the crowd, but there was no applause of welcome when he came limping back – except from the tiny pocket of Hammers' fans who made the trip.

In the 28th minute the crowd were silenced for the first time. Peters, who was now limping at centre-forward, took advantage of a mistake by Stefanskos to break away on the left. As Millissis came across, Peters' shot struck him and was diverted past Fronimidis into the net.

With Geoff Hurst working prodigiously in defence, West Ham were gradually taking control. In the 53rd minute, Sissons, with a superb dash of skill and courage, evaded the chopping boots of two defenders, and centred for Peters to head home on the far post. The silence from the stands was deafening and where there had been taunts, insults and a barrage of fireworks, there were now only cushions thrown. The Greek fans had given up. It was all over.

And although the home players hadn't quite thrown in the towel, scoring with an own goal and an "iffy" penalty; West Ham had proved their mastery to move into the last eight. West Ham: Standen, Kirkup, Charles, Bovington, Brown, Moore, Brabrook, Peters, Byrne, Hurst, Sissons.

Back in League action, West Ham were still involved in a relegation scrap, as were their next opponents at the Boleyn, Everton; unfamiliar territory for them. When they revealed their change in tactics, however, the reasons for their presence in the lower echelons was easy to see. The Merseysiders had never been taken as an easy ride, but they plumbed new depths of foul play in this encounter.

It was clear from the outset one of their main targets for the "treatment" would be Johnny Byrne, playing his first League game for eight weeks. Luckily, as Budgie fought off the over-robust challenges inflicted on him by the visitors, a back-to-form John Sissons was able to take over his mantle of goalscorer-in-chief for the day.

In a morass of cloying mud, it was Byrne – fed by Peters – who set the flaxen-haired winger up for the first goal in the 36th minute. Byrne, cleverly evading the attentions of Colin Harvey, provided a perfect centre which was headed over a bunch of Everton defenders by Sissons to leave Andy Rankin stranded.

With incidents on the field having quietened down, it was the turn of sections of the crowd to turn nasty. A few fireworks from November the fifth fizzed and spluttered and a bottle was tossed into the Everton goalmouth from the North Bank. The fans changed their tune in the 81st minute though, when their favourites bagged the goal that put the result beyond doubt. Kirkup halted an Everton attack, but in doing so blatantly handled the ball. This was missed by the officials, however, and the homesters immediately broke away on the right. A cross from Brabrook went right through a pack of Everton men to where his opposite flank man, Sissons, volleyed it home. Six minutes later, Sissons returned the compliment by crossing to Brabrook who thudded his header into the net in a fashion reminiscent of his goal against Olympiakos three days earlier. Game, set and match.

The humble Football League Cup competition, so often the catalyst for improving the Hammers' League form in the past, was once again proving to be the fillip needed away from the strains of League duty. Leaving little time to put their feet up, the Hammers were back in action two days after beating Everton for the quarter-final replay against Third Division leaders Grimsby Town under the Boleyn bulbs.

Having already been behind twice in the original tie a month earlier, when goals from Charles and Hurst had cancelled out strikes by the Mariners' deadly duo, Matt Tees and Rodney Green, the Hammers were well aware that the Blundell Park men would be no pushover as they had previously disposed of Crystal Palace, Bolton and Preston in the competition. They were also well respected by manager Ron Greenwood, who rated them "The best Third Division team" he had ever seen. "Grimsby play a very useful 4-2-4 system", he added. "And make no secret of the fact that they base their ideas largely on West Ham's".

With just ten days to go before the Christmas of 1965, the fixtures were coming up fast and furious with Town proving to be a tough nut to crack, as predicted.

The very healthy crowd of 17,500 which assembled for the tie were rewarded with a sporting and entertaining match in which the visitors were far from over-awed. After missing a host of chances, it became evident that just one goal might decide the issue and so it proved when Hurst struck the only counter ten minutes from time to preserve his record of scoring in every tie so far.

The Town team bitterly contested that solitary goal of the evening and it was difficult not to sympathise with their frustration when the advantage rule was applied by the referee even though a linesman flagged for a foul by later-to-be England manager, Graham Taylor, on Peter Brabrook. The Mariners' momentary hesitation proved fatal as the winger was able to elude the attentions of his opponent to lay on the pass from which Hurst scored the winner.

Next stop was Hillsborough, Sheffield, where only 12,996 showed up to witness the 0-0 stalemate with Wednesday. The Owls had only dropped three points at home all season, but as they had done a couple of weeks previously in another 0-0 draw at Old Trafford (when Byrne hit the woodwork in both halfs), West Ham missed a golden chance to take two points back to E13.

The culprit was the normally deadly Hurst, after just eight minutes play when he left England

The West Ham team just before kick-off to face Borussia Dortmund in the second-leg of the ECWC semi-final in Germany. Back row (L-R) Ken Brown, Martin Peters, Jim Standen, John Charles, Eddie Bovington, Bobby Moore. Front row (L-R) Peter Brabrook, Ronnie Boyce, Geoff Hurst, Jimmy Bloomfield, Johnny Byrne.

keeper Ron Springett stranded in the mud with a superb dribble, but delayed his shot too long to enable a defender to clear his shot off the line. Within minutes Byrne had a fierce drive beaten away by Springett and then Sissons hit a post with a typical effort.

But that was virtually all the offensive work the Hammers could muster as they fell back on defence under wave after wave of Wednesday attacks for the rest of the contest. Bearing in mind the Owls had only previously lost at home once – to Liverpool – and the only other point to elude them was against Leeds, Hammers' hard gained point seemed all the more valuable.

The first-leg of the League Cup Semi-Final versus Second Division Cardiff City on a deep, dark Monday evening just five days before Christmas '65, illuminated by the Upton Park floodlights and a brilliant first-half performance by Irons, has lasted long in the memories of those present.

Not just, I must add, because they'd witnessed another West Ham wonder show, but also the home team's refusal to respond to Cardiff's diabolical strong-arm tactics in kind.

Instead, they opted to reply to the kicking dished out by the visitors by playing football, which earned a 4-0 lead by the 75th minute. By then, Bovington, with a superb header, Brabrook, who dispossessed Peter Rodrigues and 'keeper Bob Wilson, Byrne, with a well-placed shot and Sissons, set up by Byrne, had seemingly made the second-leg academic. But it wouldn't have been West Ham if some old failings hadn't resurfaced and they let the Bluebirds back in the game in the 86th and 88th minutes when George Andrews scored twice. Luckily, Hurst restored the scoreline to a more realistic margin in the 89th when he kept alive his record of scoring in every tie so far.

The majority of the 20,013 present were scathing in their criticism of City's tactics and as Trevor Smith noted in his *Recorder* match report: "The visitors enjoyed, if that's the right word, the rare experience of being booed and jeered off the West Ham ground at half-time – which gives some indication of just how stupid their first-half display was". David James in the *Daily Mail* also commented: "In two years crusading across the continent, West Ham have been hacked by experts... Thus the attempt to succeed with the heavy stuff looked so naive it would have been laughable if it were not so dangerous".

Meanwhile, the youth team were involved in their own protracted saga with Spurs in the Second Round of the FA Youth Cup.

Having eliminated the Tottenham youngsters from the London Youth Cup at the end of October by the narrowest of margins in extra time at the Boleyn thanks to an unstoppable drive by inside-right Keith Miller with a few minutes left, the Hammers' lads had no illusions about the task ahead.

Another attempt to settle the tie was made at Upton Park on Monday evening January 3, 1966 after previous attempts on December 8th (postponed at White Hart Lane), 14th (Cheshunt, abandoned 78th minute with Spurs leading 2-1) and 21st (Cheshunt, 1-1 draw).

This proved to be a thrilling contest – one of the best seen at the ground in 1965-66 – watched by an appreciative audience of 5,020 spectators. A lot of this number arrived late and missed the first goal scored in the third minute by Keith Miller, but they had plenty to enthuse over during the remainder of a see-sawing encounter. The visitors equalised five minutes before the break with the score staying 1-1 at the end of 90 minutes play. Extra time proved to be a test of endurance, but when the Hammers went ahead for the second time with only seven minutes to go, they looked the likely winners after the Spurs keeper fell into the net while holding the ball from Dennis Walker's header. Yet still the Lilywhites were not to be beaten and in the 116th minute they levelled the score again – 2-2. West Ham: Death, Grozier, Lampard, Brooking, Heffer, James, T. Clements, Miller, Simmons, Cross, Walker.

So, after winning the toss for choice of ground for the second replay, the two teams were back at Upton Park 12 days later to do battle again, this time before 5,670 hardy fans who were willing to brave the freezing weather.

Once again it was a long night for them, with the fourth attempt to settle the tie again going into extra-time in the long-running saga to find a winner after playing a total of 408 minutes, spread over nearly five weeks, at three different venues.

This time Spurs drew first blood when they scored after a corner in the 13th minute, The equaliser arrived ten minutes before the break when the Spurs' 'keeper misjudged a centre by Cross, and Walker ran the ball in.

After the second-half remained goalless, it was agreed to give the frozen youngsters a deserved break before the period of extra-time. With defences dominating, a decisive goal looked unlikely, but four minutes into the second-half of extra-time, a linesman flagged for a handling offence in the Spurs' box. Miller took the spot-kick, and although his shot was saved, he managed to hammer home the rebound for the winner.

As the tie had dragged on so long – across two calender years in fact – Hammers already knew their next two opponents should they progress further. Watching with interest from the stands was Gillingham FC manager Basil Hayward. Also present were a contingent from Charlton Athletic Colts, who were due to meet the winners of the Gillingham-Hammers tie in the Fourth Round.

Pouring rain kept the attendance down to 3,094, but among this number were a good few who'd made the journey through the Blackwall Tunnel to cheer on the team at Priestfield Stadium. They were well rewarded by a runaway 5-0 win through goals from Cross (2), Simmons (2) and Miller. Karl Minor took the place of T. Clements for the only change in the line up from the Spurs tie.

So once again, a small, but growing, army of fans made their way over, under or on the Thames (via the Woolwich Ferry) to see the Hammers youngsters – two of whom, Frank Lampard and Trevor Brooking, would join the Pantheon of Upton Park legends – take on Charlton's Colts at the Valley in SE7.

The tie drew an attendance of 4,077, a record number for a youth team fixture at the massive ground which could hold 75,000 comfortably. The West Ham youngsters emerged from another thrilling encounter with great credit and a passage to the quarter-finals, against an XI which included three players with First Team experience and had defeated Chelsea in an earlier round.

From a free-kick in the 27th minute, Walker squared a ball to Minor, the Hammers' Australian centre-forward, who made it 0-1. Seven minutes later it was 0-2 when Miller took a through ball from Walker and neatly placed the ball between two advancing defenders into the net to the restrains of a chorus of "Bubbles" floating eerily around the almost empty ground.

Then came the fledgling Robins' fightback which started eight minutes before the interval when John Stenson headed home. An equaliser arrived five minutes after the break from Dennis Booth and Charlton commenced to put the young Irons under pressure for a long time. However, they stood firm and the best goal of the evening settled the issue. Miller's corner was headed on by Walker, and Minor rocketed his header home to earn his team a place in the quarter-finals to be staged at Upton Park on Monday evening, February 21, against QPR.

In contrast to their would-be successors, the first team had a terrible start to the New Year, 1966 – losing 0-3 at home to Nottingham Forest, whose victory was their first away success of the season and enabled the Trentsiders to complete the "double" over the Irons with an overall goals haul of 8-0.

On the day after Boxing Day the game at Villa Park had been abandoned after 30 minutes in wintry conditions with the score at 0-0. I was there, standing on the massive terrace of the Holte End with my father George and brother-in-law, the West Ham fanatic, Christopher Seltzer, who was married to my dear sister Valerie – among a crowd of 30,382.

Following a 2-1 defeat at Newcastle (Byrne, 90), a fortunate 2-2 draw with Everton at Goodison (Hurst, Peters), after twice surrendering the lead and a dismal 1-1 home draw with Northampton Town (Hurst, pen), it looked like the team were reverting to bad habits.

The FA Cup provided a welcome diversion, however, although Greenwood was said to be "livid" after the lucky Third Round replay 2-1 (Hurst, Brabrook) win over Third Division Oldham

West Ham fans in Magdeburg.

Athletic in front of the biggest home crowd of the season – 35,330 – who roundly booed them off the field following the 2-2 draw at Boundary Park (Burnett, Hurst) three days before.

Then came respite in the form of a 4-0 home win over WBA (Hurst 2, Sissons, Peters) which is a dress rehearsal for the Football League Cup Final as long as Hammers can overcome Cardiff City in the second leg of the semi-final at Ninian Park, which they do in a canter with goals by Hurst (2), Peters (2) and Burnett. So Hammers were in their third major cup final in as many years with a 10-3 aggregate victory.

Yet still the team continued their predilection with conceding five goals in its next match against Leeds United at Elland Road. Appropriately perhaps, the fifth time goalkeeper Jim Standen had had to pick the ball out of the net five times this bizarre campaign after the 5-0 reverse in Yorkshire.

Then came salvation in the form of six victories out of the next eight fixtures. Quite what caused the reversal of fortunes remains a mystery as Greenwood resisted the temptation to make wholesale changes.

The revival began just two days after the Leeds debacle with a 2-1 win at Aston Villa in the re-scheduled game which had been abandoned on December 27, thanks to goals by Hurst and Sissons in each half. Hurst's goal in the 40th minute, ensured that he kept his crown as England's top scorer in all competitions with 31.

It was back to the FA Cup again the following Saturday, when bottom-but-one Blackburn Rovers were the visitors to Upton Park. But if Hammers thought this an easy passage into the Fifth Round because of the Lancastrians lowly position in the First Division rankings, they were in for a rude awakening.

The magic of the FA Cup drew a crowd of 32,350 of which I was one. From my vantage point in the West Enclosure I witnessed a six-goal thriller unfold before me, with Hammers levelling the scores three times in the 3-3 draw.

When Rovers' England international play-maker Bryan Douglas was crocked after just 12 minutes play and reduced to a virtual passenger from then on, the odds looked stacked against them, even though they were already a goal to the good after inside-right John Byron put them one up in the eighth minute.

Bloomfield, now showing better form, scored the first equaliser in the 25th minute and it was Greenwood's gamble of playing him instead of Byrne that kept Irons in the competition. The left-side triangle of Moore, Sissons and Bloomfield had lifted home fans out of their initial gloom – and seats. Bloomfield's eye for a chink in Rovers' defence enabled him to dive to head home Moore's knee-high cross for his first ever goal for the First Team. Yet it seemed to be academic when Sissons' second equaliser, hit from a seemingly impossible angle out on the touchline and the goal-of-the-game, had been nullified by Byron's third in the 71st minute. It was also the third time he had scored a hat-trick against West Ham. But as the homesters stormed into attack to launch a late siege, it was Bloomfield again – aided by Peters – with a deft flick between tightly-packed defenders who set up Hurst for the final leveller. West Ham: Standen, Burnett, Burkett, Bovington, Brown, Moore, Brabrook, Peters, Hurst, Bloomfield, Sissons.

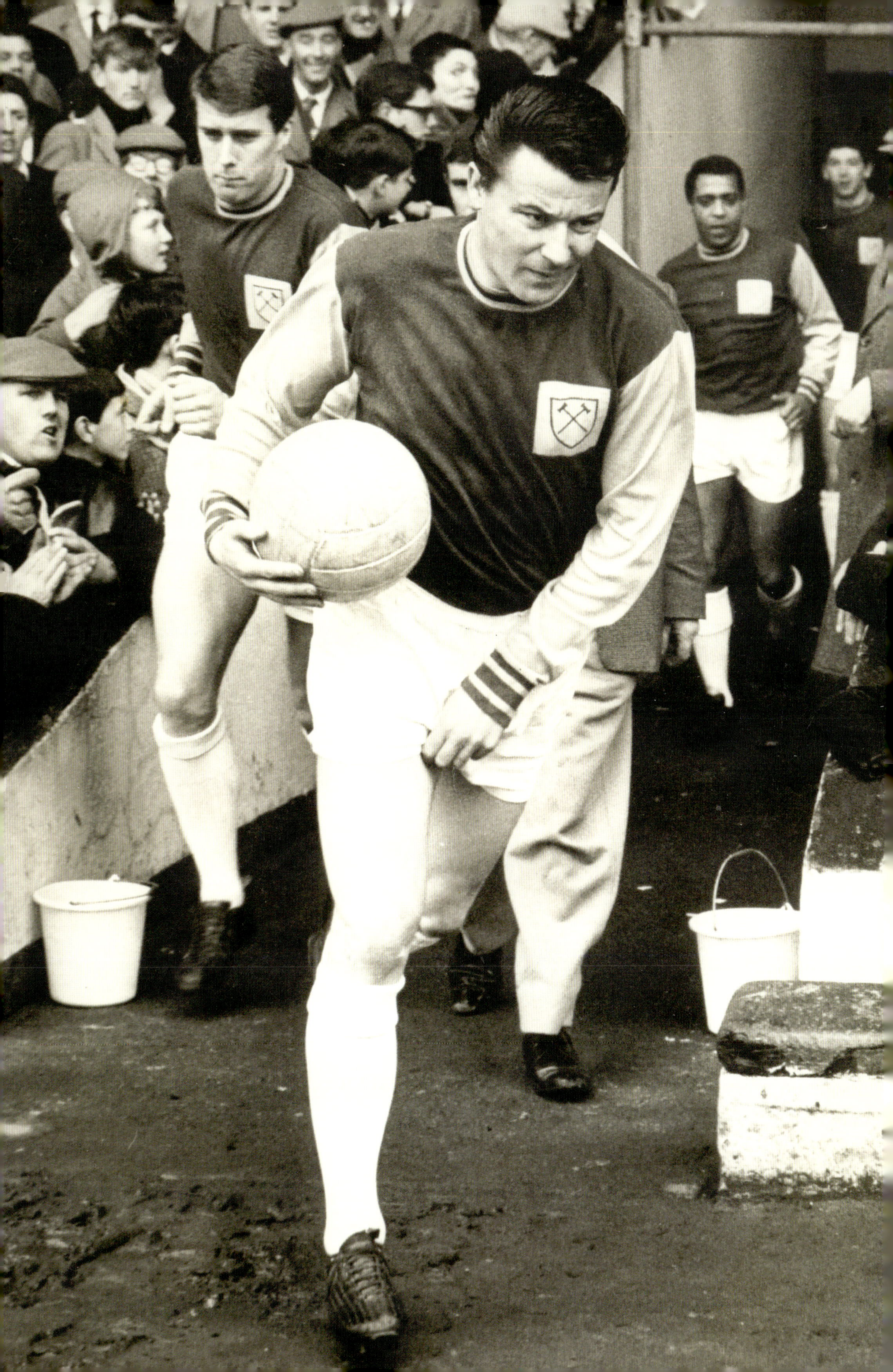

So the few hundred or so West Ham fans who travelled north for the Wednesday night replay to the land of Lancashire hot-pot, whippets and pigeon-fanciers from their own equivalent world of pie and mash, jellied eels and greyhounds, must have felt some trepidation. If indeed they did, it was proved to be well justified, for although Hurst countered Andy McEvoy's 14th minute opener, it soon became apparent their team were in for a torrid time under the Ewood Park floodlights.

Rovers' torrent of attacks started from the kick-off. Standen needed attention after diving at Malcolm Darling's feet, Byron struck a post and McEvoy headed over within the first five minutes. It was Hammers' tormenter-in-chief at Upton Park, Byron, who put his side into the lead in the 34th minute when he turned in a shot by winger Harrison. Then, in the 41st minute, Moore misjudged his headed clearance and McEvoy, outpacing Bovington, drove in a superb third goal from 20 yards. Only three minutes later he gave Standen no chance as he thundered in Harrison's cross to score from 25 yards to complete his hat-trick and make it 4-1 at half-time. That's the way it stayed, but it would have been more but for shots from McEvoy, Byron and Harrison hitting the woodwork and a superb performance by Standen.

So it was Rovers and out.

Surprisingly, there was no hang-over and the team bounced back to inflict a comprehensive 4-0 defeat on Sheffield United at the Boleyn three days later. Helped initially by a bizarre own-goal by the visitors' left-half Reg Matthewson who ushered the ball back to Alan Hodgkinson in goal, who slipped on the wet surface and ended up flat on his face with the ball in the net. When Moore put Brabrook clear for the second at 23 minutes gone and Hurst added another ten minutes later, West Ham were cruising at half-time. When Peters scored the fourth goal 17 minutes from time the points were in the onion bag. But if both sides had not missed so many chances due to the treacherous surface, the final score might have resembled that of a rugger match.

Featuring six of the XI who had defeated Millwall by 3-0 at Chadwell Heath the previous Saturday, the Youth Team faced another London club – QPR – in the Quarter Final of the FA Youth Cup the following Monday evening at Upton Park (21/2/66) and lined up: Death, Glozier, R. Jarman, Brooking, James, Lampard, T. Clements, Simmons, K. Minor, Miller, Walker.

I think it best to allow programme editor Jack Helliar's match report to convey the details of what transpired that night in his usual concise and inimitable fashion via the match programme for the Aston Villa game on Saturday, March 5:

"The manner of our exit in this Quarter-Final tie was unsatisfactory in more ways than one, for it seemed that the dice were loaded against us from the start. During the preceding weekend the 'flu-bug' struck Paul Heffer and Roger Cross from our ranks and it was only some sterling work by Bill Jenkins which made Stephen Death fit enough to play after a morning-of-the-match scare. We thus had a considerably re-arranged side and although the West Londoners made something like five late changes in their announced line-up, the incoming players only served to add to their strength.

"However, the Hammers were not deterred by these initial set-backs and attacked with such vigour in the opening spell that it came as a surprise when the visitors broke away to score in the ninth minute. With a linesman clearly flagging for offside, play was allowed to go on and the ball was in our net after a couple of quick passes. It is true that our youngsters did not appeal, but although the linesman stood his ground for a while he continued to be unnoticed and we were one down.

"An attack at Rangers' end was cleared after the ball had fallen vertically from the underside of the bar and soon afterwards the 'keeper was bustled into the net as he caught a centre on the line. Then, almost on the strike of half-time, a great flying save once more prevented the equaliser.

"Rangers kept playing a steady game, but whilst defending well against wave after wave of attacks they had more than one stroke of luck in retaining a clean sheet. But prevail they did and although we were disappointed by losing by the only goal we must give them credit for often showing that the League and Combination experience of several of their players was a decisive element in their progress to the Semi-Final.

"To the younger Hammers we give a most deserved pat on the back and they can look back upon a fine game which we felt might well have earned a replay.

"Our expectations of a gate approaching five figures proved to be correct, the number present being 9,120. During the day we had several calls asking if the game was still on and but for the effects of the week-end rain, which raised these doubts, we believe that the attendance would have been more".

That attendance figure was trebled for the next cup-tie at Upton Park, however, by the 30,620

The West Ham bench in Magdeburg: L-R Alan Dickie, John Charles, Peter Bennett, Johnny Byrne (an interpreter), Ron Greenwood (with umbrella), Albert Walker and Bill Jenkins.

who gathered there for the long-awaited visit of East German team FC Magdeburg in the quarter-finals of the ECWC (2/3/66).

On paper, the part-timers appeared to pose little threat, but ever mindful of the previous season's encounter with Belgian minnows La Grantoise, manager Greenwood was taking no chances, he accorded them the utmost respect and flew out to East Germany to attend their Oberliga match against Olympic Berlin, which was lost 2-1. His caution proved to be well founded.

Although Magdeburg were involved in a relegation battle in their domestic league, they had progressed well in the ECWC, disposing of Spora of Luxemburg in the Preliminary Round (1-0 at home and 2-0 away) and then waltzed into the next stage on the back of an impressive 10-2 aggregate victory over FC Sion of Switzerland. The contest was virtually settled in the 1st leg in Magdeburg which the East Germans won by an 8-1 margin with Manfred Eckhardt, Joachim Walter and Gunter Kubisch scoring twice and Wolfgang Sequin and Hermann Stocker getting the other two. The away leg was drawn 2-2 when it was Rainer Wiedemann's turn to score a brace. Maybe the team their fans called "Der Club", wouldn't be such a pushover after all. Let's let Steve Richards take up the tale via his match report in the next morning's *Daily Mail*:

"West Ham, the human yo-yos of English football, last night took up an uncomfortable position on the edge of the cliff in the European Cup Winners' Cup.

"I have seen Ron Greenwood's young men step over far better opposition than this with contemptuous ease. Last night, assisted by the German's refusal to pull down an iron curtain defence, they created more chances than any of the 31,000 fans would have the right to expect

Byrne cracks home the last minute winner against WBA in the first-leg of the Football League Cup Final to make the score 2-1, but Hammers lost the second leg 4-1 at the Hawthorns.

in two First Division matches.

"But they scored only one goal, a hook shot by centre-forward Johnny Byrne in the 47th minute after one of West Ham's few flowing moves. They only got my sympathy when Geoff Hurst, particularly, was having to snatch at half chances and, as an England new boy, was having to suffer humiliating derision from the crowd. Once, poor Hurst crashed the ball over the stand behind the German goal – and out of the ground.

"Yet there were many other occasions when West Ham had time – and missed inexcusably. Later the West Ham fever spread fatally to the German forwards and two excellent chances were tossed away when the Hammers' defence was showing gaps through the team's desperation in trying to increase the lead.

"Unexpectedly, the most consistent finishing from West Ham came almost at the end when a Byrne header and a 20-yard drive by Peters were both saved creditably by goalkeeper Wolfgang Blochwitz. Few teams have attacked so much and scored so little. Few teams except West Ham, who have such exasperating moods peculiar, it seems to themselves.

"Magdeburg should be interesting!"

Indeed it was, but this time it was Magdeburg's turn to suffer in front of goal.

Under the banner headline in the *Stratford Express* which proclaimed: "SISSONS LIFTS SIEGE OF MAGDEBURG. Sports Editor Peter Faulkner reported on the match:

"West Ham stepped up their bid for a double entry into Europe next season after holding Magdeburg's fighting soccer army to a 1-1 draw in the open-air Ernst Grube Stadium on Wednesday.

"Today they bear the cruel scars of this European Cup Winners' Cup quarter-final – a sad reminder of Magdeburg's 90-minute battering.

"Praise Hammers for their brilliant defensive display that halted an East German march deeper into Europe and kept Cockney cup hopes alive.

"Magdeburg proved to be a side that never accepted defeat, a side that wanted to make this a game to remember and a side that can hold its head up proudly on the European soccer circuit.

"Despite their incessant goal pounding, Magdeburg couldn't break down Hammers' great defensive wall. They were forced to shoot at long range – and showed up their lack of target practice.

"The 200 loyal Hammers fans braved biting winds and a tiring 1,500 mile round trip to cheer their cup heroes. But the cheers were lost in the frenzied white-hot heat of 35,000 fanatical, firework throwing, East Germans.

"This massive stadium erupted when centre-forward Walter erased Hammers' one goal, first-leg lead with a 78th minute scrambled goal.

"But within 30 seconds the mad, cheering mob of fans were shocked into deadly silence as Johnny Sissons crashed home the equaliser. Hurst moved the ball to Brabrook who crossed for Sissons to slip the ball home. All that could be heard in this massive bowl was the faint, but faithful hoarse and happy cries of victory from those 200 cockneys.

"It was all over. Magdeburg needed three goals to earn a place in the semi-finals, for under the new Cup Winners' Cup ruling the team that scores most goals away from home is awarded another goal.

"The rain began to pour down, but East London's own fans still stood and applauded every move until the referee's whistle signalled the end. The misery was over for Magdeburg."

Manager Ron Greenwood claimed post-match:

"If we had gained a bigger lead in the first leg this match might have been more attractive. Our eight man defence played magnificently though."

Johnny Sissons: "It was a great feeling. The crowd was so quiet when we scored it seemed something was wrong."

Ernst Kuemmell, manager of Magdeburg: "West Ham were lucky. We went all out for goals and had our shooting been more direct we would have swamped them."

West ham's fans had to have an armed police escort into the war-shattered city. High ranking police officials, worried in case any West Germans had hidden in any of the five coaches followed the convoy down the autobahn and into the city. Every car, lorry and coach was checked and a traffic jam began building up as police armed with luger pistols searched luggage racks, seats and boots for any defecting Germans. Magdeburg itself was still re-building from the devastating effects of the Second World War. In January, 1945, an allied bomber force wiped out the centre of the city in 45 minutes killing 16,000 people. All that remained was the shell of the 14th century church.

After defeating Villa and Blackburn at Upton Park, it was back on the road again to the bread and butter fare of fighting for relegation avoiding points at lowly Blackpool, where only 10,559 turned up at Bloomfield Road to see the Tangerines gain a rare 2-1 victory thanks to goals from Ray Charmley and Alan Ball – the latter who would join Hurst, Moore and Peters in the England side for the World Cup Finals in the summer. Local schoolboy fans did jigs of joy on the pitch at the end.

Then came three more home games in a hectic seven days. The first was won handsomely to the tune of four goals (Burkett, Byrne, Brabrook, Hurst) to Aston Villa's two which gave Hammers their first League "Double" of the season – as was the third versus Blackburn by 4-1 (Dear, Brabrook, Hurst, Burkett) to give Irons revenge for the FA Cup defeat and also their second "Double". But it was the match in the middle of the sandwich which the team really needed to score a hatful of goals – in the Football League Cup Final, 1st Leg, against WBA.

Largely referred to as the "Forgotten Final" of West Ham's history, it nevertheless carried a massive caveat for the winners – entry into the lucrative Inter-Cities Fairs' Cup competition for the first time. So this was arguably the most important pair of fixtures this crowded campaign. Certainly the record League Cup crowd of 28,323 seemed to think so as they waited expectantly for battle to commence with old foes Albion, no mean cup fighters themselves.

I was occupying my usual vantage point on the North Bank that night – right behind the goal about 20 steps up the terrace. I remember the initial carnival-like atmosphere suddenly turning ugly as Albion packed their defence with nine men to frustrate Hammers' ineffective efforts to break through. It was still stalemate at the interval during which fighting broke out around me and two fans were ejected by the police. But Albion were not completely dedicated to defence as Bryon Butler explained in his match report in the *Telegraph*: "Given possession they blossomed quickly and effectively into attack with their three strikers Brown, Astle and Clark, often stretching West Ham's battle-proven defence to breaking point. Albion even contrived to score first. Clark made the opening and Astle, back in the side after three month's absence with cartilage trouble, swept exuberantly on to the ball to score with a fierce, low, 18-yard drive.

"West Ham, frustrated but not, to their everlasting credit, prepared to concede defeat, threw themselves at Albion's defensive wall even more frenziedly, it was not pretty, but it was to prove effective.

"Moore had not been looking like a captain of England, but, in the 71st minute, he took a return pass from Dear and from 35 yards, swung the ball into the middle.

"It might have been intended as a shot, it was probably meant as a centre, but what happened was that Potter sensed danger too late, groped awkwardly and turned just in time to watch the ball dip under the bar.

"A goal by Byrne in a moment of magnificent confusion just 20 seconds from the end gave West Ham a barely deserved victory.

"Potter looked to be obstructed, two West Ham players were enmeshed in the back of the net and another, I thought, handled the ball.

"Byrne suddenly found himself in possession, unmarked and facing an open goal. He glanced round as if seeking someone to pass to, thought better of it and stabbed the ball into the net."

Despite Budgie coming to the rescue again, the team had still left themselves a mountain to climb in the 2nd leg two weeks hence. West Ham: Standen, Burnett, Burkett, Peters, Brown, Moore, Brabrook, Boyce, Byrne, Hurst, Dear.

Then came the return with WBA, where victory or even a draw would guarantee Hammers a copper-bottomed insurance policy for European competition during the 1966-67 season, via the Inter Cities Fairs' Cup.

Alas, it was not to be. On one of the darkest nights in Hammers' history – illuminated only by the brilliance of Albion's remorseless attacking football and the Hawthorn's floodlights – the match was over as a contest after just 34 minutes during which time the Throstles were 4-0 ahead through goals from Kaye, Brown, Clark and Williams. Peters got the worthless consolation goal late in the second half.

On a brighter note, it was announced in the home programme for the Fulham match on March 26, that Geoff Hurst would be joining team mate Bobby Moore in the England team to face Scotland at Hampden Park in April for his second cap at full international level.

But that's where the good news ended. With the counter attractions of the Grand National, the Boat Race and the FA Cup Quarter-Finals all being staged on the same afternoon, only 18,977 turned up to watch the First Division clash with relegation-fighting Fulham at Upton Park.

Those that stayed away missed another inept display from Hammers, who were obviously still suffering the after-effects of the West Brom debacle. The Cottagers 1-3 win made it four victories on the trot for them. It was 0-3 after 67 minutes through goals from Earle, Barrett and Leggatt with only Hurst replying for Hammers in the last quarter.

Although there were no counter-attractions this time, only 17,635 turned up for the following week's home game against second placed Burnley. With Moore and Hurst on international duty, Greenwood drafted in Dawkins and Dear. With Brown out injured also, the 1-1 draw was not too shabby. Brabrook put Hammers ahead after 60 minutes, but Irvine levelled for the Clarets to leave them seven points behind leaders Liverpool with seven games to go.

Then came the big one: West Ham United versus Borussia Dortmund, ECWC Semi-Final, 1st Leg on Tuesday, April 5, 1966 at Upton Park. This was the encounter that would decide the destiny of both clubs for this and the following campaign.

With no less than seven full West German internationals in their 19-man squad, Dortmund represented the strongest challenge Hammers had faced so far in their two ECWC campaigns.

Six of the protagonists on duty – Moore, Hurst and Peters and Tilkowski, Held and Emmerich – would do battle again in the World Cup Final at Wembley on July 30, but, for now, the prize at stake was the handsome silver trophy sitting tantalisingly close in the West Ham trophy room.

BVB, as they were nicknamed (after the Ballspielverin Borussia club formed in 1909) would be redoubtable opponents for sure. The teams lined-up – West Ham: Standen, Brown, Charles, Peters, Boyce, Moore, Brabrook, Bloomfield, Byrne, Hurst, Dear. Dortmund: Tilkowski, Cyliax, Redder, Kurrat, Paul, Assaur, Libuda, Schmidt, Held, Sturm, Emmerich.

Although I was there, on the North Bank that amazing evening, I must let Bryon Butler relate events via his contemporary match report in the *Daily Telegraph* under the headline, "GERMAN'S LATE RAIDS ROB WEST HAM".

"Two goals in the last four minutes by Lothar Emmerich, West Germany's leading scorer, provided a thunderclap of a finish to a brilliant and combative first leg of the European Cup

Skipper Johnny Byrne leads out the team for the second-leg with Borussia Dortmund.

Moore before the second-leg in Dortmund.

Winners' Cup Semi-Final at Upton Park last night.

"His priceless opportunism means, sadly but almost inevitably, that West Ham have lost this trophy they won so memorably last season.

"It is unthinkable that they can make up so must lost ground in Dortmund next week against a team of crushing efficiency, wide skill and indomitable spirit. Remember, too, that away goals count double in this competition if aggregate scores are level after two legs.

"But nothing must be allowed to detract from the magnificence of this match. It throbbed with all that is best in football.

"Nobody, quite obviously, had told Borussia that teams playing away from home in European competitions are supposed to defend. They took the game to West Ham at every conceivable opportunity.

"But West Ham are an odd lot. After weeks of tepid muddling in the league they suddenly shed all their inhibitions, rediscovered their old spark, their old co-ordination, and became a team of which English football could be proud.

"Yet the night did not begin too promisingly. Byrne was captain and Moore, the man he deposed and the man whose days are numbered at Upton Park, was booed as – as last but one – he took the field. How churlish it was.

"Moore, however, was soon to win the crowd to his side in the best way he knows how, by stamping his authority with strength and fervour on the night's events. This was the Moore England will need this summer.

"He was not alone. Bloomfield was at his foxiest, Byrne darted about incisively, Brown stuck relentlessly to his job and Peters was at his ubiquitous best.

"Alf Ramsey, England's team manager, was there to see it all and if Peters is not at the moment included in his first list of 40, the West Ham player's performance last night might well lead to a discreet amendment. Peters proved beyond all doubt that he has the perception and range of skill to tax the best. Peters scored West Ham's goal seven minutes after half-time. Bloomfield gave Peters the ball midway in Borussia's half and with Byrne running free on the left it looked as if the movement would continue that way. But Peters suddenly cut inside, drifted past two defenders and scored with a crisp, low drive.

"West Ham drove remorsefully for the second goal they needed, but it did not come and as they stretched forward in the last minutes Borussia hit them once and then twice with shattering efficiency.

"First Libuda, a wraith-like figure, gave Emmerich the chance to score from 12 yards; and with only two minutes left Held crossed from the left and Emmerich, waiting by the far post, slid the ball smoothly past Standen.

"Whoever wins the Liverpool-Celtic semi-final must gird themselves to meet a very, very good side in the Final at Hampden Park on May 5."

In the aftermath of this shattering defeat, manager Greenwood was philosophical, yet still hopeful of salvaging the tie: "The way it ended was cruel but a game lasts 90 minutes. We have not given up hope.

"Dortmund are a good side, but they were not in it. I told my players how good this West German team were to buck them up. But we did not let them be good.

"I thought Bloomfield was the best player on the field and Byrne has been appointed captain for the rest of the season".

Deposed skipper Bobby Moore told the German players: "You will still have a hard game over there".

At this time there was an impasse between Greenwood and Moore as impenetrable as the iron curtain with Moore claiming to have struck a gentleman's agreement with his boss to keep quiet about him wanting to continue his career elsewhere until the season was over. Greenwood, however, let the cat out of the bag at the worst possible time – on the eve of the semi-final with the Germans – claiming: "The public had a right to know".

Still there was no let up for Hammers' battle-weary bravehearts from this, the most arduous of campaigns, as they prepared for the visit to Tottenham on Good Friday – just three days after losing to Dortmund – and Chelsea the next day.

With Moore sitting fuming in the White Hart Lane stand (he was rumoured to be joining Spurs for a peppercorn £80,000 in the summer), West Ham turned in their best away performance of the season to win 1-4 and confound the pre-match forecasts which all favoured the home team.

I was there (I'll have to get the T-shirt) standing just to the right of the Paxton Road end goal about three steps from the boundary wall. I had to go and support the lads after their heroic efforts against Dortmund.

It was a case of "Oh, no – here we go again" when Gilzean scored for Spurs after 16 minutes at the Park Lane end to make it 1-0.

But Hammers hit back – hard. Five minutes later they were level. Byrne collected a through ball from Peters to find himself with just Bill Brown to beat in the Spurs goal close in. He sadistically delayed his shot until Brown dived and then lifted the ball over the Scottish international's sprawling, grounded body into the net for the cheekiest of goals.

Just two minutes later, Hurst scored his 39th goal of the season when the shaken Spurs' keeper dropped the ball after a fumble almost at Hurst's feet. Right in front of me, Geoff slammed the ball home with an angled shot – 1-2.

Immediately after the break, Redknapp – playing his socks off on the right flank – thrashed the ball past a statuesque Brown from 28 yards. Ten minutes from the end Byrne, whose skilful display silenced the Spurs fans' jeers, slid the ball through to Boyce. Brown never moved as the ball hit the back of the net from 30 yards out for the fourth goal.

One black spot was the running feud which had developed between Spurs' defender Alan Mullery and Johnny Byrne. The latter was booked 20 minutes after the break for what reporter, Barrie Keeffe, described as a "glorious south-paw elbow hook to Mullery's nose" and added: "I don't advocate the rough stuff, but I do sympathise with Byrne. He took a tremendous amount of ankle thumping and shirt-tugging without a single free-kick.

"There is a limit to how much anyone can take without retaliation. Mullery was duly booked in return for avenging his bruised nose five minutes later with a less spectacular haul from behind. It followed five minutes of hounding of Byrne by strong man Dave McKay. Only trouble was, he was too slow to catch bouncing Budgie".

Roy Peskett saw things differently in his report in the *Daily Mail*: "Bill Nicholson, Spurs manager, will speak to Alan Mullery before the £70,000 wing-half takes the field at Hillsborough today.

"In the 19th minute of the second-half Mullery hurled Johnny Byrne, West Ham captain, to the ground then stamped on his prone body in full view of the crowd.

"Fifteen minutes earlier Byrne had his name taken when he appeared to strike Mullery.

"Nicholson said after the game: 'There was obviously a bit of needle going on, but certain things happened with which I don't agree. There is no need for that sort of stuff in our game.

"I haven't talked to Mullery yet, but I will do so".

The protagonists were due to meet again two weeks later in the return bout at Upton Park.

Greenwood rang the changes the next day at Stamford Bridge – seven in all. Burkett replaced Charles at left-back, Dawkins took over from Bovington at right-half, Moore from Peters at left half, Brabrook from Redknapp on the right-wing, Bloomfield for Boyce at inside-right, Bennett for Byrne at centre-forward and Dear for Hurst at inside-left.

To be fair, Greenwood had earlier notified his intention to use two different line-ups over Easter to give match practice to as many of the senior squad as possible. But the embarrassing 6-2 defeat must have made him question his own wisdom. As a fan, I felt cheated by his selection, as did many more when Chelsea went 4-0 ahead after just 28 humiliating minutes in the quagmire conditions.

The rain kept falling and so did the goals as Osgood set up Graham with an audacious overhead kick for the first goal after five minutes. Then Venables sent Standen the wrong way with a penalty two minutes later after Dawkins had handled. Two Tambling goals in the 14th and 27th minutes completed the first-half rout.

Four minutes after the break, Graham hit the fifth before Ron Harris, standing unmarked, slammed in the sixth for his first goal of the season in the 80th minute. Sixty seconds later he got a second – but in the wrong net as he turned a Brabrook shot past Bonetti. Bennett scored another consolation for the demoralised Hammers two minutes from time.

It was West Ham's biggest defeat since Blackburn won 8-2 at Upton Park on Boxing Day, 1963, and the first time Chelsea had beaten Irons at Stamford Bridge for five years. Hardly a result to take to Dortmund.

And so, after the 6-2 shambles at Chelsea, it was on to the 2nd-leg of the ECWC semi-final at the Stadion Rote Erde to face Dortmund.

It must have felt like a visit to the dentist – hoping for a filling but knowing deep down that a molar will be extracted. For there was no way the holes in West Ham's defence – once almost impregnable in European combat – could now be repaired. It took Dortmund's goal-hungry forwards, buzzing around the visitor's goal like so many black and gold coloured wasps just 25 seconds to provide the "sting" that proved the point.

A mazy run down the left flank by Siggi Held sparked the early knock-out when he cut the ball back to Emmerich whose thunderous shot cannoned back off the bar back to the burly motor mechanic's head which finished the job without a West Ham player touching the ball. It was as good as over.

It was definitely "finis" when the man they call "Emma" scored again with a 22nd minute free-kick which swerved round, or went through Hammers' badly formed wall depending on what match report you read. The goal was a signal for the German fans to unleash the whole gamut of their armour, screeching sirens, deafening horns and thundering chants as many ran onto the pitch despite a patrolling posse of German Shepherd guard dogs.

Then, just before half-time, Hammers gave their loyal band of 200 or so travelling fans a glimmer of hope. Brabrook burst through the Dortmund defence to cross hard for Byrne to head into goal.

Now showing glimpses of the form they displayed at Tottenham, a second-half revival nearly got them back into the tie and brought them the glory they wanted – but only nearly. Peters hit a volley onto the top of the bar, then headed just over with the black garbed Tilkowski beaten.

Then Moore's pass found Hurst unmarked, deep in Borussia's penalty area. He brought the ball down with his chest, but hesitated fatally and the chance was lost. Hurst should have scored again late in the game when he blasted the ball over the bar from close in, but by then it was too late – Dortmund had already booked their place at Hampden Park.

Minutes from time, right-back Cyliax hammered the final nail into Hammers' dreams with a shot that deflected off Brown's shoulder and over Standen's head for the third goal. West Ham: Standen, Bovington, Charles, Peters, Brown, Moore, Brabrook, Boyce, Byrne, Hurst, Bloomfield.

A crest-fallen Johnny Sissons said post-match: "Dortmund played well. We were off form. Had we got that first goal, I think it could have changed the course of the game". Realistic as ever, Greenwood said: "We were lucky only to be two goals down at half-time. Dortmund deserved their place in the Final".

It was "Auf Wiedersehen" to Europe. Ten years would elapse before West Ham returned to competitive combat on the continent and another European Cup Winners' Cup Final with different players, but holding the same dreams of glory.

Hammers' deflated, battle-weary troops had precious little time to feel sorry for themselves, however, as just three days later they were back in First Division action at Upton Park to face Arsenal – their first opponents in a five-match frantic finale to this crowded, crazy campaign.

The fact that only 26,022 turned up might have been an indication of the strain the number of matches had put on the home fans' wallets and also the waning fortunes of the Gunners, who would languish in 13th place at season's end.

Still seething after the Dortmund disaster, the homesters were in no mood to help their cause and in the first 80 seconds, hit the bar twice. First Sissons flicked the ball on to the woodwork, following a cross from Burnett and then Moore, from 25 yards out, struck the underside of the bar.

Arsenal's defence was all over the place in the opening minutes and goalkeeper Furnell was lucky when a shot from Sissons hit him and rebounded clear. Then, after the deadly duo – Byrne and his compadre Hurst – tried speculative shots, Furnell just got a hand to the ball to turn aside a shot by Peters.

The Gunners were hardly in the game, but after ten minutes, Baldwin missed a sitter. After Skirton had crossed from the right wing, the centre-forward, standing less than a yard from the goal-line, failed to get a touch.

West Ham were clearly superior and after 12 minutes they went ahead when Neill brought down Hurst in the box and Byrne scored easily from the spot, sending Furnell the wrong way. It was the fourth penalty conceded by Arsenal in the last three games. Yet Arsenal levelled the scores seven minutes later. Moore tripped Court on the edge of the penalty area and from Eastham's quick free-kick Baldwin dashed forward to stab the ball into goal to make amends for his earlier miss. Undaunted, Moore had an effort well saved by Furnell and Neill deflected a shot by Hurst round a post as the Hammers continued to make most of the running.

Much of the tackling from both sides was over-robust and several heated exchanges occurred with the referee looking on indulgently.

Ure, never a favourite at Upton Park due to his run-ins with Byrne over previous years, again earned the wrath of the crowd for two over-zealous tackles on Budgie and the game began to deteriorate amid a series of unsavoury incidents.

Four minutes before the interval, Ure fouled the effervescent Byrne again. Budgie took the free-kick himself, pushed the ball to Burnett and from the full-back's centre, Brabrook headed home a fully deserved second goal for Hammers.

With Peters and Brabrook in outstanding form, the home team nearly scored again four minutes after the break. Brabrook, controlling the ball well in a confined space, pushed it through to Hurst whose shot struck the advancing Furnell and cannoned over the 'keeper's body towards the net. Just as the ball was going over the goal-line, Neill raced back and hooked it out from under the bar.

Then Hurst raced on to a through pass from Byrne but Neill again got a foot to the ball to put it behind for a corner, only for the referee to award a goal-kick – much to the derision of the crowd.

It was a vital win for Irons which kept them out of relegation trouble. Also back in the news was our old mate Charlie Williams who played his part in the SECL clash with Millwall Juniors at Chadwell Heath. The young Irons beat the Lion Cubs 3-0 with goals from J, Sutton (pen), J. Bean and an own goal.

Unsurprisingly, as the country's leading goalscorer, Geoff Hurst was voted "Hammer of the Year". Second was his England team mate, Martin Peters and third, Peter Brabrook.

Those other North London giants, Spurs, were the penultimate visitors to Upton Park on a Monday night under the lights and if the newspaper reports had it right, White Hart Lane would soon be the destination for Bobby Moore – as outlined by Albert Sewell in the next morning's *Daily Telegraph*. "Fine football, most of it from West Ham, flowed at Upton Park last night with the only incongruous note is the fact that both goals came from penalties from Johnny Byrne.

"So, West Ham completed the double they began by winning 4-1 at White Hart Lane on Good Friday. Yet it need not have proven a totally lost night for Spurs.

"Manager Bill Nicholson saw Bobby Moore give such a commanding display that, with a gigantic rebuilding problem on his hands and the necessary money in the kitty, he would be making a sound investment in the England captain even at a likely fee of £100,000.

"West Ham are resigned to Moore leaving when his contract ends in June. Ron Greenwood says they must prepare to do without him and intended doing so last night until Bovington went down with an 'infection'.

"Moore used the situation to produce one of his peak performances of the season. Whenever needed, he was there at the heart of the defence; constructively, he hit some immaculate 30 yard through balls to Hurst and Byrne and followed up close behind the strikers in a magnificent all-round display.

"If this was Moore's last game for West Ham, he certainly gave Upton Park supporters something to remember him by. One of his long through passes led to the first penalty after four minutes. Byrne ran on to it, Mullery impeded him from behind and Byrne slammed in the penalty.

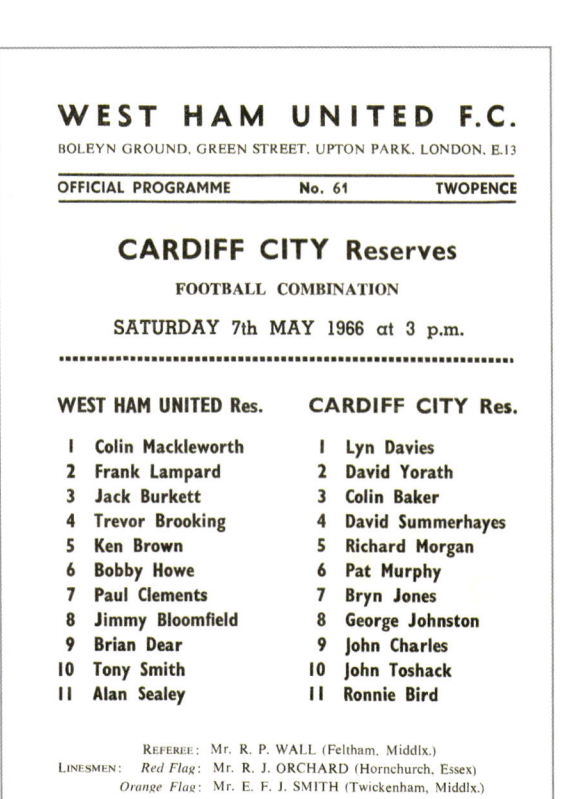

"His second was driven home just as surely 10 minutes from the end when Kinnear handled on the line. And between Byrne's goals there might have been half a dozen others in a 4-2 ratio to West Ham.

"Greaves was Spurs best forward, closely shadowed though he was by Charles. After his long illness he is gradually finding his old spark and that vital extra yard; it was good to see and gave hope for a top form Greaves again in time for the World Cup. With, let us hope, none of the ill-luck he experienced last night. In the first-half, he saw a point-blank header strike

---

WEST HAM UNITED F.C.
BOLEYN GROUND, GREEN STREET, UPTON PARK, LONDON, E.13

OFFICIAL PROGRAMME   No. 61   TWOPENCE

CARDIFF CITY Reserves
FOOTBALL COMBINATION
SATURDAY 7th MAY 1966 at 3 p.m.

WEST HAM UNITED Res.	CARDIFF CITY Res.
1 Colin Mackleworth	1 Lyn Davies
2 Frank Lampard	2 David Yorath
3 Jack Burkett	3 Colin Baker
4 Trevor Brooking	4 David Summerhayes
5 Ken Brown	5 Richard Morgan
6 Bobby Howe	6 Pat Murphy
7 Paul Clements	7 Bryn Jones
8 Jimmy Bloomfield	8 George Johnston
9 Brian Dear	9 John Charles
10 Tony Smith	10 John Toshack
11 Alan Sealey	11 Ronnie Bird

REFEREE: Mr. R. P. WALL (Feltham, Middlx.)
LINESMEN: Red Flag: Mr. R. J. ORCHARD (Hornchurch, Essex)
Orange Flag: Mr. E. F. J. SMITH (Twickenham, Middlx.)

Standen's shoulder and go over the bar, and in the second, almost unbelievably he hit the fallen goalkeeper from two yards". But the man destined to fill Greaves' role in the World Cup – Hurst – came even closer to scoring with a superb 25-yard shot which rebounded to safety from the inside of a post.

Also staking a claim for World Cup selection was the versatile Martin Peters, who did his chances a power of good with a superb performance against Manchester United in the last match of the season at the Boleyn, watched by England manager Alf Ramsey.

Certainly, Clive Toye in the *Daily Express* was in no doubt about the validity of his right to be selected as he expounded the Dagenham-born midfielder's virtues:

"Martin Peters must be teetering on the edge of England's team, and I hope manager Alf Ramsey calls him in to face Yugoslavia on Wednesday night.

"Peters of West Ham, the slender silent player of such clean and classical skills, had much to take the attention from him in West Ham's 3-2 beating of Manchester United.

"Yet it was Peters you saw, placing a pass, reaching the right spot without seeming to hasten. And more important, it was Peters that England manager Alf Ramsey saw again.

"The crowd also witnessed Bobby Charlton, flourishing his first 15 minutes' football in the grand manner of a man newly elected Footballer of the Year.

"His fans chanted: 'We've got the Player of the Year', until Bobby Moore, once given that accolade himself, gathered his defence around him and stopped the chants... and Charlton.

"Moore made his debut against United eight years ago on this ground. This match was his last for West Ham at home and the crowd appreciated the poignancy of the moment.

"But it was Peters who had a hand in the first two goals and he might have scored a couple himself. All this danger from a player chosen mostly for his midfield virtues. United had no one to match him".

Steve Richards had this to say about the match that brought the curtain down on the season at Upton Park:

"Former Chelsea captain Terry Venables picked Spurs as his next club instead of West Ham and maybe nine out of ten players would have made the same decision.

"But writing off West Ham as an unfashionable club would be as misguided as the hooliganism of some Manchester United fans who were rightly thrown out of the ground by police.

"I think West Ham will go places under the astute leadership of Ronnie Greenwood, who is one of the best, if not the wealthiest, managers in the game.

"Now that they have got their worst season for injuries in years behind them they can topple the best in the land, as they showed in outwitting Manchester United.

"West Ham had many outstanding performers in one of their more direct displays and none more polished than Burnett".

As the Fleet Street boys have had their say about what transpired on that gloriously sunny spring day 51 years ago, I feel it only fair that I should give my own take on the match and the somewhat unusual events that unfolded around me via an article I penned for *Hammers News* magazine in May, 1996:

"What is it about Manchester United? Love them or loathe them, 'house full' notices invariably go up whenever they're in town, as was the case on the occasion of the visit to Upton Park for a First Division fixture on Saturday, April 30, 1966.

"Despite the fact that nothing much was at stake – Hammers occupied a safe mid-table position while United were in fourth place – the gates were locked on a season's best crowd of 36,416, half-an-hour before kick-off.

"Thousands more were locked out, among them yours truly. Milling around outside the main gates in Green Street, I was approached by two Manchester lads who asked if I knew any other way into the ground.

"There might be a chance round the Chicken Run side", I guiltily replied and with segregation still the exception rather than the rule, an unlikely looking trio went off to explore the possibilities of gaining entry by fair means or foul.

"As I feared, the Chicken Run was 'chock-a-block' and the turnstiles well and truly closed. With kick-off agonisingly close and the chances of witnessing Moore, Hurst, Byrne and Peters pitting their skills against Charlton, Law, Best and Crerand receding by the minute, caution was thrown to the wind when a loose board was spotted some eight feet from ground level.

"This is definitely out of order, I thought as I was propelled upwards with one foot on each of my Mancunian partners-in-crime's shoulders.

"I pulled, then slid the board sideways to be met by a deafening blast of sound as the teams came out.

"Cheekily shouting 'next' I went through head-first, but horror! – the ground level on the other side was a lot lower than the pavement on Priory Road. And worse still, there was a 70-year-old steward guarding his patch of the longest latrine in the country against just the eventuality which was now taking place, armed to my dismay, with a stout walking stick, which he proceeded to bring down on my head as hard and rapidly as a septuagenarian is able.

"To his credit, blood was soon drawn, as I came down the wall head first with one hand holding on to a drain pipe, Spider-man like, and the other trying to fend off the blows to the Hogg bonce.

"Summoning up my last reserves of rapidly waning strength, I managed to grab the stick and, uttering dark oaths, look sufficiently threatening to put my assailant to flight despite by now being totally 'done in'.

"To complete my grand, if unorthodox, entrance all I had left to do now was to perform a hand-stand next to a dangerously overflowing trough, followed by a forward roll before some startled patrons of the West Ham WC and I was 'home and (almost) dry'.

"Not standing on ceremony, I made straight for the square of light at the top of the wooden steps (everything was wooden in the old 'run' except the corrugated iron roof and the steel girders which held it up) and due to my wild-eyed disorientated state, the crowd miraculously parted for me just as Denis Law took his place on the half-way line to share pleasantries with the locals.

"The match was the 60th of long, hard season for Hammers and the last home match, but they were up for this one, having defeated Arsenal and Spurs in consecutive home games.

Hurst in action against United (watched by Hoggy in the crowd)

"With the 1966 World Cup Finals just a month away and three players from each side due to play a part in England's triumph on view (Bobby Charlton, Nobby Stiles and John Connelly for United and Moore, Hurst and Peters for West Ham), the match quickly followed the pattern of a true West Ham/Man Utd classic encounter with play ebbing and flowing from end to end.

"Watched by England manager Alf Ramsey from the stands, Bobby Charlton celebrated his selection as Footballer of the Year with a 'magical performance' as one paper reported: 'mesmerising and splitting the West Ham defence at will'.

"But in an atmosphere more like a cup-tie than an end-of-season league match, it was West Ham who took the lead on 28 minutes when Hurst scored in a goalmouth scramble after a John Sissons effort was blocked.

"Despite being outplayed at times, Hammers increased their lead when Johnny Byrne

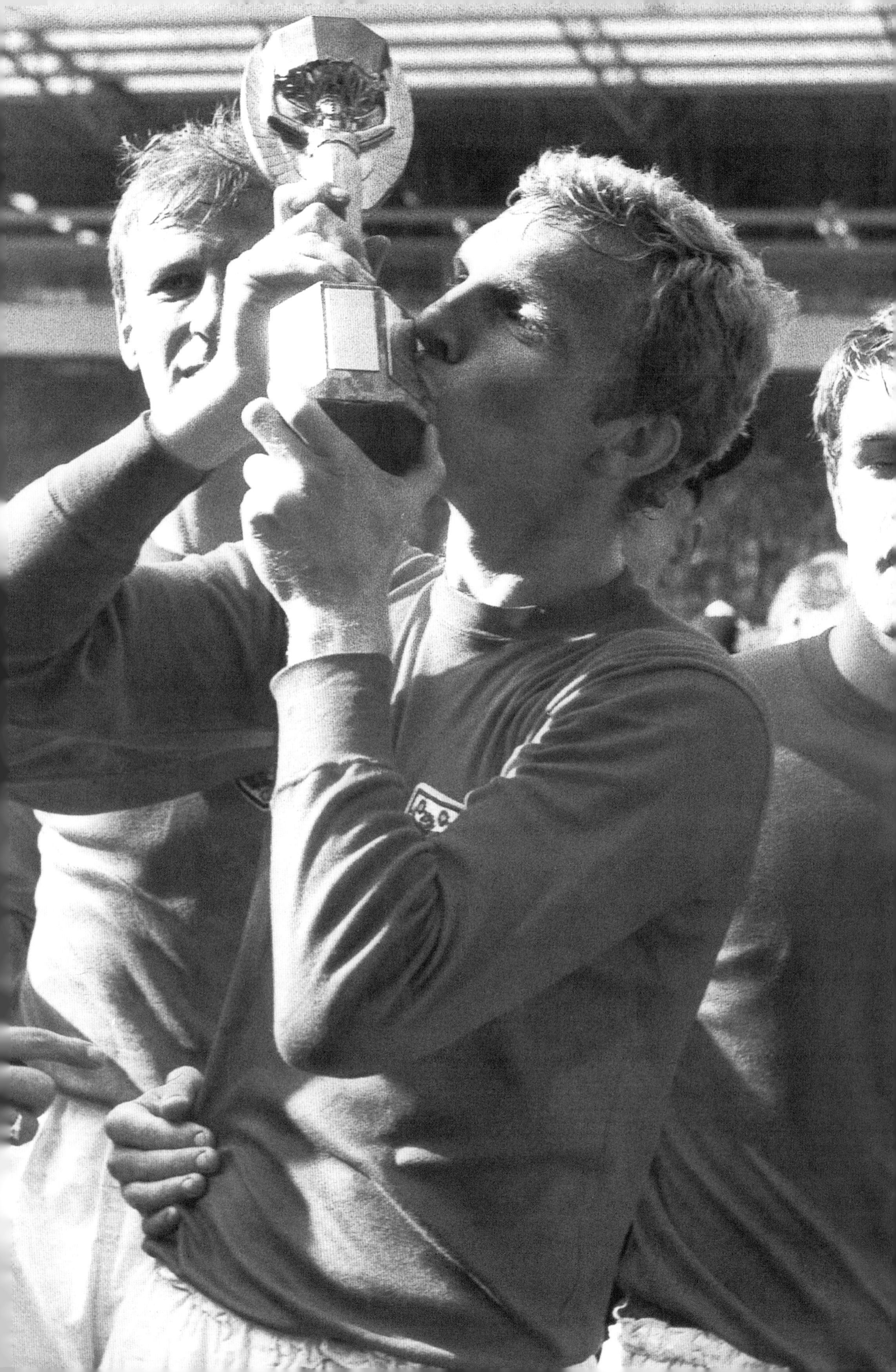

converted his fourth penalty in three consecutive home games in the 42nd minute, after Shay Brennan felled Peters just inside the area.

"Former West Ham captain and Ireland international full-back Noel Cantwell, who moved to Manchester United from Hammers for a record fee for a full-back of £30,000 in 1960, reduced the arrears for the Red Devils in the 63rd minute, but Hurst, heading in a Sissons corner, restored West Ham's two-goal cushion ten minutes later.

"Although United winger John Aston made it 3-2 12 minutes from time, Hammers held out to win the day – and make mine'.

West Ham: Standen, Charles, Burnett, Peters, Bickles, Moore, Brabrook, Boyce, Byrne, Hurst, Sissons.

United: Gregg, Brennan, Dunne (Herd), Crerand, Cantwell, Stiles, Connelly, Law, Sadler, Charlton, Aston.

Footnote: Now that he has come clean and admitted his guilty secret after all these years, Tony Hogg has promised to send a postal order for 3/6d to the West Ham ticket Office – Ed.

Although no trophies were won, the club recorded a record profit in 1965-66.

Here, the minutes from the AGM of the following year, tell why:

"From the playing point of view, season 1965-66 was one of near misses, as we reached the Semi-Final of the European Cup Winners' Cup and the Final of the Football League Cup. However, from the financial angle, these two competitions alone netted £52,500 and gave yet another very welcome boost to our Revenue Account income and enabled that Account to show a profit of £33,500. This revenue profit together with the very healthy surplus on transfer fees of £60,500 are the main items providing us with a record profit of £96,000.

"It is timely, therefore, to remind ourselves that for the past two or three years our financial structure with its heavy wage bill has been very largely geared to success on the field. Your Directors are very conscious of this and we can assure you we will be watching this aspect with great care.

"However, we are justly proud of our success on the field during the last ten years and we are equally proud that it has enabled us to spend approximately £175,000 on improving our amenities. This figure is, of course, in addition to the normal items of repair and decoration which are, with a stadium like ours to maintain, a very heavy recurring item each year. The figure of £175,000 includes the purchase of a freehold and provision for the new Main Entrance, access stairways, etc., cover to the North Bank and the new floodlighting installation, the provision of new and modernisation of existing toilets to the West Stand and the South Bank, construction of the new 'A' Block to the West Stand, new seating to 'B' Block, the new Press Enclosure and re-surfacing of the North Bank terracing. On top of all this, we have built a new suite of offices which would be a credit to any organisation.

"We must never forget, however, that our first priority is, and always will be, continued success on the field and provided we secure this we hope to continue with our programme of steady improvement to the stadium and better amenities for our spectators. We also have high hopes of building a new East Stand in the near future. There are problems with building licences, etc., still to be resolved, but we are hoping to be in the position to make a definite statement shortly. This will be far the most ambitious capital project we have undertaken and it should be remembered that it can only be paid for in the final analysis out of taxed profits".

So the final shots were about to be played out of this, West Ham's most successful, unsuccessful season of all time. It was also the most exhilarating, exasperating, frustrating and downright infuriating in the club's rich history.

With just two matches to go, the season fizzled out in anti-climax with disappointing defeats at Stoke (1-0) and Leicester (2-1, Byrne) the team failing to better their points total of the previous campaign.

There would be no silverware for the West Ham players to hold aloft and parade through the teeming, banner bedecked streets of East London this year.

But there would be gold for a chosen three of their number, called to do battle on a higher stage, where immortality awaited them.

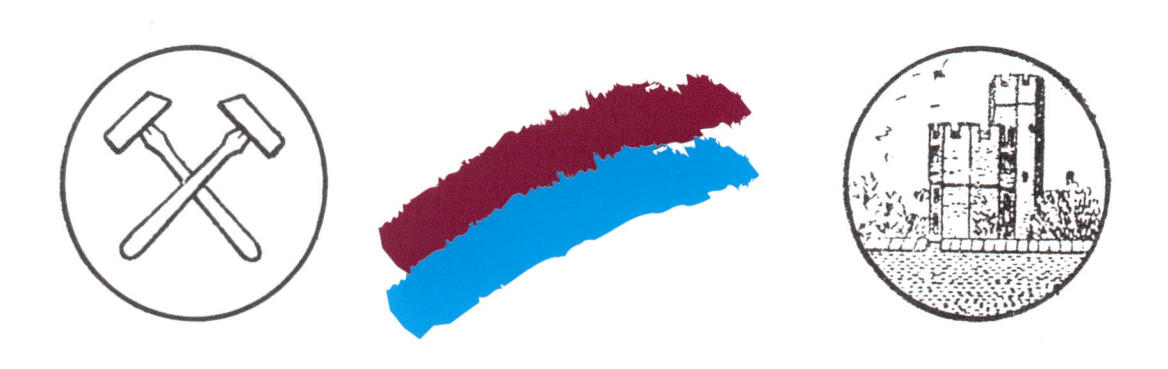

To be continued...

Above: Action from 1959-60 season. Noel Dwyer saves from that man Greaves at Stamford Bridge, watched by team mates (l-r) Malcolm, Brown, Cantwell and Bond.

Above: Dwyer is beaten as Chelsea score in the 3-2 win (l-r) Greaves, Tambling, Brown and Cantwell (3). Below: Dwyer is beaten again by Bolton's centre-forward, Dennis Stevens, with (l-r) Kirkup, Moore and Brown (5) in attendance.

The Fan Who Wore the Shirt

In his own words - John Buttwell

TEA IN THE BOOTROOM

John Buttwell, was born in Canning Town, East London in 1959 into a West Ham family.

First Experience: *I remember going to the Greengate, Plaistow to see the West Ham coach on its parade after winning the FA Cup in 1964.*

My first game was at age 6 at Upton Park with my Dad and older brother David. We went regularly after that.

I remember at some matches the Dads would pull us up through the gap into the South Bank, lots of youngsters got in that way. Monty would make us jump behind the goal when he blew his bugle/trumpet. We would look for Paddy the groundsman to come out and wave, we knew then the players would come out onto the pitch led by Bobby Moore, to the strains of the Leyton Silver Band playing the "Post Horn Gallop".

OTHER MEMORIES: *The marching band at half time, getting soaking wet on the wall behind the goal, looking for the half-time scores, muddy pitches and seeing legends from all the clubs, Moore, Hurst, Byrne, Charlton, Law, Best, and great games played by proper footballers.*

I was lucky to play at the original West Ham ground, **THE MEMORIAL GROUND** *at Canning Town. We used the old dressing rooms. It was eventually closed and left for years.* **I WAS SCOUTED** *by Wally St. Pier and went to my club West Ham United for the 1973/74 season after playing for my district, Newham Boys. My coaches were Ronnie Boyce, Tony Carr, Bill Lansdowne Snr, Pat Holland and Frank Lampard. I loved the training at Upton Park: Tuesdays and Thursdays in the small gym at the back of the dressing rooms, outside at the front of the ground with the main gate shut, being chased by the coaches in the new Chicken Run through the seats, then the whole length of the stand until they tell you to stop. We once had Bobby Moore watch us train. I think he came to run around the pitch for extra training. I was lucky to have known him as I got older. He was always smart and the Captain of England. Till the end, he would take an extra suit to away matches to look the part as he met people from other football clubs.*

CHADWELL HEATH *was a long bus trip from my house in Plaistow, but we got paid our expenses. There was always about 30 boys training, and sometimes balls would go everywhere during ball skills, but I loved the full pitch matches. I remember working my way into the Counties team, but was hit with some bad luck. I travelled to Chadwell Heath one Saturday to find the game was called off – I was gutted. Then I got injured in training, but went to matchday and had treatment with Billy Bonds, Trevor Brooking and Mervyn Day. That was great, but I didn't play for weeks. Rob Jenkins, then George Barwick at Clapton did the physio.*

MATCHDAY AT UPTON PARK: *I went with Youth Team players Paul Brush, Gary Sproul and Lou Murphy from Cumberland School along with Alan Curbishley and Alvin Martin. I was too young to be behind John Lyall in the dugout, but was told to keep out of the way of the players and coaches. We would go into the boot room with Jack Leslie, and get a cup of tea to stay away from the dressing rooms. We would see all the great players from different teams of the 70s.*

I was invited to the Town Hall in 1975 when we won the FA Cup. Then Wally St. Pier's testimonial. I remember being in a circle of players talking football: Moore, Hurst, Peters, Byrne, Bond and a couple of my age. No selfies in those days. I would have loved a photograph of that moment in time. That night I met all the West Ham legends of the 1960s and 70s when the '64 team played the '75 side.

MY TIME AT WEST HAM *came a bit early and I couldn't progress into a side 2 or 3 years older than me. My attitude was to blame for me getting the boot.*

I went to Orient and played in Alan Stephenson's reserves in the Midweek League. George Petchey was the Manager. I left when I didn't get an apprenticeship, so went to Building College. I played non league and good standard of leagues. The experience of professional clubs made me a better player. I played in Germany and Holland against FC Karlsburg, Shalke 04 and FC Den Haag Youth, with ex-West Ham players Terry Sharpe, Kevin Lygo, Lou Murphy, Ron Barham, Alan Durrant and Clive Beauchamp.

ONE STRANGE *thing happened after I left West Ham. I went to a West Ham away game at Chelsea with my mates to a mad day out at Stamford Bridge in 1977. Trouble all over the place! We were in the Shed when police got about 20 of us into a group and marched us down the pitch whilst the game was going on. I remember walking past John Lyall sitting on the bench. The police put us in the West Ham end.*

MY CLARET AND BLUE BLOOD *is the cause of my 50 years of collecting everything to do with West Ham United. It is sad to see no more football at Upton Park. "It don't bear thing about!" It's a big move, a big gamble – will it equal the buzz of a night at the Boleyn Ground? I don't think so.*

SOME THINGS I HEARD *of about West Ham.* **STAN BOTHAM:** *Head Groundsman for 25 years. I worked for him and we would talk for ages about West Ham.*

(1) He said when West Ham beat Liverpool in the 1963 FA Youth Cup Final, he took a tray of teas into the Liverpool dressing room. Bill Shankly was shouting at the players as they lost the Cup, whilst 2 players were on the floor fighting. Stan put the teas down and shut the door behind him.

(2) He asked the players of the 60s to paint some of the ground with Claret & Blue paint during their daily work. Someone dipped a tennis ball in red paint and threw it hitting Johnny Sissons on the forehead!

(3) **RON GREENWOOD** *once asked Stan to get rid of a cupboard of so called junk into the ground's skip. Stan said items included old leather football bags with boots in from the 30s/40s with players names on them, plus shirts, paperwork, etc., to redecorate. Imagine what they would fetch on eBay today!*

JOHN LYALL: *John was always a nice person. I never saw him lose his nut. I was once standing around the players' dressing room as the game finished. We won. John was praising the team. About six of us were just inside the door with shirts thrown into the middle of the floor. We had a tea, then stood outside. No-one asked me to get out of the way, I knew I took liberties, but meeting all the players, old and young, on matchday was just being part of the club.*

STRATFORD SNOOKER HALL, ALVIN MARTIN: *I went some afternoons to Stratford Snooker Hall with Lou Murphy and met up with Alvin Martin and Alan Curbishley. They were Youth and Reserves players. I mentioned this to Alvin years later and he said "Good days".*

ERNIE GREGORY *said they had meetings about the players and they said: "shall we let Alvin go back to Liverpool or keep him?" Ernie said put him in the side, give him a run. So Alvin stayed, the rest is history.*

NOTABLE MEMORIES:

(1) When I got the chance to go to first team matches, I would walk through the car park and go into the little door with PLAYERS above it. Go down a long corridor to the dressing rooms and stand there. Others would be there too – groundstaff, reserves, youth.

I got to see **THE GREAT LIVERPOOL SIDE:** *Keegan, Toshack, Hughes, Newcastle's Macdonald. Each team had quality players. Then walk out of the tunnel before kick-off and get in the corner of the dugout area behind the players' bench.*

(2) I will always remember **THE BUZZ** *in and around the club when we had signed Billy Jennings, Keith Robson and Bobby Gould. We scored 20 goals in four games: 6, 6, 5, 3. I wonder if we will ever repeat that goal tally in the future?*

RON GREENWOOD: *After Ron Greenwood retired, there was an evening in the ground to honour him, hosted by Geoff Hurst. Ron got to the door and security stopped him as he had no pass. Geoff ran across and said this Ron Greenwood's night – and this is Ron Greenwood! They then let him in.*

KENNY DALGLISH: *I was told that Kenny had a trial at West Ham when he was 17 and the coaching staff and manager weighed up whether to keep Kenny or let him go back to Scotland as he was a bit young to be away from home. He went back and played for Celtic a year later. Perhaps Kenny Dalglish wasn't good enough for West Ham!*

The Founders of the Academy

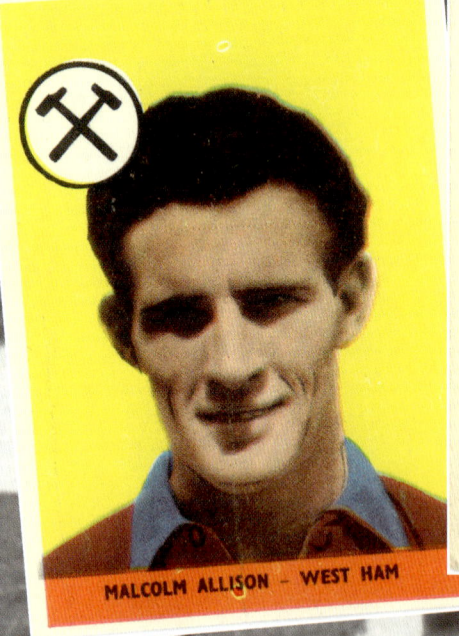

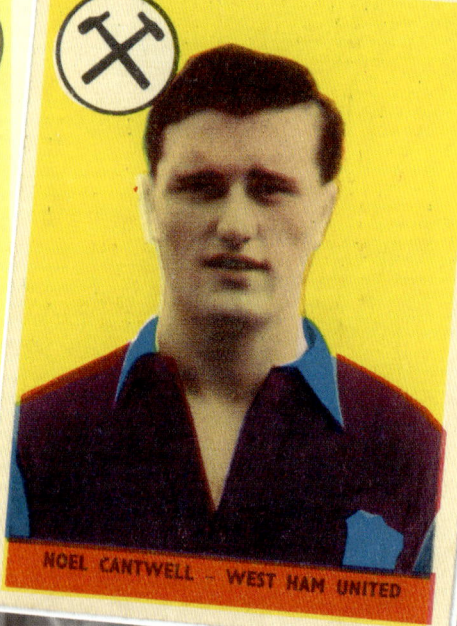

Allison Bond Cantwell

MALCOLM ALLISON — WEST HAM

JOHN FREDERICK BOND — WEST HAM

NOEL CANTWELL — WEST HAM UNITED

Peter Chiswick saves whilst shielded by John Bond.

Above: Penzance August 2000.
Below: Rotterdam 1992 or was it Liverpool or Rome?

The author's pal Barry (in cap) says "one lump or two Sir?" to Brian, as they meet the locals in Volkenburg during the Euro 2000 Football Championships in Holland and Belgium.

Barry Nunn: Surely the oldest goalkeeper ever to play at West Ham and one of the last, in a specially arranged match at Upton Park in the Summer of 2016, before the ground was demolished.

'Well I guess that these heroes always live there
where you and I have only been'
Leonard Cohen

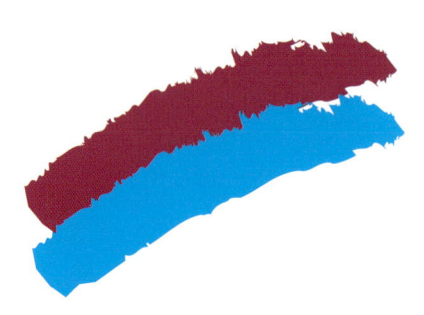

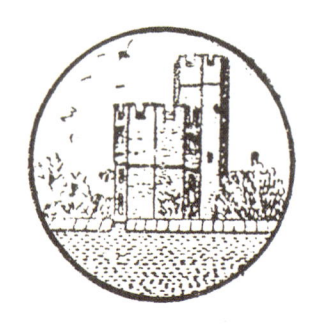

Books by the same author

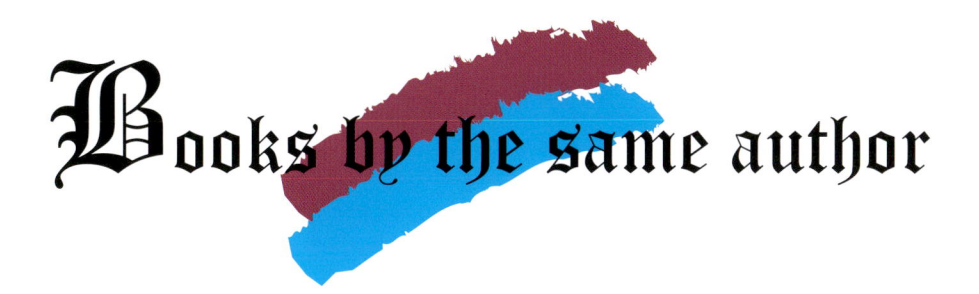

Who's Who of West Ham United, 1900 to 1986 (With Jack Helliar) *Helliar (1986)*

The West Ham United Quiz Book, *Mainstream, (1988)*

1895-1995 Hammers 100 Years of Football (With Tony McDonald) *Independent Magazines (UK) Ltd (1995)*

West Ham United Who's Who: Centenary Edition, 1895-1995: A Player by Player Guide to West Ham United F.C. (With Tony McDonald) *Independent Magazines (UK) Ltd (Dec. 1995)*

The Essential History of West Ham United FC: The Complete Story from 1895 - 2000 (With Kirk Blows) *Headline Book Publishing; First Edition edition (3 Aug. 2000)*

The Essential History of West Ham United FC: The Updated Edition (With Kirk Blows) *Headline Book Publishing (2002)*

Who's Who of West Ham United, 1895 - 2005 - Celebrating 100 Years at the Boleyn Ground. *Profile Sports Media Ltd (2005)*

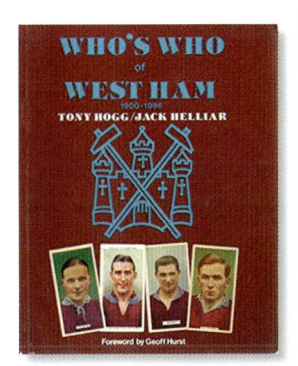

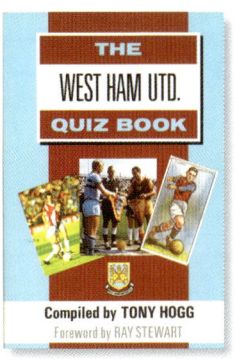

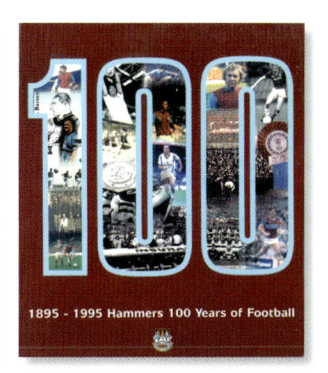

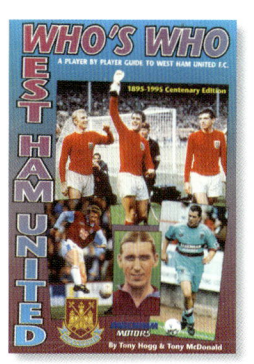

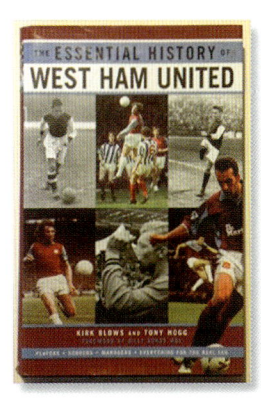

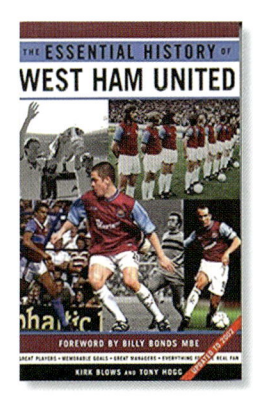

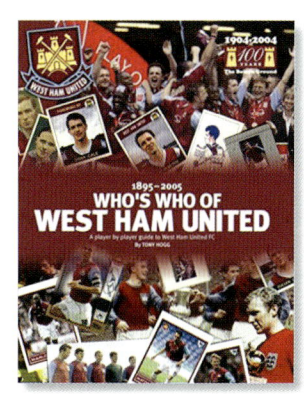

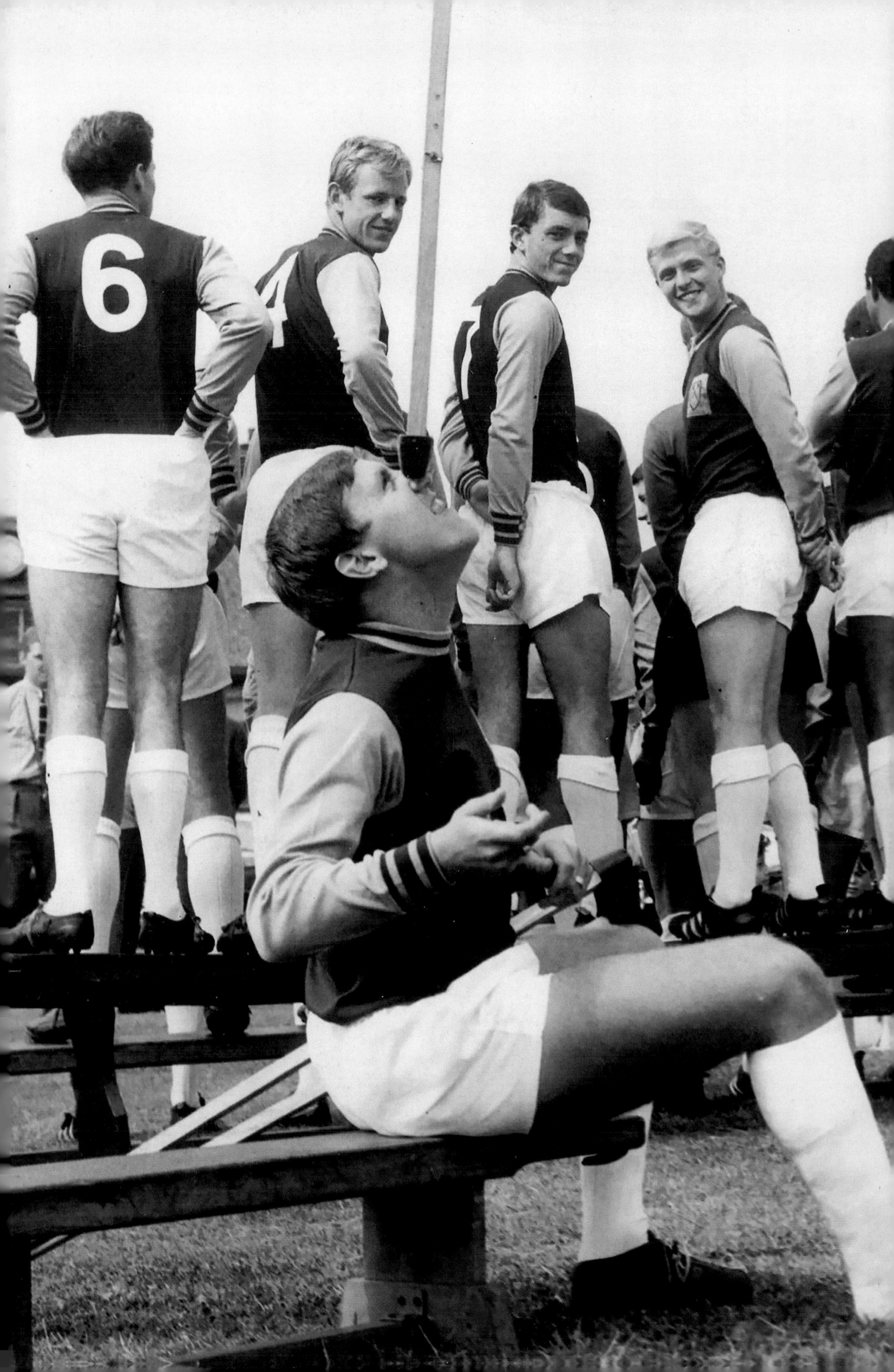